ERRATUM

Line 6, jacket text, for "ethnological" read "ethological."

Human territoriality

New Babylon

Studies in the Social Sciences

33

MOUTON PUBLISHERS · THE HAGUE · PARIS · NEW YORK

Human territoriality

Survey of behavioural territories
in man with preliminary analysis
and discussion of meaning

Torsten Malmberg
Department of Social Geography
University of Lund, Lund, Sweden

MOUTON PUBLISHERS · THE HAGUE · PARIS · NEW YORK

ISBN: 90-279-7948-0

© 1980, Torsten Malmberg, Lund, Sweden

Printed in Great Britain

To Aimée

Preface

In the summer of 1970 Professor Torsten Hägerstrand of the Department of Social Geography, University of Lund, asked me to give a lecture on human territoriality. This was made in October the same year in connection with a conference, "Urbanization – planning human environment in Europe", held at the castle of Ham, Belgium, under the auspices of the European Cultural Foundation, Amsterdam.

At that time I had already collected material for some years on the behavioural territories of man, and after the conference it was decided that I should make a thorough survey of available information on the matter with some financial support of the Foundation – which is gratefully acknowledged – and as a prerequisite for further research. The result could not be presented until now, because an immense literature – hopefully fairly well covered up to 1975 – from many different disciplines had to be examined and the writing had to be done along with my ordinary duties as a biologist-geographer.

It is self-evident that the work could be done only with the aid of many librarians, particularly the always helpful staff of the University Library, but also the personnel of the Geographical, Pedagogical, Psychological, Sociological and Zoological Department libraries of the University of Lund.

Some colleagues and friends should be thanked for valuable assistance in different ways, above all for critical views on parts of the manuscript: Professor Per Brinck, Ecological Unit of the Zoological Department, University of Lund; Professor Anne Buttimer, Graduate School of Geography, Clark University, Worcester, Mass.; Professor Eric Fabricius, Ethological Unit of the Zoological Department, University of Stockholm; Dr. Michel van Hulten, Secretary of Transport to the Dutch Government, Lelystad; Dr. Fritz Lienemann, Systemplan E.V., Institut für Umweltforschung und Entwicklungsplanung, Heidelberg; Professor Paul Leyhausen, Max-Planck-Institut für Verhaltensphysologie, Wuppertal; Professor Arne Müntzing, Department of Genetics, University of Lund; Professor Gudmund Smith, Department of Psychology, University of Lund; Dr Gösta Wennberg, College of Education, Uppsala; Professor Torbjörn Westermark, Royal Institute of

Technology, Stockholm; Professor Olof Wärneryd, Department of Social Geography, University of Lund.

Some persons have, however, particularly facilitated the completing of this book: Torsten Hägerstrand, who not only took the initiative but also furthered the work in all possible ways, Paul Leyhausen who presented indispensible comments on crucial parts of the manuscript and my son and wife, Ole Malmberg and Aimée Malmberg, who made many valuable suggestions and together with my daughter Birgitta Malmberg gave me unlimited help, support and encouragement.

Torsten Malmberg,
Lund, November 4, 1979

Contents

1. Introduction

Mankind today faces an environmental crisis of hitherto unparalleled proportions. Rapidly diminishing resources, augmenting levels of pollution and a deteriorating quality of life all loom large on our horizon. Space conditions on earth largely contribute to these problems, and one of the reasons seems to be this: "Man is a territorial animal and territoriality affects human behavior at all scales of social activity" (Soja 1971: 19). Despite their obvious importance in human affairs behavioural territories represent a seriously neglected field of research. We have made this survey in the hope that it will stimulate to new investigations and to international cooperation in the field. In fact, the study of human territories demands a cross-disciplinary approach, and great efforts have been made to cover, in this book, most vital aspects of the subject. But the obstacles have been considerable, not the least those of a terminological nature.

"The matter is, of course, tentative. It has been, and will be, difficult to gather data about human territoriality or non-territoriality which satisfies many of the criteria of evidence. None the less it would be very unwise to discount the possibility that a territorial propensity exists and is in part the basis for a variety of human behaviours and institutions" (Tiger 1969: 60). It is the more recommendable to collect such data, as many earlier studies on the matter have mainly inferred from observations of non-humans and have often been criticized for this. Recently it was also stressed that "the process of conceptual refinement and proliferation should be accompanied by a survey process or the gathering of extensive distributional data and rate measures" (Willems and Campbell 1976: 138).

Some valuable books have already treated substantial parts of the enormous field of territoriality (e.g. E.T. Hall 1959; Ardrey 1967; Sommer 1969; O.M. Watson 1970; *Environmental Psychology* 1970; *Spatial Behavior of Older People 1970; Behavior and Environment* 1971; Greverus 1972; Bakker and Bakker-Rabdau 1973; Altman 1975; Scheflen and Ashcraft 1976). But as far as we know none of these earlier works have aimed at a scientific survey of the whole realm of physical human territories. Given the current stage of knowledge, what this book presents is, however, predominantly a compendium of examples from different territorial sections, unequal both as to frequency, coverage and importance. A more exhaustive and definitive treatment must be left to detailed reports on particular aspects of the field. The study of territories is still in its infancy, profound analyses of natural and cultural elements are rare exceptions, and in one of the few attempts it was underlined that, "What, essentially, is missing, is a comparative natural history of territorial groups" (Stanner 1965-1966: 3).

The working method has largely been that of quoting and reviewing existing literature in order to show, as objectively as possible, the criteria of behavioural territoriality, whether the authors cited have been aware of this aspect or not. Quotations from sources not in English are translated by the author. Frequent references have been made to non-human animals according to the statement: "If we were to study the experience of space in humans only, we would have no hope of arriving at essentials" (Esser 1971b: 1). In order to avoid misunderstanding it should further be stressed with the words of Konrad Lorenz: "You can't explain everything in terms of territory" (Sheehan 1968: 73). And we do not join a recent formulation by Scheflen and Ashcraft (1976: 4): "The study of human territoriality is the study of human behavior", albeit we are convinced of the great range and importance of the former concept.

It has been deemed wise not only to give territory examples from many different contexts, particularly urban, but also to present and define their adequate background. Further, we have tried to analyse the material as far as it seems possible today. There is also at the end of the book a discussion of presumed effects and functions as well as an effort to put human territoriality into an evolutionary perspective. In spite of more or less inevitable mistakes and fallacies it is the hope of the author that this attempt to follow a rather new and promising line of study will be of value. The matter seems to be fundamental in connection with the solving of different kinds of pure and applied spatial problems in a world where satisfactory rooms to live and work in is nothing but a dream for millions of human beings.

2. Basic concepts

2.1. Space and its perception

2.1.1. Space and environment

The importance of defining spatial parameters is in the territorial context self-evident. First among crucial concepts comes environment, as territory both includes part of, and means adaptation to, the milieu. Unfortunately there is as yet no unanimity about an adequate definition and a unified theory of the nature of the environment (cf. Proshansky, Ittelson and Rivlin 1970a). This phenomenon can, however, be presented as an open, dynamic system, which is structured as well as constantly changing. We might also agree with Cain (1967: 203): "Environment consists of all of the things, conditions, and forces to which living matter is sensitive and capable of reacting to, including changes in the intensity and direction of stimuli".

In any case we have to realize that environment is multi-dimensional in different senses. Primarily we speak of three-dimensional, geometric or physical space (cf. Whitrow 1955-1956), to which the fourth dimension of time – now most often treated in the language of space – should be added. But it is also possible or, rather, necessary to distinguish between geographic, internal, social, and, at least for humans, cultural environments (cf. Frank 1943: 344). Without doubt three-dimensional space is on the whole identical with the geographic environment, but this point should be penetrated a little further.

Albert Einstein (1969) remarked about the concept of space that "it seems that this was preceded by the psychologically simpler concept of place. Place is first of all a (small) portion of the earth's surface identified by a name". He contrasted the historical concept of space as positional quality of the world of material objects against that of space as container of all material things and continued: "The victory over the concept of absolute space or over that of the inertial system became possible only because the concept of the material object was gradually replaced as the fundamental concept of physics by that of the field... That which constitutes the spatial character of reality is then simply the four-dimensionality of the field" (as to the philosophy of space and time, see Cassirer 1957, Reichenbach 1958).

Thus space in modern physics is not an absolute and static entity but relative to a moving point of reference, for instance, the body of man (cf. the later treatment of "personal space", e.g., section 2.2.4.). It is well known how this has influenced thinking in many different disciplines, not the least geography, as historically and conceptually analysed by Blaut (1961) and Abler, Adams and Gould (1972: 72-82). It is without doubt symptomatic of this rather intricate matter that the first-named author finally arrived at the statement that "we are still without a spatial notion which qualifies as a suitable basic organizing concept" (p. 6).

2.1.2. How space is perceived

One reason for the definition difficulties could be this: "The term 'space perception' is unfortunate because it suggests that space is something that we perceive. Only objects are perceived, and these objects possess a number of attributes – qualitative, intensive, and spatial. The term refers to the perception of the spatial attributes of objects, viz., their size, shape, stability, motility, and their distance and directional locations in reference to each other and to the perceiving subject. Space as distinct from these spatial attributes is a conceptual construct" (Carr 1966: 1).

Concerning the perceiving agents, Lorenz (1935: 138) stated that "the senses which localize stimuli in man are chiefly those of touch and sight. Thus we speak about spaces of tactility and vision, but in audition localization is much less exact, so that a human space of hearing is seldom suggested". Koffka (1935: 121) confirmed that the perception of spatial characters is supported by other than visual forces, notably those which arise in the vestibular organ of the inner ear and those which derive from so-called deep sensibility in humans. And E.T. Hall (1969: 39-60) discerned both visual, auditory, olfactory, thermal and tactile space.

In his interesting book on congenitally-blind persons who were investigated before and after operations which made them sighted, Senden (1932: 266-298) emphatically asserted that humans born blind have no awareness of space and that it is surgical treatment alone which can change this situation. However, the author himself underlined that the whole conceptual framework of spatial phenomena is constructed and the examinations performed by sighted persons, and for these and other possible biases the philosopher G.J. Warnock (1960) could not, on logical premises, agree with Senden's conclusion. Russian experiments with blind persons even suggested that "It is locomotion in space and not vision which is the necessary and crucial condition for emergence" (Shemyakin 1962, cited after Stea 1970: 145). Yet, "Vision is certainly our most powerful organ for exploring space around us, and it gives us good cues for distance in the form of: (a) the disparity of binocular images; (b) the muscular effort needed for convergence and accommodation, and (c) the phenomenon of parallax as we move about" (H. Davis 1956: 188). The fact that about two thirds of all the nerve fibers that enter our central nervous system come from the eyes (Gerard 1957: 429) also suggest a strong influence of vision on spatial and other perception.

2.1.3. Life space

It should be stressed that physical space is not the same as life space, experienced by every animal species in a specific and, at least among humans, in an individual way, too (cf. Beck 1967). According to the definition by Ittelson (1960: 34) "perceiving refers to the process by which a particular person, from his particular behavioral center, attributes significances to his immediate environmental situation. It is this attribution of significance which transforms a neutral environmental 'happening' into a meaningful event". This is certainly not far from the 'Umwelt' of Uexküll (1909: 5-6), that is, the special world to which every organism is adapted according to the requirements of its morphology and physiology (cf. also Mühlmann 1952, G.J.W. Smith 1962).

Here it seems suitable to note that human spatial behaviour is also strongly dependent on the individual's cognitive maps of the environment. Such a map could be defined as a convenient set of symbols which we all subscribe to and employ, resulting from our specific and individual prejudices and experiences (cf. Downs and Stea 1973: 9). Without doubt these maps are also influenced by the social and cultural environment: "Human space perception is biologically rooted, but the level at which it functions in the individual is not reducible to innate capacities or maturational development. The process of socialization contributes experiential components that must be considered. Some of these acquired components of space perception are a function of the cultural milieu in which the individual has been reared. The cultural patterns of different societies offer different means by which spatial perceptions are developed, refined, and ordered" (Hallowell 1955: 201-202; cf. also Sorokin 1943: 97-157).

We should not forget, either, that space on earth, of course, is bounded, which seems particularly important in the field theory of life space developed by the psychologist Kurt Lewin (e.g., 1936: 118-135). Boundaries could be natural as well as cultural and have valuable functions in connection with our information about space (Cox 1972: 119-140; cf. also J.G. Miller 1965: 342-344). It was vindicated by Goldfinger (1941: 129) that the spatial sensation is influenced both by the enclosing agent and the enclosed space (cf. also Hutton 1972; Goodey 1973).

Concerning the two opposite schools of atomistic and holistic scientific thought it was rightly argued by Lorenz (1951: 159) that "particularly the behaviour student must maintain an absolute readiness to use both methods; which of them has to be applied at a given moment is a question that cannot be settled by methaphysical speculation or by the dogmatic misapplication of a slogan, but one that must be answered by patient inductive research, separately for each individual object and at every single step of the investigation".

In another context he stressed that "It is a pre-eminent characteristic of that phenomenon of perception, to which alone the term '*Gestalt*' should be applied, that it is largely independent of the elementary parts out of which it is built up" (Lorenz 1950: 225). "*Gestalt*" as a product of pregnant organization has the meaning of a concrete individual and stringent entity, existing as something detached and having a shape or form as one of its characteristics (cf. Köhler 1947: 102-105). "Tacit acceptance of the organism's capacity to make unity out of diversity is general, especially since Gestalt psychology asserted that such a capacity is innate". However "This has not led to an understanding of how the unique interrelations within each unity are integrated into a unique unit" (Riesen 1958: 445).

Maybe there is, however, a valuable clue in the observation, first made by Piaget and supported by the above-mentioned experiments with blind persons, that the representation of space arises from the coordination and internalization of actions. Our adult understanding of space results from extensive manipulation of objects and from movements in the physical environment rather than from any immediate perceptual copying of this milieu (cf. Gibson 1950: 223-230; see also the review by Hart and Moore 1973, especially p. 261-262). Thus "Lived, action space is built into the organism by behavior; distance spanned by habit becomes part of organismic expectancy and rhythm" (E. Becker 1964: 31).

This leads us to the definitions of territory.

2.2. Territory definitions

2.2.1. Definition situation

It was claimed by Uexküll (1957: 54) in 1934 that territory "is an entirely subjective product, for even the closest knowledge of the environment does not give the slightest clue as to its existence". Ardrey (1972: 196) presented a similar view: "A territory, for example, cannot exist in nature; it exists in the mind of the animal". Even though these statements are in principle correct, they do not of course exclude the observation of natural or cultural territorial phenomena, e.g. in the form of physical boundaries and markings. Perhaps we have here, however, one of the reasons for the difficulty in defining and describing territories.

In a splendid review of territoriality C.R. Carpenter (1961: 229) gave the following pessimistic expression of the definition situation: "Behavioral systems change over periods of time. Those which constitute territoriality in animals are so complex, and involve so many adaptive and even nonadjustive mechanisms, that they defy adequate description by condensed definitions. Fully systematic and analytical descriptions are required". That the conditions were much the same ten years later became evident from the paper "Is territoriality definable?" by J.H. Kaufmann (1971) with its final conclusion that "No simplified definition or explanation of territory yet advanced can cover all of the related kinds of behavior known, and perhaps it is naive to look for one".

Nevertheless, we will here survey some of the more important attempts to define territory, the main part of which are for non-human animals, particularly birds. Altman (1975: 105-106) summarized some general themes of territory definition: "First, there are consistent references to places or geographical areas. Second, many definitions imply various needs or motives that territorial behavior serves – such as sex and mating, food gathering, child rearing, and the like. Third, all definitions convey the idea of ownership of a place. Fourth, territoriality seems to involve personalization of a place by some marking device – for instance urination, glandular secretions, signs, or fences.... A fifth quality of territory is that it can be the domain of individuals or groups.... A sixth quality of many definitions concerns territorial intrusion and defense".

The first zoological pioneers of the territorial study gave no quite clear definitions. Heape (1931: 28), however, said: "All discussion upon the movements of animals must be based on the fact that they occupy at one time or another a definite area which they regard as a 'home'. This home area I have called their 'home territory'. It is essentially associated with the deposition of eggs, or parturition, and with the rearing of young; it is almost invariably recognised as a sanctuary, though not always respected". And Mayr (1935: 31) proposed the following definition: "*Territory is an area occupied by one male of a species which it defends against intrusions of other males of the same species and in which it makes itself conspicuous*".

2.2.2. The defense problem

Thus the dominating definition characteristic of defense went into territory theory, and it was later supported by a great many other eminent scientists, even though they differed as to formulation and main weight laid on various activities. Among these authors the following should be named: Tinbergen (1936: 5), Crawford (1939: 419), Nice (1941: 441), Hediger (1942: 19), Jenkins (1944: 39), Dice (1952: 234-235), Bourlière (1952: 199), Kendeigh (1961: 184), Barnett (1964: 179) and J.L. Brown (1969: 199). Such a broad consensus of students on different species could seem to be a most assuring one, particularly as the crucial criterion of defense gives a clear limitation to the concept.

Already Hinde (1956: 341-342), however, stressed not only that all types of territory depend on basically similar mechanisms. He also made this statement: "Defence may of course be by threat, song or any other behaviour pattern evoking avoidance in other individuals, as well as by actual combat ...". It was, however, Emlen (1957: 352), who started questioning territory as a necessarily defended space, and Pitelka (1959: 253) went a step further: "The fundamental importance of territory lies not in the mechanism (overt defense or any other action) by which the territory becomes identified with its occupant, but in the degree to which it is in fact used exclusively by its occupant" (cf. also Schoener 1968: 124-126).

Fretwell and Lucas (1969: 26) agreed, saying: "Territorial behavior is defined as any site dependent display behavior that results in conspicuousness, and in the avoidance of other similar behaving individuals. Territorial behavior is specifically not restricted to defensive and/or aggressive behavior nor are they excluded". These new ideas were also reflected at the international symposium on the use of space by animals and men, during the 1968 meeting of the American Association for the Advancement of Science (*Behavior and Environment* 1971: 46-52).

An extreme position was taken by Etkin (1964a: 21-22), who defined territoriality "as any behavior on the part of an animal which tends to confine the movements of the animal to a particular locality", while Odum (1971: 209) included "under the heading of territoriality any active mechanism that spaces individuals or groups apart from one another...". That at least the first of these two definitions is too broad because of lack of exclusiveness in the formulation was demonstrated by Brown and Orians (1970) in their valuable investigation on "Spacing Patterns in Mobile Animals", where relevant terms and opinions were discussed. As to the crucial point of defense the authors said (p. 242) that two categories are included, namely "1. actual defense, such as attacking, chasing, and threatening rival intruders, and 2. identifying acts that designate the defender and that make his presence conspicuous to his rivals; these include certain vocalizations, displays, and scent markings. When such acts typically fail to keep rivals out, the area should not be designated a territory".

Different meanings of the term "defense" are evidently in operation. Recent authors often wholly avoid the word and define territoriality e.g., as "any space-associated intolerance" (Eibl-Eibesfeldt 1970: 309), and territory as "a field of repulsion (and sometimes attraction) fixed in space" (Kummer 1971: 223). One of the best definitions in the zoological realm is that by Anderson and Hill (1965: 1753): "Territoriality...is any behavioral phenomenon which effects the exclusion of some category of conspecific organism from space inhabited by the territorial individual or group". However, it is doubtful if any form of behavioural exclusion can function for long without a background of possible active defense.

2.2.3. Human definitions

In spite of the fact that information on behavioural territories in man becomes more and more plentiful, particular definitions for *Homo sapiens* are still scarce. That of Lowenthal (1961: 253) told us that territoriality is equal to the ownership, division, and evaluation of space. Parr (1965: 14) was of the opinion that "Territory is the space which a person, as an individual, or as a member of a close-knit group (e.g., family, gang), in joint tenancy, claims as his or their own, and will 'defend'".

Altman and Haythorn (1967: 171) argued that they use the actual term not only in the case of intrusion and defense but also in connection with preferences for areas and objects, and Kuhn (1968: 395) talked about "Territoriality or the sense of possession of a given space and the urge to protect it against intruders". Sommer (1969: 14) reported with reference to Hediger that territory represents an area "which is first rendered distinctive by its owner in a particular way and, secondly, is defended by the owner", stressing that the major components of this definition are personalization and defense. And Lipman (1970: 69) defined territory as just *"possessed locality"*.

Thus even in the case of human territories definitions have long stressed defense. Soja (1971: 19), however, used the term territoriality for *"a behavioural phenomenon associated with the organization of space into spheres of influence or clearly demarcated territories which are made distinctive and considered at least partially exclusive by their occupants or definers"*. Proshansky, Ittelson and Rivlin (1970a: 180) put the matter this way: "Territoriality in humans, defined as achieving and exerting control over a particular segment of space, seems always to be instrumental to the achievement of a more primary goal". Similar thoughts seem to lie behind the definition by Eyles (1971: 2) stating that territory is "the space which may be continuous or discontinuous, used by an individual or group for most interactions and which, because of this, goes a long way towards satisfying the needs of identity, stimulation and security". Kälin (1972: 47) asserted that studies have shown definitions of territory as a defended area to be too simple in a context of human psychology. According to Greverus (1972: 382), territory is first an entity of identification, but it functions also as a space of action and protection. And Bakker and Bakker-Rabdau (1973: 271) defined territory as "Any object of territorial behavior. It may be a stretch of land, an idea, a function, or anything else that holds a person's fancy to such a degree that he seeks to own it".

After several earlier comprehensive formulations Altman (1975: 107) presented the following definition: "Territorial behavior is a self/other boundary-regulation mechanism that involves personalization of or marking of a place or object and communication that it is 'owned' by a person or group. Personalization and ownership are designated to regulate social interaction and to help satisfy various social and physical motives. Defense responses may sometimes occur when territorial boundaries are violated" (cf. also Edney 1974: 962-963).

2.2.4. Definition for the present survey

My own earlier definition (Malmberg 1972: 10) is here somewhat changed: *Human behavioural territoriality is primarily a phenomenon of ethological ecology with an instinctive nucleus, manifested as more or less exclusive spaces, to which individuals or groups of human beings are bound emotionally and which, for the possible avoidance of others, are distinguished by means of limits, marks or other kinds of structuring with adherent display, movements or aggressiveness.* Because unrestricted and reserved use of resources seem to signify the everyday aspect of territory, more than defense and aggression, certain cases excepted, this formulation is thought to be useful and will be a guideline for the present survey.

It remains to detail some practical information about what is treated and what is left aside in this study. Only physical entities are included, and thus not imagined territories, and only spaces large enough to contain the human body are relevant. Excepted from this rule are some play and game territories as well as one example of a material, symbolic representation of physical space. As to political, economic and similar territories delimited by custom or decision it does not, of course, matter if the distinguishing characters are natural or artificial, old or new, only the actual definition is applicable, e.g., in the instance of a national state (cf. Haggett 1975: 444-446).

The whole problem is very well visualized by Goffman (1972: 52): "'Territories vary in terms of their organization. Some are 'fixed'; they are staked out geographically and attached to one claimant, his claim being supported often by the law and its courts. Fields, yards, and houses are examples. Some are 'situational'; they are part of the fixed equipment in the setting (whether publicly or privately owned), but are made available to the populace in the form of claimed goods while-in-use. Temporary tenancy is perceived to be involved, measured in seconds, minutes, or hours, informally exerted, raising constant questions as to when the claim begins and when it terminates. Park benches and restaurant tables are examples. Finally, there are 'egocentric' preserves which move around with the claimant, he being in the centre. They are typically (but not necessarily) claimed long term".

Both the "fixed" and the "situational" territories doubtless belong to this investigation, and even the "egocentric" ones show evident signs of behavioural territoriality. These latter forms, which may be summarized as "personal space", are said to be distinguished from real territories by their being carried around, by having the body as their centre and by being as unbounded as invisible (Sommer 1959: 248). The first two criteria seem not to prevent application of our definition and some display features would be enough to make up for what is said to be lacking in the third. For practical reasons, however, we have mostly concentrated on territories which are not constantly changing (cf. Willems and Campbell 1976: 128) and which are not only structured by display (as to extremely temporary and portable territories, see, e.g., Becker and Mayo 1971; Cheyne and Efran 1972; Efran and Cheyne 1973).

In this connection it should once more be underlined that "Territory and locality are not the same. The relations between a group and its territory are among other things ecological relations. The relations between members of the group in respect of the territory, in itself, or as a locality of a larger entity, are among other things social relations. Territoriality and sociality lie in different systems of relations. The conventional approach to local organization has tended to compound and thus to blur the distinctions. The result has been a certain ambiguity and confusion. The study is inherently interdisciplinary. It may be said in Radcliffe-Brown's terms to fit in between the studies of the first and second of three connected adaptive systems – the ecological, the institutional or social and the cultural" (Stanner 1965: 1).

Here it may be fitting to include a short digression on the use of some territorial terms.

2.2.5. Some terms with territorial connotation

Indubitably much of the disagreement and confusion in the territorial realm is of a terminological nature. It seems therefore suitable to give a few comments on some terms related to the concept of behavioural territory, which in French mostly has as a counterpart "territoire" (Richard 1970: 4-6) and in German "Revier" or "Heim" (Uexküll 1957: 54-56).

It should be underlined that the term "home range" has been used in the past without distinction from that of "territory" (Burt 1943). Home range "refers to the total area occupied by an organism during a given period of time..." and "is likely to be of greatest conceptual value in the study of the human use of urban space..." (Porteous 1971: 166). Another designation for this same phenomenon is "orbit", and this is "a term I use to define the much wider concept of the space through which an individual habitually or occasionally roams" (Parr 1965: 14). Not seldom home range and territory coincide, which can explain the fact that the German "Territorium" can be used for both territory (Revier) and home range (Streifgebiet). The last concept in French is called "domaine vital" (Bourlière 1951: 73). This concept is defined for a certain period only and covers all the places frequented by an individual or a group during this time (Richard 1970: 1-4).

Stanner (1965-1966: 2) in his investigation of aboriginal territoriality in Australia discerned from an ecological point of view the three concepts "estate", "range" and "domain". "The evidence allows us to say that each territorial group was associated with both an estate and a range. The distinction is crucial. The estate was the traditionally recognized locus ('country', 'home', 'ground', 'dreaming place') of some kind of patrilineal descent-group forming the core or nucleus of the territorial group. It seems usually to have been a more or less continuous stretch. The range was the tract or orbit over which the group, including its nucleus and adherents, ordinarily hunted and foraged to maintain life. The range normally included the estate: people did not usually belong here and live there but, in some circumstances, the two could be practically dissociated. Estate and range together may be said to have constituted a *domain*, which was an ecological life-space". It seems to be a reasonable guess that "estate" here is a concept not far removed from that of behavioural territory.

With these prerequisites we proceed to the discipline implications of our matter, that is, to the sciences of territory.

2.3. Sciences of territory

2.3.1. Cross-discipline aspect

From the definitions of human behavioural territoriality it is already evident that different disciplines have interests in the phenomenon. So it has been found desirable to give an account of this matter, particularly as the scientific claim to or acceptance of an item is often decisive for its treatment and exploration. There are many examples showing that facts at the border between separate sciences run great risks of being neglected. And "All this comes about through the authoritarian notion that no specialist is entitled to observe or interpret anything that might seem the province – or *territory!* – of another specialist" (Russell and Russell 1961: 422).

First of all territoriality has suffered from the classical division of the learned world into "The Two Cultures" (Snow 1965), science and the humanities. This means that all social and cultural aspects of man have been placed on one side of the gap and all biological aspects on the other. There has also, up to the present day, been no real, established discipline of human biology, while medicine has been almost totally engaged in the indispensable task of curing the ill. By education and by custom the humanists have not been interested in biological man or, worse, have denied him, as did Ortega y Gasset in his remarkable words: Man has no nature, what he has is history (Dubos 1965a: 4). In fact both the natural and the historical side of human territoriality make fascinating fields of research, the last one still practically unknown (cf. sections 4.1.4.1., 4.1.4.2., 4.2.1., 4.3.1).

"The orientation of the behavioral sciences to the history, structure, and dynamics of social relationships has tended to obscure the potential significance of the nonhuman environment generally and, more specifically, that aspect of the nonhuman environment which we may designate as significant space" (Fried and Gleicher 1961: 311). At the same time biologists have preferred to concentrate on non-human animals and on what could be called fundamental biology, while "the aspects of biological science which are most relevant to the interests of the humanist are probably those which deal with the response of individual human beings to their total environment" (Dubos 1965a: 7).

2.3.2. Anthropology and geography

Fortunately there are now signs suggesting that bridges over the gap are being built from both sides. And it is no wonder that the anthropologists, who more than others have to study all facets of human life, are among the forerunners. Eickstedt (1950: 6-7), in his introduction to the first volume of the journal *Homo*, advocated the study of human biology, "*die dritte Biologie*", as a special science equal to that of plants and that of animals. And Laura Thompson (1961: 230) had support from several distinguished colleagues when, in her book *Toward a Science of Mankind*, she stressed the demand that such a discipline must be biologically based. Anthropologists are, of course, also responsible for a lot of valuable cross-cultural observations of territoriality, and some of them have made special studies on the matter (e.g., E.T. Hall 1968, 1969; O.M. Watson 1970). They have largely contributed to the very intense modern study of the behaviour of man's nearest relatives, the primates, too (cf. e.g., *Primates* 1968).

Up to this century anthropology and human geography were just parts of the same science, with the concept of culture as common denominator and with Friedrich Ratzel, originally a zoologist, as common ancestor (Lowie 1937: 119-127; Mikesell 1967: 618-619). It would be fair to think that human territoriality had a place in modern geography, particularly when we are reminded of "Geography as the study of environment" and of "geography's unique position as a discipline devoted to both natural and social science" (Berry et al. 1974: 16). For some reason, however, we have not found this subject in most handbooks of the discipline (however cf. Haggett 1975: 427-456).

But the geographical, perhaps here better termed spatial or chorological, realm (Hägerstrand 1967: 6-7) has many sub-sections, and some of them have discovered the phenomenon under discussion. One is ekistics, the science of human settlements (Doxiadis 1968b), manifested in a journal with the same name and including architecture. Another is political geography, which has produced one of the most important among papers on human territories, namely that of Soja (1971), as well as good contributions to the study of the boundary concept, which is central for territoriality (S.N.B. Jones 1959; Kristof 1959). Here we should not forget the neighbouring area of jurisdiction, where territorial limits seem to be laid down everywhere (Roos 1968).

Yet, behavioural geography is the most self-evident subdepartment for territory in the discipline. It has grown out of "increasing dissatisfaction with 'economic man' concepts as explanations of human spatial behaviour" and its goal seems to be that "Human geography is being reunited in a behavioural framework" (Doherty 1969: 1-2).

2.3.3. Psychology and ethology

If geography is the leading science of spatial matters, psychology is, of course, the central one treating behavioural phenomena and thus also a crucial discipline for territory. But apart from students of animal behaviour this area has long been neglected by psychologists with rather few exceptions, some of whom are Sommer (e.g., 1969) and Altman (e.g., 1975). In fact it has been possible to penetrate standard textbooks on psychology as well as a special volume on *Ecological Psychology* (Barker 1968) without finding any reference to human territoriality. This state of affairs is, however, now changing fast, and as an interesting proof it could be mentioned that from 1973 onwards "Territoriality" has been a main word in *Psychological Abstracts*. A still better omen is the publication of two magnificent volumes, *Environmental Psychology* (1970) and *Behavior and Environment* (1971), both with territory as a central theme.

"Psychology and Ethology as Supplementary Parts of a Science of Behavior" was once used as the title of a discussion contribution by one of the founders of the last-named discipline (Tinbergen 1955). Concerning animals Tinbergen concluded that psychologists had mostly worked experimentally and in order to trace direct causality, while ethologists had preferred making observations in the field as well as studying survival and evolutionary aspects. In fact "Ethology is a convenient word to denote behaviour study in the widest sense..." (Thorpe 1954: 101), and it has also been defined as the "Complete Analysis of Behavior" (Hess 1962) and as "the comparative study of behaviour" (*Zeitschrift für Tierpsychologie 1973*: 429). But the best and most simple definition is probably that of Tinbergen (1963: 411): "*the biological study of behaviour*".

Comparisons have mostly been made through the application of animal evidence to man, and ethologists have with few exceptions not been much engaged in research involving human subjects. It was asserted not long ago that "Human ethology seems at present to lack adequate definition as an academic discipline" (Crook 1970b: 207), and at the same time an anthropologist questioned most ethological interpretations of social man in a book called *Ethology and Society* (Callan 1970). But from another side it was maintained with direct reference to psychology that the "features of ethology augur favorably for tremendous advances in the formulation and analysis of behavior systems, in the near future and for a long time to come" (Hess 1962: 254). In any case we have today a rapidly increasing amount of information on human territoriality, and it seems to be quite natural to classify adherent behaviour as ethological. This kind of observation has shown itself to be of great interest even for the medical profession, particularly for psychoanalysts, as demonstrated, e.g., at the "Symposium on 'Psychoanalysis and Ethology'" (1960), and for general psychiatrists (Ploog 1964; *Behaviour Studies in Psychiatry* 1970).

2.3.4. Sociology, ecology and territorology

The implications of psychoanalysis and psychiatry as well as those of sociology raise important questions in the dynamic field covering that behaviour and environment-relation of individuals and groups which we call territoriality. This is why even sociologists have been interested in the phenomenon (e.g., Goffman 1972). In fact modern sociology was established some fifty years ago with biological ecology as a model (Timasheff 1957: 212-215). The central study area was in the beginning conditions of city societies, and the discipline was initially called human ecology. This concept was thus once restricted to community and particularly urban sociology (e.g., Wirth 1956), but it has also been used in medicine for environmental relations of disease (Bruhn 1970) and for the whole realm of geography (Barrows 1923), as well as for all parts of the science of man (Bews 1935: 13-14).

Functionally, territory in animals as well as in man is an ecological phenomenon, while as aforementioned it relates organisms to their milieu (cf. Pitelka 1959: 253). This process is, however, dependent on behavioural traits and thus ethology is the next science to bring in. The basic roles of territoriality, which will be discussed later (sections 3.3., 4.6.), and its central place among spatial disciplines can well defend the pretension to a special name. After considering such terms as human topology, chaology, oriology, chorology etc. E.T. Hall (1968: 83) chose proxemics as a suitable designation for "the study of man's perception and use of space".

But it seems more natural to stay closer to "territory" and state that "territorology" today has become "a broad and fairly well-cultivated field of science, in which ethology, animal psychology, and ecology are successfully combined. It seems to me that ethnology, physical anthropology, and sociology can also gain in various ways from territorology, especially since human behavior can never be understood as something isolated, but only in its phylogeny as revealed by comparative studies" (Hediger 1970b: 34-36). For the moment it is, however, quite enough to assert that the study of human territoriality is multi-disciplinary, albeit primarily a part of ethological ecology.

Other basic questions involve the relations between territoriality on one side and instinct and aggression on the other, and this matter will now be discussed.

2.4. Instinct and aggression

2.4.1. History of instinct

That there is, at least in vertebrates, a phenomenon called territoriality is hardly denied by any scientist today. But controversies still occur over the eventual instinctive background for observed behaviour of this kind, provided with more or less aggressive attributes. This is, of course, a cardinal point in the context, because an inborn mechanism involves quite another solidity, unchangeability and importance for territoriality than if it should be just a question of cultural, learned superstructures (cf. Ardrey 1967: 102-103). So we have first to look briefly at the content and use of the concept of instinct – coming from the Latin verb *instingere*, to prick and in a figurative sense to excite or urge – in order to see if it is applicable to territorial behaviour phenomena in non-human and particularly human animals.

The Greek language has no special word for instinct (S. Diamond 1971: 325), but it seems probable that the control of the movements of animals to their advantage, proclaimed by the classic Platonists and Stoics, should be of an instinctual character. Later on the instinct concept was adopted by the Christian church, but from the Renaissance onwards it was criticized by various scholars in England, France and Germany. David Hume, however, in his rather modern natural philosophy from the eighteenth century, held instinct in esteem. The term was later wholly rejected on different grounds, by such authorities as, e.g., the field naturalist Alfred Brehm and the physiologist Jacques Loeb, but was revived by the vitalists of the last century.

Darwin gave the instinct theory a new and solid basis. He was the first to state that instincts imply some inherited modification of the brain, that they do not separate but bring animals and men together and that they originate and function within the field of variation and natural selection (Ziegler 1920: 1-75). Darwin (1963: 228) himself did not attempt to define the concept of instinct in *The Origin of Species*, first published in 1859, but he gave sufficient examples so that "every one understands what is meant...".

At the beginning of this century a rather good definition was, however, given by a quartet of well-known experts (C.L. Morgan, J.M. Baldwin, K. Groos and G.F. Stout 1901-1905: 555). They classified instinct as "An inherited reaction of the sensori-motor type, relatively complex and markedly adaptive in character, and common to a group of individuals". Further they stressed that "This definition makes instinct a definitely biological, not a psychological conception" (cf. also C.L. Morgan 1895). At about the same time C.O. Whitman (1898: 328), one of the forerunners of ethology, stated that, "Instinct and structure are to be studied from the common standpoint of phyletic descent, and that not the less because we may seldom, if ever, be able to trace the whole development of an instinct".

But Whitman was too far ahead of his time, and the phylogenetic approach got no immediate response. Some years earlier William James (1892: 391-414) had declared that "*Instinct is usually defined as the faculty of acting in such a way as to produce certain ends, without foresight of the ends, and without previous education in the performance*". He even maintained that instinctive actions all conform to the general reflex type, that every instinct is an impulse and that every instinctive act, in an animal with memory, must cease to be 'blind' after being once repeated – dubious arguments which have strongly influenced later schools of thought.

James B. Watson, like most other behaviourists, denied the effect of instincts, because experience is a fact from the first day of life of the individual, and concentrated instead on the roles of learning and motivation. This "war over instinct was fought more with words and inferential reasoning than with behavioral evidence" (Beach 1955: 404). It should, however, not be forgotten that some scholars like Craig (e.g., 1918) and Tolman (1932: 305) defended instincts, the latter speaking of them as "varieties, or phases, of response primarily due to innate endowment plus a biologically provided normal or standard, environment".

In Europe instinct was long a very broad concept. The well-known German psychologist Wilhelm Wundt (1892: 430-446) regarded as instincts all mechanically running, more complicated actions. He even divided them into inborn and acquired, the latter group probably identical with what is now called conditioned reflexes. Ziegler (1920: 94), however, asserted that instincts are innate and that only actions which are not learnt or acquired by exercise should be designated as instinctive.

2.4.2. Ethologists and anti-ethologists

When Konrad Lorenz (1937), taking up suggestions from C.O. Whitman and Oskar Heinroth, first published his instinct theory, it was primarily in the form of an attack. He questioned the belief of Herbert Spencer and Lloyd Morgan that instinctive action cannot be clearly distinguished from other types of behaviour and that through experience it develops into intelligence (cf. Rivers 1922: 40-51). Further he rejected McDougall's classification of instinctive action as purposive behaviour, and he upset the chain as well as the conditioned reflex theories of Ziegler and others. Lorenz (1939) described instinctive action as a behaviour depending on an inherited, specific, stereotyped motor pattern.

Nikolaas Tinbergen (1958: 112), the second founder of ethology, defined instinct in 1951 as "a hierarchically organized nervous mechanism which is susceptible to certain priming, releasing and directing impulses of internal as well as of external origin, and which responds to these impulses by coordinated movements that contribute to the maintenance of the individual and the species". Tinbergen called the first chapter in his book *The Study of Instinct*, published in 1951, "Ethology: The Objective Study of Behaviour". So it was particularly this seeming pretension to sole objectivity which was sharply attacked by Kennedy (1954), who stressed the subjective character of some ethological terms and their kinship with those of psychoanalytic theory while at the same time defending the reflex explanation of instincts. In using the word, "objective," however, Tinbergen (1953: 126) meant "with the assistance of the traditional methods of the natural sciences".

At about the same time "A Critique of Konrad Lorenz's Theory of Instinctive Behavior" was presented by Lehrman (1953), who concluded his treatise in this way: "Any instinct theory which regards 'instinct' as immanent, preformed, inherited, or based on specific neural structures is bound to divert the investigation of behavior development from fundamental analysis and the study of developmental problems. Any such theory of 'instinct' inevitably tends to short-circuit the scientist's investigation of intraorganic and organism-environment developmental relationships which underlie the development of 'instinctive' behavior".

Very useful was a series of confrontations between European ethologists, stressing the importance of inborn behaviour, and representatives above all of the American school of behaviourists, emphasizing the role of learning, which took place in the years 1954-1958 (*Group Processes* 1955-1959; *L'instinct dans le comportement des animaux et de l'homme 1956*). The result was a better mutual understanding, preferably as to terminology, and a growing consensus about the importance of both the innate and the learned in most, if not all, behaviour, but no settling of the controversy.

Thus it was said (Potash 1966: 95): "There is no such thing as an instinct in animals or men (either in the sense of an innate drive or in the sense of an innate pattern of behavior)". And recently Freedman (1975: 31-32) maintained that "it seems unlikely that animals have built-in instinctive territorial instincts" for the reasons that "animals seem to like physical contact", that "controlled studies on reactions to lack of space have produced mixed results" and that "the amount of space has little or no effect, while the number of other animals present does". Detailed evidence on the great frequency, permanence and rigidity of territorial phenomena will, in the coming treatment, hopefully, give more than enough counter-evidence to these views. Meanwhile, the general attitude now seems to have changed, for "Although behaviourists in the past have tended to regard the development of behaviour as entirely determined by experience, they seem nowadays to be moving away from this concept, even in America" (Vowles 1970: 19).

In his book *Evolution and Modification of Behavior* from 1965 Lorenz (1973: 101-109) argued that there are "in the machinery of behavior, quite considerable self-contained units into which learning does not enter, and which, in the hierarchical organization of appetitive behavior, are intercalated with links that are adaptively modifiable by learning.... No insight into the physiological causation of behavior can be gained without knowledge of the source of the information contained in any of its adaptations to environment. Neither the close cooperation between phylogenetic adaptation and adaptive modification of behavior nor the close analogy between the 'methods' by which both processes extract information from the environment must ever make us forget the basic difference in their physiological causation".

In spite of the remaining lack of unanimity as to the value and use of the crucial term of instinct and its alternatives (cf. e.g., Lehrman 1970; Leyhausen 1974) it must be underlined: "There is a good excuse for naively using a word of common parlance even if one cannot give an exact definition of the concept corresponding to it: very usually there is a real natural unit corresponding to a concept for which the natural growth of common language has developed a word" (Lorenz 1956: 633). And without doubt a leading British expert was right when he asserted: "This inflexible instinctive behaviour is so over-whelmingly apparent as to constitute one of the ethologist's most attractive subjects for analysis. So he finds almost incomprehensible the reluctance of the psychologist, both 'human' and 'comparative', to take seriously this stereotyped behaviour and to pay due regard to its major theoretical impli-cations" (Thorpe 1961: 87).

2.4.3. Instinct in man

Looking more specifically on man we will first note that the term instinct, for more than a thousand years up to about 1270, was just used in relation to humans (cf. S. Diamond 1971: 326). Its meaning in anthropological con-nections has always been changing, even during this century (cf., e.g., Bühler 1926 and Lorenz 1953). As an extreme example it could be noted that Bernard (1924: 220) in his book on *Instinct* tabulated no less than 5,759 classes of human instincts, while in a later work (1942: 562) he enumerated only 23 true and 23 false instincts – modes of procedure which undoubtedly gave a ridic-ulous touch to the matter.

Those authors who have emphatically denied the possibility of applying the term instinct to man are here represented by an anthropologist, a psychiatrist and a sociologist: (a) "It is a misapplication of the word 'instinct' to use it about human conditions ..." (Sombart 1938:9); (b) "The time is now long overdue for psychiatry, and particularly for psychoanalysis, to divest itself of the inaccurate concept of instinct as applied to human behavior. In the past quarter of a century the advances made in the fields of experimental psychology, biology, and anthropology leave little doubt that this concept has diminishing scientific validity at each stage of ascent in the evolu-tionary scale, and least of all when applied to man" (Marmor 1942:515); (c) "Apparently all of the specific direction of behavior required to satisfy demands of the physiological mechanisms is supplied by habits acquired in experience, and mainly in organized social experience. Custom does the work formerly thought to be performed by instinct, and adequacy of the culture supplants 'wisdom of the body' " (Faris 1966: 29).

Probably still more behaviour students have, however, long recognized the value of and the realities behind the instinct concept, also for man. The psychologist J.R. Kantor (1920: 51) showed clearly that the function of human instincts is to adapt the person to the various surroundings in which he is found, pending the development of the intelligent responses usually required for such adaptations. These modes of instinctive response develop in the organism during its interaction with the environment. Consequently there is an entirely natural genesis of the instincts paralleling the growth of the human being in the evolutionary course of the animal species to which he belongs.

In his book *Instinct in Man* the sociologist Ronald Fletcher (1957: 303) asserted: "The theory of the instincts must conclude that the major ends of human activity are rooted in the instincts, and that instinctual experience is, indeed, an extremely extensive and important feature of human nature, exerting a far-reaching influence upon conscious and rational activity in both individual and social life". That instinctive actions are commonly performed in the human context, not only by children but also by adults, and are perhaps most often and most easily seen in mental deficiency patients has recently been shown by the psychiatrist Pilleri (1971).

As earlier suggested it seems evident that much of the divergence of opinion, not the least as to numbers of instinctive phenomena, is rooted in differing terminology, e.g., confusion of "instinct" and "drive". Speaking of children Barnett (1962: 2) summarized the meaning of these two concepts, saying that there are well-defined, characteristic, stereotyped behaviour patterns (instincts) as well as fluctuating, internal, emotional states (drives) influencing behaviour. Most often instincts are accompanied by drives. The common view that instinct and experience are incompatible and that man's great capacity to learn must imply only few and insignificant instinctual relics was clearly rejected by Lorenz (1973: 29), who stressed that "all learning is performed by mechanisms which do contain phylogenetically acquired information".

Leyhausen (1969b: 81) also thought false the old supposition that the higher mammals and man in particular should be more and more deprived of instincts. "The great multiplicity of experienced and learned behaviour which phenomenologically appears predominant in humans is not compensation for lack of instincts or even adaptive superstructure on a rigid and closed instinct system. Instead, this abundance of behaviour elements is actively built upon a much more diversified and complex armoury of instincts, compared with lower vertebrates and invertebrates" (cf. also the valuable survey "The Instinctoid Nature of Basic Needs" by A.H. Maslow 1953-1954).

Maybe the truth in the instinct controversy was best summarized by the Swedish zoologist Hans Wallengren (1927: 254) who, taking issue with a French animal psychologist, vindicated: "Even though one as Bohn kills the concept, it rises without his knowledge from the dead and pushes itself forward".

2.4.4. *Aggressive behaviour and instinct*

Moving on to aggression, this term is most often not defined, probably because its meaning is supposed to be known to all. But it was declared, e.g., that "An animal acts aggressively when it inflicts, attempts to inflict, or threatens to inflict damage on another animal. The act is accompanied by recognizable behavioural symptoms and definable physiological changes" (Carthy and Ebling 1964: 1). It looks as if there is less violence in the term of agonistic behaviour, which, however, likewise can be broadly interpreted as falling in the range from attack through threat to passive defense (cf. Vowles 1970: 7). According to Ardrey (1972: 257): "There is aggressiveness, arising from the competition of beings, without which natural selection could not take place. There is violence, that form of aggressiveness which employs or effectively threatens the use of physical force. And there is war, that particular form of organized violence taking place between groups". Of special interest now is that "Aggression within animal species is almost always associated with competition" (E.O. Wilson 1971: 185) and that this competition establishes the type of organization which best satisfies environmental requirements, i.e., that which is most adaptive (cf. Collias 1944; Goldsmith 1974: 125).

Speaking of humans the psychologist H. Kaufmann (1970: 10-11) after thorough reasoning presented the following definition of aggressive behaviour: "1. It must be transitive; that is, directed against a living target (as opposed to being purely autistic). 2. The attacker must have an expectation or subjective probability greater than zero of reaching the object and of imparting a noxious stimulus to it, or both". This formulation is not very far from that of Tinbergen (1968: 1412), who explained that for him "aggression involves approaching an opponent, and, when within reach, pushing him away, inflicting damage of some kind, or at least forcing stimuli upon him that subdue him. In this description the effect is already implicit: such behavior tends to remove the opponent, or at least to make him change his behavior in such a way that he no longer interferes with the attacker". In the last definition the connections between aggression and territoriality are clear, and it could be mentioned that the psychiatrist Bilz (1967: 167) coined a special term for this defensive behaviour: *"Territorium-Verteidigungs-Aggressivität"*.

As to an instinctive background for aggression the social psychologist Berkowitz (1962: 24) held the following opinion: "Animal aggression arising from obvious competition clearly does not stem from a constantly operative (i.e., entirely internally based) instinctive drive to hostility. Such hostility is primarily either instrumental aggression or a reaction to frustrations" (cf. also Berkowitz 1969). And the ethologist J.P. Scott (e.g. 1958: 20) came to the conclusion that aggressive behaviour in animals has to be learned or at least mostly depends on experience.

Such views seem to be common to all of the authors of the book *Man and Aggression* (1970), predominantly a horrible squib against ethology. It is here indicated, for instance, that " 'Aggressive instinct' is a catchy phrase, but its usefulness for an understanding of interpersonal aggression is quite limited" (H. Kaufmann 1970: 13). And it is maintained in another connection that "Accounts of human aggressiveness must include the process, specific to the human species, by which man learns and responds to external stimulation in accordance with verbally formulated rules or generalizations" (Sherif and Sherif 1970: 567; cf. also Aronson 1976: 141-171).

More balanced is this argumentation: "The social learning theory of human aggression adopts the position that man is endowed with neuro-physiological mechanisms that enable him to behave aggressively, but the activation of these mechanisms depends upon appropriate stimulation and is subject to cortical control. Therefore, the specific forms that aggressive behavior takes, the frequency with which it is expressed, the situations in which it is displayed, and the specific targets selected for attack are largely determined by social experience" (Bandura 1973: 29-30). The sociologist Berghe (1974: 779), however, recently underlined: "What seems no longer tenable at this juncture is any theory of human behavior which ignores biology and relies exclusively on socio-cultural learning as an explanation, as does, for instance, Bandura (1973) in his theory of aggression".

That animal aggression has an instinctive basis as well as a species-preserving function was stressed by Lorenz (e.g., 1965: 119-152). According to his reasoning aggression is a true instinct with its own endogenous excitatory potential and appropriate appetitive behaviour. And Eibl-Eibesfeldt (1961: 112) declared: "Investigators of aggressive behaviour, often strongly motivated by concern about aggressive impulses in man, have usually been satisfied to find its origin in the life experience of the individual animal or of the social group. Aggressiveness is said to be learned and so to be preventable by teaching or conditioning. A growing body of evidence from observations in the field and experiments in the laboratory, however, points to the conclusion that this vital mode of behavior is not learned by the individual but is innate in the species, like the organs specially evolved for such combat in many animals" (cf. also Tinbergen 1968; B.A. Cox 1968).

Indubitably the existence of such animal phenomena as tournament fighting indicates how strong the selection pressure is in favour of inherited aggressive behaviour. Otherwise counterselection would have bred it out, where damage to conspecifics is possible. Instead, the most complex fighting techniques have evolved in order to allow fights as spacing-out mechanisms (cf. Eibl-Eibesfeldt 1970: 325). Most interesting were the experiments (Wuttke and Hoffmeister 1967) which showed that certain psychopharmacological agents could stop reactive fighting which depended on external influence, but could not stop spontaneous, unprovoked aggression (cf. also Avis 1974).

As late as 1909 Sigmund Freud would not accept the existence of a special instinct for aggression in man. It was not until after much additional clinical and historical evidence had been analysed that he came to the final conclusion that the tendency to aggression is an innate, independent, instinctual disposition. This conclusion is now one of the basic postulates of psychoanalytic theory (cf. Freeman 1964: 109). "In the human species, it seems likely, aggressive behavior evolved in the service of the same functions as it did in the case of lower animals. Undoubtedly it was useful and adaptive thousands of years ago, when men lived in small groups. With the growth of supersocieties, however, such behavior has become maladaptive. It will have to be controlled – and the first step in the direction of control is the realization that aggressiveness is deeply rooted in the history of the species and in the physiology and behavioral organization of each individual" (Eibl-Eibesfeldt 1961: 122).

2.4.5. Function of aggression

In spite of steady and intense critique from different directions, not the least the psychological (cf. e.g., Ginsberg 1952), against the actual use of the word instinct, this concept "has acquired new and significant meaning in the study of animal behavior, and its elaboration has provided insights into the nature of social behavior that are indispensable for modern views" (Etkin 1964b: 167). It should be stressed that "The most general dispersing mechanism in vertebrates is intraspecific aggression and its counterpart, escape" (Kummer 1971: 222) and that "Ownership of territory is frequently a prerequisite for the occurrence of aggressive behavior" (Eibl-Eibesfeldt 1970: 312). But it must also be underlined that the constraints on aggression are so great that even when it functions" as a genetically determined trait it can be expected to be programed in such a way as to be brought into play only when it gives a momentary advantage" (E.O. Wilson 1971: 199; cf. also Fabricius 1974).

Without doubt there are still scholars who, like Freedman (1975: 105), do not hesitate to state about people that "they show no hint of territoriality in the sense of an instinctive aggressive response to a lack of space". But still more seem to realize with Berghe (1974: 778) that "Homo sapiens scores higher on territoriality, hierarchy, aggressivity, and population pressure than most mammals, and nearly all of our nearest relatives, the higher primates". And this author proceeds: "The common element to the two solutions of territoriality and hierarchy is that, while they regulate competition and thus aggression they also require a great deal of aggression both to maintain and to change. Boundaries and pecking orders are constantly tested, i.e., they are both challenged and defended. Aggression, then, is a mechanism making for both stability and change, the two ubiquitous sides of social organization".

Thus human aggressive behaviour occurs in a variety of contexts with a number of different patterns and functions with both innate and acquired elements contributing to the final results (cf. the very good survey by Freeman 1971). A correlation has further been established between hormones and aggression, and those areas of the brain which are involved in agonistic behaviour have been fairly well identified as ranging from the midbrain through the hypothalamus and the thalamus to the limbic structures of the forebrain and neocortex. It has also been possible to show experimentally that stimulation of these areas can evoke aggressive emotional feelings. Actual knowledge supports the idea that isolation effects changes in the brain, leading to a heightened responsiveness to stimuli which can elicit aggression. The result is evident. "Territorial behaviour is, of course, manifested by aggressive or defensive actions against intruders and this would presumably be parallelled by the physiological changes described above" (Vowles 1970: 15-33).

Consequently it seems very probable that main parts of the aggressive behaviour in man are instinctive and that territorial defense is based on this instinctive aggression. Having examined concepts basic to territoriality we now present a summary report on animal territories.

3. Animal territories

3.1. Characteristic features

3.1.1. Territory types

It is a fundamental mistake to believe that mobile animals have a complete spatial freedom. As stressed especially by Hediger (e.g., 1942: 15-24) they are limited first by range – here similar to distribution area – second by habitat and third by territory according to species and other demands.

As stated earlier the concept of territory is a dynamic one, and McBride (1964: 76-77) suggested "that the basic expression of the social dimension is a type of 'extension of self' in space to create a field of social force associated with an animal . . . . the territories represent social force fields fixed in space". Later on this author changed his terminology, using "personal field" instead of "social force field" (McBride 1971: 55). Such views supported by the great variability of the phenomenon are probably the background for statements like this: "Territory is not space, it is behaviour" (D.S. Peters 1962: 163).

Considering the fact that territory is a space-time system it is remarkable how often the temporal aspects are neglected. In practice there are all grada-tions, from exclusive spaces in permanent use during the whole lifetime of an individual or group to quite ephemeral spaces. Most often it is a matter of season, at least in the sense that territories are more evident at certain times of the year than at others. Sometimes it even happens that the same space is the territory of different individuals at dissimilar times of the day (cf. Leyhausen 1971a). This relative nature of territoriality does not, however, diminish the strength of the concept as much as perhaps could be expected.

For even though an animal holds or grows up in a territory during a rather short reproductive season, this space is often central or decisive for its be-haviour during the rest of the year, perhaps sometimes during its whole lifetime, determining the migrations and other movements away and back. In fact it is sometimes tempting to apply the term "home" here, and "homing" has long been the word for the migratory journeys towards the native or reproductive place, this locality having a special attraction. But this does not mean that territories cannot be held, even repetitively, in other regions too (cf., e.g., Dorst 1962: XV-XVI).

As to the limitation of territory it is, as mentioned, often impossible to trace it in the field without the presence of the holder, but there are many cases where conspicuous traits of the environment separate the territorial units (cf., e.g., Watson and Miller 1971: 373). Without doubt territory often functions as a system of biologically significant, more or less connected points rather than as a bounded space (Hediger 1946: 242-247; *Die Strassen der Tiere* 1967; Fischer 1971). It could be that these path habits, at least partly, are based upon conditioned responses worked out during the animals' exploration of their life space (cf. Lorenz 1973: 67-70). The most important point in the territorial path system is, of course, the eventual nest or den, but also other refuges as well as preferred feeding, drinking, perching or resting places are valuable in the context.

Self-evidently we are here highly interested in the marking places, which are crucial for the exclusiveness of territories and can be placed at their periphery as well as in the centre. The marking animal can make its territory conspicuous by means of mechanical changes of the environment, by excretions of various kinds and particularly by display of its voice and morphological characters (cf. Hediger 1970b: 39-42). Perhaps not all marking behaviour is related to territory, and undoubtedly the communication value of some markings is still not demonstrated enough (cf., e.g., R.P. Johnson 1973), but the principle seems to be quite evident.

3.1.2. *Form, size and exclusiveness of territory*

As to the shape of territory there are, of course, strong variations, even though a more or less circular form is the easiest one to supervise and defend and therefore the most common, provided that environmental or other conditions do not prevent it. Territories may be fixed in space or portable, as for nomadic animals, and there are totally exclusive as well as overlapping types. Concerning size it is clear that the normal magnitude of territory changes between different species, so that larger animals often keep larger territories (e.g. Schoener 1968). In fact it is most often impossible, beforehand, to state any details about the measures of the regular territorial space of a certain species. This depends i.a. upon the fact that not only quantitative but also qualitative aspects are in operation, above all that the structure of the habitat and the frequency of the local population are significant factors (cf. Dice

1952: 247-254; Wynne-Edwards 1962: 98-101; Hediger 1970a: 526; Soja 1971: 23-28).

According to the rubber-disc theory of J.S. Huxley (1934) territories are compressed with increasing number of settlers, and this is often seen in the field, but there must always be minimum as well as maximum sizes for the territorial space of a species. It should also not be overlooked that "Territorialism obviously can not be manifested unless the species is sufficiently common so that there is the necessity of defending the territory. Abundance then is a prerequisite, not for territorialism, but for our recognition of territorialism" (D.E. Davis 1941:93). The intolerance to crowding that territoriality implies seems to underlie the definiteness of threshold values often recorded for given species on given areas (Errington 1946: 228).

Well known is the formulation by Margaret Morse Nice (1941: 468) about territory: "*It is based primarily on a positive reaction to a particular place and a negative reaction to other individuals*". There is also a wealth of information supporting the fact that single animals often have quite exclusive territories with no trespassing permitted. Particularly for males before and during reproduction time this is a common phenomenon, and after pair-building both parties join in display and defense, even though the male with few exceptions is dominating in this respect. Unpaired animals also sometimes hold territories, but these are mostly small compared to those of the breeders (cf. O.M. Watson 1970: 20-27; Kälin 1972: 32-40).

Overt physical aggressiveness and defense in connection with territories seem in most cases to be uncommon and concentrated around the time of establishment. It is even stated that "we may include in the term 'territorial behaviour' anything that can be shown to reduce a competitor's aggression" (Assem 1967: 144). Marler (1976a: 240), however, believed that "the violence of animals has been underestimated". It should also be stressed that aggression phenomena, frequent or not, are all but unimportant, and it is often demonstrated how they increase, in the case of intrusion, towards the centre of the territorial "property" (cf., e.g., Iersel 1953; Meyer-Holzapfel 1952: 7-9). But when individual holders and limits are known to neighbours, violence is generally substituted by display of some kind. It is trivial that former combatants meet quite peacefully on neutral feeding ground (cf. Richard 1970: 3-4), and extreme cold in spring can upset the whole territorial system for a while and cause the animals to assemble in winter flocks. Temperature can also influence the magnitude of territories (cf., e.g., Jenkins 1944: 43). Kalela (1954: 6-8) gave examples implying that there are many exceptions to the rule of negative reaction towards other individuals, even among holders of normal, exclusive territories.

Here it should be noted that there is, as a counterpart to personal space in man, a concept of individual space or individual distance ("*Individual-Distanz*", Hediger 1941: 43), which means that, irrespective of other spatial preference, every individual animal is separated from its conspecifics, even its own mate, by a certain distance, varying between different species. In social context this has a counterpart in group space (cf. Brown and Orians 1970: 243). In the past it was often said that colonial animals have no territories but it is now known that most often every member has a quite small but strongly defended individual territory and the whole colony a special group territory (Wynne-Edwards 1962: 158-160). Individual territories are, of course, evidence of a more or less unrestricted spatial domination, which with little available space and many individuals can be easily changed into a hierarchical power system.

3.1.3. *Instinctiveness and origin of territoriality*

That animal territoriality is instinctive was presupposed by most authors treating the subject (e.g., E. Howard 1948: 65-66; Hediger 1956; D.E. Davis 1962: 319). According to Walter Heape (1931: 31): "Amongst a large proportion of the animals capable of locomotion, even amongst many gregarious animals, the instinct for the preservation of individual territorial rights prevails with increased force and vigilance during the breeding season. Thus, it is a main attribute of family life, the preservation of which is indeed one of the most primitive of all instincts, and is perhaps the most solid part of the foundation on which our own civilisation is built".

A possible explanation for the origin and diversity of territoriality was advanced by Leyhausen (1971a: 23-25), who found that the overall motivational state of the animal varies with circadian, seasonal and other rhythms and also because of interference by non-rhythmic factors. The kind of halo which surrounds an animal as a result of keeping individual distance and of ranking is, therefore, not rigid but pulsates, as it were, more or less regularly and rhythmically. "Remembering that this pulsating halo of rank-determined individual distance is individual with respect not only to the owner but also to its relationships with each individual member of the group, and that in this respect the halo resembles somewhat the common field of gravity of two celestial bodies, it becomes obvious that the function of space in shaping the social interactions within the group is far from being straightforward and easy to understand, and that the extension into the fourth dimension is partly rhythmically repetitive and partly not.... If an individual becomes home-conscious, if it attaches itself to one place or district, the fact of individual distance will result in an area, a fixed area, a geographically definable area, instead of a moveable halo around the animal; and this is called territory".

Thus, it could be stated that behavioural territoriality is a spatially as well as temporally strongly varying, but nevertheless definite and concrete phenomenon of general distribution in the animal kingdom. It is known from different invertebrate groups and from all the classes of vertebrates. Now we will concentrate on a presentation of territories in birds, where the matter was first studied and is best known, and in non-human mammals, which, of course, are of particular interest in this context.

3.2. Territories in birds and mammals

3.2.1. Discovery of bird territories

More than two thousand years ago Aristotle wrote that "a pair of eagles demands an extensive space for its maintenance, and consequently cannot allow other birds to quarter themselves in close neighbourhood" (D.W. Thompson 1910: 619a). And in 1622 G.P. Olina published in Rome a book in which it was said: "It is proper to this Bird at its first coming to occupy or seize upon one place as its Freehold, into which it will not admit any other Nightingale but its mate and where it usually sings". If these two descriptions were the first known of behavioural territories, the latter term was in its actual meaning initially used by Oliver Goldsmith in 1774: "The fact is, all these small birds mark out a territory to themselves, which they will permit none of their own species to remain in; they guard their dominions with the most watchful resentment; and we seldom find two male tenents in the same hedge together" (Nice 1941: 442-443).

But the first scholars giving comprehensive accounts of the matter were J. B. T. Altum in "Der Vogel und sein Leben" from 1868 (Mayr 1935) and Eliot Howard in several works but particularly *Territory in Bird Life* from 1920 (E. Howard 1948). It should, however, not be forgotten that C. B. Moffat (1903) also presented a scientifically outstanding treatise on the subject, where only the underestimation of bird mortality was a flaw. The facts that birds are common and conspicuous, that they especially during breeding time proclaim their lands by singing and display and that at certain times they regularly chase each other and fight at the territory boundaries are probably responsible for the fast growing interest in territoriality during the last fifty years, first awoken by Howard's books.

Without doubt territorial behaviour is a very general phenomenon in birds, and these animals, like fishes, have, literally, spaces for territory and not merely areas or path systems. In practice this means that with few exceptions they are capable of three-dimensional movements, that they can easily visit all parts of the space and that they can really survey their territories from song and perching-posts or when flying in the air. Another important factor is, of course, that reproduction is fixed to a nest with eggs and young, which cannot be moved. Thus bird territories are very often mating and nesting ones (cf., e.g., D.E. Davis 1952: 174-175). The sexual background is, in these cases, also evident from the fact that doves injected with testosterone propionate enlarged their previously held artificial territories. But the hormonal control is surely not complete, for partially or wholly gonadectomized birds still won test encounters while in their home area (cf. C.R. Carpenter 1961:232-235).

3.2.2. Variations of bird territoriality

Territory seems to be most studied in non-migrating or migrating passerine birds, among the latter of which males usually come to the breeding grounds in spring several days before females. When these arrive, the males have in most cases already established territories and are in full song, thus advertising to other males their reclaiming of land and at the same time attracting females. After mating the two birds of the pair can join in defense of their territory, but in some species the male alone performs this task. There are also cases in which male and female arrive mated from migration and establish their territorial space together (cf. The Ibis 1956: 340-530).

But if the male is dominant in choosing and limiting the territory, the female normally decides the place for the nest, hole-nesting birds excepted. The male in this case seeks a suitable hole and fights for it as for territory (Haartman 1957). A general feature also seems to be that territorial urges become less strong as reproduction proceeds, and when the young grow up, the parents have little time for exclusion competition. After the breeding season the birds often abandon their territories and join flocks with just males, females or young or of a mixed composition (cf. Dice 1952: 235-241).

An exception to one of the rules above is, not unexpectedly, the European cuckoo, *Cuculus canorus*. Here the female locates and defends a space, incorporating territories of a number of that bird species, which this individual exploits as host for its eggs. And in hummingbirds both sexes establish and guard separate territories during the whole breeding season. Rather peculiar also are those species, such as the American woodcock, *Philohela minor*, which defend just their mating territory, to which females come for copulation but where neither feeding nor breeding take place. Of the same character are the wellknown communal "lek" territories of northern galliform species like the American ruffed grouse, *Bonasa umbellus*, and the European blackcock, *Lyrurus tetrix* (cf. Dice loc. cit.).

Of special interest from a territorial point of view are those birds which live in colonies. For marine species the feeding grounds are in the sea, while the nesting territories on land for some terns, e.g., are just the nest and adjacent space as far as the breeding bird can reach with its bill. For colonial land birds like the rook, *Corvus frugilegus*, there are all-purpose social territories as well as small, individual nesting ones. The rookery is situated within such a social area, claimed as a mostly exclusive feeding ground for all the birds of the colony, but functioning more according to custom and mutual avoidance than by means of daily boundary fighting. This dispersion pattern is in nonmigratory populations partly followed even in winter, but then the birds from several rookeries, evidently following a hierarchical system, join in larger and larger flocks in the afternoon to roost – predominantly in an old, cardinal, used or deserted rookery. These roosts represent a kind of collective night territory, which is visited most of the year outside the breeding season (cf. Wynne-Edwards 1962: 158-159; Malmberg 1971).

3.2.3. Mammalian territory traits

We can agree with Alverdes (1935: 199-202) that many mammals claim a certain territory for their residence and mark it in different ways. The very phenomenon of marking has long been in the centre of interest for Hediger (e.g., 1955: 19): "A particularly important type of locality in the animal's territory should not be overlooked, the so-called demarcation places, found with deer, and many other mammals. These exist usually on prominent twigs or branches, or tree stumps, or stones, to which the owner of the territory applies its own property marks, so to speak, in the form of a self-produced scent. We must remember that most mammals are macrosmatic, *i.e.*, they have a literally superhuman sense of smell, by means of which they recognize faint traces of scent, which are quite beyond our powers of detection, as conspicuous signals" (cf. also Hediger 1949).

As suggested earlier it is possible that the importance of scent marking has sometimes been exaggerated. "It seems probable, however, that although scent marks do not cause avoidance, they may signal that an animal is in foreign territory and predispose withdrawal in the presence of the resident animal" (R. P. Johnson 1973: 528). Concerning, e.g., the house mouse, *Mus musculus*, it was stated that this animal uses primarily visual information and only in the second hand olfactory means to recognize territory boundaries (Mackintosh 1973: 464-470), which without doubt is astonishing in such a night-active mammal. It could further be mentioned that not long ago there was a rather general consensus among workers that in this species territorial behaviour was absent or most weakly developed, both in wild and laboratory strains. But then Anderson and Hill (1965) showed experimentally that territoriality is a well-developed part of the social repertory of the animal.

Concerning the frequency of territorial behaviour in mammals the opinions are divergent. Burt (1943: 350), citing Heape, emphasized that nearly all scientists who have critically studied the behaviour of wild mammals have found territorial traits inherent in the species with which they have worked. But D. E. Davis (1949: 251) concluded that although territorialism in birds is quite well understood, the situation in mammals has not yet been clarified. He referred to the difference between nest and den with pertaining behaviour and the difficulty in observing the mostly nocturnal mammals defending their space as compared with the easily seen, more or less aggressive display of the preponderantly diurnal birds.

During the last decade considerable new information about the territoriality of different mammalian groups has become available. Thus Walther (1967) asserted about African ungulates that females are not a prerequisite for the foundation of territories, which are held by the lonely males long before the mating period. Writing of rodents L. E. Brown (1966: 134) demonstrated that the territory of a clan of *Apodemus* is protected by the males and maintained by the females and that a dominant male limits the territory of the community by means of his activity. And J. F. Eisenberg (1967: 99) underlined that there will be active territorial defense and fighting only when strangers dispute about food, nests etc. with dominant male rodents. It was further stressed (Leyhausen 1965a: 257-258) that "Only after studying a population for a long period and following the individuals at all times and through all situations will one be able to make a correct and proportional assessment of their social interaction and relationships".

Gustav Kramer (1950) seems to be the first author to stress that in territorial animals the fixation of an individual to a definite locality obviously facilitates the recognition of this individual by its neighbours. Hence they probably "label" the conspecifics encountered by the locality where the encounter took place. This is perhaps of minor importance in species like most songbirds, where neighbours are in almost continuous vocal and auditory contact, but it is likely to play a major role under conditions prevailing for solitary mammals.

The best synthesis of actual knowledge on the territories of non-social mammals seems to be that published by Leyhausen (1964: 394): "The basis for some kind of communal relationship in solitary mammals is modified territorial behaviour.... The owner usually cannot, like a bird, survey his whole territory almost simultaneously, and so cannot always immediately spot and drive out an intruder. Consequently mammalian territories usually overlap considerably, communal use of pathways by neighbours becomes tolerated, priority rights on occasional encounters are established and a ranking order based on territory ownership develops. Gradually the spacing-out function of territory is counterbalanced by a tie of mutual tolerance, attraction and sometimes even friendship. The keynote of communal organisation in solitary animals is therefore neighbourliness. The difference shows clearly when a stranger instead of a neighbour trespasses" (cf. 4.3.8.1.).

3.2.4. Primate territoriality in general

Of great interest for the sake of human territoriality is, of course, the territorial situation in the mostly group-living primates, close relatives to man. Particularly here, however, the scientists disagree. Thus Yerkes and Yerkes (1935: 999) maintained that no more impressive instance of territoriality had been described than that shown by the howler, but they admitted that many primate types frequent a certain limited range and on occasion defend it. And Scott (1969: 634) still claimed that territoriality, in the sense of permanent occupation of a specific area and defense of its boundaries, occurs relatively rarely among primates, a view which has been widely distributed.

But according to C. R. Carpenter (1952: 231), one of the most experienced experts in the field, "There are no known exceptions to the generalization that organized groups of monkeys and apes live in, occupy, possess and defend limited ranges of space or territories". And recently Schultz (1969: 237-238) concluded that "Social groups of primates generally live within territories of their own with fairly definite boundaries, not transgressed by others at least in the presence of the troop occupying the particular area".

Somewhere in between, Washburn, Jay and Lancaster (1972: 250) expressed themselves cautiously, stressing variability: "Populations may be capable of a wide variety of behavior patterns ranging from exclusive occupation of an area which may be defended against neighboring groups to a peaceful coexistence with conspecifics in which wide overlap in home ranges is tolerated. Because local populations of a species may maintain their ranges in different ways it is necessary to investigate all variations in group spacing in diverse habitats before attempting to describe characteristic behavior patterns for any species".

As to actual concrete knowledge, indubitable territoriality, according to modern and here applied definitions, has been confirmed at least in: howling monkeys, *Alouatta palliata*, (C. R. Carpenter 1934: 43-55) and in red spider monkeys, *Ateles geoffroyi*, (C. R. Carpenter 1935: 175-176) of Panama, in monkey species of the genus *Callicebus* of Colombia (Mason 1968: 214-216), in vervet monkeys, *Cercopithecus aethiops*, (Gartlan and Brain 1968: 277-278) as well as in species of the genus *Colobus* (Marler 1972: 179-180) and in patas monkeys, *Erythrocebus patas*, (K. R. L. Hall 1968: 54-60) of East and South Africa, in *Galago demidovii*, *Perodicticus potto* and *Lepilemur mustelinus* of central Africa and Madagascar (Charles-Dominique 1974), in *Lemur catta*, *Lemur macaco* and *Propithecus verreauxii* of Madagascar (Petter 1970), in hanuman langurs, *Presbytis entellus*, (Sugiyama 1967: 224-225) of India and in the macaque, *Macaca fuscata*, of Japan (Imanishi 1957-1958: 48).

Strongly territorial are, further, the two gibbon species, *Hylobates lar* and *Symphylangus syndactylus* (C. R. Carpenter 1941; Ellefson 1968), which are closely connected with the anthropoid apes. Ellefson (op. cit. p. 199) made a unique attempt to trace the evolutionary background of territoriality in these primates: "It is impossible to know whether territoriality was present in the ancestors of modern gibbons prior to the series of anatomical changes that led to their present-day specializations. However, it seems reasonable to assume that as trekking became more and more difficult because of these anatomical changes, the establishment and maintenance of a territory gained in adaptive value. Territoriality is as old in the gibbon lineage as the feeding-locomotor specializations that allow them to exploit a terminal branch-feeding niche efficiently. Given these features (anatomical specializations and territoriality) small group size is a necessity. The lack of variation in gibbon group size indicates that there continue to be severe selection pressures acting to maintain this state. The present-day success of gibbons in numbers and distribution suggests that this constellation of traits evolved and was highly successful in the distant past".

3.2.5. Territories of anthropoid apes

The three species of anthropoid apes belonging to the family *Pongidae* are close relatives of man and therefore highly important here. It has often been argued that they are not territorial at all, but this assertion must be modified.

If we first look at the orangutan, *Pongo pygmaeus*, new field investigations of this little-known animal have recently been made in undisturbed areas on the isle of Borneo during a period of more than one year. Contrary to earlier evidence it was now shown that the species is not without social organization, and the material "tends to support the tentative conclusion that males occupy discrete ranges and that long calls function to maintain spacing" (Rodman 1973: 189).

In his valuable monograph on the gorilla, *Gorilla gorilla*, in East Africa it was reported by Schaller (1963: 129): "Direct observations of the actions of groups near each other never revealed the slightest indication that a certain section of forest was defended directly by fighting or indirectly by aggressive displays against intrusion of another group. Although groups frequently hesitated to mingle and individuals occasionally behaved aggressively toward one another... no attempt was made to restrict movements into a certain area. This evidence suggests that territorial behavior is absent in gorillas".

Some years later the formulation was less affirmative (Schaller 1972: 100-101, 123): "The almost complete overlap of some ranges and observations on peaceful interactions between groups indicate that gorillas have no territory in the sense of an exclusive area defended against others of the same species". Concerning group encounters it was said that "Some join readily, others merely approach each other closely, and a few behave antagonistically toward each other".

These accounts make it not too difficult to give reasons for the supposed absence of territoriality. With the very small recent populations of gorillas, members of groups in contact are surely most often well acquainted with each other, some young animals perhaps excepted, and if spaces were divided between groups long ago, there is no need for actual, overt, territorial defense or display. It could also be, as Louis S. B. Leakey suggested in a discussion – emphatically supporting the territoriality of gorillas – that the troops studied by Schaller were just parts of a larger territorial group (Barnett 1967: 53).

Concerning the chimpanzee, *Pan troglodytes* – biochemically our nearest relative – the territory question is not quite settled either. The most comprehensive field investigations of this species were made in Tanzania by Jane van Lawick-Goodall (1968: 333). She admitted, however, that since the chimpanzee population of the Gombe Stream Reserve comprises only one loosely organized social group, she had no data on interactions between different troops of chimpanzees. Sugiyama (1973: 392-393) described encounters among more stable groups in Uganda:

"In the overlapping part of their ranges mixed parties of members of two adjacent groups were sometimes observed together without the occurrence of any agonism. However, I twice observed that when many chimpanzees of neighbouring groups met, they mixed together excitedly, ate exaggeratedly leaves and fruits which they seldom eat, ran and leaped about the ground and branches, drummed and beat the buttresses of the huge trees and uttered their desperate cry and bark. After nearly one hour of noisy booming clamour, the chimpanzees of each group returned to their own proper ranges. During the time no direct aggression against the other group between animals of separate groups could be observed. Although chimpanzees of neighbouring groups are acquainted with each other and have neighbourhood relations, they usually avoid mixing as whole groups".

The same reasoning seems to be quite possible here as for the gorilla (cf. Chance 1967: 130-131). Thus it was stressed by Marler (1976b: 260): "Most recent research suggests that there is territoriality in both species, and that adult males take a prime role in territorial defence in both the chimpanzee and the gorilla. In the former the territory is maintained by a group of males, while in the latter the onus tends to fall on one silverback male".

Particularly decisive in all these cases is, of course, the magnitude of the population, and examples from the hanuman langur are in this context very instructive (cf. Ardrey 1972: 221-223). First Jay (1963) studied the species in certain forests of central India, where it is fairly scarce, and the result showed that each troop had a range of about two square miles, that there were no evident boundaries between groups and no defended territories. Later Ripley (e.g., 1967) investigated troops of about the same size in Ceylon, where they had one-half to one-eighth of a square mile each, unchanging borders and defended territories. Finally Sugiyama (1967) made research on hanuman langurs in forests of Western India, where the territories averaged 8.9 hectares, both territorial order and dominance order were poor and the situation not far from that of a "behavioral sink" (Calhoun 1962a). The number of animals per square mile in the three studies was about 20, 150 and 300, respectively.

3.2.6. *Primate territoriality concluded*

We can conclude that not a few primate species have already shown themselves to be clearly territorial, and without doubt their number will increase
with more thorough investigations and a perfect consensus as to terminology.
It seems, e.g., very probable that the core area reported for many primates
cannot be sharply distinguished from, and is in several instances equal to,
territory (cf. Jolly 1972: 102-107). Perhaps these predominantly vegetarian
animals give more attention to the centre than to the periphery of their territory, as many mammals do. Further, there are indications that most primate
species, if not all, are capable of territorial behaviour if their living conditions
begin to deteriorate (cf. Gartlan and Brain 1968: 278) and under such circumstances the territorial behaviour can be exceedingly defensive (Dolhinow
1972: 360).

In fact present-day primates show a variety of distinctive behaviours acting
to create or support territorial inclinations. "Presumably, these behaviors are
reflected in many basic adjustments – ecological, social, and spatial. When a
greater number of territorial species are known, it may be possible to view
primate territoriality...as one element in a more general pattern of adaptation" (Mason 1968: 202). That this must be of great importance is taken for
granted by Hooton (1946: 332): "In short, it seems to me that the term,
'territoriality', indicates a finding in regard to infrahuman groups of our order
that is possibly the most significant discovery of students of primate
sociology".

We then have to look more deeply into the presupposed significance of
animal territories.

3.3. Significance of animal territories

3.3.1. *General context*

Behavioural territoriality can be looked upon as "one means of relating the
needs of animals to the environment" (D. E. Davis 1962: 317). Its widespread
occurrence and manifold forms give hardly any doubt as to its "important
relationships to the adaptive, selective, and survival mechanisms of animal
evolution" (C. R. Carpenter 1961: 244). It is thus possible to evaluate territoriality as part of the great evolutionary communication system of animals
(cf. Crook 1970c: 156-167). First the discrimination of individual and place

must have developed in relation to the complexity of the central nervous system. Then territoriality, above all among dispersed animals, and dominance hierarchy among members of an aggregation, have followed gradually (cf. Sugiyama 1973: 406) when the population of a given area increased, making it profitable to spend energy on defense and exclusion (cf. Stokes 1974: 296).

But even though it is easily inferred that the effect of territories is to space out individuals and groups of animals competitively, the modes of procedure and significance of this spacing can be interpreted in many ways. Thus we could mention that C. R. Carpenter (1961: 242-243) listed 32 different functional explanations from the literature. It is supposed, too, that territory should operate for the fitness of the individual and the regulation of the population and that these ultimate goals can be arrived at via proximate factors (cf. Baker 1938) connected with feeding, breeding and so on. Some of the crucial theories are summarized below, the emphasis as before on birds and mammals.

To begin with the pioneers, Altum (Mayr 1935: 34) thought that territoriality in birds would safeguard a food supply sufficient for the successful rearing of the young. E. Howard (C. R. Carpenter 1961: 226) added to this that territory ensures mating by providing a focus for reproductive activity, that by means of fighting it eliminates the weakest birds from breeding and that it limits the number of pairs. Lack and Lack (1933-1934: 196-197) criticized above all the importance of territory as feeding ground and maintained that it was "nothing more than an affair of the male bird, and its real significance seems to be that it provides him with a more or less prominent, isolated headquarters where he can sing or otherwise display". Mayr (1935: 37) took an attitude in between: "*Territory was originally developed only in connection with the mating, but it has acquired in certain passerine species a secondary significance as the food providing area*". And Nice (1941: 470) centred on safeguard: "*The chief function of territory is defense – defense of the individual, the pair, the nest and young*" (cf. also Nice 1933).

Introducing a symposium on the territorial behaviour of birds Hinde (1956: 364) stressed that the functions thereof are extremely divergent and that simple answers could not be expected. He admitted, however, that there is circumstantial evidence that the familiarity with an area following site attachment may assist in feeding, in escaping from predators and in increasing fighting potentiality. And he found strong evidence that territoriality can regulate density in favoured but not in all habitats, that it facilitates the formation and maintenance of the pair-bond, reduces interference by other members of the species in various reproductive activities and that in most species the food value of the territory is not significant. According to Tinbergen (1957) site attachment enables the animal to become intimately acquainted with the topography, the survival value of spacing through hostility is acknowledged and, as to the population limitation by available food, it is vindicated that selection acts when situations are critical (cf. also Gibb 1961: 438-441). And it should not be forgotten that a dispersing of the population must involve a reduction of predation too (cf. Hinde 1956; Tinbergen 1957).

3.3.2. Population regulation

The crucial and difficult problems about territorial behaviour and population regulation have been reviewed and re-evaluated, particularly for birds, during the last decade. J. L. Brown (1969: 320-321) concluded that part of the confusion is due to the basic questions. "Rather than ask about the 'functions' of territoriality..., it would be more to the point to state directly that our primary interest is in the evolutionary origin, development, and maintenance of territoriality and that we approach this problem through a study of the effects of territorial behavior on gene frequencies. One of the dangers in speaking of the 'functions' of territory is that the mechanisms of selection by which a particular function might act on the gene pool of the species are often left vague and unspecified.... The fitness differential between territorial and non-territorial individuals is so great and so widespread – in potentially every territorial species – that we are justified in seeking a general theory for the evolution of territorial behavior based on individual selection".

Starting with a new theoretical development (Fretwell and Lucas 1969) on the influence of territorial behaviour and other factors on habitat distribution in birds, Fretwell and Calver (1969) first tested their models on the sex ratio variations in the dickcissel, *Spiza americana*. The result was consistent with the theory that territorial behaviour in the males of this species limits their density. Then Fretwell (1969) used the models on the breeding success in a local population of field sparrows, *Spizella pusilla*, with results suggesting that territorial behaviour neither effects nor affects the distribution. Zimmerman (1971: 610), however, likewise contended that his investigations of the dickcissel clearly showed that territoriality in this species had a density-dependent effect on population size.

"To demonstrate that territorial behaviour really limits breeding stocks, it is necessary to show: (a) that a substantial part of the population consists of surplus non-territorial birds which do not breed; (b) that these are prevented from holding territory and breeding by the established territory-holders; and (c) that they are able to take territories and breed, if they are given the chance by the removal of the established birds" (A. Watson 1967). In fact all these three prerequisites were filled in an experiment with red grouse, *Lagopus lagopus*, in Scotland during the years 1960-1966 and the author finished one paper on the matter saying: "These results show experimentally that territorial behaviour in red grouse sets a limit to the size of the territorial population during the winter months and of the subsequent breeding stock" (op. cit.; cf. also Watson and Jenkins 1968; Watson and Miller 1971). Thus we now have examples demonstrating with great certainty that territoriality is able to regulate populations in birds.

As to mammals the specific explanations of territory significance are rather few. Burt (1949) assumed that in those animals which display territoriality the young are forced away by their parents in most cases. The result would be a tendency to maintain a population near or below optimum in the preferred habitat and to drive the excess, gradually, into other areas, thus possibly also involving adaptation to new types of habitat in the service of survival. This might be an important factor in determining the rate of the spread of a species, once it is established. The movement of individuals from one sector of a population to another and, perhaps, to new areas means the dispersal of genes throughout the population. This most certainly has a direct bearing on the genetics of the total population and on the rate of evolution within the species. In fact more and more experiments are materializing supporting the contention that territorial isolation is equivalent to reproductive isolation (cf., e.g., Thiessen and Dawber 1972).

Hediger (1970b: 53-55), the eminent expert on zoo mammals, asserted that "territory enables us to grasp the grandiose simplicity of the systems of animal communication, especially if we take into consideration the concept of social distance and the importance of imitation and of the contagiousness of emotions. . . . Thus, territorial behavior of a group insures the right degree of distance and contact within its biotope; and social distance, the right degree of distance and contact between the individuals within their territory" (cf. also Hediger 1965: 330-332).

Speaking of social dynamics in rodents Barnett and Evans (1965: 246) found it to be a reasonable assumption that the survival value of territorial xenophobia is dispersal and regulation of density and that threats and displays make this possible without injury to conspecifics. Thus social stress may kill in the absence of physical wounding. This raises difficult questions of physiology and psychology, as practically nothing is known about fluctuations in the readiness to perform stereotyped territorial behaviour, e.g., of the internal process which ends an activity such as fighting.

Students of population dynamics have mostly concentrated on birth, death and migration data, combining them with climate, food, disease, predation and other conditions. Even social interaction *per se* can, as we have mentioned, have drastic effects. Experimenting with pseudo-natural cultures of inbred strains of house mice John B. Calhoun (1956: 102) showed that as population density increased, continued disruptions of homeostasis transformed a genetically determined, stable physiology into a phenotypic unstable one with accompanying extensive alterations of behaviour. Operating with enclosures of different magnitude he got this result (Calhoun 1968: 7): "In the larger universes the more classical picture of territoriality and hierarchies developed with the overflow of stressful situations affecting females to the extent of reducing conception and interfering with proper maternal behavior. In contrast, this feedback loop, which functions to inhibit population growth, has hardly materialized in the smaller universes. We suspect that these divergent cultural norms will persist and lead to the larger universes expressing reduced rates of population growth as well as suppressed final levels of population" (cf. also Calhoun 1971: 335-344).

In further investigations on Norway rats, *Rattus norvegicus*, Calhoun (1962b: 49-51) found that the rats organized themselves in groups of twelve individuals each as a mean and that this was the maximum limit of group membership with maintenance of harmonious living. Also in this species overcrowding implied social stress, which led to different pathological conditions as to histology, physiology and behaviour (in the last case called "behavioral sink") and relevant to all but the dominant males, which behaved normally. Comparable facts are noted in the field, e.g., with Sika deer, *Cervus nippon* (cf. Christian 1963: 592-602). This is of great interest, particularly in the light of this fact: "Social stress is often, perhaps usually, a result of territorial behaviour: that is, of the defense of a region against intruders" (Barnett 1964: 212).

Concerning man's near relatives it was stated: "Social animals, such as many primates, may have group territories rather than individual ones, and in such cases agonistic behaviour seems to have two distinct separate functions – in keeping groups apart, and in leading to smooth organisation within the group" (Vowles 1970: 13). As stressed by M.W.C. Fox (1968: 33): "Territoriality prevents overcrowding in that a given area cannot be indefinitely compressed, so that subordinate animals that have lost the fight over acquiring territory do not breed. Thus, the environment supports only those animals that have breeding territory", which is in accordance with the earlier mentioned bird experiments by Adam Watson.

In this connection it could be of interest to note the very strong difference between forest and urban populations of Rhesus monkeys in India. "When forest monkeys were placed together, they were relatively relaxed and uncombative. Urban monkeys, however, generally fell to fighting, regardless of whether the strangers to which they were introduced were urban monkeys or forest monkeys. Their battles were violent, usually resulting in severe injuries, and two of the combatants were actually killed. In experiments in which the monkeys competed for food we found that the forest monkeys generally yielded to the urban monkeys. Indeed, although male monkeys are usually dominant over females, in the urban versus forest matchings forest males often gave in to urban females" (Singh 1969). Among possible explanations for this behaviour difference the principal one suggested was "The restrictive urban environment", which should be remembered when urban conditions come to the fore (in section 4,3. 12.).

3.3.3. Animal territoriality importance concluded

Reviewing critically available information on the significance of territories in animals Klopfer (1969: 83, 86) tabulated three advantages of territoriality: "1. An increase in the efficiency by which natural resources (e.g., food, refuges, etc.) are utilized as a consequence of activity being restricted to a discrete and familiar area. 2. A limitation in the intensity of competition for food (or nest sites) since the number of territories will set a limit on the total breeding density of the population. 3. Enhancement of pair formation and pair-bond maintenance because of the existence of a common 'home'". He even vindicated that "as long as some lower limit governs size of a territory in a given area, a limit which is periodically manifested, territories can be considered to be incompressible, and thus they can serve to regulate population size".

Barnett (1964: 211-213) summarized general consequences of territorial behaviour in this way: The numbers of a species rarely become so great that there is excessive consumption of food or over-use of other resources. Infertility or death intervene for some individuals before debility can overcome the whole population. Hence intraspecific conflict constitutes a negative feedback regulating density, being an example of a density-dependent factor which governs population growth. It may be the most important of such factors among at least mammals and birds.

The well-known diversity of territories is often said to be an argument against the assumption of a unitary selection pressure behind territorial behaviour (cf., e.g., Klopfer 1968: 399). But J. L. Brown (1964) reconciled the apparently strongly varying avian phenomena, contending that territoriality is most accurately regarded as site-dependent aggressiveness. The aggressive behaviour itself is likely to be favoured by natural selection when its employment enhances survival. Aggression could be linked with defense of food, mates, mating places, nests, or any other requisites, for survival or reproductive success. Whether the aggressive behaviour actually is employed to defend any or all of these resources, depends on their availability and accessibility to each individual and on the cost in time and energy of obtaining and defending them. The character of the territory that evolves thus depends upon the economies of site-dependent aggression.

McBride (1971), too, admitted that aggression is the most common behaviour used to control spacing. But animals normally have reactions which prevent aggression by neighbours or halt it once it has started. Such behaviour is called submission, and a common form is avoidance or flight to the edge of the controlled space. This may be to the border of a territory or to the limits of a personal area around the individual. Thus the "relationship between dominance and spacing appears to be a general one. An individual territory is a hierarchy of one with the owner dominant over all others entering the territory, but subordinate when it moves off this space.... The behavior may be genetically coded by natural selection, or the society may be so organized that appropriate and inappropriate behavior are positively and negatively reinforced. More commonly, both coding systems operate together". (op. cit. p. 59, 61).

According to Soja (1971: 23) position within a hierarchy of dominance, e.g., the familiar "pecking order", and territorial domination, size and location are all intertwined to establish the basic design of animal societies. Internal conflict is limited by the avoidance of territorial trespass or through ritualized dominant-subordinate behaviour. The group maintains its integrity and identity by means of territorial separation from other groups, while internal competition and cohesion are shaped by a system, often territorially based, of dominant-subordinate relationships. Most studies of animal behaviour have shown territoriality and dominance behaviour to be complementary and interrelated means of maintaining social order. When one is unable to function, the other tends to play a greater role.

This balance is fundamental. "An optimal dynamic stability of a population is a favorable condition for species survival, and the territorial order of the population in an area is an important condition for optimal population stability. Territoriality combined with social organization reduces stress, conflict, pugnacity, and nonadaptive energy expenditure. On the basis of these assumptions it may be hypothesized that physical-geographic changes which radically disturb the territorial order of a species population may seriously and adversely affect the survival of the species" (C. R. Carpenter 1961: 244-245).

These general, important and far-reaching aspects of animal behavioural territoriality are also of great anthropological interest and should be born in mind as we now enter the realm of human territories.

4. Territory in man

4.1. "Primitive" territories

4.1.1. Human and animal

4.1.1.1. Taxonomic position of Homo sapiens:
Behavioural territoriality was first discovered in animals and was used as a purely zoological term before its application to man. Now the concept has long been involved in the discussion about the importance of nature and nurture, that is, what is inborn and what is learned in behaviour. Still older and more controversial, however, are the questions concerning the place of *Homo sapiens* in biological taxonomy and the possibility of inferring, analogically and homologically, from animals to men. These problems should, of course, not be neglected in territorial contexts, particularly as there is no consensus, not even about the statement of Allesch (1937: 128): "The close connections between the psychology of animals and of man are well known and it would seem superfluous to talk about them at length".

It is not possible here to recapitulate the interesting history of man's changing views about himself, with the extremes labelling humans as angels and beasts (cf. F. W. Jones 1929: 45-67; Hofer and Altner 1972: 149-219). But it could be noted that some philosophers have established interesting definitions, for instance, Aristotle, who is responsible for the remark that, "Man is by nature a political animal", and Nietzsche, who claimed that, "Man is the undetermined animal". We will also mention that "orangutan" means "man of the woods", that some earlier authors used the Latin constellation *Homo sylvestris* for the chimpanzee and that it was long seriously discussed whether the great apes could be some kind of human savages.

Linnaeus (1956: 20-32) created, in the tenth edition from 1758 of *Systema Naturae*, the order *Primates*, in which he placed bats, lemurs, monkeys, apes and man. Darwin (1871: 197) stressed that "we may infer that some ancient member of the anthropomorphous sub-group gave birth to man", supporting

Thomas Huxley (1864: 103-105) in his *Evidence as to Man's Place in Nature*. The theory of evolution gave a strong impetus to new and intense investigations, i.a. in paleontology and physical anthropology, and the knowledge of the history of man has increased tremendously, during the last hundred years not the least by means of recent discoveries in East Africa. Morphological, physiological and other evidence has tied man and the other primates more and more together. Above all modern serological research (e.g., Goodman 1968; Wilson and Sarich 1969) has suggested that the relationship in time is much closer than once thought, with a separation between the lineages leading towards man and apes as recent as four or five million years ago (cf. also Simpson 1966; Washburn and Harding 1972: 347-351).

4.1.1.2. Specific characters of man:
Summarizing a bulk of evidence Julian Huxley (1948: 16) expressed his views in the following way: "The essential character of man as a dominant organism is conceptual thought. And conceptual thought could have arisen only in a multicellular animal, an animal with bilateral symmetry, head and blood system, a vertebrate as against a mollusc or an arthropod, a land vertebrate among vertebrates, a mammal among land vertebrates. Finally, it could have arisen only in a mammalian line which was gregarious, which produced one young at a birth instead of several, and which had recently become terrestrial after a long period of arboreal life".

Without doubt man is outstanding in several respects and not only as to capacity for conceptual thought. Already Bolk (1926) pointed to the "foetalization" of man, that is, the prolonging of foetal characteristics into postnatal development and adult life, thus delaying sexual maturity and giving time for acquisition of the social heritage of the species (for a critique of this theory, see, e.g., Hilzheimer 1926-1927). Several authors have stressed the great variability and non-speciality of humans, even of range and habitat (e.g., Schwidetsky 1959: 41-43), and their great tool-making skill (i.a. Oakley 1962: 11-12), unsurpassed among wild non-human species. And Lorenz (1950: 482-495) to this added self-domestication, exploratory behaviour and space perception as three important traits in the evolution of man.

Further Dobzhansky (1963) stressed that the evolutionary uniqueness of man lies in that, with mankind, a new, superorganic mode of evolution begins, which is the evolution of culture. He argued that culture is a tremendously potent instrument for adaptation to the environment and that there is feedback between genetics and culture, being an adaptive mechanism, supplemental to, but not incompatible with, biological adaptation. To be sure, adaptation by culture proved to be more efficacious, and, above all, more rapid than adaptation by genes. This is why the emergence of the genetic basis of culture is said to be the master stroke in the biological evolution of the human species.

We should, however, not forget the words of R. Fox (1971:292): "For the last time then, let me say that culture does not represent a triumph over nature, for such a thing is impossible; it represents an end product of a natural process. It is both the producer and the product of our human nature, and in behaving culturally we are behaving naturally".

4.1.1.3. The comparative method:

The background for our considerations is thus that man is a vertebrate, belonging to a group of animals, the common ancestry of which is quite clear and their joint genetic heritage therefore indubitable. Further, men are mammals, and, as we have seen, close relatives to other living primates, which is why it is extremely improbable that whole groups of inborn behavioural attitudes of apes and monkeys should be lacking in man. But this is what not a few scientists take for granted, why every ethological-ecological phenomenon traced from animals to men could be a matter of dispute.

"The relevance to a science of new data is not always immediately obvious to its practitioners. This is particularly so when these data derive primarily from other sciences and when an admission of their relevance to the science may require a fundamental critique of its working assumptions. The distinction between the biological and social sciences has been based on a limited view of human social action. Though both areas are concerned with social behaviour, their findings have not been integrated within a comprehensive theory of such behaviour" (Tiger and Fox 1966: 75).

Crook (1970a: XXXII) maintained that arguments from mental states or which use mentalistic terms in comparisons between phyla or between animals and man are very difficult to interpret as are statements about learning abilities at different phyletic levels. He admitted that it is tempting to make inferences from animal to human life in cases where social processes or factors, e.g., dominance-submission ranking, appear to be common to both. But he thought that the value of such inferences is dubious because the mediating processes of the phenomenon are poorly known in either case and could usually be expected to be different.

And Barnett (1969: 65) directly questioned the comparative method: "What use, then, is it to compare other species with ourselves? There is no great problem when, say, the effect of a drug or a vitamin is closely similar in a laboratory animal and in man. Less obviously, the contemplation of animal behaviour might, by analogy, suggest useful hypotheses about our own behavior, though whether it often does so, is doubtful. But discussions of aggression and other social behavior usually seek conclusions of wider generality than do comparisons of the effects of drugs, and of greater precision than can be derived from analogical reasoning. Explicitly or not, they often contain the question, how can we learn to control our own behavior? The answers are unlikely to be found in the behavior of other species. Their physiology, especially when we know it better, may tell us much about ourselves. But when we look for wisdom in our dealings with each other, the Delphic exhortation still holds: know thyself" (cf. also Barnett 1973).

But a great many scientists recognize today that it is both possible and necessary to infer from animals to men, even that a truly scientific perspective for understanding human conduct is to be found in the study of animal behaviour. When it, for instance, is said that "Extrapolation from animals to man must be viewed with extreme caution because of man's biologic uniqueness" (Prosser 1969: 415), this seems not to be a tenable statement. One must, of course, always be cautious when inferring from one species to another and the more so the further they stand from each other taxonomically. But the uniqueness of specific characters does not in principle prevent general comparisons, and homologies should always be possible as long as the common phylogenetic history is sure. "The essentially morphological concept of homology cannot at present be applied to behavior in any meaningful (nontrite) way because of its lack of structural correlates" vindicated Atz (1970: 69), but such views have been effectively contradicted by eminent taxonomists and evolutionists like Emerson, Mayr and Simpson (Simpson 1961: 533).

4.1.1.4. Analogy and homology:
Lorenz (1974: 230) defined homology "as any resemblance between two species that can be explained by their common descent from an ancestor possessing the character in which they are similar to each other", and he emphasized that "Strictly speaking, the term homologous can only be applied to characters and not to organs". At the same time he brought out clearly that there are no such things as "false analogies", of which ethologists are often accused, and that analogy is a most useful method in science (cf. also Oppenheimer 1956).

Hebb and Thompson (1954: 532) combated the not seldom heard argument that knowledge of human behaviour will result only from the investigation of mankind on the grounds that proving something to be true of an animal does not prove it true for man. They stressed that the latter part of this statement is both correct and irrelevant, because it implies that an empirical science proceeds by proof and disproof, which is a most misleading idea. The fact is that no scientific theory can ever be proved true, nor can we ever be quite sure of having proved one wrong. The Nobel prize winner Peter Medawar (1976: 498) goes straight into the matter, admitting that "A great deal obviously depends upon whether or not it is possible to establish genuine homologies between the behaviour of human beings and that of the collateral descendants of their remote ancestors; to my mind, there can be no question that we can do so:....".

After a thorough examination of "The Argument from Animals to Men" J. B. S. Haldane (1956: 13) came to this conclusion: "I think that the study of animals may tell us a good deal about the human unconscious, and thus about irrational human behaviour". And the editors of the magnificent volume on *Behavior and Evolution*, Anne Roe and George Gaylord Simpson (1961: 417-418), summarized their position in one of the chapter introductions: Human behaviour does clearly combine elements – and we may as well call them biological – that are phylogenetically older, more widely shared with others in the animal kingdom, and as a rule more obviously related to genetic factors, with other elements – and almost everyone recognizes them under the term cultural – that are on the whole of more recent origin, more specific to man, and comparatively independent of biological inheritance.

A last word goes to a famous psychologist and a distinguished anthropologist. The former said: "Our willingness to extrapolate to man insights gained from studies with other animals on the body physiology level, coupled with greater reluctance with regard to making similar extrapolations at the mind-behavior, particularly social behavior, level presents the possibility of our getting into a real trap if this myopic mental lesion persists" (Calhoun 1973: 96). And the latter added: "However, we should not forget that the main usefulness of these primate studies is twofold: first, they permit us to make hypotheses about early forms of incipient human cultures – that is to say, what took place about one or two million years ago. Second, they disclose facts which are so fundamental that if they hold true for primates, they also hold true for the whole of mankind" (Lévi-Strauss 1968: 349; cf. also Masserman 1973: 133).

4.1.1.5. Animal and human territoriality:
Concerning territoriality in particular the critique should first be represented

by the zoologist Klopfer (1968: 399): "Extrapolations from the behavior of animals to that of man frequently err when they assume the behavior in question to be a unitary phenomenon. For example, the territorial behavior of vertebrates, which has been cited as providing a biological explanation (and justification) for human property rights, probably has as many different bases as there are species. Extrapolations, if they are to be useful, must be accurate. This requires us to focus upon similarities in evolutionary and physiological processes rather than upon similarities in final appearances" (cf. also Suttles 1973: 118-124). And Crook (1970a: XXXII) maintained: "There are many ways in which a theorist may make inferences from animal behaviour to man. The least reliable consist in a drawing of vague analogies between poorly defined attributes (such as 'territory') which animals and men are thought to have in common".

To this we will just say for the moment that the site-dependent exclusiveness called behavioural territoriality is mostly both definable, strict and evident, and its appearance in a wealth of species and forms only underlines the strong probability for its genetic background and its great importance in all kinds of vertebrates (cf. Edney 1976; Esser 1976). We join a well-known ecologist when he stresses: "The basic requirements of man are the same as those of other organisms, and although man may attribute special properties to himself which he believes set him apart from other animals, it is possible to place man in an ecological setting and to examine his interactions with the environment" (Owen 1973: VI).

Edney (1974: 961-962) gave, partly with reference to Sundstrom and Altman (1974), eight arguments for distinguishing between animal and human territoriality, but most of them seem not to be valid. First, he said that the human use of space is very variable and not like the stereotypic spatial expressions of animals. It is true that human cultures and constructions give more possibilities for territorial variation than the living patterns of most other animal species, but the basic territorial behaviour is as rigid in man as in non-human animals. Second, it is stated that the association between territory and aggression is not so clear-cut in humans as in animals. This is absolutely wrong, for aggression is in both cases normally averted by suitable behaviour, and overt, aggressive territoriality is not at all rare in man. Third, it is maintained that territories primarily serve biological needs in animals, whereas in humans they also have secondary purposes, e.g., in connection with recreation. In animal as well as in primitive and advanced human societies territories respond to biological needs, of course including those called recreational. Fourth, it is vindicated that animals mostly use one single territory for continuous periods of time while humans have several territories in different locations. Here we will only refer to migrating birds and other wandering animals, which can hold territory not only in winter and summer quarters but also at resting places in between. Fifth, it is reported that temporary territories are rare in animals but frequent in humans. This might contain some truth, but the same counter-evidence as before can be presented. Sixth, it is asserted that total invasion of one group's territory by another is rare in animals but common in human war. Even this is dubious, but it is as impossible here as in the former case to compare frequencies. Seventh, it is, of course, true that modern man with modern weapons can engage in warfare without trespassing, but maybe it could be vindicated that this is exactly what every singing male bird does. Eighth, it is claimed that humans are the only territorial organisms which routinely entertain conspecifics on home grounds without antagonism. As earlier argued this is absolutely wrong and neighbourliness is a key feature for territorial animals which have settled their controversies and have begun to know each other well.

It is self-evident that there are differences between animal and human territoriality. "Thus human-response repertoires seem to be richer, more variable, and more complex than animal territorial responses" (Altman 1975: 109). Above all, artificial structures are, of course, much more important ingredients in human than in animal territories. But the similarities seem to be still more obvious, which, hopefully, will come out, when we now start searching for behavioural territoriality, first in children and the mentally deficient and then in early man and "primitive" societies. We thus follow suggestions from Hediger (1940: 313) and Katz (1953: 174) in looking for primitive, basic traits in such areas, but we are quite aware of the pitfalls involved.

4.1.2. The background for territory in children

4.1.2.1. Development:
There is no generally accepted theory about the phylogeny of the human space-time perception and conceptions based upon it. Nor is the ontogeny of these phenomena – fundamental in connection with territoriality – fully understood. But the biogenetic law which says that ontogeny recapitulates phylogeny, although today strongly criticized by some, might be applied to the mind as well as to the brain (cf. Esser 1971b: 3-4).

Even though we have evidence that very small infants respond to visual, auditory and other stimuli, there is no sure information about whether there are correlated experiences, and if so, about what kind these are and what they mean to the child (Munn 1965: 281). As nobody can recall a time in which the different sensory aspects of an object were spatially unrelated, we may conclude that these relations are native or established before the time of memory, i.e., during the first few years of life (Carr 1966: 9). The philosophical schools of empiricists and nativists have long debated whether spatial perception is learned or inborn. There is now dominating evidence for the nativistic theory, except that the localization within space seems to be empirically based (Rohracher 1960: 115-119).

Already Karl Bühler (1922: 142) distinguished between three stages in the development of the spatial conceptions, namely "*Mundraum*" in connection with nursing, "*Tastraum*" or "*Greifraum*" covered by the extremities, and "*Fernraum*" discovered by means of locomotion. These entities are put together by psychoanalysts with three stages in the development of the child and its ego, and it is said that "the awareness of space completes the differentiation between ego and environment" (Bernfeld 1925: 256).

Concerning depth discrimination, which seems to be largely maturational, there is no evidence on this aspect of perception of objects until the age of 36 weeks. First, as infants near the age of one year they discover that "the tridimensional world consists of minute distances, as well as of far reaches. And it is the minutiae of this world of intimate near vision with which the infant is preëminently concerned during the closing months of the first year. With his inquisitive index finger he punctures and penetrates the third dimension" (Gesell, Ilg and Bullis 1950: 97).

It was Kurt Lewin (1936: 12) who defined psychological life space as "the totality of facts which determine the behavior of an individual at a certain moment". He used a need system as a basis, where some areas of the environment have a positive valence, that is, contain conditions in which the needs could be satisfied, and some a negative one. All significant aspects of the environment are determined in part by what could be called an environmental filter (cf. also T. Alexander 1973: 5-6). Lewin stressed that the boundary between the self and the environment is less defined in the child, that the child to a greater extent is a dynamic unity and that personal fields of force are more prominent dynamic features of the child's environment, as compared with adults. "Not only other persons but other objects may have a close psychological relation with the self of the child. To the 'I' in this sense there belong not only the child's own body but certain toys, a particular chair, etc. Such objects are dynamically somewhat like his own body in that they represent points of special sensitivity to invasions by environmental forces" (Lewin 1935: 110).

Of great interest in the actual context is, of course, the notation by Piaget that the concept of unitary space begins as an active manipulation of objects near by (Piaget and Inhelder 1956; cf. also p. 4, 6). The authors think that the child's awareness of proximity, enclosures and boundaries is the beginning of the understanding of spatial relationships. Immediately following sensori-motor activity, tied directly to perception, the action is recalled in imagination subsequent to being performed physically. This gives rise to thought which reproduces action with all its concreteness and irreversibility. And they continue: "From this process arise concrete operations (from 7-8 to 11-12 years) when the schemata are co-ordinated sufficiently to be combined, and consequently, for each one to be mentally explored in alternate directions. This type of reversible combination represents the initial equilibrium state reached by internalized actions and thus constitutes the first truly operational system. . . . Thus the child now disposes (about 11-12 years) of abstract operations, capable of being expressed in propositional form. This marks the final stage in the development of intuition and the beginning of a type of thought which, whilst being the culmination of the continuous internalizing of actions, at the same time prepares the ground for the elaboration of abstract spatial concepts as a result of its increasingly logical discursive character" (p. 454-455).

If conceptual space should be a necessary prerequisite for real behavioural territoriality, there would hardly be found any such phenomena below the age of 7 years. This might be in accordance with the fact that "the need for territory is manifested in the child at the age of 7 years" (Sivadon 1965: 490). Recent investigations show, however, that interpersonal distance behaviour and thus personal space has been acquired in children by five years of age (Bass and Weinstein 1971). Territorial effects of instincts maturing long before this time combined with strong and fixed perceptions should either not be overlooked and are even highly probable, as suggested by animals. This leads us into the phenomenon of imprinting.

4.1.2.2. Imprinting:
It was discovered by Heinroth (1910: 633-634) and confirmed by Lorenz (1935: 163-173) that goslings and other young birds, hatched from eggs in the absence of their parents, react to their human keeper or to the first other relatively large mobile object seen by following behind, as if it were their mother. This imprinting process is confined to a definite and brief period in the beginning of the individual life, possibly also to a particular environment. It is often very stable and sometimes perhaps totally irreversible, leading first

to an ability to respond to the broad features of a situation and later even to finer discrimination (cf. Thorpe 1956: 115-118).

Imprinting is often completed long before the various specific reactions to which its behaviour patterns should be linked are established. It is a supra-individual form of learning and centers on just the broad characteristics or "Gestalt" of the species. The first stage of imprinting, as it was originally understood, consisted of approach and following responses to sources of intermittent stimulation and thus not to stationary objects. Thorpe (1944: 80-81), however, suggested that attachment by imprinting and not only by conditioning to a home environment could be also acquired, and this has now been shown to be the case in different kinds of animals. Changes of the environment make the attachment to familiar figures and features still more evident and striking and evoke fear of new conditions (cf. Sluckin 1972: 65-57, 86-95).

Several reasons could be given for the statement that early experience is different from later. First, it is postulated that the cells of a young organism are very sensitive to direct physical and chemical changes and that they may be exposed to wide fluctuations in body chemistry because of imperfect functioning of homeostatic mechanisms. Second, there must be a gradual shift with age in the probability that any specified response will occur when an animal is confronted with a novel situation. And third, there could be progressive changes in the possible complexity of stimulus control of behaviour (Fuller and Waller 1962: 242-244). In any case it now seems to be commonly agreed upon that imprinting involves a special form of arousal (Rajecki 1973).

The significance of imprinting depends i.a. upon its being a form of unrewarded learning, a means of developing and changing motivation and a special and sometimes very rapid process for restricting the stimulus situation – setting off a particular response. Further, imprinting is an example of a sensitive period in learning, not seldom showing similarities to the initiation of cyclic rhythmical behaviour. Finally it is primarily concerned with parent-offspring, that is, with social relations (cf. Thorpe 1961: 167-174). It is true that the human application of the imprinting model (see, e.g., the discussion in Brody and Axelrad 1971: 213-215) as well as the whole imprinting concept (Salzen 1970) have recently been questioned. But is seems nevertheless quite clear that there is in birds and mammals, including man, – whatever name should be designated for the process – a territorial fixation of the early environment.

It has been suggested that the critical period for imprinting in humans should range from the age of about six weeks to that of about six months, beginning with the onset of learning ability, continuing with the smiling response and ending with the fear of strangers (Gray 1958: 161-164). As to environment in general and territory in particular this seems, however, to be quite too short and too early a period, particularly with regard to the infant's limited capacity of locomotion at the age of six months. It would be more likely to put the territorial phase of imprinting as equal to another development phase: "The separation-individuation process, which takes place over approximately two years (from six to thirty months), has maturational and developmental, autonomous and conflictual, intrapsychic and environmental components" (Mahler 1969: 220). This would be more probable, even though the definite result in the form of complete behavioural territoriality often does not show until much later.

Here it may be of interest to look at the reciprocal relationship between attachment and what could be called detachment in the child. Investigations have shown that already 10-month infants, given the opportunity, will leave their mothers to enter a new and strange environment, moving about freely with no distress, in contrast to situations in which they are placed alone in the same milieu. The mean farthest distance travelled from the mother was, in 1-year olds, 6.9, and in 4-year olds, 20.6 meters. This separation is of great biological importance for the individual and for the species, allowing the mother to care for the other offspring, giving the child greater familiarity with the environment and increasing the possibilities of interacting with it (Rheingold and Eckerman 1971). Probably it also constitutes the practical basis for the later development of spatial consciousness, preceding that of time (cf. Estvan and Estvan 1959: 259).

Bateson and Jackson (1964: 271) maintained that parent-child relationship and territory are two important, closely interrelated themes of complementary interaction, which could perhaps be conveniently understood by regarding territory as an extension of the body. They further said that the archetypal definition of territory might be "that area defined by mother's presence within which the infant has an autistic or absolute right to safety". Such a view of the relations between parenthood and territory is of great interest and might explain such metaphors as "motherland" and "patria" and the differential degrees of confidence shown when one is on, or off, one's territory.

In any case the usual effects of imprinting are that the child first develops an attachment to its mother, which grows stronger and stronger with time. "It is possible that a systematic, profitable exploration of the environment by the child can begin only when a secure bond of this kind has been created.... Likewise, we can only wonder whether attachment to one's home environ-

ment, or even one's country, does in any way depend on some form of imprinting. .... In spite of the omnipresence of human curiosity the positive
attractiveness of the familiar often comes to the fore" (Sluckin 1972: 143-
146).

The term hospitalism designates harmful psychic effects of institutional
care for infants deprived of their mothers at an early age (Freund 1910; Spitz
1945-1946; cf. also Flint 1966). In the old days often not far from 100 percent
of the babies in foundling homes died during their first year of life, many
without any sign of disease and probably as a consequence of lacking maternal or equivalent stimulation. "Motherless children fall more quickly into
mortal danger the younger they are. Even a temporary separation will
seriously affect the child, who is completely adjusted to its mother. If the
separation continues for a long time, the fate of the child is most favourable
if another woman takes the mother's place. Institutional care of the child
cannot be a substitute for his mother" (Peiper 1961: 652).

That hospitalism is here taken up in connection with territoriality depends
on the condition that there now seems to be a "need for more definitive
research on the role of many 'nonmaternal' variables, variables relating to the
characteristics of environmental stimulation and variables dealing with organismic sensitivities" (Yarrow 1964: 347). And it was recently stated by one
of the most eager critics of the phenomenon of social deprivation in children:
"The original evidence for the long term effects of maternal deprivation can
now be seen to be less secure than was thought at first. Both long term environmental effects and the considerable effects of genetic endowment must
be evaluated and allowed for in interpreting results" (O'Connor 1971: 76).

So it seems reasonable to list lack of adequate home environment and
environmental imprinting – most probably basic foundations for early territoriality – among the causes of hospitalism.

4.1.2.3. Child territoriality:
Unfortunately few investigations of healthy children's territories are as yet
available, and part of the material will be treated together with that about
adults in coming chapters on rural and urban territories. Here we present only
a couple of examples, some of which are connected with proximity studies and
which take up the conditions according to advancing age.

As to small infants in a playroom an interesting technique, suitable to
computer analysis, has been indicated by Herron (1971: 115-117), who moun-
ted an automatically-operated camera in the ceiling. He then, at intervals of

ten seconds, photographed the whole floor (masked with tape into Cartesian coordinates) in order to get a picture of the spatial movements and relations of the playing children. One result was that unfriendly action strongly related to mean distances maintained in 180 Australian kindergarten children 3-5 years of age (King 1966), which is in accordance with theories of personal space and territorial aggression.

Indubitably the creation of a secondary home is extremely important for those human beings, especially children, who have lost their natural homes – as happened on such a terrible scale in the Second World War – and have thus been the victims of uprooting with all its evils. Those charitable organizations which took over the rescue work of children of this sort noticed repeatedly a significant fact. The well-meaning care given to these children in beautiful and spacious community rooms turned out to be insufficient. All kinds of psychological deficiency symptoms kept on appearing until the idea of dividing up the rooms, advocated among others by Professor S. Bayr-Klimpfinger, was adopted. It consisted, in short, of splitting up the spacious day-rooms into separate territories, and in particular of making habitations inside these compartments within which small groups of children could in a real sense feel at home (cf. Hediger 1955: 21-22).

Here we can refer to similar observations by Hutt and Hutt (1970: 150-154) of children between 3 and 8 years of age. As long as they were in open, large, rectangular rooms no behaviour that could be called territorial was seen. But when they were moved into new localities with three separate play areas, each approximately ten feet square extended from a central passage area of about six feet square, the investigators suddenly noticed the appearance of territorial behaviour. "The normal children in particular now spent between 14 and 17 percent of their time in trying to prevent any encroachment or intrusion upon the area of which they were in possession.... It thus appeared that even the physical rudiments of territory (walls, and corners) were necessary before territory could be demarcated psychologically". The experiences of these children suggest that a territorial demarcation is necessary for full psychic health.

Further, an investigation of 116 kindergarten children in the United States showed that the experimental design in case – building of a miniature village on presumed own and foreign property – could induce territorial identification in the infants, and when combined with a perceived threat to the territory, this identification could lead to increased manifestations of aggression (Kurtzberg 1973: 5000-B). Other American experiments with same-sex pairs of children, aged 6-16 years, indicated that they needed more personal space as they grew older and that adult proxemic behaviour was acquired at the age of 12 (Aiello and Aiello 1974).

Some interesting and pertinent remarks were made by Grant (1965: 31-32): "The child who writes his name on his personal belongings is marking territory and, as in other species, any threat or potential threat to his security will increase this behaviour. This behaviour may be shown in different ways; the child of a friend of mine would place articles of his own clothing at various parts of the house, and the probable explanation of this behaviour occurred when it was seen that he would place them on new things that came into the house and on visitor's bags". It should also be stressed that children have a strong aptitude for trespass, and that "Indeed, children are among the most regular and innovative creators of home territories from the space and material available to the public in general" (Lyman and Scott 1968: 239).

Valuable facts as to sexual differences of spatial behaviour were disclosed among the Bantu groups Gusii and Logoli in western Kenya (Munroe and Munroe 1971). Boys between 5 and 8 years old went on the average further from home than girls of the same age, and those children being furthest away were also the most skilful at spatial tasks. It was thought that the herding by the boys was less binding spatially and thus allowed for expanded investigative behaviour, "an interesting example of child training which may act upon an innate predisposition" (Nerlove, Munroe and Munroe 1971: 9). In this connection some words of Bronson (1971: 63) should be recalled: "My present leaning is towards hypotheses that assume young males to be more permanently affected than females by the quality of early experiences, but the exact nature and timing of these events, and why this should be so, I find hard to specify".

Remembering how the territories of non-human mammals are often characterized more as systems of paths than as real spaces (p. 28) we finally underline that children – as well as adults – often use exactly the same well-known routes every day on their way to school and other places and that all forced deviations are felt by them as negative and distressing (Hinsche 1944).

We have thus in this section concentrated on the basis for and the development of behavioural territoriality, matters which are of great importance for the following treatment, not the least of the mentally deficient.

4.1.3. Territory in the mentally deficient

4.1.3.1. Abnormality and instinct:
It is not easy to give a short and good definition of mental abnormality. But

with Wegrocki (1964: 11) we find it convenient to stress in psychiatric patients the characteristic *"tendency to choose a type of reaction which represents an escape from a conflict-producing situation instead of a facing of the problem"*. Essential elements are also that the conflict is, at least predominantly, unconscious and that it is not the mechanism used but its actual function which is abnormal (see further Offer and Sabshin 1966).

Often it is presupposed that instinctive behaviour is practically extinguished and replaced by cultural, moral and other behaviour restraints in modern man. An overwhelming evidence is, however, against such an opinion, not the least if we look at the mentally deficient. "While in healthy people such original behaviour is often suppressed by self control, it is much more evident in the mentally abnormal. During the last ten years this knowledge has caused a number of psychiatrists and psychotherapists to emphasize the importance of animal psychology and ethology to psychiatry in special and general essays" (Meyer-Holzapfel 1964: 256; cf. also Pilleri 1971).

4.1.3.2. Psychopathological children:

If we begin with psychopathological children it should first be noted that "the absence of territory, as imposed by crowding and promiscuity, is expressed through regression" (Sivadon 1965: 490). Maybe this can be one of the factors leading to the infantile syndrome of autism, characterized i.a. by impairment of emotional relationship, unawareness of own identity, pathological preoccupation with particular objects, sustained resistance to change, excessive anxiety, distortion and stereotopy in motility patterns and serious retardation. From an ethological point of view it has been suggested that *"the core of the problem would seem to be found in desparate frustrated attempts at socialisation combined with constant and intense fear"* (Tinbergen and Tinbergen 1972: 34).

Some observations suggest territorial influence in the context. Studies of autistic children show that they, compared with normal children, exhibit under increasing density a very strong tendency to retreat to the periphery of available spaces, thus seeking the safety of the boundary, in this case the room wall (Hutt and Vaizey 1966). This is in accordance with the behaviour of domesticated or other fenced animals in foreign, unstructured environments. We will here also refer to one carefully observed case of temporal lobe damage, inflicted at the age of nine months but not treated until the age of seven years. It is interesting to note that the little patient tried to combat his very pronounced loss of boundary feeling by trying to enclose space in all possible ways and that "space binding became the most prominent feature of treatment" (Sarvis 1960: 466).

Maybe it is appropriate to mention how important clothing can be, especially for mentally disturbed children. It was said that the effected closeness could give a reminiscence of the early life in the womb. This is not impossible, but a more adequate interpretation seems to be that it is here, as in earlier cases, a question of limits for the creation of a minimal personal space or territory. In any case it is astonishing that, for instance, enuretics can be much improved or cured by means of very tight and solid clothing. This implies that in the actual children the consciousness of the solidity of "walls" is strengthened. As soon as this is arrived at, a curing of enuresis is sometimes attained with astonishing rapidity (Heymann 1943: 19-23). We will come back to this issue later (4.2.2.5.).

Very interesting observations were made on territorial behaviour in mentally deficient, institutionalized American boys, mostly with an IQ of 50 or less. It is assumed that the difficulty psychotics have in cognitive processing of the complex environment leads to a heavy reliance on primitive behavioural modes such as territoriality. This results in more order through the establishment of consistent spatial patterning between individuals, a patterning that has been demonstrated to be simple enough for them to process (cf. Esser 1968; Paluck and Esser 1971a, 1971b).

Some of these severely retarded boys were studied in a playroom with square grids marked on the floor and different, spatially structured areas which could allow territoriality. The children were divided into three groups, of which each was observed from 8.30 A.M. to 4.00 P.M. every day during two weeks, and the location of every individual as well as all interactional behaviour was noted every ten minutes. By custom aggression was verbally reprimanded in the institution, and this practice continued during the investigation in the first group, while all reprimands were cancelled in the second and in the third they were used just for aggressive, territorial acts. The result was evident. Territorial behaviour was a universal attribute of these 21 boys, who were chosen without reference to spatial preferences. It seemed to have the importance of an immediate need, for all the boys had defended territories within a week. And while other forms of aggression diminished with punishment, the territorial offensive and defensive acts did not.

These facts suggest that territoriality reaches its own level rather independently of different social reinforcement conditions, which were effective according to other criteria. Behaviour which runs its own course despite attempts to influence it is probably very primitive in nature. In addition it may be crucially adaptive. "A look at the confusion and helplessness on the boys' faces when they first entered the room, or a look at the terror in their faces when attacked by a bully, suggests that a tremendous need is generated in these situations to reduce complexity and gain control. As blind people accentuate the use of other senses in an effort to process their environment, so it seems plausible that mental defectives should accentuate the use of whatever innate ordering programs are still available.

Territoriality is one such program which reduces complexity. A severely retarded individual can be master of his own territory, both in terms of being able to code its physical aspects and in terms of knowing that interpersonally he can be left alone there. . . . We propose that the need to create order through territoriality is a motivational construct which accounts for the boys' relative lack of response to the spatial aspects of the conditioning; that is, territorial behavior may be of such importance that the drive for its expression is stronger than the punishment procedure used in an attempt to suppress it" (Paluck and Esser 1971a: 28).

After twenty months a new study was made of the 5 boys still available in the institution. These children more or less immediately staked out and fought for the specific territories they had possessed during the first investigation in the experimentally designed room, which was, of course, not used in the meantime. A boy was designated as controlling a particular territory when the number of times he was observed in that area during the week in case was greater than two standard deviations beyond the mean of observations concerning the other children. As a most important fact improvements of psychic health were related to the move from isolated or uncontested territories to popular or contested ones as well as following the move from fixed territorial ownership to participation in the staff power structure as an expression of dominance (cf. Paluck and Esser 1971b).

In a subsequent study of 22 retarded boys from the same institution, divided into two equal groups, base-line spatial and aggressive behaviour was first chartered for 14 weeks in identical playrooms and then during 8 weeks with four special, two-story structured habitats in each room and two social reinforcers for 7 weeks in one. It was found that both groups had eight individual territories as a weekly average and that thus not all children had own territories. But this was a consequence of social and candy rewards for shared use of space. The more the adult reinforcers picked out favorite habitats, the more the group contracted its use of space and the more aggression occurred. The number of territories was inversely correlated to the number of aggressive acts, and it was quite clear that some other aspects of the environment than people was responsible for the generally reduced aggressiveness in connection with territoriality (cf. O'Neill and Paluck 1973; see also Esser 1973).

It could thus be summarized with Bettelheim (1955: 17-41) that disorganized use of space – without doubt including lack of adequate territories – is an index of disease among mentally disturbed children.

4.1.3.3. Abnormal adults:
During the last decades there has been, as we have mentioned, a growing interest in territoriality among psychiatrists. First, their studies concentrated on neurotic symptoms, but it was later evident that the psychoses are most suitable for such investigations (Ploog 1958). In fact it has even been suggested that "the schizoid evolved in a territorially dominated society, and the affective in a hierarchical society" (Kellett 1973: 860). Horowitz and co-workers published a series of papers on human spatial behaviour and found that the personal distance or what was called the "body-buffer zone" is larger in psychiatric patients than in healthy individuals (Horowitz, Duff and Stratton 1964). Among the mentally ill, schizophrenics demanded more space for themselves than depressives and neurotics, at least initially (Horowitz 1968).

It was also stated that schizophrenic patients confused boundaries between animate and inanimate objects and between the self and the nonself, and they concretized space so that it became an object rather than an abstraction. They cleverly utilized spatial cues for defensive testing or manipulative purposes, or they paid excessive attention to feelings about space, leading to fear, confusion or other maladaptive behavior (op cit. p. 25). Similar views were expressed in another paper, where it was said that "Territoriality in animals is a species-specific instinctual or imprinted phenomenon.... The body-buffer zone and the area of personal space are not instinctual or imprinted structures but rather a part of the acquired body image" (Horowitz 1965: 27).

Here we must stress that if any human territorial behaviour, judged by its regularity and affective performance, must have an innate and imperative character, it is that of the mentally abnormal, particularly that of the psychotic. "By means of its inflexible rigidity, the phenomenon of distance acquires a primitive and pathological character in the schizophrenic. The sick person has been a slave of the critical distance" (Racamier 1957: 66). The following examples are without doubt revealing.

It was Staehelin (1953, 1954) who gave the first detailed descriptions of combined rank order and territorial behaviour among 50 female psychotic patients in Switzerland. Particularly one schizophrenic lady sat day after day in a special chair, the placing of which should be fixed as to centimeters. She bent forward in a catatonic position, seemingly without interest in the environment and without saying a word. If, however, someone went too close to her, the territory owner burst out into attack, the fierceness of which depended on the rank order of the offender. As this patient because of her intelligence had an alpha-position, that is, was high in rank on the ward, such intrusions were few. Her bed was defended in the same way and could not be touched in her presence, not even by the ward personnel. Another patient who had tried to sleep in the same room was beaten to death. Only the higher-ranked doctor could take her place without risk of attack. On such occasions she first stopped in front of him, trying in different ways to get him to move, and then began to circle around at a distance of 3 meters in a stereotypic manner until her place was left free.

Yet another catatonic patient often moved stereotypically within her territory in front of the door to the garden, which was locked but was nevertheless a presumptive outlet to freedom. Encroached upon by the doctor, she first tried to escape, then retreated to the gate and at 3 meter's distance she put her backside out, hiding her face in her hands with frightful anxiety. If the offender then advanced up to 30 centimeter's distance, he was, in spite of friendly words and outstretched hand, fiercely attacked. These and similar observations of humans have exact counterparts in animal confrontations, but it was stressed by Staehelin in this study that the strength of the strange behaviour and its effects largely depend on the mood and temporary mental state of the patient, decreasing under more healthy and increasing in more pathological situations (cf. also Felipe and Sommer 1967).

During a symposium in 1958 it was reported that in the overcrowded and rather neglected mental ward of Saint Elizabeth's Hospital in Washington, D.C. space had become a genuine value because of its scarcity. The dominant alpha-patient had full control of the hall, while those below him in hierarchical order had access only to limited space. Nobody could intrude into the territory of a person more powerful than himself. At the bottom of the ladder the omega-patient could use nothing more than a bench to sleep on, could not go to spit in the drain located in the middle of the hall and had little access to the toilet. As soon as these patients were given access to a decent amount of space, 50 percent of them ceased to be incontinent (E. T. Hall 1963: 439-440; Sivadon 1965: 490).

It should be underlined here that neuroleptica were more commonly introduced into the treatment of psychotics only around 1958, and that perhaps after this time such extreme examples as those given above are now not so easily found because of medicination.

Recently, schizophrenia was considered to depend directly on territorial conflicts (Vieira 1974: 68-69). It was argued that in the development of this disease "everything runs its course just as though the schizophrenic, by an unknown force, was increasingly displaced towards the boundary of his territory. Compelled by this force that introduced spatial anisotropy, he first feels dangerously close to, then exceeds and finally loses sight of the limits of his territory. For him everything is changing. After this his actual world turns over around him. At the same time he is taken away from his group. However, close to the confines from which he now feels repelled all the elements of territory – the physical, the social and the conceptual – are questioned by him. The idiosyncracies which the schizophrenics possess are immediately identified with the different ingredients of his illness". These hypotheses demand, of course, further confirmation.

As to the maniac-depressive illness Demaret (1971) tried to compare, even in terms of homology, the all-powerfulness of the maniac phase with the behaviour of an animal territory owner and the ideas of ruin in the melancholic, depressive phase with that of a creature without territory. These are interesting but risky ideas which, however, do not wholly lack support in the form of observational evidence. It was for instance stated by Goffman (1972: 449): "The manic is someone who does not refrain from intruding where he is not wanted or where he will be accepted but at a loss to what we see as his value and status. He does not contain himself in the sphere and territories alloted to him. He over-reaches. He does not keep his place".

It is a well-known experience from different sciences that unusual or abnormal phenomena are often more eagerly investigated and more easily discovered than usual and normal ones. Territoriality is from this point of view no exception. In fact, studies of mentally deficient humans have given important results already in the pioneering stage of territorology, and with these in mind we now turn to early and "primitive" men.

4.1.4. Early man's territories

4.1.4.1. Stone Age spatial behaviour:

If we remember the judgement of territory as a subjective product it must seem difficult, if not impossible, to give propositions about the territoriality of early man. There is, however, some circumstantial evidence available, and several authors have expressed, on indirect grounds, more or less decided opinions on the matter. We will now take a look at Stone Age man, who has been the sole representative of mankind during the main part of its history and is therefore of greatest interest, even in a territorial context. In fact humans have lived on earth more than 99 percent of their time as hunters and gatherers, and it is estimated that 90 percent of a total sum of about 80 billion people existing up to our own age have supported themselves this way, while only 6 percent have been agriculturalists and pastoralists and 4 percent industrialists (cf. Soja 1971: 40).

In the famous Olduvai Gorge of East Africa a series of stones was found, placed there in a circle during the Lower Pleistocene about 1 million years ago by *Homo habilis* (Leakey, Tobias and Napier 1964; Tobias 1965). To be completely honest we should, however, admit that most experts today deem these finds to belong to a species of *Australopithecus*, but even so, this is the closest primate relative of man ever to have lived. It is not known with certainty if these stones represent the base of a hut or a fire-place but they encircle definitely the first sure, still-remaining space that was actively marked out by a man-like creature.

Finds of actual Paleolithic dwellings are rare, but in recent years new discoveries have shown that in cave settlements, too, there have been tents and roof constructions as well as arrangements for dividing the space into different compartments. The oldest known hut which one has been able to reconstruct is from Terra Amata in southern France and was used by Homo erectus between 300,000 and 400,000 years ago. It was a rather large, oval dwelling with a roof held up by posts and a series of stones around it. Inside there was a fire-place and three separate working-places (Lumley 1966, 1969).

Only one Paleolithic community has hitherto been completely investigated in every detail, namely that of Dolní Věstonice in Czechoslovakia, dated by means of C^{14} to have been inhabited about 23,000 years ago by *Homo sapiens*, our own species. The finds of ten thousands of artifacts are so concentrated within a certain area that some delimiting construction around the whole site is assumed. In the case of Alexandrovka, also called Kostjenkij IV, in Ukraine, Russia, two interesting huts were excavated, about 23 and 33 m. long and 5 m. broad, each with about ten fire-places and three compartments, divided by thresholds (Jelínek 1973: 230-274).

One of the largest Neolithic villages yet known, Barkaer in Jutland, Denmark, was inhabited more than 4,000 years ago and comprised 52 to 58 one-roomed huts, which were set close to each other, side by side in two rows with an open space in between (Childe 1950: 6, 1958: 68). And at Köln-

Lindenthal in Germany a complete Neolithic village, protected by rampart and ditch, was discovered (Schwabedissen 1962: 263). It has been assumed that Stone Age society was divided into groups of from about 35 to about 500 members (Soja 1971: 39), the first figure perhaps most applicable to Paleolithic and the last to Neolithic conditions.

It is probable that the described limiting and isolating constructions outside huts were built primarily for defense against wild animals and human enemies, but the latter purpose, as well as the division of inhabited caves and huts, at least suggest territorial implications. Klíma (1962: 201), summarizing the information from Dolní Věstonice, declared: "Through convincing arguments and especially on the basis of ethnographic material, we may assume that one of our hut types was the habitation of a consanguineally interrelated social-territorial unit: the matrilineal kin group". Most interesting excavations from a Danish Bronze Age site have, further, within the confines of a single village territory unveiled clear boundaries which are thought to mark individually-owned ground plots and communally-held grazing land (Hatt 1937: 112-136).

4.1.4.2. Critics and defenders of early territoriality:
Some anthropologists do not believe in the occurrence of behavioural territories in early man. Thus Vallois (1970: 229) claimed: "All evidence suggests that the Paleolithic bands were not territorial units, that they were capable of large migrations, and that sexual relations must have existed between them". These views were supported by Reynolds (1966), and in a recent volume of the series *The Emergence of Man* it was said: "Territoriality, likewise, is not a 'natural' feature of human group living; nor is it among most other primates. . . . It appears likely that war, covetousness, greed and cruelty were later developments, coming after man settled down on the land, became more numerous and forged cultures that encouraged individual and group pride in possessions, territories and beliefs, even as they fostered art, science and humanity" (*The First Men* 1973: 136).

Many scientists are, however, of quite another opinion, e.g., Schwabedissen (1962: 263) and Hallowell (1970: 242). In their valuable paper on "Ecology and the Protohominids" Bartholomew and Birdsell (1953: 485-486) stated: "It is clear that territoriality exists in all complex human societies, and it is clearly established that group territoriality is also important at the simplest levels of human culture. It is, therefore, reasonable to assume that protohominids similarly possessed a well-developed territoriality, presumably on the basis of the family or extended family".

This is in perfect accord with the views of Clark (1960: 312-313), who argued that since all primate groups, or for that matter all vertebrates, keep to a clearly defined range or territory, it is safe to assume that this habit had a major effect upon Australopithecine behaviour. However, a primate group living on the ground is much more vulnerable to attack by predators, so that the more restricted the territory, the more intimate would be the knowledge of it and the better the chance of escape. Moreover, Clark proceeded, to ensure the maintenance of an adequate food and water supply for the group, the territory had to be sufficiently small to be adequately protected from other groups. It may be suggested, therefore, that the Australopithecine bands, which were naturally adapted to drier open country where game was plentiful, rather than to closed bush, may have had a range somewhere between those of the herbivores and the carnivores.

Hockett and Ascher (1964: 138-140) underlined in their thought-provoking paper about "The Human Revolution" that the protohominids lived in bands of from ten to thirty, consisting typically of one or very few adult males plus females and offspring. They probably had a roughly defined nucleated territoriality, that is, they defended a core area like many other mammals, not the least primates, in contrast to the mostly perimeter-defending behaviour of birds. Thus the territories had poorly demarcated boundaries but some specific site, a "home base", from which each member of the band could orient himself as he moved about and which at the same time was his safest place (cf. also Hockett 1973: 69).

Further, Bates (1953: 709) found that since territoriality seems to be a universal phenomenon among mammals, it must have characterized man's mammalian ancestors too. The instinctive, precultural equipment, then, would include elements leading to group cohesion and territorial restriction. Thus the population of Pleistocene man may have been governed by the territorial requirements of the small tribal groups. And the frequency of violent death among early men caused by conspecifics may well indicate that territorial arrangements were maintained aggressively. Washburn and Avis (1961: 433-434) stressed that hunting might have had psychological, social and territorial influence on human behaviour. The acquisition of hunting habits must have been accompanied by a great enlargement of territory, since the source of food then became more erratic and mobile. On these grounds the authors think that human territorial habits and psychology are different from those of apes and monkeys.

Finally, Washburn and DeVore (1970: 98) concluded: "By the Middle Pleistocene there is direct evidence of hunting and indirect evidence for cooperation, division of labor, and sharing of food. This human pattern differs on each of these points from that of baboons, who do not hunt, share, or co-operate, and where there is no sexual division of economic activity.... The sources of vegetable food are normally so widespread that the overlapping of ranges does not appear serious, but with the hunting of large animals the matter is entirely different. If strangers hunt game, or even disturb it, scaring it from its normal routes, the plans of the local hunters are ruined. Hunting man requires a large area free from the interference of other hunters. When man became a hunter, his relation to the land changed from one in which a small range was adequate to one that demanded a large territory" (cf. also Young 1971: 626-628).

So it is very probable that there were behavioural territories in the early human societies, consisting of hunting and gathering bands. The stability of these societies could in part have been due to kinship relations but with much more probability it depended on what has been called "the ideology of cores-idence" (Fried 1967, cited after Soja 1971: 40), that is, on a form of ter-ritoriality with overlapping spatial systems. This primary way of life, which today is confined to not quite 0.001 percent of the world population, was certainly both flexible and egalitarian and it has been considered "the master behavior pattern of the human species" (Laughlin 1968: 304).

Here we have an interesting starting-point, as we turn to the territorial conditions in extant "primitive" societies.

4.1.5. Territory in "primitive" societies

4.1.5.1. Primitivity and knowledge of "primitive" peoples:
Coming from early man to societies of a "primitive" character could seem to involve just a short and natural step. But as shown i.a. by Hsu (1964: 173-174) the concept of primitivity as usually applied has "neither empirical validity nor theoretical utility", and "a majority give the term the meaning of simple-ness, antiquity, undesirableness, and undisguised inferiority". Mostly it is used to label peoples outside the great European and Asiatic cultures. Here we employ the concept – lacking a better one, it is adopted and put within quotation marks – for societies inhabiting more natural environments and with more natural ways of living than most of those belonging to our Western and other advanced civilizations.

We are quite aware of the fact that primitivity is not seldom a secondary condition and that it cannot always be assumed that peoples given this at-tribute are more original, culturally speaking, than others. However, it is deemed possible that behavioural territoriality could be more simply expressed or easily understood in the rather unchanged or at least not quite culturally structured habitats of "primitive" societies (concerning the space conception and space imagination of "primitive" peoples, see Haberland 1957).

If some investigations of territory in "primitive" man gave negative results, it does not necessarily mean that the phenomenon was absent. There are different possible causes for such a state of affairs.

First, in the old colonial days anthropologists were often sent by or identified themselves with the government, and lack of territorial feelings was sometimes more or less consciously provoked in order to justify measures by the white masters to drive away the "savages". Eyre (1845: 296) in his excellent report from journeys in Central Australia remarked that "It has generally been imagined, but with great injustice, as well as incorrectness, that the natives have no idea of property in land, or proprietary rights connected with it. Nothing can be further from the truth than this assumption, although men of high character and standing, and who are otherwise benevolently disposed towards the natives, have distinctly denied this right, and maintained that the natives were not entitled to have any choice of land reserved for them out of their own possessions, and in their respective districts" (cf. also "Gold in Kenya and Native Reserves" 1933).

Second, according to the "history" of the social-evolutionary theories of the nineteenth century, "allotment of land regularized in customary law" – in which formulation even territorial phenomena are probably concealed – was reported to have had its origin first in the agricultural stage (Herskovits 1940: 291) and was not sought in primordial cultures. "Contact with Europeans could bring about, often surprisingly quick, conditions appearing to suggest that the aborigines lived a wholly free-ranging life" (Stanner 1965- 1966:18).

Third and certainly most important, differences of thinking and of communication between investigators and investigated indubitably often biased or spoilt understanding (cf., e.g., Bohannan 1964: 174-182). A good example is that of the Hopi indians, who, according to Whorf (1956: 200-205), have no terms for interior three-dimensional spaces like cell, room, hall and so on in spite of the fact that they have multi-room dwellings. "One might be led to assume by this that the Hopi would then lack a sense of territoriality. Again, nothing could be farther from the truth. They just use and conceive of space differently. We work from points and along lines. They apparently do not. While seemingly inconsequential, these differences caused innumerable headaches to the white supervisors who used to run the Hopi reservation in the first part of this century" (E. T. Hall 1959: 198).

4.1.5.2. Territoriality in hunters and gatherers:
As to general views it should first be mentioned that some scientists have denied or questioned any strict territorial behaviour in the primordial cultures. Thus Sahlins (1959: 58) stated: "Territoriality among hunters and gatherers is never exclusive, and group membership is apt to shift and change according to the variability of food resources in space and time. Savage society is open, and corresponding to ecological variations, there are degrees of openness: . . . .". And Soja (1971: 41) recently maintained: "Contrary to many conventional images of hunting and gathering societies, territoriality in the form of rigidly defined and defended boundaries is extremely weak or non-existent – perhaps weaker than in any other type of human society. The basic territorial model in some respects is very much like that of several other primate groups".

Evidently we have here the same problems concerning differing terms and definitions as in animals, and the contrast between the just cited authors and the following is probably not so great. Probably everyone could agree with Carr-Saunders (1922: 203) when he found that "among all these races, without exception, groups of men are recognized as, if not owning, then as enjoying the usufruct of certain very clearly defined areas". And Forde (1934: 373) vindicated that "The food-gatherers are not homeless wanderers. Even among the least organized and the poorest in equipment the unit groups of families each occupy an inherited and adequately delimited territory". Further Linton (1964: 211, 232) admitted that every hunting band claims certain territory and stands ready to defend it against trespassers as well as that the tribe is always a territorial unit.

"Most of the hunting peoples of the world live in bands. A band is a group of somewhere between thirty and a little over one hundred individuals who own and occupy a single territory, and share food. As the population density of a band's territory is rarely more than one person per square mile, a territory may cover anywhere from about thirty to several hundred square miles, and it may include water rights to lakes, streams, and coastline, which are just as important as land in providing food . . . . the territorial band is probably older than the family and may even antedate the species *Homo sapiens*, to which we all, hunters and non-hunters, belong" (Coon 1971: 191).

Most probably the secret is concealed in the words of Quincey Wright (1942: 76), reflecting also the primate situation: "All primitive people live in defined territories which supply their economic needs, but among the collectors and hunters boundaries are usually so well recognized by neighbors, and population growth so well adjusted to the food supply available in the area, that occasions seldom arise necessitating territorial expansion or defense of one's own" (cf. also the interesting recent relation by Peterson 1975).

Most authors report only group territories in "primitive" societies. Lévy-Bruhl (1922: 521) asserted that "every social group, sedentary or nomadic, occupies a more or less spacious territory, the limits of which are, in general, clearly defined both for the group and its neighbours". And later on he explicitly stated that there is no individual possession of land, which could suggest that there is no individual territory (cf. Lévy-Bruhl 1927: 122). Less uniform was the picture given by Hobhouse, Wheeler and Ginsberg (1930: 251), who announced that of 248 different "primitive" peoples 138 had predominantly communal ownership of land, 40 intermixed, 32 private (individual and family), 26 chief and 12 noble ownership.

It should already here be stressed that property in land, which matter will be treated in detail later (4.2.1.), is not always, or even predominantly, equal to territory, of course, but assumedly the concept contains more or less evident traits of behavioural territoriality. And even though, in some cases, there seems to be a real lack of extensive land territories, e.g., in the Andamans, this very people has big huts in which every family has an exclusive part, possessed by the wife, and marked out by means of wooden pieces (Nippold 1954: 48-53).

4.1.5.3. Territories in pastoralists and agriculturalists:

It has often been claimed that pastoralists show notorious carelessness as to land. Certainly it is true that herdsmen do not often mark out individual territories and that for economic reasons they must have large common areas to graze their herds on. Unfortunately, "The analysis of conditions under which land is held and used by herding peoples is limited by the fact that less is known about land tenure among such folk than among either those with cruder economies or among agricultural tribes. It is possible, however, and from hints here and there in the literature even probable, that the application of a concept analogous to that of the family hunting band might point the way to a more adequate understanding of their systems of ownership. . . .

Until more precise studies are made, however, it can merely be said, in summary fashion, that grazing land as such is rarely if ever owned by individuals, but that a presumption of group ownership is strong. It also seems probable that the vagueness of the boundary-lines where restriction of tenure exists is a result of the seasonal nature of grazing and the large resources of land available to most herding peoples; this in turn must lower its scarcity value, making it a matter approaching indifference where a given herd grazes, since all herds can be adequately cared for" (Herskovits 1940: 301-307).

Here we have, of course, an example of the earlier mentioned phenomenon that territories are established or, rather, manifested only in cases where there is some scarcity of or competition for ground or other resources. It is also significant that Herskovits (op. cit. p. 307) stated concerning the problems in this field: "In part these may never have been resolved because of the anthropologists' tendency to treat land tenure and other aspects of property primarily as a phase of social organization, though here the remedy lies in a simple redirection of interests. More serious is the possibility that European colonization has tended to destroy the traditional divisions of pasture-ranges and that boundaries, possibly vague at best when the system was in full operation in aboriginal times, cannot be reconstructed as readily as those of family hunting bands".

Since gardeners and farmers are intimately bound to the soil, it is hardly astonishing if they have great territorial interests. In connection with agricultural peoples it was asserted: "The most important form of land tenure, if only because it is the most common, is private ownership" (op. cit. p. 312). But it is also stressed that what is prized is the exclusive right to benefit from the produce raised on a given plot. Thus "primitive gardeners assign the right of usufruct to individuals or families. In some instances, title is vested in the clan, but usually ultimate ownership is vested in the community" (Hoebel 1949: 339). The fact that property of land and behavioural territoriality are not identical concepts is probably reflected in the interesting words of Herskovits (1940: 329): "Private ownership of land, however, implies greater rights than are generally accorded in primitive systems, while communistic tenure assumes that the individual has fewer rights than are found in practice". Maybe this is an indirect description of territoriality.

We now proceed to a detailed account of presumed territorial examples in "primitive" societies. If the citations are in the present tense, it does not, of course, mean that the conditions or behaviours mentioned are still everywhere unchanged. On the contrary, as we know, there have been great revolutions in the lives of most "primitive" peoples, above all during the last hundred years. Examples are given both from Africa, Asia, Australia and America as well as from the three economic stages: the primordial culture of hunters-fishers-gatherers, the supposedly more advanced category of pastoralists and the most often higher cultures of food growers, that is, gardeners and agriculturalists.

4.1.5.4. Africa:

Starting in Africa we recognize that a regularity of territorial phenomena is already suggested here in the words of Malinowski (1945: 129): "All African tribes or tribelets, from the seminomadic Bushmen to the Baganda and the Chagga, have the right to reside in safety and in peace; the right to exploit their traditional plots or territory for a minimum subsistence according to standards which for them are indispensable".

Nippold (1954: 43), however, found in investigating the bushmen and other pygmies of Africa that the tribe did not seem to have any territorial rights, but that the local group or band was in unrestricted possession of the hunting and gathering grounds and their products: "This support area, from which the group cannot be separated, has fixed limits which are not artificially erected but are composed of ridges, rivers, woods or tree groups that are recognized by the neighbours". But as DeVore (1971: 309) collected information about the bushmen, he became increasingly aware that hunters-gatherers have no territories whatsoever in the classic sense, but only defend certain spots like water holes.

Without doubt territorial conditions in the bushmen are adjusted to the occurrence of water during the dry winter season, at which time trespass across frontiers is dangerous, although a neutral zone between neighbours averts confrontation. "The Bushman band and its territory, then, is a miniature realm; it consists of a number of families, each with its own huts, and only at the dry season are these families likely to be united in the vicinity of a water-hole" (Forde 1934: 27).

That the bushmen not only defend nucleated territories, concentrated on a well, but also areal ones seems, however, evident. "Even though there is no general political or social organization, no clearly formulated laws and rights every family group knows the exact limits of its range and is careful not to cross foreign ground. Every trespasser runs the risk of being killed by an ambush without warning" (Immenroth 1933: 79; Herskovits 1940: 289-299). Heinz (1972) confirms these facts, giving plenty of original evidence for strong social territoriality and some for individual, too. He even tries to explain the conflicting theories on the matter by means of the varying history and resources of the different bands (cf. also Tobias 1964: 81-82 and particularly Eibl-Eibesfeldt 1974, where much evidence in favour of bushman territoriality is also cited).

As to the pastoralist neighbours of the South African bushmen it is said that every Hottentot tribe has its territory, into which strangers should not intrude for herding or hunting without the permission of the whole tribe. Each kraal has its distinct pasture lands, over which the people of that section of the tribe relocate their mat huts according to the needs of their herds.

Among the Mangbetu every tribe has an accurate knowledge of the boundary of the social territory, inside which the people can hunt, move about and establish villages (cf. Carr-Saunders 1922: 208-209; see also Herskovits 1940: 302-304).

Writing of the pygmies of the Ituri forest in Congo Turnbull (1965: 93-97) stressed that "Before we can begin to understand what the Mbuti band is, we have to understand the notion of territory, which is effectively the only concept through which the band can be defined". He added that in every case investigated the band had been able to delineate its boundaries by citing rivers, streams, mountain ridges, ravines, caves, or other locally well-known natural landmarks and he ended by stating that "Territory is also used as the concept by which men and women define 'home', and it is through territorial membership that any individual has such rights as he has. Above all, it is the territory which has bounds, not the band".

It is commonly claimed that in Africa individual title to land applies just to agricultural areas. However, among the A-kikuyu of East Africa i.a. even the fallow is entirely in private hands and cannot be brought into cultivation without the owner's consent (Routledge 1910, cited after Carr-Saunders 1922: 210). This was confirmed by Kenyatta (1959: 21) in a splendid monograph on his people, where it was asserted: "While the whole tribe defended collectively the boundary of their territory, every inch of land within it had its owner". His comments on land tenure also strongly suggest the probability of population dispersal through territoriality.

In the Yoruba people of western Nigeria there is a lineage group called the Ebi. "This body of agnatic kinsmen, with their wives, also had an estate – a more or less precisely determinable area within which they traditionally farmed, and which they protected from encroachment by others" (Bohannan 1964: 180).

Regarding the nomadic Tuaregs of North Africa it was reported that "The component tribes of these federations are territory holding units under a chief whose powers are limited by traditional Tuareg egalitarianism and the countervailing power of the notables of the tribe. These tribes are commonly further divided into subtribes, each of which is under the leadership of a lesser chief and has a territorial locus" (Murphy 1964: 1261).

4.1.5.5. Asia:
In Asia we find, to begin with, that the reindeer nomads in the northwestern parts of the continent, Lapps and Samoyeds, have, or at least had not long

ago, delimited hunting territories belonging to families or clans. Thus the tundra was clearly divided, e.g., among the Jurak Samoyeds. And even though the character of reindeer nomadism sometimes demands the suspension of boundaries, it is most often so that every group migrates along certain courses and visits special pastures every year (Schmidt 1940: 14-18, 119-121, 156-159).

Not very dissimilar are the conditions of the Chukchi and Tungus reindeer herdsmen more to the east. For the Tungus it was said that every family demands a not-too-small territory to earn their living from hunting and fishing and – just as important – enough pasture for their reindeer, which represent their main or sole wealth (Müller 1882: 46). About the same people it was even said: "The territory of a group of co-operating or intermarrying clans is felt as its property, and it is defended if necessary by force" (Forde 1934: 361).

In central Asia the nomadic Kazak, Kirghiz and Kalmuck tribes live with their herds of sheep, goats, horses and camels. Earlier their steppes were divided in meridional direction between the different tribes, which migrated north and south within rather narrow ranges. The fact seems to be that only the critical winter pastures are thought of as territorial possessions, and they are claimed and protected by the clan (Forde 1934: 332-334; Schmidt 1940: 192-196). In fact there is also, e.g., among the Buriats, Yakuts and Altai peoples, a strong tendency to guard crucial pastures for the herds in a territorial way. There are all transitions from collective tribe property to purely individual property as well as from totally unmarked grazing areas through those marked out by natural features, cairns, stakes and the dung of the cattle to fenced land, where the grass is cut for winter food (cf. Forde 1934: 332-334; Schmidt 1940: 193-208; see also Herskovits 1940: 304-307).

Among the many rice-growing peoples of southern Asia there are, e.g., in the Philippine Islands, territorial units for the dominating kinship groups as well as for individual families both in the Ifuago and the Kalinga, although the principle is much more advanced in the latter people. Here, however, territoriality is rather feeble in the area of domestic affairs but hard as flint with respect to foreign relations, expressed as clearly defined boundaries and involving citizenship for the regional unit (R. F. Barton 1949: 137-217, 253-255; cf. also Hoebel 1949: 338).

Long houses with territorial sections were already built by early man, and those of recent Borneo rice-growers have a length of up to 400 yards. They are divided by transverse walls, at intervals of some twenty or thirty feet, so as to form a single row of spacious chambers of approximately equal size. Each such chamber is the private apartment of one family with eating and sleeping places for father, mother, daughters and younger sons. Within each chamber there are usually several alcoves, more or less completely screened or walled off from the central space (Hose 1926: 71-80).

Among Asian primordial cultures the negrito people of Semang, Malaya, live in large family groups composed of parents and grown children with their families. Every group has a small traditional territory of some twenty square miles in which its claim for the quite valuable fruits of a certain tree species is recognized by its neighbours. As to hunting and collecting of roots all are free to wander over the lands of adjacent groups, but they always return to gather the heavy, green, prickly fruits of the tall durian tree in their own territory (Forde 1934: 12).

The peoples of the Andaman Islands west of the Malayan Peninsula build communal huts, essentially not unlike a number of windshields encircling a common central area and touching each other at the edges. Thus each family builds only its own part of the hut and is responsible exclusively for the maintenance of that part. Starting from the "windshield" edges each family also marks out an area of the hut floor with stones, shells, etc., into which only family members may enter without being formally invited (Leyhausen 1971a: 30-31).

Good and detailed information about the territorial conditions among the Veddahs of Ceylon was published nearly one century ago (Sarasin and Sarasin 1884-1886: 457-477): "The whole Veddah-region was divided into hunting areas, of which every family had one each. Schematically the country was like a net or a chessboard where the squares were hunting grounds. The hunting areas had different sizes according to their more or less favourable position. If we could make an exact map of this organization we would find that the meshes of the net radiated towards certain centres, which were or were not connected with adjacent centres. The boundaries of the hunting grounds were made up of special large trees or rocks or of rivers and were carefully observed. Such an area was jealously guarded by the resident family against encroachment by the neighbours." During the rainy season these peoples lived in caves, often two or three families in each, the cave being divided into compartments by means of branches, pieces of bark and so on, all of which, as we may remember, is behaviour known from early man (4.1.4.).

4.1.5.6. Australia:
Arriving in the Australian sphere we look first at the mainland. Long ago

Nind (1831: 28) communicated that the natives of King George's Sound "who live together have the exclusive right of fishing or hunting upon the neighbouring grounds, which are, in fact, divided into individual properties; the quantity of land owned by each individual being very considerable. Yet it is not so exclusively his, but others of his family have certain rights over it; so that it may be considered as partly belonging to the tribe". And Eyre (1845: 297) confirmed after his extensive expeditions in central Australia that the tribes had separate hunting grounds, which were further parcelled out among individual members, who could always point out the exact boundaries of their land.

Lowie (1921: 379) stressed that in the Dieri "the territorial unit co-exists with and is independent of the kinship unit", a most important statement. Much evidence on territoriality in family groups as well as within individual families among the tribes of southeastern Australia was published by Schmidt (1937: 242-250). In his book on Australian tribes Wheeler (1910: 35-46) summarized: "We have seen that each tribe has a defined territory, and that this is subdivided into smaller areas owned by subgroups. . . . The unit would generally be the undivided family, but there are a few indications that the ownership might even be vested in single persons within a family other than the head". It could also be mentioned that for the Australian aborigines a simple exponential relationship has been demonstrated between mean annual rainfall and the size of the tribal territory (Birdsell 1966: 87).

Hiatt (1961-1962) criticized the old picture of territorial organization in Australia. Relying on evidence earlier discussed and rejected here (3.2.5.) as to presumed lack of territoriality in different crucial ape species, he came to the conclusion (1968: 99-102): "Modern ethology thus raises no difficulty for an account of aborigines which implies that they lacked territorial instincts". He further presented some data on the Mararagidj patriclan with 25 members, who seemingly moved about unrestricted, and he summarized: "The evidence is clearly against the existence in aboriginal clansmen of an instinct to occupy and defend their territory". However, he immediately went on: "But it points to a strong impulse to establish and maintain territorial ownership", and he ended his paper by the statement: "Ritual responsibility was undoubtedly a factor, but another component was an emotional bond with the land itself. The source of this emotion is not clear".

This source is, however, not difficult to find for a student of behavioural territoriality with its affective binding, the phenomenon Hiatt in fact gave a good description of. The same feelings undoubtedly lie behind some interesting findings from Western Australia: "Dying persons, especially those dying from old age, generally express an earnest desire to be taken to their birth-place, that they may die and be buried there. If possible, these wishes are always complied with by the relatives and friends. Parents will point out the spot where they were born, so that when they become old and infirm their children may know where they wish their bodies to be disposed of" (Dawson 1881: 62).

Concerning an emotional attachment to the soil it was recently said: "The religious and totemic ties that united not merely whole groups with their group areas, but the individuals constituting each group with one or more defined mythological centres within each group area, were of the utmost importance.... Hence, paradoxical though it may seem, the desert nomads in the pre-'white' days were linked socially, ritually, and emotionally with even the most arid portions of their group territory by ties strong enough to keep them contented with their homeland in normal seasons, and eager to return to it after drought-caused absences as soon as the rains came" (Strehlow 1965: 126-128).

Summarizing the matter Stanner (1965-1966: 16-19) in his very interesting and valuable analysis stressed: "We are being too sociological and insufficiently ecological for the matters at issue" and came to the final con-clusion that among the aboriginal peoples of Australia: "(1) Some sort of exogamous patrilineal descent-group was ubiquitous. (2) It had intrinsic con-nection, not mere association, with a territory. (3) There was a marked ten-dency towards, though no iron rule requiring, patrilocality and virilocality. (4) The group thus formed was basic to both territorial and social organi-zation, however concealed by other structural groups (e.g., phratries, moie-ties, sections, etc.) or by dynamic emphases".

Territorial conditions similar to those on the mainland are known from Tasmania (Bonwick 1967: 83) and also from New Zealand: "Land was held primarily by tribal right; but within this tribal right each free warrior of the tribe had particular rights over some portion. He could not part with the land because it was not his to give or sell, but he had better rights to certain portions than others of his tribe" (Tregear 1890: 106). From the Fiji Islands it was reported that when the British took over in 1874 and peace was estab-lished between local fractions, the clan hamlets of Lau moved out of the bush and settled in coastal villages. Each clan hamlet occupied a section of the village but kept its proprietary clan rights in land. Volcanic islands, like Mothe, continued to be divided into pie-shaped sections, "*hoag*", bounded by natural ridges between the fertile valleys, by lines between certain trees or prominent rocks, posts and even stone walls. Thus each local clan retained the use of the garden lands, uplands, and fishing grounds of the section wherein its hamlets had formerly been located (cf. Gardiner 1898:481-486; L. Thompson 1961:116-117).

In the Chimbu of the New Guinea highland we can distinguish two types of territorial unit: first the tribe or subtribe territory, that is, a distinct block of land, generally compact and defensible, surrounded by a no-man's land and then the descent group segment, which holds several parcels of land within this block, interdigitating with those of other segments and containing a share in all available land classes. The territories of subtribes lose some of their distinctiveness as compared with those of tribes by the total or partial absence of a no-man's land (Brookfield and Brown 1963:157; cf. also Sahlins 1968:52-53).

On the Trobriand Islands east of New Guinea it is believed that every man and woman by birth and descent is connected with a definite spot, and through this with a village community and with a territory. In all cases the natives can point out the precise and actual landmarks, and the stability of territorial boundaries is regarded almost as a natural fact. "The first principle gives every man a right of residence, a right to a portion of land in it, a real asylum and a place from which he can never forcibly be moved" (Malinowski 1935:341-381; for territorial conditions on other islands in the Pacific, see Herskovits 1940:314-321).

4.1.5.7.   America:

Passing over to South America we find in Tierra del Fuego, the southernmost part, the Ona or Selknam people demonstrate, even within recognized tribal territory, the existence of more or less definite, marked off family hunting grounds. Every unallowed trespassing of the boundaries is punished by the defenders, but permits to neighbours are most often given, particularly if they have coveted goods for exchange (Carr-Saunders 1922:207; Schmidt 1937:185-187).

It is reported from Peru that some of the least developed tribes, e.g., the Chibcha, have both communal and individual ownership of land (Lowie 1921:210). As to the Boro and other tribes of the western Amazon Forest, their clans form autonomous territorial and social units with boundary marks, even in the densest jungle. They build big common houses, not unlike circus tents, in which each family has its own fire-place against the wall; and the space is sometimes divided into separate quarters by means of matting partitions (Forde 1934:134, 145).

For North America north of Mexico it was summarized that "while the land claimed by a tribe, often covering a wide area, was common to all its members and the entire territory was defended against intruders, yet individual occupancy of garden patches was respected" (*Handbook of American Indians north of Mexico* 1907-1910: 308). The lines dividing territories belonging to different tribes of the famous Indian League were not boundaries between enemies. "The Iroquois were exact about their internal boundary lines, because it served to keep each member of the confederacy distinct and independent, and enabled the idea of home rule to be properly carried out. They always knew just whose ground they were on, just as we know today which county or State we are in" (Dellenbaugh 1901: 411).

About the Blackfoot buffalo hunters of the Great Plains it was said, e.g., that most of the year they lived in smaller groups or bands, fundamentally economic and social units, each with a delimited territory (Forde 1934: 50). The Maidu of California had clear communal or village territories for common hunting, fishing and plant gathering. The boundaries between these areas were not only very fixed but watched over by special guards with bow and arrows and were never given up, not even temporarily (Schmidt 1937: 129-130).

In a now classic study Speck (1915: 3-7) described the family hunting territories of the Algonkian bands in the Ottawa Valley, later also those of Nova Scotia and Newfoundland (Speck 1922: 83-138). Here all the male members of the individual family shared the right of hunting and fishing, and boundaries were formed by rivers, ridges, lakes, swamps or other natural marks. Hunting outside the territory was punishable, occasionally by death, if permission had not been obtained. The Montagnais even carved out good maps on pieces of birch bark, with territories identified (cf. Schmidt 1937: 137-155, 1940: 365-368). It has been suggested that the size of these hunting territories depended on the abundance of game and thus was ecologically adjusted (Hallowell 1949: 43). Some authors, summarized by Leacock (1954), assumed that the hunting territories were just a result of the fur trade during recent centuries, but their main arguments had been rejected already by J. M. Cooper (1939) and Speck and Eiseley (1939).

The Sitkan indians of Alaska had no interests in the interior parts of the country but the coastline and particularly the margins of rivers and streams were duly divided among the different families. These tracts were regarded as strictly private property, and on some parts of the coast cornerstones and stakes were set up to define the limits of territories (Elliott 1886). About the Athapaskan Dogrib indians of northwestern Canada it was claimed: "The total territory yields sufficient materials for the necessities of life (famine periods excepted) so that within its domain the regional band can endure as an identity for generations" (Helm 1968: 119-121).

This fundamental formulation is the last one in a series meant to show that behavioural group territories of the tribe, most often also of the clan, the band, the large family and the restricted family, have world-wide distribution and must be regarded as normal and common features in "primitive" societies. Manifestations of truly individual territoriality of this kind are not so frequent in the available literature, which, however, does not necessarily mean that the phenomenon is very rare in real life. There will already be reasons to return to this question in the following treatise on rural territories.

4.2. Rural territories

4.2.1. *Property in land*

4.2.1.1. Concept of property:
Of special interest in connection with rural and other territoriality is the concept of property, particularly, of course, with reference to land. Without doubt it is the question of an old phenomenon: "thus it would appear that the feeling of ownership of real estate or of a certain habitat area is a very ancient primate inheritance" (Hooton 1946: 332). We can also agree with Hoebel (1949: 329) that property is a universal trait of human culture, a part of the basic fabric of all society. "In Western societies, however, perhaps more so than any others, 'property' has become rigidly and territorially defined, it has developed an existence independent of the predominant forms of social and cultural organization, and has pervaded the perception of how the larger space is politically organized' (Soja 1971: 10).

It is also notable that most people think of property only as material things, which is, in fact, its least important element. The genuine nature of property is found in its qualities as a social institution. "Property in its full sense is a web of social relations with respect to the utilization of some object (material or nonmaterial) in which a person or group is tacitly or explicitly recognized to hold quasi-exclusive and limiting connection to that object" (Hoebel 1949: 329; cf. also Herskovits 1949: 283-284).

"Land is a *sine qua non* of human existence. It is therefore the most important single object of property. All societies are territorially based, and most sustenance is drawn from the soil, either directly or indirectly" (Hoebel 1949: 331). In her interesting book *The Human Condition* Hanna Arendt (1959: 58-67) rightly remarked that prior to the modern age, which began with the expropriation of the poor and then proceeded to the emancipation of the new propertyless classes, all civilizations have rested upon the sacredness of private property. "Wealth, on the contrary, whether privately owned or publicly distributed, had never been sacred before. Originally, property meant no more or less than to have one's location in a particular part of.the world...".

Charles Darwin judged from his observations of the natives in Tierra del Fuego that indispensable requisites of civilization and social evolution are the possession of property, a fixed abode, and the union of many families under a chief. Thus sexuality, struggle for existence, social organization and the acquisition of property sum up Darwin's essential requirements for organic and social evolution (cf. Freedman and Roe 1961: 463).

4.2.1.2. Instinctive character of property:
Now the question is whether property in land – or, as some authors prefer to say, possession of real estate, implying above all the exclusive right of using the ground – is a universal feature not only of human culture but also of human nature (as to the history of the natural right theory of property, see Schlatter 1951). Beaglehole (1931: 315) in his exhaustive treatise of the matter devoted nearly a hundred pages to animal properties and was quite sure that similar human phenomena have an instinctive background, even though "the study of property interests in man emphasizes the fact that these are more than the resultant of a blind instinct to keep that which satisfies fundamental needs".

Some anthropologists do not agree with the theory of instinct foundations for property and possession in man. Thus Herskovits (1940: 288) suggested: "There may be an instinctive basis for ownership in animals that can be likened to the drive for possession in man, just as techniques of communication, found between members of the same group of social animals, are sometimes interpreted as being derived from another 'instinct' which, in man, finds expression in language. In both of these instances, however, the relationship between the phenomenon in animals and human groups is so tenuous, and, as far as its range of form in human societies is concerned, of so broad a nature when contrasted to its restricted manifestations in animal societies, that for purposes of scientific study the hypothesis of a possible instinctive basis can be regarded as of negligible value".

Hallowell (1955: 248-249) argued in a similar way, going out from the question of whether aggressive defense of certain objects in animals could be compared with the socially recognized and sanctioned rights concerning valuable objects that characterize property in human societies. He maintained that there are no social sanctions in animal societies and no attitudes comparable to human ones because there are no rights to be sanctioned, as we cannot properly speak of rights, obligations and privileges among animals. The individual animal cannot take the attitude of other animals because he has not been socialized in terms of common traditional values. Consequently, an individual animal or a group of animals must be prepared to meet any threat to food, nest, or territory by the exertion of physical force, while members of human societies are secured against the necessity to defend valuable objects from others by physical force alone and thus have a social order.

It is easy to see how false this reasoning is. Behavioural territoriality, which we think lies behind – without being identical with – the different forms of land property, has even the practical function of making acts of physical aggression unnecessary in non-human as well as human animals by means of instinctive, socially recognized attitudes. Nevertheless Tiger and Fox (1971: 119), comparing the sense of property in animals and men, maintained that "most of this analogizing misses the important point: an animal simply *defends* its territory and would never give it up unless forced; humans use property to *exchange* for other property". But even this argument is not very strong in the case of real estate because of the fact that such handling of land is rather new in Western countries (cf. Thomson 1946: 37) and is practically unknown in most "primitive" societies, where soil is not thought of as something that could be sold or rented or in any way given up (cf. Tregear 1890: 106; Goody 1962: 296-298; Bohannan 1964: 175-176).

Drever (1921: 187-190) remarked about the acquisitive tendency that in spite of numerous studies of the collecting habit there was no good systematic psychological discussion of the instinct itself. He also stressed the difficulties in penetrating the various perceptual situations which can evoke interest for nearly all kinds of objects. But Rivers (1922: 266-273) vindicated that the most striking evidence in favour of the instinct of acquisition in man is the manifold regressive property behaviour in cases of mental pathology, from the psychotics' collecting of different odd things to kleptomania.

Summarizing, Meyer-Holzapfel (1952: 27) declared that "all forms of property, be it land, movable objects or living creatures, are rooted in instinctive, emotional behaviour but can during the history of man and even of a single individual lead to more spiritualized gradations without loosing the connections with basic drives". And Ploog (1964: 345) concluded that the demand for space and the defence of property belong to the instinctive behaviour of man.

4.2.1.3. Individual and social landownership:

It is not without interest for our main theme to inspect for a moment the old controversy between the two schools of primary landownership; one which claims it to have been in general communal and the other which finds it individual in origin.

To begin with the "social" school, G.L. v. Maurer (1854: 3) stated, knitting together the threads from Grotius and Rousseau, that the first cultivation had been performed not by single persons but by whole families and tribes. Viollet (1872: 503) likewise asserted after a careful historical examination that in India, Greece and Italy, just as in the Teutonic countries, land had been common property before being the domain of the individual. And L.H. Morgan (1878: 527-528) in his famous *Ancient Society* contended as to "Property in the Status of Savagery" that "Lands, as yet hardly a subject of property, were owned by the tribes in common..." (cf. also Engels 1966; Schurtz 1900).

As a representative of the "individual" school, Fustel de Coulanges (1889: 437-439) reported after having scrutinized some papers of the "social" school that their interpretation and argumentation were not valid. "We do not pretend", he stated, "that it should be forbidden to believe in a primitive community. But in fact, unsuccessful attempts have been made to support this theory based on historical texts. It is this attitude of false scholarship that we reject". He was followed in his critique by, e.g., Cathrein (1892), Rachfahl (1900) and A.S. Diamond (1935: 268-276).

In an evaluation of the two schools (*A Systematic Source Book in Rural Sociology* 1930: 574-576) it was underlined that the so-called collective land system in almost all early stages has been merely a family system, no more collective or socialistic than undivided family property at the present; that no definite and universal sequence in the change of the forms of land possession and ownership has existed; that from the earliest stages at least of agricultural man there have been different land systems with individual, family or tribe ownership; and that if any, family possession has predominated.

This was confirmed by Schmidt (1937: 288 ff.) who concluded that "the bearer of land property was most often the original large family. This form of landholding is distinguished as the oldest by existing in all parts of the primordial cultures, usually predominant but sometimes not". And Leyhausen (1973a: 104) added that particularly common is the way that every social community, small or large, and above all the individual or the head of the family strives to reserve one certain area as its property and to repel any intrusion by others.

In fact individual property in land is thought to have been as underestimated as the related concept of individual territoriality in "primitive" societies. Of particular interest is, e.g., that a member of a people could have private property rights on foreign tribal ground. "Thus a person might have a certain right in the lands of another tribe if he happened to have been born thereon, if his blood had been shed there, if an ancestor of his were buried there, . . ." (Beaglehole 1931: 149).

It could well be worth listening to a competent, native observer explaining that "the term 'communal or tribal ownership of land' has been misused in describing the land, as though the whole of it was owned collectively by every member of the community. . . . In fact, there was not in any part of the Gikuyu, as far as memory goes, any land that belonged to everybody, or what is called 'no man's land'" (Kenyatta 1959: 25).

4.2.1.4. Terminology and territorology:
When presenting the attributes and functions of an Indian tribe L. H. Morgan (1878: 112) laid out seven necessary conditions for tribal life, the first of which was: "*The possesion of a territory and a name*". In fact even the denominations of certain kinds of property are of special interest. Both the Latin "*possidere*" and the German "*besitzen*" mean "sit on" and were originally used primarily for land, real estate. This matter is treated in detail by Meyer-Holzapfel (1952: 3, 18) with reference to Grimm's *Sprachwörterbuch:*

"Thus he who acquired ground did not neglect to possess it physically, that is by symbolically sitting down on a chair. Hereby the strange property was handed over and the jurisdictional representation seems to emanate from this ritual. Probably the throne is such a symbol for the possession of the country. But the right of disposition alone cannot make ground into property. First the feeling of social threat – that the ground could be lost – and the readiness for defense in the form of symbolic sitting or real warding off can give a genuine sense of space possession". From these words it becomes still more evident how closely related behavioural territory and property in land really are.

It could be added that the Greek word for law, "*nomos*", derives from "*nemein*", which means to distribute, to possess and to dwell (Arendt 1959: 63). And it is true that property and law are so closely associated, at least in the Western mind, that in legal theory, attributed to Hobbes, Montesquieu and Bentham, they are considered historically inseparable (Hallowell 1955: 245). According to Schmitt (1950: 36) one could give the word "*nomos*" a still more important position in relation to territorology. This scholar has found, searching the classical authors, that some basic evidence can be summarized in this way. "The Greek word for the first ground measuring, the first division and distribution of land, from which all such standards are derived, is *Nomos*". Maybe this concept, even identified with the boundary space between two households, thus covers realities not far removed from those of territory (cf. Arendt 1959: 63).

From these old conditions we follow the jurisdictional line straight into modern times. In a very interesting and rather unique paper, called "Property, Possession and Permanence: A Field Study in Human Territoriality" Edney (1972a) demonstrated a significant relation between property defense and duration of residence on land in the U.S.A. Even stronger connections were found between property defense and expected length of further residence. Property ownership, on the other hand, was not reliably associated with defense in this sample, and supplementary analyses showed that ownership alone could not account for the actual territoriality, which is in accordance with suggested opinions in this survey (cf. also Edney 1972b).

Unfortunately not much is known about how modern man reacts spatially in natural surroundings, but in a disclosing paper, "Territorial Spacing on a Beach" (Edney and Jordan-Edney 1974), it was i.a. shown that group territories do not grow regularly with group size but that space claims per person tend to decrease as group size increases, that females tend to claim smaller territories and are found under higher local density conditions than males and that certain territory characteristics tend to change with time.

As an example from quite another type of civilization we will refer to the weighty commentaries made by a student of the children and other inhabitants of Israelian kibbutzes, where everything is communal and no private property is allowed: "Nowhere more than in the kibbutz did I realize the degree to which private property, in the deep layers of the mind, relates to private emotions. If one is absent, the other tends to be absent as well" (Bettelheim 1969: 261). In the chapter "A Private Piece of Ground" the author described the often desperate efforts by the kibbutzniks to acquire a garden plot to care for or, on the whole, something uniquely their own. These experiences were summarized thus: "But I could not help thinking of 'Mother Earth' – as if the kibbutz-born was trying to find in nature an undemanding acceptance that was absent from his childhood where there were always those demands that come with living forever with others. Yet if this was so, and it seemed so for both sexes, I wondered why it seemed much more marked in the male" (op. cit. p. 265-269).

Ardrey (1967: 110-117) also studied a kibbutz, economically successful but yet in this same respect inferior to a private farm in the neighbourhood, when the number of persons involved was considered. He went on to look at the effectiveness of communistic Soviet *colchoses* as related to private American farms, the last of which, he said, produced twelve times as much as the former. Ardrey has been criticized for this statement of presumed territorial value difference between contrasting political systems (cf., e.g., Freedman 1975: 52-54), and it is true that many factors must be analyzed before it will be possible to draw definitive conclusions in such a case. But without doubt it is remarkable if, as stated, "private plots occupy about 3 percent of all Russian cultivated land, yet they produce almost half of all vegetables consumed, almost half of all milk and meat, three-quarters of all eggs, and two-thirds of that stuff of Russian life, potatoes" (Ardrey 1967: 115-116), even though the total areas for these products are not reported.

Lately, this evidence has been confirmed by figures from official Russian sources (H. Smith 1977: 180-181): According to a newspaper article in March 1975, about 27 percent of Soviet agricultural production comes from private plots, which occupy less than 1 percent of the cultivated area, and the Soviet Economic Yearbook for 1973 said that 62 percent of potatoes, 32 percent of other vegetables and fruits, 47 percent of eggs and 34 percent of milk and meat derives from private ground. Explanations given by Smith are that the big crops are cultivated collectively, that the farmers get higher prices for their own products and that most of these they consume themselves. However it seems probable that affective bonds of behavioural territoriality contribute to the much greater interest for private than for collective cultivation.

In a recent survey, *Eigentum und Freiheit. Zeugnisse aus der Geschichte* (1972: 131), facts presented were summarized thus: "The communistic model has, by trying to abolish individual possession and to create a new kind of human being, evidently disclosed one peculiarity of man's hereditary equipment, a deeply rooted demand for private property". Maybe this is mirrored by the fact that the Soviet government has considerably modified the policy of abolition of private property instituted by the Revolution. "Individuals in the U.S.S.R. still may not own land, but they are allowed property rights to their own dachas (suburban or country houses). A Soviet citizen may buy a cooperative apartment, and increasing numbers are doing so. The Soviet government may take over private property for public purposes, but it must pay the owner a fair compensation for the property. In short, the U.S.S.R., like other countries, is slowly coming to recognize the universal longing and need of each person for a place of his own" (Abrahams 1965: 160).

Taking together available facts it seems to be quite clear that there is in many vertebrates, including man, a basic property instinct, which implies a desire to collect movable things, probably originating in feeding, and to secure vitally necessary, non-movable objects, in the form of real estate. Behavioural territories, which as we have suggested are closely related to, without being identical with, property in land, have inter alia in common with their counterpart that they are limited and marked, and thus boundaries and markings will be the natural theme of the next section.

4.2.2. Boundaries and markings

4.2.2.1. Boundaries and frontiers:
It is self-evident that "Every *being-in-space* is differentiated from that space by some demarcation – his skin. It is this that makes it possible for him to relate to objects as a subject, and to become an entity distinct from the *world* in which he lives. A great deal of time and effort is spent in psychiatry in promoting just such object relations. Lewin and others have shown that the barrier is not only porous but dynamic, and that there is a constant ebb and flow. It is mandatory for the individual to distinguish his space from that of his neighbors' and there is the question of his inner and outer space. Thus the barrier is a spatial barrier in that it governs how much space comes in and out of the organism" (Burton 1964: 297). Without doubt these fundamentals of demarcation are of interest also in connection with normal territoriality.

Of course the human holder of a substantial territory cannot always survey all parts of it at the same time. Thus there is a need for markings of some kind, especially along the boundary. This term is here the right one because boundaries indicate certain well-established limits or bounds of a given unit and all that which lies inside is bound together. Thus the boundary is inner-oriented, centripetal, while the term frontier has an outer-oriented, centrifugal meaning, the borderland that is in front of somebody or of something, like the "*limes*" of the Roman empire or of Western civilization. That is why the frontier is an integrating, the boundary a separating factor (cf. Kristof 1959: 269-274).

"With increasing population density in an area there is, as I have already mentioned, also an increase in the tendency of the individual or the family to mark off all the more distinctly what space is left to it, to erect fences and walls around land and build permanent living quarters, to bolt house doors and to greet any intrusion by strangers – 'unauthorized persons', as it is so tastefully expressed – with distrust, even with open antagonism. Under such circumstances the instinctive reaction of defense of territory is continually exposed to excessive stimulation by the 'unbiologically' close and constant proximity of one's neighbor and by strangers frequently passing through one's territory" (Leyhausen 1973a: 107).

Further it was stated that man is the only animal to surround his territory by a delimited frontier which is to him a matter of life and death, regarded with a sentiment which is almost religious in its intensity (Keith 1948: 30). In these words, without doubt, the emotional strength of instinctive territoriality and its markings comes to the fore, notwithstanding in connection with inadequate formulations, because man is not unique in this respect and the term frontier, as we have seen, is not very suitable.

Indubitably, an easy and effective way to reorganize space is to put up a wall or a fence. The room becomes divided, gets a new shape, a new character and shows smaller and perhaps more useful units. But there are also, as we have just heard, two other distinct and different basic reasons for putting up the mentioned or other effective kinds of boundary: to keep intruders out and to keep one's own possessions in. These two reasons represent mutually antagonistic ways of organizing space – one of them is likely to replace the other (cf. Jackson 1969: 33) but combinations are, of course, possible.

This limiting of more or less natural territories is certainly a very old custom, as suggested by philologists: "It begins with the fence. The world of man is profoundly influenced by the boundary. The enclosure shapes the sanctuary by setting it aside, by putting it under special law and by handing it over to divinity. In a sanctuary nothing is so old as its fence and nothing is so necessary. The holy places are named after their enclosures, even after the links of their chains" (Trier 1942: 232).

As to development, it was noted that the boundary was originally very simple, a "natural fence of twigs and branches. In the beginning of the 9th century it was still the same or it could also be constructed with thorns. Sometimes it was made by a stone wall with doorways of wood or of normal fences connected with walls" (G.L. v. Maurer 1854: 23).

4.2.2.2. Acquisition of virgin land:

Of special interest in this context is the means used to acquire virgin land. Charles John Andersson (1856: 115) remarked about the pastoral Damaras in South Africa that in spite of the fact that their whole country in principle was public property, "there is an understanding that he, who arrives first at any given locality, is the master of it as long as he chooses to remain there, and no one will intrude upon him without having previously asked and obtained his permission". Here the first and foremost mark of territory, the human body, comes to the fore.

In the former British Central Africa there was unlimited freedom to select sites for new gardens if they were marked by tying bunches of grass into knots or twisting some grass around tree trunks. Once this was done, no one could interfere (Werner 1906: 179; see also Tremearne 1912: 189-190). Among the A-kikuyu of East Africa it was said that a man could pre-empt an area of unoccupied waste land as long as he marked the boundaries by felling a tree here and there along the proposed boundary line and by cultivating a small patch within the pre-empted area. The boundaries of estates were mutually agreed upon and marked out by adjoining landowners. They met and killed a sheep, then took numbers of cuttings of bushes which were suitable for the purpose, smeared the ends of the cuttings in the contents of the sheep's stomach and planted them along the boundary agreed upon (Hobley 1910: 83, 137; cf. also Kenyatta 1959: 37-40).

From the Norwegian colonization of Iceland about A.D. 870 there is good evidence about the procedure of "*landnam*" (taking land). In order to survey the region one first went up to a high point, and if the landscape seemed to be promising a territory was marked out. The boundaries were predominantly natural, as sea-coasts, rivers and mountains, but artificial markings were also used, as hacks of an axe in birches or poles, as an eagle or a cross. "*Landnam*" was celebrated by a circling around the territory, most often with burning fire, called "*at fara elldi um landit*". In this way territories were consecrated and reserved. At first the immigrants claimed very large areas, but when the population increased it was necessary to control "*landnam*". Thus it was said that no colonizer should take more land than he could walk around during one day's light (K. Maurer 1852: 50-60; cf. also the "rubber-disc" theory of animal territories, 3.1.2.).

From Central Europe we have evidence of a free occupation right to unowned land as late as about A.D. 1000. In a well-known case of the year 955, Count Pago took a non-inhabited wood into his possession by fencing and circling it with his men. Such celebrating of the occupation is also known from later times in connection with the take-over by a new proprietor or the placing of new marks. In Germany during the Middle Ages "the marking and enclosing of different types of land was achieved by using stones, poles, posts, crosses or by fences, trenches, dams and trees of different kinds" (G.L. v. Maurer 1854: 222-223).

From more recent times we can refer to one of the Swedish immigrants into North America, Gustaf Unonius (1950: 162), who around 1840 settled at Pine Lake in Wisconsin, U.S.A.: "We needed to take no steps to insure our claim except to inform our neighbors that we were planning to make our home here, and as a sign of our intention, start some improvement to indicate that this part of the section had been occupied. Pearmain, as an experienced settler prepared for any eventualities, had brought his axe. As Columbus on first landing in the new world had raised the Castilian flag inscribed with *F & I*, the initials of his sovereigns, so we chopped down a few trees, and into the bark of a couple of others cut a big *C*, signifying 'Claimed', a sign that we in our name had taken possession of the W $\frac{1}{2}$ of Section 33, Township 8, Range 18, *in hac altera mundi parte* [in this other part of the world] with full and complete legal right of possession, to be inhabited, settled, and held by us and our descendants forever".

4.2.2.3. Peripheral markings:
In considering modern conditions we will first refer to individual farming, about which it was declared that in all places, where the peasant lives in isolation, he builds an enclosure. It is a means of protecting himself, of guarding his cattle, of separating fields and pastures, of marking the boundaries of his property. "Whether this boundary be a hedge, a ditch, or a wall of earth, the enclosure contains some trees; there are rows of trees, often planted close together; which give the appearance of a grove. The grove is a human product, an artificial arrangement of nature, which indicates a particular mode of occupation. Direct contact between the house and the individual field thus ends in a transformation of the landscape by this association of trees and occupation of the land" (*A Systematic Source Book in Rural Sociology* 1930: 302).

Without doubt the fence is a particularly important example of marking. Visitors from England and Australia are often struck by the lack of fences in American suburbs, a phenomenon which they find hard to explain. The front fences in their own countries perhaps give no real, visual or acoustic privacy, but they symbolize a barrier. A British fence manufacturer said: " 'it's man putting his own stakes into the ground, staking out his own little share of land. No matter how small, he likes his own frontier to be distinct. In it he's safe and he's happy. That's what a fence is'" (Rapoport 1969: 133-134). Even from America Doxiadis (1968b: 23) reported a case in a large city where he had planned a housing development with fences between the single units. But this was refused with the argument that the American citizen does not like fences surrounding his property. Two years after the people had moved in more than half of them had erected fences themselves and more were following their example.

Maybe it is no wonder that the marking tendency was not so common everywhere earlier in a sparsely populated settler country like the United States. But evidently the recent change in connection with strong population increase and dense habitation is effective: "More and more homeowners, it seems, are fencing themselves in. A Boston fence-maker estimates his sales are rising at the rate of 45 percent a year, while his counterparts in Washington, D.C. describe their business as 'fantastic'" (Newsweek, Nov. 7, 1966, cited after Sommer 1969: 3).

Here it can be added that man, in a unique way, uses the territorial aptitude of another species as a means of marking and defending his own territory. This is the function of the watch-dog on a farm (Berghe 1974: 780), but it should be remembered that it is very common among animals that one territorial species warns other ones of danger.

4.2.2.4. Central markings:
Well-known marks like flags and coat of arms as well as signs warning strangers approaching foreign territory, like "Keep Out", "No Trespassing", "Private Property" etc. (Edney 1972a; cf. F.D. Becker 1973) could be placed both in the centre and at the periphery. But predominantly central marking seems to be involved when people, mostly young, write or carve their names or initials on trees, caves, houses, desks and different private belongings. About the street-gangs of Chicago it was, for instance, reported that "Most groups paint their names on a street or wall near their hangout. It is a rank insult to do the same near someone else's hangout" (Suttles 1968: 115).

It is quite remarkable the way strong feelings can be evoked in connection with the marking and holding of even temporary and recreational territories. In the summer of 1975 there was a lively press discussion in Sweden about the Minister of Justice, who on a common beach not far from his summer villa had marked a sandcave with a handwritten "Private" card and had said in defense of his action, that he and his wife had been working with the cave for ten years.

Here we have mostly referred to outdoor marking, but there are, of course, also indoor signs of this kind, both of a more permanent character like dormitory room decorations (Hansen and Altman 1976) and quite temporary ones. This last category is most common, "being objects that announce a territorial claim, the territory radiating outward from it, as when sunglasses and lotion claim a beach chair, or a purse a seat in an airliner, or a drink on the bar a stool in front of it, or chips on a 21 table the closest 'slot' and the attendant exclusive right to make bets from it" (Goffman 1972: 66).

In a most astonishing way markers like jackets, notes and borrowed library books can protect a person's temporary territory in a study space, a lunch counter or a drinking pub. It was found by means of a series of experiments that a relatively impersonal marker was able to keep a space vacant, that the legitimacy of the marker was recognized by two-thirds of all neighbours and that the strength of the defense was related to the length of time that the former occupant had been away (cf. Sommer and Becker 1969; see also Hoppe, Greene and Kenny 1972; Shaffer and Sadowski 1975).

Becker and Mayo (1971) as well as Becker (1973) claimed after similar marking experiments in cafeterias and libraries that territoriality was not involved here, because most persons did not actively defend their marked places when they returned and found them invaded by others and their markers pushed away. It was suggested that jurisdictional control was a better term in connection with temporary use of space for a specific purpose. For modern definitions of territory active defense is, however, not necessary, and by the way, conclusions drawn seem reasonable only if no other places than those marked had been free in the neighbourhood.

Thus we think that these results are expressions of real territoriality, which might be evident also from the fact that "Territorial markers can be a serious management problem in public areas. Unless management forbids it and instructs some employee to specifically collect all coats and personal belongings draped over empty chairs, a third of the seats in a cafeteria can be out of use because of packages and coats left on the chairs to hold space for a person in line. The same practice will convert poolside chairs into towel racks. Because the principles governing reserved space in public areas are not explicit, they can be a source of friction" (Sommer 1969: 55).

4.2.2.5. Enuresis and encopresis in children:
We have earlier described how in higher vertebrates intestinal and renal ex-

cretions, besides their normal physiological functions, have communicative ones, too, especially in connection with territoriality (cf. Hediger 1944). Remembering that the terrestrial mammal has still to be found in which urine does not play a role in a social context or in marking the environment – scent having an important role – it seems probable that at least traces of such a behaviour should be found even in man. Freud and his disciples stressed that children do not have the same negative attitude towards excreta as adults, and psychoanalysts have reported about infantile use of these products as well as of their presumed sex and property meaning (cf. Beaglehole 1931: 267-268). But the best evidence comes from psychiatrists trying to cure enuresis and encopresis.

In his thorough investigation of enuresis Christoffel (1934) underlined the manifold importance of urination, its very positive connotation for the little child, and the clear territorial aspect, when for instance a new-comer has to stand inside a circle of a group of boys urinating at him from all sides (p. 81-82). That a diminishing of anxiety, which most often is the cause of enuretics without organic background, usually effects a decrease in abnormal urination speaks also for the functioning of urination as an exaggerated territorial marking.

Among the charges leveled at child-rearing practices in the Israelian kibbutzes, the great incidence of thumb-sucking and enuresis there has been looked at as neurotic symptoms stemming from the deprivation of parents and family. Astonishingly enough, there is a laissez-faire attitude towards bed-wetting on the part of the personnel, sharply contrasting with a strong inhibition about thumb-sucking (Bettelheim 1969: 80-81, 146-150). It seems very reasonable that the high incidence of enuresis among these communally-raised children primarily depends on lack of not only attendant parents but also of own, adequate territories.

Concerning encopresis much the same could be said. Glanzmann (1934) reported about a boy of three years, who, having lost his beloved nurse, began to leave excrement in all corners of his dwelling. It seems very probable that this marking was a sign of increased anxiety and insecurity and a therefrom emanating augmented need for territory marking. Recently, similar cases have been known, where, e.g., another little boy put his faeces in a room inhabited by visiting strangers, preferably on their possessions.

According to Heymann (1943: 19-21) the abnormal excretion habits of children without organic insufficiencies can be interpreted in a territorial way. "But also such difficulties which particular children raise as bed-wetters are not seldom connected with changes in the experience of the 'house'.

For the 'house' has 'doors' which cannot be closed enough and one cannot even trust the solidity of the 'walls' ". This could be related to the dynamic character of the skin boundary, particularly in children, as well as to excretion marking presupposed (cf. p. 54).

4.2.2.6. Adult excretion, criminality and territoriality:
In adult humans direct evidence of this same kind is not at all frequent. One example, however, comes from the Pangwe-people of western Africa, where a special syringe was used to spread excrement over the fields in order to frighten away thieves (Tessman 1913: 258). The author thought it to be a sign of shame, but it seems much more probable, particularly in the light of the data below, to classify it as a kind of territorial marking. African tales about urination and defecation in territorial context are also known (cf. Kohl-Larsen 1937).

Most often excreta are a taboo subject in Western societies and therefore, at least nowadays, not willingly mentioned (cf. Bilz 1967). But only a glance at the large work *Handwörterbuch des Deutschen Aberglaubens*, where the article "Kot" covers twenty columns, gives a good impression of the position of human faeces in folk-medicine and folklore since old times. Some evidence is also here of territorial interest, especially that of "*grumus merdae*" (piles of excrement) left by burglars at the place of crime (Bargheer 1930-1931, 1932-1933). This phenomenon is earlier described above all by Hellwig (e.g., 1914) in a series of papers. The behaviour is known from several European countries and the United States (A.B. Friedman 1968) but is today not common. A policeman in New York reported as late as in 1967, however, that he had encountered the situation two dozen times during three and a half years' work on burglary.

The German folk-names of "*Wächter*", "*Soldat*" etc., speak of the belief that no one could wake up and chase away the thief as long as the excrement he left was warm and soft. Friedman (loc. cit.), in his interesting survey of these and other scatological superstitions, gave several possible psychoanalytic explanations and concluded that "*grumus merdae*" could be a consequence of vengeance (if the booty was inadequate), of destructiveness or of general nervousness. Even though such elements might be involved, we think that the phenomenon basically represents a marking of territory, which for outlaws in unfamiliar and dangerous environments could function as acts of social release and personal integration.

Referring to the fact that man, as well as his nearest relatives in the animal world, does not seem to have, under non-civilized conditions, any fixed defecation and urination points Hediger (1970b: 41) asserted: "It is therefore quite wrong to conclude that careless defecation among schizophrenics or bed-wetting (enuresis) among maladjusted children is based on the unhealthy decay of human instincts.... Such an instinct [of localized urination and defecation] has never existed in man or in his nearest animal relations, the higher primates. These unhealthy disturbances can therefore on no account be the consequence of any decay of human instinct of any kind. The localization of a water closet in human habitations is the result not of any instinct but of modern hygiene".

As earlier suggested it is, of course, crucial that the excretions are detached from the body and can really act as substitutes and place-reservations in the absence of the originator, that is, as "*pars pro toto*" (Bilz 1940: 70). It seems not to be so important if special localities are used consequently or not. In fact the excretions of man are sometimes placed in such a way within limited areas that with great probability they are manifestations of instinctive, territorial behaviour just as in most other mammals. This point of view gets further support from extremely interesting research made recently in the United States.

Hereford, Cleland and Fellner (1973) investigated nine profoundly retarded, institutionalized adult males, who exhibited chronic enuretic and encopretic behaviour and who, with one exception, showed strong territoriality. The authors suspected that the abnormal habits could be examples of an exaggerated territory-marking with excrement and urine. The patients slept, together with others lacking the same pathological symptoms, in a 25-person dormitory. The 16 non-experimentals were removed so that the remaining 9 beds could be rearranged with equal space between them, resulting in a 64 percent decrease of crowding.

This individual spatial expansion had the effect that there was a proportion of dry beds the following morning. When the total space was visibly divided into equal areas by means of broad coloured tape strips on the floor, the wetting and soiling diminished still more. A return to the initial conditions in the dormitory did not lead, however, to a complete restoration of the original abnormal behaviour, and it is thought that the reason could be too short a time for observation afterwards or some kind of learning, making the return to pathological behaviour incomplete. Nevertheless, "It is entirely possible, then, that this type of behavior is being used as a very rudimentary form of communication of territorial needs" (p. 430).

Thus there is good and varied evidence of boundaries and markings supporting the theory that the limited and indicated spaces mentioned belong to or at least are influenced by behavioural territoriality. More such facts, will emerge in our treatment of urban realms. But we will now first have a look at the farm, the village and other rural units.

4.2.3. Farm, village and larger units of land

4.2.3.1. The farmyard:
Social vertebrates have to know each other personally. This is possible not only because individuals differ sufficiently as to physical and behavioural traits but also because of "the very good memory for places possessed by most vertebrates, since memories bound up with places are of great significance to them. A neighbor linked to a locality is no doubt easier to recognize as 'always the same one'. Now, if in man's case, and particularly in the early days of our own civilization, it was (and is) perfectly usual to call people after their locality, after the farm on which they lived, after the village from which they originated, it certainly does not seem absolutely out of the question that this is based on similar internal connections. This no doubt explains why even today a large percentage of our family names still indicates where their bearers originally came from" (Leyhausen 1973a: 106).

Further it was underlined by Fraser (1968: 47) that the more sedentary groups become, the greater their emphasis on land and property and the more inclined they are toward fixed spatial organization. Thus it is very probable not only that man in the old days was most often signified by his territory but also that agriculture during the last circa 10,000 years has augmented further the inherent aptitude for territoriality in mankind.

G.L. v. Maurer (1854: 239) stated, citing Tacitus, that "in old times the free Teuton was master in his own house and of his own family and this was not changed when he took up a fixed abode. Even though the first settlements were started by communities, every single individual measured and fenced an area, necessary for his habitation. By this enclosing, a space for house and yard was taken away from the common field and at the same time released from herewith connected constraints. This also meant prohibition of entrance without admission, later valid even for civil servants".

Here we already find the behavioural elements of rural territories clearly expressed, and they are as evident in a modern example: "To the farm family, home means not merely the house but the whole farm. It is a little world – a homestead – encompassing the domestic sphere with the domains of other families fenced out" (Sims 1940: 309).

Often it is stated, as above, that there has been a development from col-

lective toward private ownership of land, particularly in the case of farmland.
To our earlier discussion of these things (section 4.2.1.3.) we will now just add:
"As a matter of fact all these forms – private ownership; tenancy; small and
large holdings; concentration of land in few hands and its parcelling out
among small landholders; private and public property in land; state, city, or
church property in land; or the processes of the nationalization or denational-
ization of land – may exist in the earliest stages among various peoples, and
we find all of them existing at the present moment" (*A Systematic Source
Book in Rural Sociology* 1930: 575-576).

4.2.3.2. Villages:
As pointed out by Jean Brunhes (1947, cited after Briault and Hubbard 1963:
395) the difference between isolated farms and a village can be defined just by
means of the length of the road separating the agricultural units. However,
villages are most often sited in relation to some local natural or cultural
advantage, not uncommonly a cross-road. In this way something of a special,
socio-territorial interest originated, namely "the inner-village area consisting of roads and open places designated for cattle pens where the cattle
were driven in and out and where there were villlage wells, watering-places,
ponds, session-stones and other public institutions" (G.L. v. Maurer 1854:
35).

This open place was in the old days mostly traversed by the crossing roads
and surrounded by the bounded farm-yards. Even the whole village was often
fenced or provided with outer graves, and the entrances from the roads were
not seldom, just as in towns, equipped with gates. Such village bounding is
known today from many parts of the world (Forde 1934: 226; see further
Keith 1948: 278-286).

The Kabylian tribes of North Africa have three frames for their social
life: the territory, the village and the house. And "the village is the most
important unit, the basic element of Kabylian society, indeed a little fortress.
It has a territory that is different from other common properties of the tribe,
the limits of which are familiar and which are predominantly made up of
pasture" (Maunier 1927: 316-317, 330). Without doubt there are in many
such cases both individual and group bindings of a territorial character, and
then conflicts are inevitable, particularly if the collective units grow too
large and crowded. Thus it is said that "Frequently, in a nearly instinctive
manner, the peasants attempt by slow degrees to free themselves from the
concentrated habitat" (*A Systematic Source Book in Rural Sociology* 1930:

295), exemplified by the enormous villages in Hungary and perhaps a result of inadequate private territories.

Before leaving this matter we should like to say a few words about the constellation caste and territory in India, studied predominantly in the villages of the Malabar Coast. It seems that a necessary correlate of the rigid caste system is a territorial segmentation, evidently of a behavioural character which promotes localized interdependent relations between castes, especially at the village level. This even supports the hierarchical order of castes by permitting greater mobility and a greater spatial range of intracaste connections. Thus "the caste system survives most strongly where the territorial cleavages are least impaired" (E. J. Miller 1954: 419; cf. also Dumont 1970: 152-166).

4.2.3.3. The state and other large units of land:
One of the difficulties with the actual study is this: "Territorial claims are or were, vested in the nation, the tribe, the family or the individual, and not infrequently in various ways in all these categories at once" (Wynne-Edwards 1962: 187). The larger units of land and the terms covering them, however, often go back to and reflect the smaller agricultural ones, at least in Europe. "In the first settlements, all revolved around the agricultural stock-raising. So it is difficult to find an old village where, together with the fields, there are not smaller or larger pasture areas. The common name for such ground was 'Mark', up to the northernmost parts of Europe. To all Teutonian peoples this word originally meant limit sign, later the boundary itself, and finally that area enclosed by the marks. The areas called 'Marken' were equivalent to the valleys in the Alps and in other connections to neighbourhood, district, province or country" (G.L. v. Maurer 1854: 40, 53-54).

As to larger social units than the village, it could often be "that territoriality has simply become more complicated, diffuse, and discontinuous" (Soja 1971: 36) and thus is not always easily recognizable. Quite evident are, however, the fishing right territories, claimed in particular areas along the coast of central Maine, U.S.A. by lobstermen from different communities. Although their claims are unrecognized by the state they are well established and backed by repetitive violence. There are two kinds of lobstering territories, termed "nucleated" and "perimeter-defended", which differ as to fishing rights maintained (Acheson 1975: 183). In fact "the relatively open areas of the coast where territorial boundaries are weak have suffered from overexploitation of the lobster resource. If lobster fishing and fishermen are to survive in these areas, Maine will have to impose more controls on lobstering. The state would do well, when it prepares new legislation on lobstering, to take into consideration the lobstermen's unwritten rules of territoriality" (Acheson 1972:69).

We will here also refer to the famous standard marketing areas of China, which existed at least up till 1949: "a cluster of small villages surrounding a locally important marketing town. The marketing community of these towns formed a discrete areal unit. No smaller town or village traded outside it, and social and political as well as economic life focused on the standard market town. Given this territorial confinement of activity, the local community became a tightly knit socio-political unit" (Skinner 1964-1965, cited after Soja 1971: 36). It is interesting, indeed, that these areas tend to conform with the marketing, transport and administration principles of the central place theory (Christaller 1933).

The modern concept of the state seems to have its origin as a designation of a rather small area of practical value for, and surveyable by, the individual. Surely this is crucial for judgements on the relations between behavioural and political territorology, which are thought to be non-existent by some authors, e.g., Fried (1967: 46): "What we cannot accept is the implication that the territoriality that underlies state formation has any but superficial resemblance to the kind of territoriality that seems quite definitely to be much more ancient than the cultural recognition of kinship". But many oppose to this view, stressing the spatial component, even in the development of kinship feelings (cf. Lowie 1927: 51-73).

Thus it was stated: "Although the territorial principle of social organization is much weaker, much less often in the people's consciousness, than the tribal or kinship principle, it is of almost unexaggerable importance, since it is the progressive principle, the one from which the state arises. The generalization is sound that human society develops by forming ever larger units, based on new principles and loyalties, which engulf and unify the older, smaller, and contending units" (Barton 1949: 137). Yet, the growth of the state form of organization has not entirely replaced the older, lesser units, for if a full replacement had taken place, the very active minorities, which we know today, would not exist (cf. Wagley and Harris 1967: 242).

Maybe we can say that a state is a sound unit only if it represents a natural, collective behavioural territory, and this is, as we know, not always the case either in modern Africa, where artificial, colonial boundaries are still dominating (cf. Ardrey 1967:313), or elsewhere. "If the law of nations is not to deny itself, it must defend not the actual, more or less accidental territorial status of a certain historical moment, but the basic 'Nomos' and its spatial structure as a unity of order and area" (Schmitt 1950: 157; cf. p. 88). Discussing what is meant by a nation Keith (1948: 298) gave some reasons for the establishment of one of the first real states in the modern sense, Ancient Egypt, among which was this: "The love of an Egyptian for his home-territory – his patriotism – extended to all parts inhabited by his fellow subjects".

4.2.3.4. Political systems and territoriality:

Sometimes real hierarchies of boundary walls delimit territorial units of increasing magnitude. It was for instance said about Old China: "Beyond the city walls were the walls that demarcated the limits of states, as these existed during the Eastern Chou period; and beyond the state walls was the Great Wall, that, after the unification of the empire, defined the limit of civilization. Each wall, on its level, separated orderly life within from the threat of disorder without, whether the 'without' meant the alleyway, the thoroughfare, the countryside, or the steppe. The importance of the idea of enclosure serving both the need for protection and for definition is preserved in the structure and meaning of words. . . . The word for 'country' or 'nation' is *kuo*: it is the word *yü* (made up of the signs for weapon and residence or citadel), surrounded by a large square which by itself, means enclosure" (Tuan 1968: 240).

It was also stressed: "Political organization and political action have always a territorial basis" (Wagner 1960: 54). According to Soja (1971) the most far-reaching developments within the human social and political realms came about when localized kinship or residence groups became territorial units within a political system. All social groups have a spatial dimension, but all are not characteristic territorial groups. This transformation probably took place among the more settled and agricultural "tribal" or "ranked" societies, where localized residential patterns and mutual cooperation based on proximity increasingly began to play an important role in maintaining societal cohesiveness. With the origin of the state the role of kinship decreased relative to the growing importance of territory and property as institutional grounds for societal organization. One of the central characteristics of the state is, in fact, the clear emergence of the polity as a territorially-defined unit, not necessarily linked to any other organizational structure. "The nation-state is probably also the most territorial of human political organizations" (op. cit. p. 11-17), undoubtedly a most interesting statement.

It should also be remembered that the territorial pattern of collective life is largely a result of the friction of space as manifested in time-cost distance. The proximity which interdependence requires varies under different conditions. "Even though a single index should prove usable, it will remain that community boundaries are zones rather than lines. They are formed where the territories of neighboring communites converge and overlap, where the integrating influences emanating from different centers meet in competition, and where, in consequence, the communal attachments of the local residents are not only divided but in a state of flux" (Hawley 1950: 249).

Without doubt Kristof (1959: 277) was right when stating about the political form of the boundary concept that it involves a meeting-place for two socio-political bodies, each having its particular interests, structures and ideologies. Each of them generates loyalties and also imposes duties and constraints for the sake of internal harmony and compactness and of external separateness and individuality. "Two neighboring states do not need to be engaged continuously, or at any time, in a struggle for life and death. They may compete peacefully and, in general, minimize their conflicts of interest. Still, the very existence of the boundary is proof that there are some differences in ideology and goals, if not of a virulent present-day character then at least embedded in the historical heritage" (cf. also Boggs 1940).

In fact this is in good agreement with demonstrated essentials of behavioural territoriality, the state conflict aspects of which will now be considered specifically.

4.2.4. War

4.2.4.1. Innate factors:
We begin with an important statement: "As for human nature, it contains no specific war instinct, as does the nature of harvester ants. There is in man's make-up a general aggressive tendency, but this, like all other human urges, is not a specific and unvarying instinct; it can be moulded into the most varied forms" (J. S. Huxley 1948: 190; cf. also Hoebel 1949: 400). Thus the argument of Andreski (1964: 131): "If men had an innate propensity towards war, similar to their desire for food or sexual satisfaction, then there could be no instance of numerous nations remaining at peace for more than a generation" is not very weighty.

For the crucial point is whether other innate factors than special war instincts are involved. Scott (1969: 131), however, maintained that "in both agonistic and allelomimetic behavior, the principal behavioral components of warfare, there are no physiological mechanisms which could produce stimulation through internal metabolic changes, such as occurs in hunger. In allelomimetic behavior the emotional distress caused by isolation is a direct reaction to the situation. Likewise, in the case of agonistic behavior, the emotion of anger arises from external situations" (cf. also Fromm 1973: 114-123, 129-151).

Arguments of quite another kind were presented by Berkowitz (1962: 4), referring to the correspondence between Einstein and Freud (1933) about ways to deliver mankind from the menace of war, where both of them vindicated that man has an inborn "lust for hatred and destruction". In this context Berkowitz asserted: "But aside from its theoretical significance, Freud's hypothesis has some important implications for human conduct. An innate aggressive drive cannot be abolished by social reforms or the alleviation of frustrations. Neither complete parental permissiveness nor the fulfillment of every desire will eliminate interpersonal conflict entirely, according to this view. Its lessons for social policy are obvious: Civilization and moral order ultimately must be based upon force, not love and charity".

This citation seems to be correct except in its final conclusion. Without doubt the pioneer primate investigators Yerkes and Yerkes (1935: 1030) gave a true formulation when they said: "What is wrong with the world is that many things are wrong with human nature". But from this it does not follow that our civilization must be based just on force. It is not only so that aggression and love have much more to do with each other and have both many more positive and negative sides than is usually thought. There are also a lot of adaptive features which can avert aggression (Lorenz 1965: 239-308; Eibl-Eibesfeldt 1966: 502-503). But the best evidence showing that Berkowitz is incorrect must be that of territoriality, where in spite of the valuable role of instinctive aggression in the service of survival, it is the rule that a weaker territory owner is able to dominate over and can exclude a stronger territory intruder.

4.2.4.2. Aggression theory:
Thus we support the largely misinterpreted and misunderstood views of Lorenz (1965; cf. also Tinbergen 1968) and join the opinion that the aggression instinct theory of war "has some considerable degree of truth" (Flugel 1955: 376-377). At least there seems to be a growing consensus that "war is not merely a human problem; it is a biological problem of the broadest

scope, for on its abolition may depend life's ability to continue the progress which it has slowly but steadily achieved through more than a thousand million years" (J. S. Huxley 1948: 191; cf. p. 23-26).

Let us here first have a look at the principal position of Durbin and Bowlby (1950: 28) in their valuable book *Personal Aggressiveness and War*: "This then is our theory of international war. War occurs because fighting is a fundamental tendency in human things – a form of behavior called forth by certain simple situations in animals, children, human groups, and whole nations. It is a fundamentally pluralistic theory of international war. If the theory is true, then it follows that nations *can* fight only because they are able to release the explosive stores of transformed aggression, but they *do* fight for any of a large number of reasons. They may fight because of simple acquisitiveness, or simple frustration, or a simple fear of strangers. They may fight because of displaced hatred, or projected hates or fears. There is no single all-embracing cause – no single villain of the piece, no institution nor idea that is wholly to blame".

In 1932 the 528 members of the American Psychological Association were asked: "Do You as a psychologist hold that there are present in human nature ineradicable, instinctive factors that make war between nations inevitable?". 346 replied "No", 10 "Yes", 22 gave ambiguous answers and 150 did not reply at all (J. M. Fletcher 1932: 142). This does not, however, say very much: the last six words of the question are such that nearly everyone has to give "No" as an answer. That there are in human nature instinctive factors which can lead to war is, as earlier suggested, not the same as saying that wars are inevitable. On the contrary there are a lot of adequate brakes, control devices and submissions which, in most cases, are able to prevent war.

Nevertheless "it must be remembered that the destructive instincts which, when all is said and done, are the greatest single cause of war, are instincts and that they are impossible to eradicate altogether, greatly though they may be modified" (Strachey 1957: 266). And "man's ferocity to man does have one clear biological counterpart in territoriality. If war has any innate, 'instinctive' basis, it may most likely be found to be a derivative of the reactions associated with defense of territory, so widely characteristic of the vertebrates" (Bates 1955: 129; cf. also Eyles 1971).

From the above it will be clear that the pure economic as well as the pure ideologic explanations of war are at best only half-truths. But "The value of land and other property as symbolizing people is stressed and such terms as 'motherland' taken seriously" (Durbin and Bowlby 1950: 149), which suggests that emotional behaviour of an instinctive nature has its proper place in the context. Therefore we can now account for the strange terms in which a national talks when he thinks of his country as a land.

"Thus, if it is invaded he thinks of it as being 'violated' or 'raped' quite literally, as he thinks of a woman – in this case *his* woman and his great mother into the bargain, as well as his feminine self – being raped and desecrated, and he responds with frenzied rage. He even violently resists a peaceable partition of his country, however just and even advantageous, because it means a cutting up of the beloved land made up of its fields, trees, houses, streams, mountains, plains and seas which is at once his own great self and his still greater parents" (Strachey 1957: 204). Or if we put it another way: "When our own tribe engages in this behavior we call it patriotism; when another does the same, we call it nationalism or aggression" (Stea 1965: 13).

4.2.4.3. Territoriality and character of war:
With territoriality as an anticipated, if not always directly admitted (e.g., Swanton 1943: 15-16) background factor in connection with warfare, the frequency of this phenomenon is of great interest. Schmidt (1952: 406-409) and some other distinguished anthropologists advocated a return to the myth of a golden age of peace on the ground that most "primitive" peoples were said to be gentle and harmless. But "The antithesis between war and peace is really inapplicable to the simple conditions in which these peoples live. Anything like the organized and aggressive warfare which we find in early history and among the more advanced of the simpler societies can have no place in the life of the simplest societies, for this implies organization, discipline and differentiation between leaders and led which the people of the lowest culture do not possess. But if these do not have war, neither have they peace. We must think of war not as a genus uniquely opposed to peace but as a species of violence opposed to social order and security" (Glover and Ginsberg 1934: 287).

In their examination of 311 "primitive" societies Hobhouse, Wheeler and Ginsberg (1930: 228-233) found that 298 showed war and feud behaviour distributed through all the grades while in 9 certain and 4 doubtful cases war was not known. Wright (1942: 527-561) surveyed war practices and other characteristics in more than 650 different peoples and recognized four basic varieties of war: defensive, social, economic and political. He found the hunters least warlike, the agriculturalists intermediate and the pastoral peoples most warlike, while the peoples organized into clans were least warlike, those organized into villages more so, those with tribes still more warlike and those organized into states most warlike.

Nobody will, of course, maintain that the strength of territoriality is the only factor leading to war, and so the evidence above cannot be used as an argument against the instinctive nature of martiality as implied by Fromm (1973: 149). If it is true that pastoralists are more warlike than agriculturalists, the reason could be that the latter as sedentary peoples have more fixed and more easily respected territory boundaries than the former, who also when moving around more often have the chance to come into contact and conflict with strangers. Sorokin made an index of European wars as to duration, size of fighting force, number of casualties, number of countries involved and proportion of combatants to total population. This index came up with the figure 18 for the 12th century and the figure 3,080 for the 20th century (Wright 1942: 655), which gives counter-evidence to the statement that "we have every reason to believe that modern society controls aggression much more effectively than did the corresponding societies of the Middle Ages" (Scott 1962: 175). That, in spite of such terrifying statistics, war is not the normal daily condition in most peoples today is probably dependent i.a. on ritualisation and sublimation of aggressive drives (e.g., Goldsmith 1974).

But "history is full of examples of human fighting originating from the fact that more than one human group had identified itself with the same patch of land" (White 1966: 103). And even in such cases as the Bantu, the tribal boundaries of which usually seem vague and undecided, there is in times of war a tendency "to peg down the country", keep out invaders and recognize boundaries (Schapera 1956: 13-14). Concerning one of the latest and most observed cases it was reported: "All of this makes psychologically interesting the apparent assumption of a great many American militants that South Vietnam is self-evidently 'our' (the Free World's) territory, that North Vietnamese Communists who cross the line as we have defined it are self-evidently invading 'another country' rather than, as they claim, trying to 'liberate' their countrymen from foreign rule, and that to regard our presence in Vietnam (from 1950 to now) as an infringement on Vietnamese soil is fantastic" (White 1966: 105).

No less striking is the detailed territorial behaviour during active war service as described from one of the camps of the American Special Forces in the jungle of Vietnam, otherwise controlled by the Viet Cong (Bourne 1970: 114-116): "When the men are confined within the barbed wire perimeter of the camp by the threat of attack, the relative inactivity and passivity they are forced to accept is antithetical to their usual self-images. Tied down to the defense of a fixed piece of territory, the military initiative must be abandoned and with it their preferred style of behavior. . . .

Attempts to achieve physical and psychical space between each other produce an overt pattern of territoriality in the camp. One might anticipate that
with little ground space available in the camp the team members would share
equally that which they had. This was not the case, and individual team
members would jealously guard those areas of the camp to which they felt
they had a special claim. The two radio operators would refuse entry into the
communications bunker, the medics allowed no other team members into
their dispenśary, and even the weapons specialists felt that they had personal
ownership of any area in which ammunition was stored.

At times this behavior reached ludicrous proportions, as when one man
posted a sign stating that he would shoot any intruder into his area, and when
one medic claimed that he felt other team members brought germs into his
already inevitably dirty and fly-infested dispensary. It is perhaps of
significance that these men, whose job was to defend a small piece of territory
with their lives, should behave this way toward one another when frustrated
by the enemy's failure to attack. A need to gratify an aroused urge toward
territoriality seemed to exist" (cf. also Mehrabian 1976: 117-118).

In sum we can state with Durbin and Bowlby (1950: 3, 25) about war,
defined as organized fighting between large groups of adult human beings,
that it must be regarded as one species of a larger genus, the genus of fighting.
This in turn is plainly a common, indeed a universal, form of human behaviour. It extends beyond the borders of humanity into the types of mammals most closely related, in the evolutionary classification, to the common
ancestors of man and apes. War between groups within the nation and between nations are obvious and important examples of this type of behaviour.
Since this is so, it must follow that the simplest and most general causes of war
are to be found in the causes of fighting, and here territoriality plays a most
important role. "Fighting and peaceful co-operation are equally 'natural'
forms of behaviour, equally fundamental tendencies in human relations.
Peaceful co-operation predominates – there is much more peace than war –
but the willingness to fight is so widely distributed in space and time that it
must be regarded as a basic pattern of human behaviour" (loc. cit.).

War is thus one of the most spectacular manifestations of aggression and
territoriality, and this last phenomenon seems also to be significant in home-
love, migration and homesickness, which will now be examined.

4.2.5. Homelove, migration and homesickness

4.2.5.1. Homelove:
The well-known English proverb "A man's home is his castle" makes it hard

to doubt the character of home as a possibly defended territory. In order to give an example of definition we cite this statement: "Home territories are areas where the regular participants have a relative freedom of behavior and a sense of intimacy and control over the area" (Lyman and Scott 1967-1968: 238). The outstanding importance of the phenomenon becomes evident when one hears that the average person of all ages and both sexes spends about three quarters of his lifetime at home, at least in Western civilizations, the percentage of time, e.g., being 76 percent for U.S. citizens and 75.3 percent for the people of Athens, Greece (Doxiadis 1968c: 22).

In space as well as in time, home-binding forces seem to be common. "The struggle for home, an individual habitation, be it a garden, a yard or a manor, the struggle for a common territory, the native'place or the fatherland, the struggle for obtaining food and clothing safely, the struggle for the possession of a spouse, for the care and safeguarding of children, all these reactions have been repeated for thousands of years" (Meyer-Holzapfel 1952: 17). It is summarized that even in man the drives for resting conditions attainable at home and the appetitive reactions directed toward home play an extremely important role and influence his whole social life (Holzapfel 1940: 267; cf. also Greverus 1972).

Eighty years ago G. S. Hall (1897: 388) postulated that there are two tendencies in children, one centripetal inclining the individual towards home and one centrifugal inclining away from home. Maybe this is reflected also by the "two types of adults, as far as attitude to the home is concerned; the attached and the independent" (Hediger 1955: 21; cf. also Kline 1898). Or rather it is so that the two tendencies are of varying strength in different persons at different times. However, it is hard to doubt that the former is normally dominant, meaning that territoriality is more fundamental than the migratory urge, particularly in childhood. "Judging by his whole mental make-up, the human baby is just as dependent upon a home, in the biological sense, as an octopus or mouse, a fox or hippopotamus. In their psychotopes, a home is a basically important element, so much so that the lack of it may give rise to serious deficiency symptoms" (Hediger 1955: 21).

We have earlier tried to explain one of the foremost factors behind the great influence of the childhood home, namely that of imprinting (4.1.2.2.). This phenomenon is probably the biological reality behind the words of the sociologist Brepohl (1952: 17): "It is decisive for the value of the home that it represents the first reality in a world characterized by endless variants. The unit of home is mirrored in the awakening mind. It will then constitute a prototype and later experience develops by transformation of this first witness of the world."

It may be recalled from our earlier discussion (4.1.5.) that the territorial binding to home is very great among "primitive" peoples, and the use of tools has hardly influenced this urge as suggested by Nicolai (1917: 218-220). To this author's astonishment, even many "civilized savages who had seemed already well adapted – and for example had completed their university studies with distinction – at first opportunity ran away into their bush and became naked savages." For further illustration we can refer to the Kabylians, one of whom was quite aware of the disadvantages of staying in his destroyed mountain village but yet refused to move into the plain with the explanation: "C'est un amour" [it is love] (Doxiadis 1966: 313).

There are also lots of instances from non-primitive peoples of a love for home stronger than death. We need only cite the Icelander Gunnar of Lidarände from the tale of Nial, who about a thousand years ago, was killed by his enemies after having refused to go into exile. His famous words were: "How fair is the valley. It never was so beautiful before. I will go home and never leave again". Or we can think of the many persons during the Second World War, who instead of fleeing remained in their homes, committing suicide when enemy troops arrived (cf. also Stavenhagen 1939; Bausinger, Braun and Schwedt 1959: 156-193 and particularly Greverus 27-55).

4.2.5.2. Migration and mental problems:
As we all know there is another proverb stating: "*Ubi bene, ibi patria*" (Where I fare well, there is my fatherland). Even though the childhood home is of incomparable territorial importance, man has a greater or lesser power to take a movable territory with him or to build up new territories after leaving the old ones, following the exploratory urge. "Migration is not, however, to be identified with mere movement. It involves, at the very least, change of residence and the breaking of home ties" (Park 1927-1928: 886-887), which could be compensated for in a more or less satisfactory way.

As to definitions it is said: "Migration is defined broadly as a permanent or semipermanent change of residence. No restriction is placed upon the distance of the move or upon the voluntary or involuntary nature of the act, and no distinction is made between external and internal migration.... However, not all kinds of spatial mobility are included in this definition. Excluded for example, are the continual movements of nomads and migratory workers, for

112									TERRITORY IN MAN

whom there is no long-term residence, and temporary moves like those to
the mountains for the summer" (E.S. Lee 1966:49; cf. also Hägerstrand
1957).

The individual territorial problems involved in human migration are of
enormous proportions, which is easy to understand if one penetrates a summary chapter like "The Great Migrations" (Borrie 1970: 85-127; cf. also K.
Davis 1974). Just two figures should be given here: more than 50 million
Europeans have permanently left their continent since the sixteenth century,
and between 40 and 50 million people have been reshuffled across international boundaries as refugees or in migration during and since the Second
World War. It is reasonable to assume that at least some of the voluntary
migrations originated in a more or less conscious desire to leave crowded
areas with territorial difficulties in order to fill up remaining "open spaces"
elsewhere (cf. Forsyth 1942).

Of interest in this context is the fact that "the longer the distance, the
larger the area to which one belongs. One is adherent to the house, the block,
the district, the town, the province and the country. All this can be home; it
depends on the distance" (Mackensen, Papalekas, Pfeil, Schütte and Burckhardt 1959:21). Further it is certainly so that "Geography and the territorial
organization of society get their importance from the facts that social relations are determined largely by physical distances and that social stability
is insured when human beings are rooted in the soil. On the other hand, the
most drastic changes in society are likely to be those that involve mobility
and particularly mass migrations of peoples" (Park 1952: 120-121; cf. also
Trewartha 1969: 135-145).

Soon after voluntary migrations mental problems seem to increase. As
Faris (1944: 738) stressed: "The conclusion most harmonious with the above
data is that the high rates of various types of defectiveness in populations
which have undergone migration is not due to their previous inferiority, since
the differences noted are more in the direction of superiority. It is more
probable that the migration, which resulted from ecological forces, caused the
behavior abnormality by disorganizing the social system.... The ecology of
behavior abnormality, then, is largely a matter of the consequences of migration" (cf. also *Mobility and Mental Health* 1965).

Thus Dayton (1940: 80-143) showed that in the state of Massachusetts,
U.S.A., the admission to mental hospitals between 1917 and 1933 was highest
in the foreign-born population and that younger migrants tended to be afflicted sooner than older ones. Hyde and Chisholm (1944) found among 60,000
army recruits from Boston in the same state a high incidence of psychopathy

in Negroes, Irish and Italians. And Tyhurst (1951) discovered in Canada, among mostly displaced persons from Europe, a high percent of frustration, helplessness and aggression as compared with the native population. The causes given for these disturbances were change of cultural atmosphere and xenophobia, but it seems reasonable that strongly contributing factors have been loss of childhood and homeland territories and difficulties in getting adequate new ones in the foreign country (cf. also Ödegaard 1932).

Particularly in the case of refugees the situation is troublesome, because these people often have no hope of return. In her chapter "Aufbruch aus der Heimat," Pfeil (1948: 12) describes the circumstances. "The refugee enters a road into the unknown. It has no goal, it leads away from a home that cannot give protection, and it has no end. The fugitive will get to a place of safety but he suspects that there is salvation for him only insofar as his fleeing removes him from the immediate threat".

Ebermann and Möllhoff (1957) found five times as many psychopaths among the refugees from eastern countries in southern Germany than among their normal clientele. And Soviet-Russian refugees in Switzerland during the Second World War had the same kinds of illness. "To deprive them of their homes meant taking everything, for their bonds were to the earth. Undoubtedly the common ideology was important, but first of all these people were space-bound. The Russian earth, the Russian air was for them 'Biotope' and 'Archetope'" (Pfister-Ammende 1949: 253; cf. also Pfister-Ammende 1950, Champion 1958).

4.5.2.3.   Homesickness – the Swiss disease:
The primary mental troubles connected with absence from the well-known, original, more or less imprinted territory are, of course, those summarized as homesickness. Pfeil (1948: 107) reported laconically: "The refugee is home-sick", and Frost (1938: 801) gave an interesting example, stating that "Immigrant psychoses arise among foreign domestic servants usually within eighteen months of their arrival in Britain". Self-evidently it is just a matter of terms and seriousness, if we speak of immigrant psychosis or of homesickness – phenomena which are in most cases non-morbid but which under certain conditions and in certain individuals can be pathological and even lead to crime. It has long been known that especially girls in a foreign country some-times commit arson or murder, not to say suicide, in their masters' home as a desperate means to be freed from their terrible situation, far from their own and known territories (op. cit.; cf. also Jaspers 1909).

Homesickness is hardly experienced before the age of six months, probably because the newborn child has not enough contact with the physical environment to react to changes, provided that its normal needs as to human care and nearness are satisfied. But after the age of half a year it is a common phenomenon in infants, showing symptoms like anxiety and sorrow, later even silence, immobility and withdrawal. But the longing is in the beginning mostly for the parents, especially the mother, and so it can even happen that the child shows symptoms at home, if near relatives are absent for a long time. First at an age of 6-7 years there are sure signs of real homesickness, directed not only toward human beings but also toward a place, the home and its surroundings (Peiper 1961: 652-659), which is in accordance with the earlier mentioned age for beginning definitive territoriality (p. 55). It has been shown that rural children were more affected by homesickness than urban and that the phenomenon could influence the psychic development (Schwab 1925; see also 4.1.2.).

Homesickness was primarily classified as a pediatric disease. "It is true that as a violent longing for a return to places of one's childhood and to customs which have grown dear it occurs mainly in young people. They have been too dependent on their fatherland and mother country. Even the best things in life cannot compensate for the old beloved habits and habitats" (Boette 1930–1931: column 1990).

But we have already mentioned symptoms also among adult migrants and refugees. It is interesting to note that it was once thought, for instance, that a piece of earth from home carried by the migrating person could protect against homesickness: "and thus it was thought that the wanderer was followed and surrounded by a piece of home" (op cit. column 1689; cf. also Marbe 1925).

McCann (1941: 165) introduced his survey "Nostalgia: A Review of the Literature" with the following words. "It has been argued that nostalgia is older and more fundamental than human nature itself . . . and that all people of the world, all ages, and all temperaments, weak and strong, are more or less susceptible to it. . .". But in spite of examples back to Homer and the Bible, homesickness was long called "*Schweizerkrankheit*" and it was not until 1774 that nostalgia was described as a sickness of other peoples than the Swiss. It is difficult to explain this fact, but it might be that a strongly structured landscape gives a more permanent territorial imprinting of home than another one (op. cit. p. 169-174):

"Thus typical homesickness is particularly evident in the inhabitants of mountains and is a purely individual affection. Perhaps it depends on the

conspicuous differentiation of the landscape – which must fascinate consciousness – above all the spot on earth where one has lived and to which one
has belonged. Broadly speaking, there is no reason why mountain tribes
should love their homes more than peoples of the plains. But evidently one's
emotions always tend to be more impressed by the strongly structured
mountains, where every point is unique, than by the plains, where all the
points are similar. Therefore we also have more home-feeling for an old,
irregular town with many nooks and corners than for a modern, perfectly
uniform one" (G. Simmel 1908: 622).

Concluding his survey McCann (op. cit. p. 178-180) found that the essential
features of nostalgia are: (1) an "away from home" situation; (2) a strong,
emotionally charged desire to return to the home situation; (3) thwarting of
this desire; (4) failure of escape mechanisms; (5) frustration; and (6) the arousal of emergency emotional behavior with its various symptoms. Like many
other American psychologists McCann was of the opinion that "The instinct
theories, are, of course, purely metaphysical and without any value whatsoever". But his very formulations strongly suggest that territoriality with
instinctive background must be involved in nostalgia.

In a world where millions of people are still on the move with unsatisfactory
territorial bindings as a result, nostalgia must be a very general phenomenon.
This has also been discovered by the entertainment industry. In 1956 a song
called "*Heimweh*" was the greatest hit up to that time on the German record
market. This fact was commented on by Berghahn (1965: 111) in this way:
"Where the entertainment industry gives the promise of a house and a home,
it is not made convincingly but is full of anxiety. It clutches at a straw.
Somewhere, the films and hits tell us, one should be able to feel at home.
In what could we otherwise believe or to where could we otherwise escape?
The paradoxical situation arises that human beings, between their own four
walls, can feel like strangers and yet be afforded consolation by the promise
of being carried home!"

This situation is easy to explain if we remember not only that lots of people
have migrated or escaped as refugees from one country to another but also
that more or less dominating parts of the population in our towns and cities
are strangers there, displaced persons from the countryside. Thus the consequences of homelove, migration and homesickness are probably most serious in the urban realm, an important section of society, which will now be
scrutinized from the point of view of behavioural territoriality.

4.3. Urban territories

4.3.1. Historical comments

4.3.1.1. Definitions and terms:
History builds the Town, the title of a book by Arthur Korn (1953), is a self-evident remark that calls for some historical facts, introducing our treatise on urban territories. First, however, we will try to give some definitions, remembering that "The concept of 'city' is notoriously hard to define" (Childe 1950: 3).

One of the most influential is the explicitly tentative, early definition by Ratzel (1912: 293): "If we talk about a great, concentrated accumulation of habitations of humans who are not wholly nourished by the surrounding agricultural fields but who also live by trade, industry, transport, government and garrison, then we have suggested essential characters of towns without giving an exhaustive treatment of the matter".

Maunier (1910, cited after *A Systematic Source Book in Rural Sociology* 1930: 159) put territoriality into the definition, saying that the city is a *"complex society whose geographical base is particularly restrained for the size of its population,* or *whose territorial element is relatively meager in amount compared to that of its human elements"*.

Still more information, even as to modern cities, seems to be hidden in some definitions of ancient urban units. Thus Mumford (1938: 3) stressed that the city, as one finds it in history, is the point of maximum concentration concerning the power and culture of a community. "It is the place where the diffused rays of many separate beams of life fall into focus, with gains in both social effectiveness and significance. The city is the form and symbol of an integrated social relationship: it is the seat of the temple, the market, the hall of justice, the academy of learning".

The definition by Hamblin (1973: 11) seems to be a most comprehensive and probably also a most useful one: "By these criteria it is possible to define a city as a permanently inhabited place whose residents form a group larger than a family or a clan. It is also a place where there are both opportunity and demand for a division of labour, which creates social classes that recognize a differentiation in function, privilege and responsibility. The size and specialization are both cause and result of the unique rôle the city plays in the region. It must perform services important to the lives of those who live in and around it or travel to it. These services may be religious, administrative, commercial, political, defensive, or may involve the maintenance of water or food supplies.

But whatever their form, the services must be in such demand that they give the city control over the surrounding area – on which it must depend for food to support its concentrated population". Here we get a clear suggestion not only that the city *is* a territory but also that it *has* one.

We should look for a moment at the relevant terms, too. The Latin *"civitas"* originally signified a district organized by the Romans but later, during the Merovingian and Carolingian empires, referred to the centre of an area in which was a bishopric, in France called *"cité"*. By the twelfth century the term *"civitas"* was related to a settlement that had a special law, a wall and a marketing, industrial and commercial centre, independent of magnitude. This meaning is now reflected in the French *"ville"*, the German *"Stadt"* and the English "town".

"Cité" was thus in the beginning an ecclesiastic centre and is still used in this sense, but the term "city" has acquired a wider modern connotation as a major locality for institutions, administration and organization, cultural life, social contact, production, commercial activity and transport (cf. Dickinson 1967: 15-16). The well-known magnitude difference between "city" and "town" has thus historical reasons, and it is, e.g., quite possible to state about a Babylonian king that "Sargon and his successors can therefore claim to have been 'founders of cities' even where townships had existed long before them" (Childe 1948: 175). The words in case are, however, often used as synonyms in this survey.

4.3.1.2. The urban origin:

As remarked i.a. by N. Carpenter (1931: 17-18) there are both material, technical, political and strictly human factors behind the first urbanization. Agriculture and cattle-raising were the foundations of a settled community life as well as of a growing population, but the special grounds for cities were trade, worship and particularly defense against enemies. Thus Mumford (1956: 385) stressed that the earliest meaning of 'town" is an enclosed or fortified place, and Ennen (1953: 35) agreed that the city should be called "a particularly well-defended settlement, a fortress".

These views are consistent with the historic explanation of Keith (1948: 293): "At the beginning we have village communities spread over the marshlands of Babylonia, each community being an independent unit, owning its territory and capable of its own defence. As tillage improved villages would increase in number and also in size of population. With these increases came the struggle between adjoining village communities, weaker villages combining against the stronger neighbour, until, finally, some one village, because of the courage and enterprise of its chief or of the natural fertility of its territory, or because of its favourable situation for trade, or of a combination of all three factors, became a central power, and the foundation of a city-state".

A complementary background was presented by the earlier cited famous archeologist V. Gordon Childe (1950: 8) in "The Urban Revolution": About 5,000 years ago – in the light of later facts some millennia should be added – irrigation cultivation combined with stockbreeding and fishing in the valleys of the Nile, the Tigris-Euphrates and the Indus had begun to yield a surplus large enough to support a number of resident specialists who were released from food-production. Water-transport, supplemented in Mesopotamia and the Indus valley by wheeled vehicles and in Egypt by pack animals, made it easy to gather food stuffs at a few centres. At the same time dependence on river water for the irrigation of crops restricted the cultivable areas, while the necessity of canalizing the waters and protecting habitations against annual floods encouraged the aggregation of people. Thus arose the first cities, units of settlement ten times as great as any known neolithic village, and it can be argued that all cities in the world are offshoots of those in Egypt, Mesopotamia and the Indus basin.

In another context this author (Childe 1948: 153) added: "The centre of each city was the sacred *temenos* or citadel containing the temples of the city god and other deities.... The magic force which man had sought to compel would be personified as a god who must be helped and conciliated. Before history begins, society has projected its collective will, its corporate hopes and fears, into this fictitious person whom it revers as Lord of its territory" (cf. also Adams 1960). In Egypt the early urbanization was probably not much pronounced, but settlements developed around temples, palaces and tombs. It is not unlikely that as early as the middle of the fourth millennium B.C. "some villages grew into 'central places' as the 'capitals' of the *nomes*, the clan divisions, exerting at the same time a certain protective function for their territory" (Gutkind 1953: 20; cf. also p. 88).

Reviewing the papers from a symposium on the theme "Courses toward Urban Life" Mumford (1963) stressed that the reaching out for variety is one of the significant traits of the city, which distinguishes it from the more self-subsistent village. Further: "one aspect of the city is that of a container – a container of people, of crafts and trades, of distant products and resources – another equally important aspect is its role as a center of cosmic and kingly powers, exercising a life and death control over large populations, intensify-ing their energies, unifying their activities, absorbing for the benefit of a ruling minority the goods that once were distributed more evenly within the smaller community. . . . If we understand the present uses of the two primeval aspects of the city, that of the magnet (paleolithic) and that of the container (neolithic), we shall view with skepticism the suggestion that our complex civilization can be carried on in small, specialized pseudo-urban enclaves that lack even the complexities of a village" (cf. also Smailes 1953: 7-22 and p. 3).

4.3.1.3. Oriental and Greek cities:
Turning to specific examples it is, of course, very interesting that the oldest town yet discovered is the one that lies next to the modern city of Jericho not far from the Israel-Jordanian border and that this place has been almost continuously inhabited for about 10,000 years. Among the many walls discovered here, the oldest one, made of small stones and at least 20 feet high, supplemented by a 27 feet wide and 9 feet deep ditch as well as by a 30 feet high tower, was put up about 8,000 B.C., suggesting a defended group territory at the spot from this time onwards (Hamblin 1973: 28-41).

But it was the culture in the basin of the rivers Euphrates and Tigris which built cities in any significant numbers during the following millennia. "Although the Sumerian city-states shared a common cultural root, when their energies had cleared the jungles, drained the swamps, and organized irrigation complexes, their territories began to touch and even overlap, so that frontier disputes caused inevitable friction. War between Sumerian city-states appears to have been frequent, violent and destructive, so that, in time, one state emerged victorious" (Curl 1970: 13). Interestingly enough the Sumerian word for love in use about 3,000 B.C., "*ki-ág*", also had the meaning "to measure the earth" (S. N. Kramer 1958). There are presented several possible interpretations of this fact, all with territorial suggestions (N. W. Smith 1975), but it seems most probable to think of a breeding territory for the human animal.

In any case the citadel, even though not always built just for defense, became a main point in these first urban units. And when towns had grown to cities, it was, e.g., said about Babylon – for fifteen hundred years beginning about 2,000 B.C. the capital of different empires – that it had "immense fortified walls within which were fields which could produce food for the population during a siege" (Curl 1970: 17). It looks as if this capital already then functioned as a territorial nucleus, for if at the time one wanted to express the concept of "the Babylonians" one had to say: "the people (*ameluti*) of the territory (*matu*) of the city (*alu*) of Babylon" as well as "the king of the territory of the city of Babylon" and so on (Schachermeyer 1952-1953: 25).

There is a direct line from the old Mesopotamian city-states to the Greek classical ones, known under the name of "*polis*", but coinciding with this Oriental line there were also Aegean and Indo-European contributing lines. In fact a city culture already flourished in Greece in the first half of the third millennium B.C., that is, more than 2,000 years before the urbanization in the rest of Europe. But these first towns were mostly Oriental and were only slowly influenced by the primordial Aegean Civilization. The earliest true Greeks moved into Hellas about 2,000 B.C., they were Indo-Europeans and predominantly cattle breeders. It took more than a millennium to bring the three elements into complete harmony in the "*polis*".

"A generalized picture of the polis would show it as a walled enclosure, on rising ground, dominated by a fortress or *acropolis* . . . and itself commanding a view out over its own fields. A few would be found to lie on flat, or almost level land, without *acropolis*, but these would mostly be of later origin, founded after the age of the quasifeudal princes who established the high fortresses. Within the walls would be narrow streets, lined with houses, small and simply built of adobe and wood with only a sparing use of stone, a public square or *agora* . . . and a few public buildings, which alone would show any architectural distinction" (Pounds 1969: 139). As conditions gradually became less insecure and population increased, unfortified lower cities overflowed from the fortified citadels down the slopes of the hills onto the plains below. The line of the new ring-wall, usually determined by topographical considerations, was carried along ridges that provided natural defense and often included a larger space than the built-up area of the lower city (cf. Toynbee 1967: 445).

4.3.1.4. Roman cities, medieval cities and old city figures:

The "*polis*" cities were numerous but small and were found in Greece as well as in other countries around the Aegean Sea (Pounds 1969: 136). From the third century B.C. Rome took over as the centre in a strongly organized and urbanized empire with a marked hierarchy. In his address to the city of Rome, given in the second century A.D., Aelius Aristides said: "What another city is to its own boundaries and territory, this city is to the boundaries and territory of the entire civilized world, as if the latter were a country district and she had been appointed common town. It might be said that this one citadel is the refuge and assembly place of all *perioeci* [literally "those living round about'] or of all who dwell in outside *demes* [i.e., rural districts]" (Oliver 1953: 901).

Roman cities were of three kinds: colonies established on virgin sites by government decree, *"coloniae"*, settlements growing up around legionary barracks, *"cannabae"*, and in the great majority of cases tribal forts of the native Celtic and Iberian peoples, *"oppida"*, transformed by the conquerors for their use (Pounds 1969: 148-152). They all had defensive arrangements, particularly the last ones. By the second century A.D. the Roman Empire presented more than ever the appearance of a vast federation of city states, called *"civitates"* and enjoying local self-government.

As mentioned earlier the term *"civitas"* first denoted an area and normally one occupied by a tribe and independent of cities from the beginning. But "even the most rural *civitates* developed some urban centre, and in the more civilised provinces the town had from time immemorial dominated its surrounding territory. It was however the rarest of anomalies that a *civitas* should consist of a town only, without a dependent territory: the only known case is Alexandria of Egypt and here the reason was that the Ptolemies took over the administration of 'the territory of the Alexandrians' and organized it as a nome of Egypt" (A. H. M. Jones 1954: 139).

Thus there was a close bond between the city, whatever its size, and its region, so that the terms *"polis"* and *"civitas"* covered the urban settlement together with its surrounding and dependent countryside. This association was maintained throughout the classical period, and was perpetuated through medieval times by the ecclesiastical dioceses, which delimited the approximate areas dependent upon the cities, and to some extent by the medieval city-states themselves (cf. Pounds 1969: 156).

"The city, the road, the law spread together with the scheme of Roman imperial defence of the frame of the Mediterranean Sea, and it is thus from the work of the Romans that we have to trace many features of the growth of cities in Europe north of the Mediterranean, . . ." (Fleure 1936: 7). The medieval period produced its own city-states, which were political units with town-councils, guild bodies and special liberties for their citizens, while their customs and laws were distinct from those of the country districts, dominated by feudalism. Eventually, through growing trade, municipal power and successful conflicts with the feudal lords, the towns gained more control over rural areas. Thus a two-way traffic was assured with market produce coming into the towns and the work of craftsmen going out. In addition the peasants could count on the protection of the town walls in times of unrest (cf. Curl 1970: 74).

Medieval cities were in general small, but though they were usually walled, they were not overcrowded. Gardens were numerous, but, as time passed, they were gradually filled with inferior dwellings to the great disadvantage of the urban unit. "In these early walled towns it was unusual for the streets to be arranged in a regular plan. To some extent the various trades were segregated in special quarters, and the streets penetrated these quarters rather haphazardly. The chief meeting place of the town was the market square, which often faced the main church of the town" (Taylor 1949: 140). The psychological importance of this town with its wall was very great. "When the portcullis was drawn and the town gates were locked at sundown the city was sealed off from the outside world. Such enclosure helps create a feeling of unity as well as security" (Mumford 1961: 304; cf. also J. H. Johnson 1967: 8-11).

In the period of the Renaissance many changes developed which had marked effect on the town plans of the time. As artillery became more effective, the old straight walls offered little protection. Instead new-style massive, star-shaped fortifications were developed with earthwork, bastions, ravelins and artillery-resistent walls, which restored at least some degree of security to the citizens. These new fortifications were space-consuming and expensive, and the result was that as a city grew there was a more and more pronounced overcrowding – for other reasons already found in classical Rome (Pöhlmann 1884) – within the now not easily movable walls (cf., e.g., Mumford 1961: 356-363).

Apartment living was now increasingly developed in Continental cities, while England, lacking defense problems, long retained the old urban habitation traditions. At the same time, geometrical design began to be adapted, with a central core in the royal palace and straight wide streets radiating therefrom. This was the "*città ideale*", the ideals of which influenced three centuries up to the beginning of industrial and modern times (cf. Curl 1970: 88-103).

Before leaving the early cities we will try to give some very rough population figures. It should then be stressed that in urban units, probably for the first time, conditions developed which imply that the individual citizen no longer could know personally every other member of his community. The old Sumerian cities were small according to modern scales and had at the most 7,000 to 20,000 inhabitants. Babylon probably contained, circa 600 B.C., about 80,000 persons, Thebes at the height of its splendour as the capital of Egypt, circa 1600 B.C., maybe 225,000 inhabitants, while classical Athens had 20,000 to 300,000 people. The last figure, probably nearest to the truth, included some 100,000 slaves, some 150,000 free women and children and not quite 50,000 full-fledged male citizens. It is finally thought that the population of classical Rome might have approached 500,000 persons (cf. K. Davis 1955:

429-432; Mumford 1961: 153; D. Morris 1969: 18-20; Pounds 1969: 140-143).

If we try to summarize these very incomplete historical data the fact stands out that cities from their earliest times had predominantly defensive purposes, facilitated by special arrangements. Thus they without, or mostly, together with adjacent areas constituted clearly bounded and seemingly very successful group territories with behavioural background. Yet the contrast between urban and rural has been evident from the very beginning of urbanization and these conditions will now be investigated.

4.3.2. Factors of urbanization

4.3.2.1. The rural-urban complex:
Homo sapiens needs room but finds a total land surface area of 150 million square kilometers (particularly its fertile parts) strongly limited. Thus the struggle for existence for 4 billion men is, as with other organisms, above all a matter of control of space, commanding the resources of water, food and other needs. The more or less successive stages of hunting, pastoral, agricultural and industrial economy involve not only increasing numerical strength but also augmented density in spite of the ever larger areas used. In this development we have to insert the phenomena of rural and urban habitats.

Man has used terrestrial space for more than a million years. He has lived in it and tried to shape it, more and more with the effect of destroying it, and he has nearly always been on the move across it. "These actions have occupied different spatial units, from the cave (or room) to the whole earth. Such units can be classified in a system starting with man as the smallest unit of ekistic space (we should never forget that man is the measure), moving to a room (as the smallest physical space formed by man), then to the house, neighborhood, small and large cities, metropolis and up to the whole earth..." (Doxiadis 1968a: 380).

The relations between the city and the countryside are thus old and complex, monographically treated by Bookwalter (1911). They seem to be briefly and well formulated by a student of Megalopolis who asserts that "the rural exodus empties the countryside and fills the towns, which in their turn explode and spread different establishments of urban types over the surrounding rural districts" (Gottman 1966a: 37).

Some well-known sociologists, Sorokin, Zimmerman and Galpin, have reported the following differences between the rural and the urban world (*A Systematic Source Book in Rural Sociology* 1930: 239-242): First of all, in the former, nature dominates over artificial environment and agricultural over other occupations. Further, both the size of the community and the density of the population are comparatively smaller but the homogeneity of the human stock greater in the rural than in the urban field. Finally the differentiation, stratification, mobility and contact interaction are less in the first type of habitat than in the second (cf. also N. Anderson 1963).

It is, however, difficult in our time to define rural as opposed to urban, because there is an ever increasing intermingling of both, although with the urban factor as the most progressive and commanding. T. L. Smith (1951: 43, cited after Mann 1970: 6-7) gave this picture of the situation: "Rather than consisting of mutually exclusive categories, rural and urban, the general society seems to resemble a spectrum in which the most remote backwoods sub-rural [sic] settlements blend imperceptibly into the rural and then gradually through all degrees of rural and suburban into the most urban and hyper-urban [sic] way of living". These views were opposed by Benet (1963-1964: 17-19), maintaining that the idea of the continuum has not been successful. In comparisons the rural and the urban break up in splinters and the spectrum is one of jarring contrasts.

In spite of the fact that there were cities several thousand years ago the pre-urban stage is by far the dominating one in the history of mankind. The rural surroundings not only supplied all material necessary for the vital needs of man but also shaped all kinds of psychological, social and cultural manifestations and maintained the biological balance of the population. It is wise to remember that the urban world is a rather new parasite, living on and grown out from the rural, and that original rural features are hidden even in the modern urban context (cf. *A Systematic Source Book in Rural Sociology* 1932: 628; cf. p. 67).

4.3.2.2. Urbanization development:
First we state with Marcus and Detwyler (1972: 6): "*Urbanization* is the process of city establishment and growth; the term commonly connotes population increase in the city, resulting from both internal growth and immigration, as well as spatial expansion of the city". The crucial factor is, of course, that this process – often divided into symmetrical growth, asymmetrical growth and absorption (N. Carpenter 1931: 119) – during the last century and a half has gone ahead much faster and reached proportions far greater than before. It is a global tendency with strong influence even outside the urban-confined world, and it is of interest that it now usually means an excess of urbanization over industrialization everywhere. It was, however, suggested "that at all levels of size there is a saturation limit for towns, and

that this limit depends on natural conditions and financial circumstances" (Beaujeu-Garnier and Chabot 1967: 341).

But the present trend of nearly total urbanization of the countryside, e.g., in western Europe and eastern U.S.A., should not conceal the reciprocity of influence. It is true that the urban settlement spreads still more deeply into rural areas with or without the help of satellites and that the urban people build their recreation centres and second homes there. But rurality also invades the city, i.a. by means of cultivation in villa and allotment gardens, and, during wars, even in parks (cf., e.g., Clout 1972: 43-44).

Several observers, among them Osvald Sirén, have remarked that "A commonly noted characteristic of the city in North China is that large areas within the walls are open fields or cultivated farmland" (Tuan 1968: 243). And during the early stages of the Cultural Revolution in 1966 Mao Tse-Tung called for the ruralization of cities along with the industrialization of agricultural villages. This ruralization has been put into action, e.g., in the new petroleum city of Tach'ing and in the old and large city of Shenyang (Kojima 1974; cf. also the conditions in old Babylon, p. 120).

Not the least interesting are the direct connections between rural and urban, implying i.a. regular local transportations of food, raw material for industries, workers, etc., which are involved in the concepts of "*Umland*" and "*Hinterland*". One now, e.g., even speaks of "Urban Recreational Hinterlands" (Mercer 1970). These relationships are expressed in many different ways and develop more or less freely according to physical and cultural restrictions. "Even in countries with an advanced civilisation, rural-urban communications vary according to whether the country is rural or industrialised and whether the population is dense or sparse. The exigencies of physical surroundings are gradually being conquered by technical progress. Political restrictions are perhaps more hampering. Frontiers form a barrier even if no hostility exists between the nations; on the Franco-Swiss border the towns turn their back on each other to some extent, and face towards their respective countries" (Beaujeu-Garnier and Chabot 1967: 426).

In any case urbanization is first and foremost characterized by the expansion of urban people and urban land. It is of interest to note that "At any given stage of technological development, the grander the empire the grander the size and number of its cities" (Sjoberg 1964: 8). We have earlier given approximate figures for the peak population of some of the largest of the ancient cities, and it is thought that the records for Rome were not surpassed until the rise of London in the nineteenth century (cf. K. Davis 1955: 432). To give an idea of proportions it could be calculated that in 1800 about 3 percent, in 1850 about 6.4 percent, in 1900 about 13.6 percent and in 1950 about 29.8 percent of the world population lived in cities with more than 5,000 inhabitants (E. Jones 1966: 32). This percentage is, of course, still higher now.

4.3.2.3. Territoriality and urbanization:
Beginning with the simple assumption that a certain amount of land will support a town and that the larger the area the bigger the town Walter Christaller (1933) developed his central place theory, suggesting that several small tributary areas focusing on small towns would be found within a large tributary area focusing on one central city. The result was a hexagonal hier-archy of regions, each with a nodal point in the form of an urban unit in its centre (cf. also E. Jones 1966: 85-88). In spite of its character of a mostly deductive, theoretical framework with limited direct practical applicability, at least in non-agricultural and non-uniform areas, the central place theory has shown itself to be of great value (cf. J. H. Johnson 1967: 94-102) and doubtless has territorial connotations.

As to the concept of the city-region it can only be made specific and definable as a geographic entity by reference to the precise areal extent of particular associations with the city (cf. *Proceedings of the I.G.U. Symposium in Urban Geography* 1962: 313-318). These associations fall into four cate-gories: trade relations, social and cultural connections, movements of popu-lation and the impact of the city on land uses. The city's spheres of influence or urban fields, combined to a more or less constructed city-region, often have close relations to the state.

"The great city, as a centre of industry, commerce, culture, and adminis-tration, and often as a great political capital, has grown up in the past, and especially in the last hundred years, through access to a unified political and economic unit, the State, and through access to the international worldwide market, . . . 'Here we have an area inhabited by producers and consumers who from a radius usually of over a hundred miles look to one big centre for marketing their products and serving their supplies,' and this region 'has grown to be a potential rival of the State' " (Dickinson 1964: 554; cf. also Gras 1926).

Territorial problems are thus everywhere involved in the connections be-tween rural and urban, but we will here just give two specific examples, the first relating to Western conditions: "The physical effects of contact between agricultural areas and the edges of towns can, then, be quite bad or quite bearable, depending on the type of farming and the type of community. There will be trespass problems but these can be canalised to footpaths in one or two fringe fields without undue effect on crops or stock if the children and parents of the nearby houses can be educated as to the reasons behind normal farming activity. The situation is also improved if the urban development is at a reasonably low density so that gardens of fair size, open spaces and safe roadways are available to the people, and particularly to the children, who live there....

Trespass, both of human beings and dogs, is always said to be serious where the edge of a town abuts on commercial farming, though it is difficult to get unbiased and factual evidence on this point. It is curious, however, that there are many townspeople who would be horrified and indignant at the use of factory workshops as playgrounds and places for interesting walks, who still do not see the farm and its reaction to uninvited guests in the same light. The physical movements of individuals can be regularised by careful marking out of public footpaths, good fencing and adequate notices, especially if changes in the type of farming are being carried out" (Wibberley 1959: 68-69).

In a not very "primitive" African culture there are intricate relations between the rural and the urban field, the last here just in an embryonal stage. The highest real unit of Ibo social and territorial organization is the enlarged village, the "town" or, as it is also called, the village group. This group is the normal landholding unit and it numbers on an average from four to five thousand people. The layout of most Ibo village groups follows a very definite pattern, the broad outlines of which were drawn when the groups were founded. In every case, however, the purpose of the design remains the same, namely, to allow a number of villages to exist reasonably close together as a single local community and yet be able to expand without too much friction. It achieves this by zoning them around one or more central meeting-places and at the same time giving each village the right to occupy the land extending in a specific direction away from this centre.

"This land is of two kinds – houseland (*ala ulo*) and farmland (*ala agu*) – which form two successive zones around the group centre: an inner zone of houseland where people live and grow their oil-palm and other trees and their shade crops, and an outer zone of farmland where people farm but do not live. Each of the component villages has its own segment of this farmland and houseland, and each maintains a path, ritually cleared every year, which leads from the group centre to the village meeting-place and on to the farmland beyond. The villages are thus focused on the village-group centre while their expansion is directed away from it and from each other" (G. I. Jones 1949: 310).

It is, of course, not suggested that this is the way rural and urban territorial

differences are always established, but it is an interesting case not without
parallels elsewhere, e.g., the infields and outfields of Europe (cf. also p. 81).
In any case, with these starting-points we will have a closer look at the constellation "Cities and space".

4.3.3. Cities and space

4.3.3.1. General remarks:
When we now definitely enter into the actual towns and cities it could be wise
first to give some general spatial characteristics of the urban world. For "All
this taken together indicates the continuous but orderly processes of change
leading to the development of basic spatial patterns broadly generalizable
from city to city" (Reiss 1957a: 226).

The city consists of two primary components: urban man and urban environment. An understanding of the dynamic interactions between these two
elements is facilitated by recognizing that the city is an ecosystem, an open
system which like other multifactorial units of this kind is poorly understood
as a whole. And "space is a biological requirement of urban inhabitants that
has received slight attention until recently. It has always been obvious that
cities consume space as they grow physically. It has been less apparent, even
when the efforts of city planners, architects, and social scientists are taken
into account, that living and working space for the individual inhabitant is
also a significant biological need" (Marcus and Detwyler 1972: 14).

Among the primary ecological processes connected with urbanization we
will, with R. N. Morris (1971: 101-113), name the following complementary
pairs: concentration – deconcentration, centralization – decentralization, invasion – retreat, succession – withdrawal. The first pair is related to changes in
the distribution of the population in space. Such changes may be the result of
two processes, unequal volumes of migration and differences in the rates of
natural increase through births and deaths between one area and another. In
Western countries it has been found that concentration in cities generally
results from cityward migration, since urban birth-rates have been below
rural birth-rates and city death-rates have tended to be slightly higher than
those in the countryside.

Centralization and its counterpart refer to the increasing or decreasing
dominance by the city or its central area over the surrounding region as the
number and types of services performed within the region come to be more or
less exclusively found at the centre. While concentration therefore is primarily
bound to population, centralization depends on the location of commerce

and industry and especially on the policy-making involved in these and other activities.

Invasion and retreat arise in a situation where there is segregation of residential from commercial and industrial land or of differing types of residential areas. The first term denotes the arrival in an area of other social groups or of a new type of land user who was not found there previously, and retreat signifies the gradual movement of the established users out of the area.

While invasion represents the moving of groups through space, succession can be regarded as a movement through time within the same space. Succession also marks the final stage of the sequence which began with invasion, and together with its complement, withdrawal, it means that the recent arrivals dominate the area, that their organization and values have assumed control, perhaps even that they are in the majority numerically (cf. Ward 1964). Here this should be stressed: "First, territoriality is a major factor giving unit character to populations. Second, space is simultaneously a requisite for the activities of any organizational unit and an obstacle which must be overcome in establishing interunit relationships. Finally, space – like time – furnishes a convenient and invariant set of reference points for observation, and observed spatio-temporal regularities and rhythms furnish convenient indicators of structural relationships" (Duncan and Schnore 1959-1960: 136).

4.3.3.2. The city as a point and as an area:
In principle it is possible to look at the modern city either as a point or as an area, just as the ancient one could be regarded as magnet or container and animal territories as nucleated or areal. Concerning the first view it is said, for instance, that "The concept of urban space, thus, takes its meaning from the organization of the nucleated, interdependent set of activities whose characteristic form a millennium ago was the town, a century ago the city, today the metropolis, and a decade hence, perhaps, megalopolis" (Wingo 1963: 10). And it is further reported: "We are entitled to regard nucleation as a basic aspect of the city because relationships among units of the urban community are not spatially randomized, but rather tend to be focused or concentrated at one or a few points. The concept of nucleation is broad enough to admit of multiple nucleation, although it is often true that multi-centered cities have a single, more or less distinct, predominant center" (Duncan 1957: 357).

The process of urbanization inevitably involves a multiplication of the points of population concentration in a given territory. These points are closely integrated into networks of cities on the local, regional, national and international level (cf. Reiss 1957b: 81). Thus our cities are not only *per se* spatial, they are also placed in space in a way which does not seem to be random. A nodal point seems here to be best described as the place of greatest convenience. The value of nodality is thus determined by the number of possible services rendered, goods procured, contacts made, etc., at a certain place. "Nodality can, thus, be defined as a behavioral act of man, not simply a geometric point or circulation intersect. In behavioral terms, a nodal location is that place where the individual has the greatest freedom to interact" (Berry and Horton 1970: 170). In fact a spatial hierarchy is the specification of a nodal system, and the hierarchical structure and nodal pattern are both the consequences and the indices of the division of labour and territorial specialization.

An areal conception of urban space is, of course, also defendable, the more so as urbanization goes on. In any case it should be possible to put the case this way: "An important elaboration of the urban-place conception, which re-gards the urban unit as a regional phenomenon, assigns to each place the surrounding territory with its population and activities; and the urban region is thus conceived as the node plus its hinterland. . . . The place in the hierarchy is also a function of population size, and population size is related to the kinds of functions that are performed at the various settlements. The most spe-cialized cities serve the largest territories; the least specialized cities primarily serve the local farming areas" (Webber 1964b: 83).

It should also be kept in mind that there is a clear distinction between the natural area and the administrative area. The city is broken up into adminis-trative units, such as the ward, the school district, the police precinct, and the health district, for the purposes of administrative convenience, and the object is usually to apportion either the population or area of the city into equal units. "The natural area, on the other hand, is a unit in the physical structure of the city, typified by a physical individuality and the characteristic attitudes, sentiments, and interests of the people segregated within it. Administrative areas and natural areas may coincide. In practice they rarely do. Administrative lines cut across the boundaries of natural areas, ignoring their existence" (Zorbaugh 1926: 224).

Without doubt the most radical and far-reaching way to tackle the spatial city concept is that of the urban field. "The inherited form of the city no longer corresponds to reality. The spatial structure of contemporary American civilization consists of metropolitan core regions and the intermet-ropolitan peripheries. The former have achieved very high levels of economic and cultural development at the expense of the latter, leaving the periphery in a decadent state. Current and projected trends in technology and taste suggest that a new element of spatial order is coming into being – the urban field – which will unify both core and periphery within a single matrix" (Friedmann and Miller 1965: 312).

Regarding the dynamics behind the spatial structure of the city one can distinguish between centripetal forces of attraction and coagulation, centrifugal forces of dispersion and disintegration and forces of spatial differentiation, which result in the segregation of buildings, persons and activities in distinct areal groupings (cf. Dickinson 1967: 60).

All these structural phenomena are of great territorial interest, and we will next examine the limits and forms of the city.

4.3.3.3.   Limit and form of cities:
Of course the dynamic theories cannot conceal this fact: "Human space is limited, not boundless" (Morrill 1965: 312). And it should be remembered that: "The Latin word *urbs* is related to *orbis*, the circle. Like the English 'town' and the Slavic '*gorod*', related to 'yard' and 'girdle', it denotes as the basic characteristic of the urban phenomenon the enclosure which separates it from the open country. This is the city as it has existed through recorded history: a static unit, confined and defined by its enclosing boundary, and with a definite pattern of its internal organization, in which each part has a stable and defined relation to the whole" (Blumenfeld 1964: 75).

That this is important even from a practical point of view can be shown by means of an example. It was said about the Bangala people of the Upper Congo River in Africa: "The boundaries of a town are well defined, and the islands belonging to a town are well known to all the other towns in the neighbourhood. If an animal is killed on ground owned by a town other than that to which the huntsman belongs he has to send a portion – generally the head – to the chief of the town that claims that ground" (Weeks 1909: 123). Further, it was reported that the land surrounding a town belongs to the people who live in the town. Certain landmarks, as streams, forests, etc., are agreed upon as boundaries. Within the boundary the inhabitants of the town are free to make their farms and build their houses where they like, provided the land is not already occupied by someone else. Priority of occupation is the only title recognized (cf. Weeks 1913, cited after Herskovits 1940: 325-326).

In fact, the first act in the Etruscan ritual of city-founding, after consulting the omens, was to cut a furrow in the ground marking the new city boundary (Lynch 1954: 60). This leads us more deeply into the history of urban form. The old Egyptian hieroglyph for town was a circle with a double-line cross inside. Undoubtedly this sign represents a town plan of circular form, where the houses are distributed into four quarters with two streets crossing at right angles at the central point. This plan is nowhere said to be in accordance with that found by archaeologists, neither with more or less well-known settlements, nor with other evidence (Brunner 1957:618).

Contrary to what is said here, a circular form of towns dominated, e.g. among the Hittites, and plan layouts quite similar to the hieroglyph are known. It was even stated that "the circular and the rectangular form have long coexisted in all parts of the Old Orient", and during the Medieval Age cities with a circular ground-plan were still numerous, for example in France (Lavedan 1926: 56-63, 250-280). Without doubt, the circular form is the most natural and the easiest to defend, and it seems reasonable to assume that it has always been the primary one where conditions have so permitted. It is also in perfect accordance with territorial theory: "It will be clear that the territory will tend to take the form of a circle if there are no outside forces affecting it" (R. J. Martin 1969: 214).

The Egyptian hieroglyph was also interpreted thus: "The cross represents the convergence of roads which bring in and redistribute men, merchandise and ideas. This convergence entails a quickening of communication which is nearly always a great advantage, but may become a handicap if speed grows so frantic that the city has no time to keep its share of the incoming goods and to impress its mark on the goods it re-exports. The circle, in the hieroglyph, indicates a moat or a wall. This need not be materially erected so long as it is morally present, to keep the citizens together, sheltered from the cold, wide world, conscious of belonging to a unique team, proud of being different from the open country and germane to one another" (Lopez 1966: 27-28).

A circular form is also reflected in the concentric zone theory of Burgess and Park (1923, cited after J. H. Johnson 1967: 164), where the city is divided into five circles, as well as in the sector theory of Hoyt (1939, cited after Thomlinson 1969: 146). Earlier, in 1903, Hurd (1924: 47) presented the star theory of urban form, which is characteristic i.a. of many metropolises, and the more recent muliple nuclei theory (Harris and Ullman 1945: 13) implies that several centres have contributed to the form of the final city. It has been found that the concentric zone hypothesis is essentially supported with respect to urbanization, while the sector hypothesis fits best with social rank (Anderson and Egeland 1961).

4.3.3.4. City structure:
Besides exterior form and limit there is another feature of the city which is of

utmost territorial importance, namely interior structure. Of course not just the morphological elements are of interest but also how they function, which is reflected in the two principal aspects of the city's make-up, urban morphology and urban ecology. In his valuable survey "The Form of Cities" Lynch (1954) divided the matter into shape, size, density, grain and internal pattern. Primarily the two last of these items are included in what we here denote as structure. Lynch stressed that some primitive city types in Africa and Asia have relatively little differentiation: "Houses of all kinds are mixed together; there are few distinct focal points. It is difficult to perform large-scale functions, to locate any particular activity or to service it easily. Such a town astonishes and confuses a visitor from our own cities, which, though often called chaotic, represent a much higher level of organization" (op. cit. p. 57).

Medieval cities, however, had a well-developed sorting-out of uses, there were sharp cleavages on occupational and class lines and one or more precise focal points such as a market square, a cathedral or a castle. Thus the "grain" of such cities was relatively fine and sharp, while it is much coarser in modern ones, where there is differentiation on a much larger scale.

Of certain interest in this context is that the city should be imageable, to use the terminology of Lynch. This means that it should be so clearly organized that the resident can carry an accurate picture in his mind of the community's major spatial forms. "A stereotype of a metropolitan plan fashioned in this spirit would show a dominant central area to which major radial transportation routes led but through which major surface transportation did not unduly cut; articulated residential communities, in turn broken down into neighborhoods; industrial districts carefully bounded and, if necessary, buffered; outlying commercial centers tied in with the transportation network and centered, if possible, in major communities or sectors; and, at the outer bounds of the urbanized areas, a greenbelt, clearly marking the break between city and country and controlling lateral expansion" (Foley 1964: 68).

In American cities the boundaries between areas are often blurred and indistinct and there is a broad segregation, with residential areas broken up and separated by wide factory areas or green belts. As to the internal pattern it has to do with streets, squares and buildings, their directions, magnitudes, proportions and combinations. There is in modern cities, for instance, a tendency to make open places instead of buildings dominant. But "The sense of urbanity and the function of the city as a meeting place for large numbers would be destroyed if an entire city were given over to this new pattern. . . . The modern city requires a rhythmical balance between enclosure and openness, concentration and freedom" (Lynch 1954: 63).

Now, an important facet of man's use of the environment is his organization of it into territories. They influence behavior from one location to another since territorial transactions with elaborate cultural rules are associated with such parcels. The kinds of division and accompanying rules affect the character of each man's life space (T. Alexander 1973: 13).

Thus it could be stated that "the city, and particularly the modern city, is the consummate example of the territorial unit" (Hawley 1950: 216). "The ecological conception of the city regards it as a permanent nucleated settlement of population within a circumscribed territory..." (Duncan 1957: 357). It is, of course, possible to contend that the essential qualities of urbanity are cultural in character, not territorial, and that these qualities are not necessarily tied to the conceptions that see the city as a spatial phenomenon (Webber 1963: 30). But one cannot deny that: "An urban region, comprising an urban settlement and its surrounding hinterland, is a spatially delimited territory. Although the margins are always indistinct and overlap, at any given level in the hierarchy of urban regions each urban region is territorially discrete; except at their margins, no two urban regions encompass the same territory" (Webber 1964b: 116).

Recalling the conditions in animals (p. 28). we can in sum conclude that both the pointal (nodal, nucleated) and the areal views of the city, not to say its at least in the old days very common circular form, are perfectly consistent with the theories of human behavioural territories. Porteous (1971) even tried to divide such spatial phenomena into urban macro-space (home range), urban meso-space (normal territory) and urban micro-space (personal space), the occurrence of which will now be traced, beginning with the contrasts: little town and megalopolis.

4.3.4. From little town to megalopolis

4.3.4.1. People and density:
The presence of a large number of people in a small space is commonly accepted as a necessary part of city definitions. We can assume, then, that cities involve a special kind of relation between population and area. The significance of this relationship does not, however, depend solely on the correlation of population size and urban space. Even though all cities had the same density, the spatial structure of large cities would no doubt be quite different from that of small ones, that is, we would expect the spatial pattern of activity to be different for 25,000 persons living in 5 square miles than that

for 2,500,000 living in an area of 500 square miles. The radius of a city – supposing it to be shaped as a circle – is not proportional to its area, but to the square root of its area (cf. Ogburn and Duncan 1964: 132-136).

"Population statistics on towns terminate abruptly at arbitrary lower limits, usually 2,000 to 3,000. Many centers of less than the minimum population do fulfill urban functions and therefore belong in the functional hierarchy of towns. On the other hand, many towns that are included in urban statistics because their populations exceed the arbitrary minimum are not towns at all in function. Small towns with rudimentary urban functions may include widely varying agricultural components, so that their populations are poorly correlated with their urban functions. Lack of comprehensive data on functions of small towns both smaller and larger than the minimum required for inclusion in urban statistics precludes any attempt to measure the shape of the town-size pyramid near its base" (Stewart 1958: 231-232).

When comparing cities of varying magnitude it is characteristic that there is an increase of population density with increasing city size as measured by the numbers of inhabitants and as seen in figures for population per square mile in urbanized areas in 1950 (Ogburn and Duncan 1964: 132).

City population:	Persons per square mile:
2,500-5,000	1,765
5,000-10,000	2,226
10,000-25,000	2,721
25,000-50,000	3,339
50,000-250,000	3,869
250,000-1,000,000	4,468
1,000,000-3,000,000	6,776
3,000,000 or more	7,679

4.3.4.2. The giant city:
The last two of the just tabulated categories, at least, belong to the metropolis, a term not easier to define than other urban units. "Compared with an ordinary city, a metropolis is usually larger, denser, more powerful, taller, less agricultural, more commercial and industrial, more parasitic, more packed with commuters, and more varied" (Thomlinson 1969: 71). The Standard Metropolitan Statistical Area of the U.S.A. signifies an area containing a nuclear city of at least 50,000 inhabitants, but this is not applicable to the

general use of the concept. Metropolitan area is also defined as a concentration of at least 500,000 people living within a region in which the travelling time from the outskirts to the centre is no more than about 40 minutes (Blumenfeld 1967: 49). In fact "metropolis" is predominantly used as an economic term and is characterized by the specialization of function by place (Dickinson 1964: 10-13).

As suggested London was the first occidental city to attain one million inhabitants in modern times – probably the first ever, having surpassed Paris around the beginning of the 18th century. In the 20th there has been a dramatic increase in the number of great metropolises. Prior to 1900 suburban populations were relatively small, and census data emphasized the magnitude of central cities. But when population figures for 1950 were made known it was found that the world had 83 metropolitan areas with a population of one million or more; by 1962 this number had increased to 133 with a total of 335 million people or 11 percent of the earth's entire population (Hoyt and Pickard 1969: 198).

"To assess fully the momentous transformations now developing in the relationships between the distribution of people and the space they occupy, it may be useful to remember that while only a small fraction of mankind has lived and worked in the past at high densities, that is, above 1,000 per square mile, at present a large and rising proportion of mankind lives at residential densities of 5,000 to 30,000 per square mile and works at densities of more than 50,000 (and, in the largest business districts of great cities, at densities approaching 200,000 per square mile)" (Gottman 1969: 20). Recently, it was reported that the most crowded wards of Delhi, Bombay and Calcutta in India show almost incredible densities ranging from 300,000 persons per square mile to over 450,000 (Murphey 1969: 67).

Thus the city of former days is being replaced by a new entity, the metropolitan community, with a distribution of population shading off from extreme congestion to relative sparseness, yet with some uniformity of character. Three dimensions would be required in order to give a clear picture of this metropolitan organization of today, for some of our metropolises are regional in character, some are interregional, and one or two are international. "Neighboring metropolises compete for trade and prestige, and the boundaries between the territories they control may be as fluctuating and as hotly disputed as though each were an independent principality" (McKenzie 1968: 245).

The idea that each nodal settlement should be governed by a single, separate municipality is a clear application of these concepts, and the proposal that each metropolitan settlement should similarly be steered by a separate unit is largely a territorial expansion of the same idea. The fundamental concepts are reflected, too, in the typical general plan that recommends a segregated land-use pattern. The proposals for new towns amidst a greenbelt and for unitary neighbourhoods with sharply bounded parks and highways are probably another expression (Webber 1964b: 132- 133).

Conurbation is a term that was coined in 1915 by Patrick Geddes (1949: 14- 15) to designate a formless, undifferentiated urban mass extending for dozens or hundreds of miles with high and relatively even density. For approximately the same phenomenon Gottman (e.g., 1966b: 4) introduced the word megalopolis, which has been widely used as signifying urbanized regions containing several metropolitan areas (for a detailed definition of megalopolis, see Nagashima 1974).

The maps of distribution of urban land use in megalopolis have got an increasingly nebulous character. This is due to a desire of many people to have their residence in rural landscapes, to the vogue of the suburban way of life among certain categories of urbanites and to the advantages of decentralized location for new industrial and even bureaucratic establishments. This phenomenon, called metropolitanization in the United States, has developed in megalopolis on a scale that is so far unique in the nation and in the world. Over vast areas there is an almost colloidal interpenetration of urban and rural that gives the region a special quality. Despite this interpenetration, megalopolis has also continued to build up its several enormous nuclei of densely occupied, congested central cities (cf. Gottman 1966b: 390-392).

4.3.4.3. Attraction and repulsion of large cities:
It has been discussed whether a town, even a very large city, can be classified as an organic entity. "Even though we reject the idea that the aspect of human society called town could represent a living being in a physical-biological sense, we must agree, at least, that both its structure and vital manifestations appear as if we actually had an organic phenomenon in front of us" (H. Peters 1954: 35). In any case it is inhabited by organisms, leaving their marks on it.

Sometimes it has been maintained that the concept of home-love is not applicable to metropolitan societies, but this is denied by Schäfer (1968: 110-111): "The size of the community does not influence the intensity of the home feelings which differ only in content between persons in Paris, Berlin and Munich and inhabitants of villages or of the countryside. This difference means that home, for the people of a big city, is not limited to the surround-

ings of the house, the family and work. Home in the metropolis is not restricted to either the public or to the private sphere but develops as a
permanent interaction between both".

In an extensive German investigation it was shown that 22 percent of
people interviewed liked to live in cities with more than 200,000 inhabitants,
37 percent in urban areas with 50,000 to 200,000 inhabitants and 37 percent in
cities with less than 50,000 (Oeter 1974: 3). In view of such figures it can be
asked: What physical deficiencies make the great metropolises we know less
than satisfying as places in which to live? First and most obvious is the burden
of perceptual stress imposed by the city. The second fault is a lack of visible
identity. A third source of distress in our cities is their illegibility. The fourth
disability is its rigidity, its lack of openness (cf. Lynch 1965: 209).

"The form of the metropolis, then, is its formlessness, even as its aim is its
own aimless expansion. Those who work within the ideological limits of this
regime have only a quantitative conception of improvement: they seek to
make its buildings higher, its streets broader, its parking lots more ample:
they would multiply bridges, highways, tunnels, making it ever easier to get
in and out of the city, but constricting the amount of space available within
the city for any other purpose than transportation itself" (Mumford 1961:
544).

Among the many dangers for mankind involved in megalopolis, perhaps
the most immediate one is that we might run short of territories, of enough
space for living, that the whole area will become so crowded that people will
not be able to move freely about in it, and that there will be no choice left as to
where to live, how to stay, what to do for work and for recreation. "To have
'enough space' has often meant to individuals *the free choice of 'a place in the
sun'*, and such individual freedom to choose one's mode of life and to change it
has long been associated with free land, especially in American history. This
association of man's freedom and the abundance of free open land has underlined the whole epic of the frontier and the legend of the West. As a person
brought up with such concepts looks at what is developing in Megalopolis,
fear may arise concerning the crowding of people and the scarcity of space..."
(Gottman 1966b: 242).

In connection with metropolises, there are manifold manifestations of behavioural territoriality, even though lack of limits and nebulous structure
may often conceal phenomena and obstruct their observation on this scale,
while crowding on the other hand should stress them. Certainly it is easier to
trace these spatial reactions in lesser units, and so we now proceed to a treatment of urban cores and suburbs.

4.3.5. Urban core and suburb

4.3.5.1. Content of the core:

We have to realize first that the spatial order of the city is founded on the desires and resources of its inhabitants as these are constrained and directed by the encompassing society. In the ancient city the simplicity of the ecological and social systems was reflected in the resulting spatial pattern. Self-contained quarters and a general zonal arrangement, with central-city location being the preserve of the elite provided the basic plan. In the modern city a more complicated order is apparent. Each differentiating property tends to follow its own distinct design. The need to be within reasonable distance of work and the attraction of the central areas are reflected in the sectorial distribution of social rank. Once identified with this division, developments in a given direction tend to perpetuate (cf. Timms 1971: 252).

A standard feature in the city of the Western world is the concentration of administrative, financial, commercial, cultural and amusement facilities within a central urban core. Frequently this core coincides spatially with the city as it was before the great urban explosion of our industrial age. The typical concentration of these central activities mirrors their interdependence, and other activities are attracted to them (cf. Elkins 1973: 43-48).

The spatial qualities of the core have long been diminishing. "The attractiveness of the centre of the modern metropolis now mostly depends on its qualities as a consumer's paradise. Its remaining importance for orientation has changed. The transcience of stop-over periods and contacts, the enormous buildings, the human double role as passer-by and as user of traffic routes isolated in his car have restricted the spontaneity of the social experience of the centre" (Stöber 1964: 37).

Various, above all economic, advantages have produced great competition for a site in the urban core among those enterprises which can benefit from such a location. As a result very high land values are found in the city centre, and in turn these values have strongly influenced other features. Most notable is the high intensity of land use, which is expressed in the concentration of multistoried buildings in the central area. This indicates an attempt to erect the maximum floor space which is legally possible on these core sites. A sequel has been the three-dimensional quality of city centres, which is now a most noticeable phenomenon (cf. *Urban Core and Inner City* 1967).

"A further characteristic of city centres has been the decline of their residential population which has accompanied the increased concentration of commercial activities within them. The number of people living in the historic

cores of Western cities has been falling steadily since the middle of the nineteenth century, the precise date depending on the individual circumstances of
a particular settlement" (J. H. Johnson 1967: 113-116). This redistribution of
population has encouraged some geographers to describe the centre as the
"dead heart" of the city, but that is perhaps not an adequate description, since
far more noticeable than the absence of night-time population is the intense
concentration of people there during the working day.

4.3.5.2. Suburbs and satellites:
In fact, the last century was already an age of distinct suburbanization. The
rapid growth of cities is always a twin process to internal transformation and
readjustment combined with outward expansion. For the urban community
is a dynamic organism, constantly changing in a variety of ways to meet new
needs and conditions. This was also true during the course of the powerful
and steady increase of urbanization in the nineteenth century. Towns grew in
size and in height, too, in their central parts as new constructions went up.
Even at that time, the existing town-areas were built up to such an extent that
the growing populations were forced to seek new residential areas outside the
former city boundaries (cf. Kant 1957: 244-245).

"The attraction of new suburbs, with new houses and new standards of
amenities, is reflected in a zonal arrangement of family status. The younger
the area, the more young people; the older the area, the more old people and
the fewer families with young children. The zones in transition around the
central business district and on the rural-urban periphery provide a haven for
despised minorities and attractive location for all those who welcome the
anonymity and freedom from traditional social controls characteristic of the
urban way of life. Since each set of differentiating properties is, to a greater or
lesser extent, independent of all the others, the resulting spatial pattern is
highly complex. It is unlikely that any simple model, stressing the influence of
one or other spatial arrangement, will provide an acceptable description of
the modern city" (Timms 1971: 252).

The spectacular population growth of suburbs and the relative, often also
absolute decline of central city populations since the Second World War
suggest the emergence of new dispersed forms of metropolitan settlement. As
the U.S. Population Commission noted in a recent report, 15 out of the 21
central cities with a 1960 population of one-half million or more had lost
people by 1970. In fact, declining central cities lost more inhabitants in the
1960's than were lost by decreasing rural counties. Over half of the 1970

metropolitan population lived outside the central city, and suburban areas had captured almost all the metropolitan growth during the preceding decade.

It was, however, stated: "While these data are interesting, the exact form of this new metropolitan settlement pattern remains unclear. There has always been a tendency for metropolitan areas to expand on the outskirts, and the decline of central city populations may be due as much to a shortage of land for residential development as to a particular desire of urbanites to live in the suburbs.... Most of the recent changes in population density may be seen as a consequence of changes in the number of dwelling units. In other words, the growth of the city has been relatively synonymous with the amount of new housing units. However, population growth of areas has been checked to some extent by the trend toward a decreasing number of persons per dwelling unit" (Guest 1973: 53, 67). Yet, these explanations cannot stand for more than part of the very marked suburban development.

A working definition of suburbs is that they are "*those urbanized, residential communities which are outside the corporate limits of a large central city, but which are culturally and economically dependent upon the central city*" (Dobriner 1958: XVII). The term satellite has been used in similar context, but the difference seems to be that suburbs are primarily dormitory towns without their own production, while satellite cities provide jobs for their own residents. "In spatial terms, both suburbs and satellites are often physically indistinguishable from adjacent areas, hemmed in on all sides by other municipalities" (Schnore 1957-1958: 122).

For the moment the suburb is in a decisive transition from its traditional role as dependent "urban fringe" to independent "neocity". "The significance of suburbia was not put in proper perspective until the fires of the urban riots began to fade in the late sixties, and 1970 census figures confirmed what many had suspected about the outward movement of urban populations – that America had become suburbanized on such a scale and in such a comprehensive way as to threaten the viability of the historic city" (Masotti 1973: 15-16), a problem which today is real in many countries.

It should, however, not be forgotten that there is, in some parts of the world, also a tendency of retreat from the suburbs to the core of the city. But this is probably a consequence of the fact that suburbanized areas in a way are becoming filled or crowded too, and that their distances both from the real countryside and from the central core is steadily increasing (cf. Chermayeff and Alexander 1963: 59-67).

4.3.5.3. Suburban territories:

The territorial differences between urban cores and suburbs are, of course, evident. Mumford (1961: 487-488) reported: "Let me emphasize the demand for space, which changed the whole scale of urban planning once the protective fortification ceased to be essential for security. Whatever else the suburb has stood for, it has demanded an enlargement of the areas of open green and garden, as proper appurtenances of the city. What only kings could demand once, was now the prerogative of every commoner who could get hold of the land itself. The more constricted the old quarters of the city, the more closely packed its streets and houses, the greater was the visual relief of the suburb's openness: indeed part of the esthetic value of the suburb, its special psychological virtue, springs from the daily shuttling to and from the city, with its alternation of openness and enclosure, freedom and constriction, easy movement and clogged traffic, spaciousness and overcrowding".

It should here once more be stressed that even the old suburbs are now expanding very fast nearly everywhere with increasing personal wealth and improvements in transportation. In the United States suburban living has become the principal mode of habitation, and there can be no doubt that millions of suburbanites live where they do because they like it and that they consciously choose to be there for reasons which are very real and important to them. "How many men, given their choice, do not forsake the congested city for more wide open spaces? ... The qualities suburbanites are seeking – single family dwellings, home-ownership, private outdoor green space, open countryside, local government, easy access to the city centre ... must somehow become the raw materials of the future environment" (Junker 1971: 48, 51).

The most frequently reported changes that do take place in connection with suburbanization are not caused by the move to the suburb but are in the first place reasons for moving there. These reasons are based on aspirations for space, for ownership of a single-family house that are today satisfied only in suburbia. "Homeownership gives people the feeling of having an equity – or sharing it with the bank – more privacy from neighbors than they had either in apartments or Philadelphia row-houses, and an opportunity to improve the house and yard in their own, individual way. This not only satisfies desires for self-expression and creativity, but for joint family activity around the house that brings the family closer together" (Gans 1963: 186-187).

Still more clear become the drives of behavioural territoriality in *The Squeeze* by Edward Higbee (1960: 89-91), who stresses that suburbia is essentially the nation's year-around residential nursery, riding high on the boom of human multiplication and the protective instincts of parents, who want to give their spawn a sporting chance. "It is today's response to the old-age nesting urge which, from the beginning of time, has been the most important business of living things. Newly married parents stick to fundamentals. Instinctively discounting world-shaking threats of holocaust each young couple seeks a plot of earth on which it may rear its own. That is the essence of suburbia's popularity. It is the habitat that in our time comes closest to what the human animal requires for its basic task" (cf. p. 120).

From the environmental standpoint, the most remarkable feature of suburbia is this mass consumption of space and its ever accelerating conversion of open farm land into the more rigid pattern of residential use that for all human time is not likely to change again so drastically, except where demolition will open wider roads or remove homes to make way for commercial structures as the community grows. This is the inevitable consequence of locating families on an acre of ground that in the city might have supported a hundred apartments.

"The children in a single-family Cape Cod cottage on an ordinary 70 × 120 foot suburban house lot have more room of their own to play in than is provided for youngsters from 250 apartments in New York's new public-housing projects, where between three and four square yards of playground are the official quota for each apartment. Such are the facts of life which generate enthusiasm for suburbia. In its allocation of space for living, the modern commuters' development is a triumph of parental instinct over the inhuman forces of an urban-industrial society, which too often values the job more highly than the family that the job supports" (loc. cit.).

If, thus, there seem to be quite evident territorial urges behind the movement from urban core to suburb, the phenomena of garden city, garden colony and summer villa, which will now be inspected, must be no less interesting in the context.

4.3.6. Garden city, garden colony and summer villa

4.3.6.1. Garden and garden city:
A simple definition runs like this: "The garden is an enclosed, intensively cultivated piece of earth" (Schäfer 1968:90). In certain meanings, garden culture is without doubt much older than agriculture. Rüstow (1963:285-286) gave the tentative periods in use as about 100,000 years for the former and 12,000 to 15,000 years for the latter of the two cultivation forms. A much shorter history, of course, characterizes the garden cultivated

primarily for pleasure, even though this, too, has been a practice for several thousand years, mostly in connection with sovereigns, nobles and other prominent persons.

It can be noted here that the concept of garden together with that of park is already recorded in the first book of the Bible, and the background seems to be the following: "The Persian designation for such a park is taken over into Greek as '*parádeisos*.' From this comes the term 'paradise' for the garden of Eden in Genesis, the park where Jahve walked in the cold of the evening" (op cit. p. 288). On the whole it is very difficult to define the differences between garden – particularly in the German form "*Baumgarten*", garden of trees, above all fruit-trees – and park, but it is at least a question of rather large areas and high trees, when the latter concept is used.

An interesting development parallel with and perhaps the consequence of the great population increase on earth is that of the Chinese miniature garden over the last 3,000 years. "To sum up, the cosmic-garden was first reduced to the size of a hunting park in the suburb of the capital; then to a rich but private estate; at last it shrank into a dish, where, instead of enjoying and meditating on its several parts seriatim, the philosophically-minded might comprehend the whole construction at once. Its final form was its simplest and therefore its most perfect – a single bit of stone" (Schafer 1963: 26).

As a common phenomenon the pleasure type of garden hardly developed at all until the last few centuries and was then predominantly coupled to the city. Starting-point for the garden city movement became not only the farm garden and the feudal park but still more the industrial society with its growing population and urbanization. Especially in the oldest of the industrialized countries, England, the urban habitation situation was during the nineteenth century often terrible as a consequence of lack of regulations for building and density as well as special tax conditions leading to overcrowding and all the herewith connected problems. And the situation seemed to be not much better on the European continent (cf. Berlepsch-Valendàs 1912).

It was as a reaction against the unsatisfactory habitation conditions, particularly of industrial cities, that Ebenezer Howard launched his garden city idea 1898 and four years later he published his famous book "Garden Cities of To-morrow" (Eb. Howard 1946). Of course there were gardens earlier inside and outside cities, but this was a quite new integration of rural and urban. The first point to be observed is that the land in the garden city was not directly parceled out into individually-owned parts. Second and most important was controlled growth and limited population. The third notion introduced was that of functional balance, e.g., between town and countryside.

"Howard, in other words, not merely avoided the weaknesses of the specialized dormitory suburb and the specialized company town: he also eliminated the possibility of deterioration through success – unlimited agglomeration. Howard may be said to be the first modern thinker about cities who had a sound sociological conception of the dynamics of rational urban growth" (Mumford 1938: 397-398).

The garden city was proposed to have a population of some 30,000 people in an area of 1,000 acres surrounded by a permanent belt of agricultural land of 5,000 acres. As early as 1903 the first application of the idea was made at Letchworth, 34 miles from London, and in 1919 a second grew up at Welwyn, closer to the metropolis. Both were successful without the overdeveloped centres and underdeveloped peripheries of unplanned market towns and with enough open space (cf. Gallion 1950: 91-93). At the same time one of the architects of Letchworth, Sir Raymond Unwin, demonstrated that even from an economic standpoint there is nothing to be gained by overcrowding. He showed that "vast amounts of money had been wasted in duplicating unnecessary streets and in robbing people of garden space under the false notion that crowding houses together would reduce their costs: ..." (Mumford 1946: 31).

It was rightly vindicated that a garden or other plot of ground constitutes a *sine qua non* for perfect human habitation. "To an individual settlement should belong a private space under the sky. In its ideal state this takes the form of a yard or a garden, directly attainable from the apartment. The claim for privacy is satisfied only when there is no observation from the street or the neighbours" (Bernatzky 1974: 22). It was even stated that a garden represents man's ideal picture of his world and as most people are imprinted by the society to which they belong, the consequence is that in every epoch the garden mirrors the dream of its contemporaries. Thus the garden is created according to our own measures (D. Clifford, cited after Bernatzky 1974: 21-22).

How strong the drives for private space and ground among modern congested city dwellers are is evident from some German investigations. In Hannover, with 160,000 households at the time, about a fourth had a garden and more than a third frequented private gardens. Of the rest about half desired a garden, as many a garden colony as a house with garden. "The wish for a garden was never so strong in the city before" (Gleichmann 1963: 53). In a similar study from Münster it was shown that "nearly two-thirds of the inhabitants of the villa quarter mentioned undisturbed habitation as the most important function of the garden. Predominantly the garden is seen as a mechanism for isolating us from our neighbours. Thus it is suggested that it functions to create and maintain spatial distance and that this is aimed at through personally owned homes" (Schäfer 1968: 93).

4.3.6.2. Garden colony movement:
As to the garden colony movement, it started in Germany with the "*Armengärten*" of Kiel, 1822, but it was not until about 1850 that there was a more general progress. The units were called "*Gartenkolonie*", "*Kleingarten*", "*Laubenkolonie*" or "*Schrebergarten*", the last named after a physician, D. G. M. Schreber of Leipzig, who was interested in the physical education of youth and in health colonies (cf. Hessing 1958: 7-9). Some traces perhaps go back to the medieval cabbage lands or to the regular farming by city-dwellers up towards our own time (cf. Mangoldt 1907: 671).

It can hardly be denied that there has been a seemingly instinctive search for garden surrogates among industrialized citizens. "We all know how one encloses a small area rather simply by one's own efforts and if possible without costs on waste land or on sites that are not yet ready for building. Here one raises a little shelter of tinware or other provisional material, and then one cultivates in poor soil and with tremendous efforts one's own vegetables and flowers" (Rüstow 1963: 294-295).

But now there was an organized movement by means of which factory workers in particular could rent 100-500 square meters for cultivation during a certain time within special, fenced areas on the outskirts of or outside cities under different constraints, e.g., that no heated settlement for permanent habitation should be erected. Indubitably the garden colony movement, which has expanded above all in Belgium, Holland and the Scandinavian countries in addition to Germany, was of great economic and nutritive importance, particularly in the beginning and during wars, but there have been other and, with time, more decisive factors behind it (cf. Helle 1965).

As early as 1907 it was said that there were 30,000 "*Laubenkolonien*" in and around Berlin alone. The garden director of another German metropolis declared not long ago that "in the urban situation of today the allotment gardener is without doubt a favoured citizen who can cultivate and otherwise exploit 300 square meters of ground while most people must be content with some few square meters of open town space which statistically belong to them" (Sallman 1961, cited after Gleichmann 1963: 30).

It is also of special interest that garden colonies could be rented by everyone. "Only garden allotments are independent of one's habitation and settlement and constitute in the metropolis the only form of ground property and ground use which are theoretically open to all, even to those who belong to the lowest social classes" (Schäfer 1968: 99). It is no wonder that in Germany the demand for lots is far greater than the supply.

In spite of the possibility of expropriation by the authorities there is also now, after a period of declining interest, again a great desire for allotment contracts in the Scandinavian countries. New types of areas are laid out. Together with conventional right-angle ground plots the municipalities of Copenhagen, Denmark have, e.g., opened wagon-wheel-like clusters of 24 allotments each, arranged around a car parking lot at the hub with large, grassy, open spaces between the circles. The buildings here are so good that the families with allotments can live just outside the metropolis all summer, the colonies thus functioning as summer villas (Graves 1974: 260-261).

One of the very few modern investigations of garden colonies available (Helle 1965: 17-18) reported that in 1964 half of the allotments in Hamburg, Germany were permanently inhabited, partly as a consequence of bombing destruction during the war. The name of the study, *Squatters in Hamburg*, tells us that we have hints of a problem here, which is of great importance and which will be discussed later (4.3.8.5.).

As to the motives for German garden cultivation, the colonists predominantly (60 percent) speak of "*Naturverbundenheit*." "All the additional motives which cannot stand alone are named together with other, mostly economic considerations. They show, however, that the wish for a garden is also motivated by aspired compensation for lost proximity to nature and for monotonous and unpleasant professional work" (Hessing 1958: 55; cf. also Helle 1965: 57-58). Probably one of the foremost factors in these motives is stressed by Hessing (1958: 93) when he states that "Important for the allotment gardener is also a wish to have his own piece of land, a wish coming from a natural bond with the earth".

4.3.6.3. Countryside second homes:

The custom of double habitation is an old one, known, e.g., among the Romans. In the Middle Ages the nobles, as a complement to their castles in the countryside, had houses in the city. And company owners, from the beginning of the industrial age, retired as often as possible from their settlements in the congested and unhealthy urban cores to their estates in or outside the suburbs (cf. Clout 1974: 101-104).

Around 1850 summer villas were built regularly by wealthy people, e.g., at Furusund in the Swedish archipelago outside Stockholm (Paulsson 1973: 66-72). From this time and particularly during the last decades there has been a rapid increase in second home ownership, e.g., in Belgium, France and Sweden as well as in the U.S.A. (Ragatz 1970). In Sweden about 450,000 summer villas of different kinds had been built by 1969, that is, one second home for every fifth household (Clout 1974: 107), and it has been suggested that there will be about 600,000 summer villas by 1979.

"Second homes merit geographical attention for two main reasons. First, they add new and distinctive features to the already complex assemblage of residential areas around urban cores, thereby transporting 'the city' and its inhabitants into the countryside for substantial periods each year. Second, the seasonal presence of second-home occupants gives rise to important social and economic changes in host communities" (op. cit. p. 102). As a matter of fact the highly restricted nature of second-home occupation has broken down since the Second World War, and this phenomenon represents a strengthening of the interrelationships between cities and their zones of influence. It is even stated that today "both countryside and peripheral resort settlements should be viewed simply as highly specialized ecological extensions of the city, constituting what Cracknell has termed the city's 'living space'" (Mercer 1970: 77).

Speaking of second homes, a French author gave the following sensible explanation: "Behind the origin of such a property there is a deep, nearly animal self-assertion, and for this reason it deserves interest and perhaps respect. For most people who receive, acquire or construct a second home outside the town – a place for work and exile – this house has a unique value. It expresses in a symbolic way the old descent tie with the earth as a mythical birthplace" (Brier 1970: 137-138).

In this connection we also refer to studies of some preferred weekend resorts in Holland, where it was found that every group, mostly consisting of several families, tried to reserve for itself a certain area, e.g., in a meadow. "The wish for private enclosure was always followed by anxious efforts to avoid being separated from the car and other equipment. This is thought of as demonstrating that a garden or other territorial plot is inconceivable without being coupled with some kind of habitation. The allotment garden, the second home and the trailer are just variations on the same theme. The car allows us to conquer a piece of land and here we delimit an individual area for the afternoon, the weekend or the holiday" (Gleichmann 1963: 96-97; cf. also Jonge 1967-1968).

There are unmistakable traits of behavioural territoriality in all these phenomena, which at least partly seem to be reactions against modern, ground-depriving industrialization and urbanization. It is probably not by chance that the garden colony movement started in Germany and that Sweden has the highest percentage of summer villas in the world. Both these countries had, at least until recently, their dominant habitation in flats lacking private territorial ground or garden. From here the step is not very far to the park and the other open spaces of the city, the square and the street, which now will be the subjects of our interest.

4.3.7. Park, square and street

4.3.7.1. Open space:
Not long ago the urban scene was viewed as a fairly comprehensible cityscape of a finite shape and size, in which buildings, pavements, and other man-made forms so predominated that the matter of open spaces as an urban concern hardly reached the stage of consciousness (cf. Zisman 1967: 287). But the open space of the city has today become the object of a new, quite remarkable interest. "Given the high densities for dwellings that have prevailed in big cities, it was natural, no doubt, that there should be an emphasis on the biological necessity for open spaces: . . . . But, in addition, we have learned that open spaces have also a social function to perform which the mere demand for a rural refuge too often overlooks" (Mumford 1960-1961: 1).

In fact the open space of which people are aware has three functions: it is used, it is viewed and it is felt. And: "In the midst of all this complexity of function, the physical shape of any open space sits there aloof and unchanging, a setting for a wide variety of functions. Not only is the physical configuration of open space less elusive than its function, it has intrinsic qualities which. I believe, make it the main basis for a policy and program for open space" (Tankel 1963: 58-59; cf. also Clawson 1970). How different the situation is in various capitals becomes evident from the following figures for square feet of open space per inhabitant: Paris 15.0, London 96.9, Berlin 140.0, Vienna 269.1, Washington 538.1 (Beaujeu-Garnier and Chabot 1967: 341).

Among the many different existing types of urban open space we will here just take up parks, squares and streets for discussion from a territorial point of view.

4.3.7.2. Public parks:
Beginning with parks we can, of course, find all transitions between this kind of green area and the various forms of gardens which were treated in the last

chapter. They were generally private, and we are now interested in public spaces and thus communal parks. "These free spaces do not represent a luxury which cannot be considered in towns before providing for streets and sewers. They satisfy a real need; the more a town becomes crowded with people and the more its constructions come into demand. It is enough to see how much the public parks and squares are frequented, what a benevolent refuge they offer children, to judge their enormous influence on comfort and health in cities" (Joyant 1934:50).

The development of public parks during the last decades has been all but satisfactory in many countries. "City building has not stood still in recent years, yet the loveliest city parks and the most ample public playfields are found almost invariably in the old-fashioned neighborhoods. They are holdovers from the times when people tried to make their cities attractive and when it was believed that the city could be the noblest environment in which a cultured human being might live. Nothing remotely comparable to these sometimes fabulous relics are being set aside or developed by the public in newer urban sections or in the conventional suburb" (Higbee 1960:225-226).

Reasons for this unsound development are partly financial but particularly of a social nature. As the physical and human composition of the modern community has changed, enthusiasm for public parks has been superseeded by other interests at the same time as the whole cultural pattern of living has undergone a metamorphosis. In the New York metropolitan area this is, e.g., reflected by the fact that from 1901 to 1940 some 16 acres of new park were established for every increase of one thousand people, but from 1941 to 1955 only 7 acres per thousand were laid out. (loc. cit.).

In the German investigations from Hannover it was shown that "parks were visited by 25 percent of city families. Park visits and garden property correspond to two typical forms of green area use. Between them there is an earlier unknown connection. Those who have a garden or allotment garden seldom visit public parks. As to the future of the green areas the following prognostic possibilities could appear. Park visits can decline for any of three reasons. First, the actual wishes for allotment gardens and personally-owned homes are satisfied, mainly outside town limits. Second, the demand for qualified apartments is realized, but not inside towns. And third, the immense increase in leisure traffic is the product of further motorizing. Evidence for this is the high degree of motorization of those who wish to have a garden and, above all, the desires of future car buyers" (Gleichmann 1963: 97-98; cf. also Seeley 1973: 124-132).

4.3.7.3. Territoriality in American and Swedish parks:
Unfortunately there are very few territorial studies of parks. But in his book
The Social Order of the Slum Gerald D. Suttles (1968) devoted one valuable
chapter to "The Park and the Italians", where he reported about an intrusion
of a Mexican gang into a park in Chicago: "Once established, the Barracudas
installed themselves in the northwest corner of Sheridan Park.... The
significance of this location can be appreciated only if one understands the
role of this park within the Italian section. Practically every Italian street
group in the area makes use of this park, and several of them have their
hangout there. Other people in turn refer to the Italian groups collectively as
the guys from the Park. Sometimes, the entire Italian community is spoken of
as the 'people over by the Park'. The park itself is partitioned into a finely
graduated series of more or less private enclosures, with the most private
hangout going to the reigning group and the least private to the weakest
group.

The northwest corner of the Park is the most exposed of any portion, and
this is where the Barracudas installed themselves. Even in this lowly spot,
however, they were much resented by the other groups. To the Italians, the
Park was almost a sacred charge and the Mexicans' intrusion was a ritual
pollution rather than a mere loss of space and facilities. The Barracudas were
harassed, ridiculed, and insulted. On their own part, they became belligerent
and vaunted all sorts of outrageous claims about themselves. Soon the situation deteriorated, and the Italian groups became extremely harsh with the
Barracudas. Since the Barracudas were no match for even some of the
younger Italian groups, they removed themselves to one member's house near
Racine and Harrison" (op. cit. p. 113-115).

Very revealing also were the investigations by Lerup (1972) of the park
Kungsträdgården in Stockholm, Sweden. This park is continuous apart from
one street-crossing, although many sociocultural divisions divide it, forming
different territories. The two most distinct occupy the opposite ends of the
oblong park, one centred on a restaurant close to a department store and the
other on a tea house close to a waterway and the Opera House. The former is
used primarily by Southern European immigrants, predominantly Italians,
by now longtime denizens. The other territory is dominated by students,
artists and literati, connected with the Opera, the Academy of Fine Arts
further down the street, or the University.

Among different observations of territorial interest in this park the well-
known incident with the elms is the most striking: "The new plan for the Park
includes a subway stop which was to be located under the tea house. This

152   TERRITORY IN MAN

would require the removal of the elm trees. The day the trees were to be removed the workers were confronted with a large group of demonstrators led by a retired army colonel. The elms were not cut down. The demonstrators occupied the area for several nights and days, slinging hammocks from the trunks of the elms. The government finally had to give in to the demands, and new plans were made in which the elms were saved. This incident can be seen as a milestone in a beginning struggle for a closer user-involvement in the planning of cities in Sweden" (op. cit. p. 356).

4.3.7.4. The square:
The square is, like the park, a common with ancients roots, originating in the need for a meeting-place in front of a well, a shrine, a market place or a castle. The American pioneer-time use of small Western town squares as communal, fenced, open areas for storing cattle at night as a guard against straying and depredation probably gives another clue to its descent.

In any case: "This physical and psychological function of the square does not depend on size or scale. The village green in a small New England town, the central square of a residential quarter within a larger city, the monumental plaza of a metropolis – all serve the same purpose. They create a gathering place for the people, humanizing them by mutual contact, providing them with a shelter against the haphazard traffic, and freeing them from the tension of rushing through the web of streets.

The square represents actually a psychological parking place within the civic landscape. If one visualizes the streets as rivers, channeling the stream of human communication – which means much more than mere technical 'traffic' – then the square represents a natural or artificial lake. The square dictates the flux of life not only within its own confines but also through the adjacent streets for which it forms a quasi estuary. This accent in space may make itself felt some blocks in advance – an experience shared by everyone who has ever driven a car into an unfamiliar town" (Zucker 1959: 1-2).

Just one archaic Greek "*agora*" has been reconstructed with any certainty, that of Thera; it consists merely of a broadening of the main street. The same origin is seen in many other squares, e.g., the Stortorget of Lund, Sweden, founded around A.D. 1030 (Blomqvist 1951: 330-331). Nevertheless it was this focal point which, as the place of political gatherings and legislative assemblies, made the town a "*polis*", a city-state. However, to the Greeks space meant only a medium in which to define and set off shaped volume. The creation of space, consciously handled and molded as such by three-dimensional design, was achieved by the Romans, who included the necessary limitations by means of surrounding vertical planes. Thus the Roman *"forum"* is original and different from the Greek *"agora"*.

For medieval man the town was just a place to live in, more easily defensible than an isolated house in the open country. It was not until the end of the Middle Ages that it became the symbol of any political or social idea. Before, in the city, man had hardly considered himself as an individual, still less as a citizen of a specific town, but rather as a member of a specific parish or guild and as a subject of a feudal lord. Thus quite naturally the population, not yet sharing in a general feeling for the community as such, did not see the need for public centres such as squares which would refer to the town as a whole beyond the limits of an individual parish.

Peculiarly, the yearning of the Renaissance for the clearest possible visual articulation of volume and space was realized in two contrasting ways. Within the street this articulation referred primarily to volume, and the individual structures were independent and isolated. Thus the street itself was conceived of as an agglomeration of heterogeneous buildings and not as an artistic unit. But the square, on the other hand, was unified, its single elements tied together by all possible architectural means, and here the space was articulated (cf. Zucker 1959: 97, 141).

Let us finally refer to a phenomenon on the border between the normal and the abnormal. Agoraphobia, the fear of squares and other large open spaces, can develop from a kind of idiosyncrasy among healthy people into the realm of serious nervous disease. It is characteristic that persons with the defect seem to have special difficulties in going out in the open, from their house to the street and from the street to the square, but are often not disturbed when travelling over large plains or over the open sea (cf. Scheller 1957: 573). That agoraphobia is predominantly a question of fright over leaving a known and limited place is supported by various observations of young and old, normal and abnormal individuals. And it is confirmed in severe cases, in which persons cannot even leave their homes without great mental trouble, except, for instance, when in cars with curtains for the windows. It seems not improbable that agoraphobia involves i.a. a special, abnormal form of strong territoriality.

4.3.7.5. Territorial comparison of a park and a square in Stockholm:
Quite generally the meaning of the square as a spatial experience can be grasped only by those who are aware of the fact that the human reaction toward the forms and dimensions of shaped and molded space changes continuously. This change is elemental, grows from a specific and characteristic

mode and attitude of human behaviour and can be followed not only from country to country and from century to century but also within one period and one nation. This perspective is crucial, when we now look at a modern square like the one in Stockholm called Hötorget or just "the Torg" (Lerup 1972):

"On the main concourse level, the Torg is two plazas connected by a mall. In addition to this there is an upper level with roof gardens connected by catwalks and linked to the main concourse by stairs and escalators, and a lower set of levels, which lead to the two subway stations and are also connected with the main concourse.... The context of the Torg is mainly commercial and office facilities; there are five twenty-story office towers on the main concourse.... The Torg is hard-edged and urban; there is little greenery. Materials are hard and glossy, yet lively and gay, appropriate to the atmosphere of modernity and progress intended by its planners.... The upper level is bright and arena-like with magnificent views of fountains and townscapes beyond" but there are also "cul-de-sacs off the main path, where benches and plantboxes produce quite intimate areas.... while the lower plaza at the bottom of the stairs is a 'forest of pillars' and low lighting – a pit-like atmosphere" (op. cit. p. 345-350).

Comparing the Park treated earlier and the Torg in Stockholm Lerup found it evident that both places are "pedestrian" and identified as such with walking behaviour – outside them contained, disciplined and cautious but inside irregular, spontaneous and erratic. It was further clear that the Park has a far greater variety of stable territory with fairly stable clientele than the Torg, which, on the other hand, has arenas, where physical privacy can be obtained. The old and persistent settings of the Park have groups of denizens – steady residents – who can be found at particular times day after day. A constant swarm of kibitzers make an overall variation, continuously changing. Any change will cause reaction among the denizens and their followers, as the incident with the elms indicated.

The Torg, however, has only two such "static" territories, the steps at the concert hall and the dopepushers' hang-out in the lower plaza. Both are far less established and have less identifiable and steady denizen populations. The territoriality is also far less expressive in the physical environment of the Torg. Only the stairs and the fountain by the concert hall share some of the features of the tea house and the restaurant. The territoriality established by the different users was clearly shown in the elm controversy, when the denizens of the tea house demonstrated against the removal of the symbols of their territory (op. cit. p. 354-358).

4.3.7.6. The street:
In the Baroque Period "Even in contact with nature, the axis is the compel-
ling force; architecture and natural growth are equally subordinated and
square and rondel alike become simply the means for retarding or stopping
the visual flight.... Thus it is only logical that out of the classicistic prevalence
of the axis, *the street, and no longer the square,* evolves in the nineteenth
century into the leading element in town planning, ..." (Zucker 1959: 235).

In fact the necessity of roads giving access to its various parts has naturally
always been one of the chief determining factors in the building of a town. Today it is quite the most decisive of factors. The classification of principal
streets as arteries is not an euphemism, for streets are the channels along
which the very life-blood of the urban social organism flows. Without a
satisfactory street-system no city of today can exist. If such a system becomes
clogged or in any way unhealthy, the whole body corporate must become
diseased and exhausted (cf. Sharp 1932: 178).

But it seems often to be forgotten that streets have other uses than those of
transportation. From a territorial point of view, streets are channeling that
which was called tracks in non-human animal use and paths or preferred
routes in "primitive" man. Thus the street is just a more artificial expression
for a well-known tendency. "There are also numerous indications that many
people in much of their lives follow fixed routes, visit certain locations, sit and
lie down in fixed 'spots of their own'. Such conclusions make possible further
hypotheses about people's use of space in a number of situations, allowing the
prediction of certain aspects of behavior in new spatial structures (e.g., buildings, parks) before these have been made" (Jonge 1967-1968).

The open space in the immediate vicinity of homes and workplaces is more
frequented and more experienced by the inhabitants of the city than all other
kinds of urban areas. This dominance amplifies its impact on the role of the
other levels of open space. At the street scale it is also unique because it is the
most man-made both in its quantity and design. Nature can be of some help,
but for the most part street-scale open spaces are creations of man and are
completely bound up with urban activity and urban buildings. A crucial point
in this context is the ability to find ways to combine shared use of open space
with shared ownership of it. This is an important consideration of the phenomenon along with its function and scale (cf. Tankel 1963: 62-65).

Some of the most actual and most difficult of city problems are mirrored in
the streets and their sidewalks. "Impersonal city streets make anonymous
people, and this is not a matter of esthetic quality nor of a mystical emotional
effect in architectural scale. It is a matter of what kinds of tangible enterprises

sidewalks have, and therefore of how people use the sidewalks in practical, everyday life.... Under this system, it is possible in a city street neighborhood to know all kinds of people without unwelcome entanglements, without boredom, necessity for excuses, explanations, fears of giving offense, embarrassments respecting impositions or commitments, and all such paraphernalia of obligations which can accompany less limited relationships. It is possible to be on excellent sidewalk terms with people who are very different from oneself, and even, as time passes, on familiar public terms with them" (Jacobs 1962: 57, 62).

For the most part, the street and its sidewalks thus have the character of a common group territory, available for all but primarily for the inhabitants of the neighbourhood and peripheral with respect to the private core territories in the houses. That a street can also be a perfect defended territory was shown, e.g., by the people of Istedgade in Copenhagen during the German occupation in the Second World War.

4.3.7.7. Different street uses:
There are already great differences as to street use between different districts of the same city. Thus Fried and Gleicher (1961: 312) reported: "most middle-class observers are overwhelmed at the degree to which the residents of any working-class district and, most particularly, the residents of slums are 'at home' in the street. But it is not only the frequency of using the street and treating the street outside the house as a place, and not simply as a path, which points up the high degree of permeability of the boundary between the dwelling unit and the immediate environing area. It is also the use of all channels between dwelling unit and environment as a bridge between inside and outside: open windows, closed windows, hallways, even walls and floors serve this purpose".

Very interesting was the comparison made by Appleyard and Lintell (1972) of three streets in San Francisco with similar width and buildings but with different population and traffic intensity. One, termed Light Street, had light traffic with an average 2,000 vehicles a day and was predominantly settled by families with many children; half the families were homeowners, and the average length of residence was 16.3 years. Another, Heavy Street, had heavy traffic with an average 15,750 vehicles a day; it was inhabited mostly by single persons without children who rented their apartments and had a mean length of residence of 8.0 years. A third, Moderate Street, was in all the above respects in between. The investigation showed this: "Even though legally a householder's responsibilities extend to the maintenance of the sidewalk immediately outside his building, residents on MODERATE and LIGHT STREETS considered part or all of the street as their territory. However, the HEAVY STREET resident's sense of personal territory did not extend into the street, and for some, mostly renters in the large apartment blocks, it was confined to their own apartment and no further. This pattern of territorial space corresponds to the pattern of social use of each street. The contrast between the territorial restrictions of those living on HEAVY STREET and the territorial expansiveness of those on LIGHT STREET is one of the more salient findings of the study" (op. cit. p. 94-95).

Culture differences of street use are self-evident. It is well-known that in India, e.g., the side-walks serve as habitation for millions of homeless people, mostly immigrants from the countryside. The family territories are very small and based on the house-walls, where a distance of a maximum three meters may be defended. A slanting sunshade is the roof, if any, and the limits outside the wall are marked by the few bed and cooking utensils, piles of dried cow-dung for fuel etc. Nearly every day there are quarrels or fights concerning space, water, food and toilet facilities (cf. Abrams 1964: 3-4; Friholt 1974: 7-10).

Street use variations according to sex are also common, e.g., in the Mediterranean countries. In Greece men spend much time together in open places, the *"Plateia"*, while "A woman's associations seldom extend far beyond the outside of her own house. The women generally sit and gossip just outside their house door.... They usually sit sideways to the street, which enables them to communicate with passers by without appearing to involve themselves too directly in the activity along the street. Basically the women's sense of place is restricted to her interior domain – her interior courtyard.

Very rarely do people have any private space between their house and the street. However, the public space – the street – is usually cared for by the people who live along it. The women whitewash the outsides of their houses at frequent intervals, and also paint around the edges of steps and around the joints of the paving stones. This makes them more visible at night in areas without street lamps. Each woman develops her own way of doing this.... Sometimes they even paint over adjacent rock protuberances, claiming them as part of their territory..." (Thakurdesai 1972: 334-340) and are thus in-volved in various forms of marking.

4.3.7.8. Special street group territories:
Most interesting examples of colonizing on public urban lands are the at-tempts by youth gangs to stake out streets as home territories open only to

members of their own clique and defended against invasion by rival groups. "Subject always to official harassment by police and interference by other adults who claim the streets as public territories, youths resolve the dilemma by redefining adults as non-persons whose seemingly violative presence on the youth's 'turf' does not challenge the latter's proprietorship. Streets are most vulnerable to colonizing in this manner and indeed,... streets and knots of juxtaposed streets become unofficial home areas to all those groups who require relatively secluded yet open space in which to pursue their interests to maintain their identities" (Lyman and Scott 1967-1968: 240).

The spatial restrictions seem to be still more striking in the more or less criminal gangs of adults in the big cities, and it is even known how beggars, hawkers and pickpockets "will stake out a 'territory' on the sidewalks or among the blocks and occupy it sometimes to the exclusion of all others similarly employed" (D. W. Maurer 1955: 23-24).

In the already classic monograph on "Street Corner Society" of Chicago, first presented in 1943, the experiences were summarized thus: "Territory provides one important key to the problem. While I did not see North End gangs fighting each other, this was perhaps because it was clear to everybody concerned which gang belonged on which corner. Nevertheless, I could observe the sentiments toward territory which must underlie these gang fights. The younger men of Cornerville seemed to feel that the corner really belonged to them. Furthermore, they were at home on their corner, and only there. Doc commented to me that most of the corner boys felt extremely insecure when they ventured very far away from their corners. These attachments to territory arise, of course, in an environment where there is relatively little territory in relation to the population. When the population is then shifting, the crowded conditions provide more than ample opportunity for small frictions that can rapidly build up into large-scale clashes" (Whyte 1964: 267).

Valued attempts to restrict or forbid motor traffic in certain streets of different cities the world over were referred to, e.g. by Oscar Newman (1972: 51-77) in the chapter "Territoriality" of his interesting book *Defensible Space*. The residents of one street, for instance, contracted with the city to take over the responsibility of road and light maintenance for a slight rebate of city taxes and gained the right to close a one- to two-block stretch of the street at either end. They got the impression that this led to an appreciable reduction of crime, and "the residents claim that their street is now used very differently: children play in the central roadway; most everyone claims to know, or at least recognize people up and down the block; strangers to the street are greeted by questioning glances and a cacophony of barking dogs" (op. cit. p.

60). The reduced traffic thus seems to give an augmented territory feeling to the people inhabiting the street in addition to other positive results.

In spite of still sparse investigation there are not a few evident cases of behavioural territoriality known from parks, squares and streets. Maybe conditions will be found similar, as we now are going to examine urban subdepartments.

4.3.8. Urban subdepartments

4.3.8.1. The neighbourhood:
Local areas in cities have been distinguished since ancient times, not seldom circumvallated and sealed off by night from the rest of the urbanized area. Often such city sections have been inhabited by ethnic or racial groups different from the main population. They are sometimes termed natural areas, signifying that they developed naturally and were not consciously planned. This concept, mentioned earlier (p. 131) is, however, difficult to apply to populations in cities, because social and cultural groups only seldom live exclusively in local areas but are, rather, intermingled in others. But in special cases they are segregated in residential areas by means of voluntary immigration or racial discrimination (Sjoberg 1960: 91-103; Sirjamaki 1964: 201-205).

It is often maintained that: "Sociologically, the most significant city segment having territorial aspect is the neighborhood. In certain situations, other areal units are more meaningful – wards, precincts, quarters, blocks, parishes, tracts, or districts – but the subcommunity most frequently identified as a social unit remains the neighborhood" (Thomlinson 1969: 181). The definition and analysis of this concept offers intricate problems. It was, e.g., stated that one of the major study difficulties for the social scientist is the elusiveness of the neighbourhood. If one isolates it as a piece of territory, one often finds little or no correspondence with human behaviour, and if one concentrates instead on social relationships, one finds that these do not synchronize with geography. Yet one persists in thinking that the two components are somehow crucially interdependent (cf. T. Lee 1968: 241).

"A neighbourhood is usually thought of more in geographical terms as a distinct part of a town or city, which may be distinct by virtue of certain boundaries, e.g., made by roads, railways, rivers, parks, etc., and marked out from other neighbourhoods by a certain homogeneity of housing within the area" (Mann 1970: 150). Thus a small limited area is needed and mostly personal, social relations, by means of which properties neighbourhoods are persistent forces affecting the personality and behaviour of residents at the same time as they themselves are determined by their inhabitants. For instance, Paris, with "all its formal Cartesian unity, is a city of neighborhoods, often with a well-defined architectural character as well as an identifiable social face. The Parisian neighborhood is not just a postal district or a political unit, but a historic growth; and the sense of belonging to a particular *arrondissement* or *quartier* is just as strong in the shopkeeper, the bistro customer, or the petty craftsman as the sense of being a Parisian" (Mumford 1954: 256).

4.3.8.2. District and block:

The distinction between district and block is not always very great. A block appears, however, to be something much less than a district in the city. "It constitutes a kind of elementary unit, particularly used by the inhabitants themselves. It is an assembly of streets and houses, which has more-or-less fixed limits and a more-or-less important economic centre, usually with other points of attraction. The boundaries of a block are marginal zones or frontiers. Inside a district there is a mixture of blocks, the forms of which can be difficult to distinguish but which manifest themselves to the attentive observer. The behaviour and the language of the inhabitants demonstrate where they belong. In sum, it is through a series of divisions that one discovers the truth, also of city subdepartments" (Chombart de Lauwe, Antoine, Couvreur and Gauthier 1952: 57).

Presupposed condition for such an attachment is, of course, first propinquity, but still more decisive is surely familiarity with the area and its people, which brings about the necessary ordering and patterning of impressions. In their interesting experiment "A Walk around the Block" Lynch and Rivkin (1958-1959) invited foreigners and inhabitants to go round a block in Boston and give their observations. The strangers could not find any overall uniformity but only small confused areas, while the natives organized the environment and found, often imaginary, similarities between streets, blocks, buildings and open spaces. For the latter "Not only is the block considered as one, but the facades facing the block are also drawn into the unit. Even the rectangular shape with its sharp corners cannot be allowed, and the form is distorted towards the seamless circle" (op. cit. p. 33).

In these cases it is not uncommon to find an attitude like that met with in Light Street, San Francisco: "I feel my home extends to the whole block [very emphatic]" (Appleyard and Lintell 1972: 95). It looks as if particularly the poor person may visualize city space in a distinctive manner. He is, so to say, a block dweller. He does not feel at home outside his neighborhood, perhaps not anywhere further than 10 or 20 blocks from his home. The block dweller has little interest, then, in the pattern of city space beyond his own neighbourhood. These are the things he prizes about the spatial surrounding: his possesion of it, his being enclosed by it, its familiarity, its manageability, and its intimacy (cf. Schorr 1963: 41-43).

This is in accordance with the notion of E. T. Hall (1971: 255) that in the public housing projects of Chicago there was a great deal of hesitancy on the part of women from one building to visit a community center or become involved in community centers in nearby buildings. Like the women who seldom, if ever, crossed the street and knew only the neighbours on either side these women were not venturesome and hesitated to enter what was to them another group's territory.

Most often in such a case, it is the question of a defended neighbourhood, which can be conceived of as the smallest spatial unit within which coresidents assume a relative degree of security on the streets as compared to adjacent areas. "In populations where distrust is severe, as in low income areas of the inner city, the defended neighborhood may become so limited as to include only the residents of a single building. Or, in similar circumstances, the face-block itself may become a defended neighborhood. But generally these areas are simply too small for residents to carry out the practical business of shopping and pedestrian travel to work. Thus, the defended neighborhood is generally expansive enough to include a complement of establishments (grocery, liquor store, church, etc.) which people use in their daily round of local movements" (Suttles 1973: 57-58).

4.3.8.3. Ghettos:
Of particular interest are, of course, the minority group enclaves. Once established, they either form permanent districts of stable character or exhibit the same gradual alteration more or less common to any white-majority area. Some minority enclaves have grown so large as to constitute virtual cities in their own right, for example, Haarlem and Chinatown in New York and Chicago's "Black Metropolis". These districts are much too large to be called neighbourhoods, but their residents are generally united by common bonds, strongly encouraged by the refusal of the white majority to accept them outside the ghetto. Such vast areas are subdivided, then, into smaller worlds, distinguished from one another by social class and other criteria in much the same manner as majority-group neighbourhoods (cf. Thomlinson 1969: 192-193).

"The existence and persistence of the Negro ghetto as a spatially based social community may best be explained within the framework of the social assignment of territory. Once a slice of physical space is identified as the territorial realm of a specific social group, any attempt to alter this assignment results in group conflict, both overt and covert.... The territorial acquisition by advancing Negro populations cannot always be viewed as a gain in this game of psychological warfare, for once the territory is transferred from one group to the other, it is perceived by the white population as having been contaminated and, therefore, undesirable.... The behavior described above is rapidly leading to the development in the United States of central cities within which territorial dominance is being relinquished to the Negro population. This fact has undoubtedly had much to do with the increasing demand by Negroes for black power, and logically so. If one inherits a piece of turf it is only natural for him to seek control of the area of occupance" (Rose 1970: 4-5).

Territorial differences are even still to be found between adjacent but different ethnic groups among European emigrants in the United States. Mack (1953-1954: 353) reported about an iron factory town on the shore of Lake Erie. The Swedes came first and settled in a district accordingly called Swedetown, which, however, was later invaded by arriving Italians, whereupon the Swedes moved to a nearby district called The Harbor. "Despite the fact that they are incorporated within the same city limits as Uptown, both The Harbor and 'Swedetown' constitute separate sociological communities. Their members, almost without exception, are all inhabitants of the physical space occupied by the communities. The reason that this is true is linked with the principal test for admittance: ethnic origin. A person who is not of Swedish or Finnish descent finds it quite impossible to join in community life at The Harbor, nor is anyone not of Italian ancestry ever really a member of the group in 'Swedetown' ".

Even in the dominating factory with about 400 workers, of which about 175 were of Italian, and 150 of Swedish or Finnish origin, there was an "invisible barrier between track 10 and 11", east of which Italians were busy with "light" work and west of which only Swedes and Finns did the "heavy" work. There was the same differentiation in the supply room and the lunchroom, it never happened that the division lines were seriously transcended and all kinds of personnel in both sections belonged to the respective ethnic groups. If because of the work a crane had to be loaned by one side to the other, it was necessary that an operator from the "right" side went over to fetch the crane. (cf. op. cit. p. 353-355; cf. also Wirth 1928).

It was stressed by Sommer (1969: 15) that group territoriality is expressed by national and local boundaries, a segregation into defined areas that reduces conflict. Segregation that is forced on one group by another has many undesirable consequences in stigmatizing members of the former, but it is one form of accommodation between two groups. Thus there are decisive borders between black and white areas, e.g., in New York City at 96th street in Manhattan and on Chicago's Ashland Avenue: "On the sidewalk west of Ashland there was not one black, on the east side, not one white. All this was accomplished without a Berlin wall, a freeway or railroad tracks, but by an invisible boundary that was accepted so naturally that no one glanced at it".

4.3.8.4. Slums and gangs:
The Negro as well as other ghettos are often also slum areas. Among different possible causes for the development of slums – a term which is difficult to define but which always involves bad housing – this one is of special relevance: "In the United States a very large proportion of our population fails to meet the public standards we set for measuring someone's merit, trustworthiness, and respectability. Many locality groups have avoided compromising these ideals of public morality by territorial segregation: more exactly, they have simply retreated and left valuable portions of the inner city to those they distrust" (Suttles 1968: 7).

Obviously this practice has its flaws since it tends to aggregate those who are poor, unsuccessful, and disreputable in the same slum areas. In such neighbourhoods territorial aggregation usually precedes any common social framework for assuring orderly relations. Ethnic invasion, the encroachment of industry, and economic conditions constantly reshuffle slum residents and relocate them around new neighbours. "The withdrawal to small territorial groupings and the extension of personal acquaintances are strategies which slum residents can use to embark on a search for order" (op. cit. p. 8).

In the light of the very miserable conditions predominating in the slum one might think that the inhabitants would be eager for an opportunity to move into another place. But on different occasions, e.g., in connection with the relocation of the people of Boston's West End redevelopment area (Fried and Gleicher 1961), investigations showed that the residents experienced profound satisfaction from living in their old home region, mostly emanating from the close associations maintained among the local people and from their strong sense of identity with the local place.

"We would like to call this way of structuring the physical space around the actual residential unit a *territorial* space, in contrast to the selective space of the middle class. It is territorial in the sense that physical space is largely defined in terms of relatively bounded regions to which one has freedom or restriction of access, and it does not emphasize the path function of physical space in allowing or encouraging movements to or from other places. There is also evidence, some of which has been presented in an earlier section, that it is territorial in a more profound sense: that individuals feel different spatial regions belong to or do not belong to them and, correspondingly, feel that they belong to (or in) specific spatial regions or do not belong" (op. cit. p. 312-313).

Even though there are gangs in various contexts it cannot be doubted that the slum, "the city wilderness", is the natural habitat of the gang. We have already met with the phenomenon in streets, and now we will look for a moment at the areal "Gangland". In his well-known monograph first published in 1927 Thrasher (1968) studied no less than 1,313 gangs in Chicago and its environs – divided into three great domains, called "North Side jungles", "West Side wilderness" and "South Side badlands", each of which in turn broke up into smaller kingdoms. This gangland stretched interstitially in a broad semicircular zone between the central business district, the Loop, and the better residential areas, and here feudal gang warfare was carried on more or less continuously. It was usually organized on a territorial basis, each group becoming attached to a local area regarded as peculiarly its own and through which it was dangerous for members of another gang to pass (cf. op. cit. p. 5-6, 116-119).

An example from Chicago tells us that "For persons in the Addams area only the adjacent neighborhoods are well defined.... Beyond this, their notion of established boundaries become vague and uncertain. Even when they are in unfamiliar territory, however, there is the general assumption that boundaries exist and that the area included must 'belong' to someone. Thus, the city is seen as something like an irregular lattice work from which a person's behavior and appearance can be gauged, interpreted, and reacted to depending upon the section to which he belongs" (Suttles 1968: 15).

In another book by the same author the situation in Chicago was summarized like this: The basic functions of the peer group seemed to be territorial defense and the moral enlightenment of its members. In this sense, such peer groups are vigilante gangs which develop out of the inadequacy of formal institutions that have authorized responsibility for the protection of property and lives and for moral education. The foremost adjustment required in the area was a specialization of the male-adolescent peer group into a sort of informal police power which barricaded its neighborhood for selected hours of the day and on conditions of the entrant's personal deportment (cf. Suttles 1973: 225).

When the Democratic Party convention of 1968 was held in Bridgeport, an inner city district of Chicago, a newspaper reporter asked some residents if they were afraid that the Yippies would come into the neighborhood and endanger the convention. The answer was "no", and the explanation that "the kids around here are pretty tough. They'll keep them out". On this occasion several thousand federal and state troops had already been brought into the area to protect it, but the residents did not mention them at all, relying on the territorial defense of "their kids", that is, the local gangs of boys and adolescents (cf. op. cit. p. 201).

It is self-evident that these phenomena are not indigenous just to Chicago and the United States, even though they are mostly studied there, but more or less to all cities and countries. The present author once upon a time (around 1930) took part in a long-prepared battle in a meadow between the boys of two adjacent villa suburbs in the Swedish town of Helsingborg, and as this·is written the newspapers carry reports of severe fights between motorized youth groups from the cities of Malmö and Ystad, towns also in Sweden.

4.3.8.5. Squatter settlements:
Squatter settlements are often called a form of slum. As to bad housing and conditions of living they are sometimes worse and sometimes better in comparison. But while the slum is most often an old phenomenon occurring inside a city and involving legitimate residents, squatters are illegal occupants of urban or rural land located mostly on the outskirts of or outside cities. These squatter towns have millions of inhabitants in different parts of the world, and in many a metropolis at least a quarter of the population is of this kind, with extremely limited living space. The squatters are often rather well organized, they are partly made up of peasants from economically depressed rural areas, partly of emigrants from inner city slums, and they have, contrary to general opinions, better prospects for the future than most slum inhabitants (cf. Abrams 1964: 12-24; Mangin 1967; Juppenlatz 1970: Wennberg 1977).

Squatter settlements are known from many countries under various names, "bidonville", shantytown", favella", "barriada". From the "tugurio" of Bogotá, Colombia it is reported, e.g., that: "In mid-1965 two families were offered the opportunity to leave and start new lives with adequate financial support from an agency of the municipal government. Both refused: the first, because the barrio [neighbourhood] had always been 'home' and its members wanted their roots to be maintained; the second, because of intense fear of all the unknowns of an inimical big city" (Schulman 1967: 1010).

In a way the settlements of squatters are crucial from the point of view of territorial studies. In Lusaka, the capital of Zambia, for example, there has been no call or opportunity for some kind of externally-imposed land jurisdiction or other regulative community action. "Yet there must be a guiding force which affects each man as he sets up his hut in the compound. Closer inspection on the ground reveals some interesting aspects of living in a squatter area. It might be thought that people in such circumstances would treat all things in common, since all are in need. But little rows of stones around the houses, dividing lines between public and private, between the road and 'my garden', belie this idea. Further enquiry reveals that these rows of stones are only a small, visible manifestation of an elaborate system of property tenure" (R.J. Martin 1969: 213).

There are, thus, many striking and good examples of behavioural territoriality among squatters, gangs and other ghetto and slum inhabitants – which does not mean, as we have seen, that they are lacking in the more ordinary populations of districts and blocks. We will now look for corresponding phenomena in the realms of ground, house and flat.

4.3.9. Ground, house and flat

4.3.9.1. Origin and defense of house:
We find it suitable to start with some general statements about the central human theme of the house.

"The house is an institution, not just a structure, created for a complex set of purposes. Because building a house is a cultural phenomenon, its form and organization are greatly influenced by the cultural milieu to which it belongs. Very early in recorded time the house became more than shelter for primitive man, and almost from the beginning 'function' was much more than a physical or utilitarian concept. Religious ceremonial has almost always preceded and accompanied its foundation, erection, and occupation. If provision of shelter is the passive function of the house, then its positive purpose is the creation of an environment best suited to the way of life of a people – in other words, a social unit of space" (Rapoport 1969: 46).

Without doubt this description is influenced by Raglan (1964), who derived the origin of the house from the temple and the palace. He also emphatically stated that "Anyone who wishes to study any aspect of human behaviour should start by banishing from his vocabulary such words as 'evident', 'obvious', 'natural', 'innate', 'instinctive', ..."(p. 3), which are all question-begging terms. Nevertheless we here maintain, as earlier, that phenomena which have such a world-wide distribution and manifold variation of a certain plan as the hut and the house must have, in addition to a cultural, even a natural, that is, instinctive background – maybe of the same kind as the "nest" in some primates.

Probably the shortest and surely not the least adequate definition of territory is that just given for the house, "a social unit of space", which formulation was put into its context by Rapoport (1969: 79-81). He stressed that both constant and changeable aspects may have profound consequences on the house and the city." The distinction among the different types of urban space made by some French urban sociologists – physical space, economic space, social space, and many others – can be partly understood in these terms, while architects have suggested that one can usefully distinguish between technological space, such as bathrooms and service spaces, which is changing as equipment and services change, and symbolic, largely living, space, which is constant and usable almost indefinitely. This latter type of space is related to territoriality and clarifies the concepts of 'ethnic domain', separation of spaces inside the house or tent, and separation of domains" (cf. also Buttimer 1969).

Here we could ask whether the demands of territory, which seem basic to the house, make life easier by giving cues for behaviour, and whether people, like animals, feel more secure and better able to protect themselves on their home ground. The need for security may be one of the reasons why man has to defend his place, and Anglo-Saxon law, as well as other legal systems, recognizes this by protecting the home from intrusion, even permitting killing in its defense.

The house as a defended territory has certainly always played and still plays an important role, i.a. influencing form and structure, and not only in fortresses and castles. Already the use of stockades, palisades and fences has, of course, defensive implications, and, clearly fortified houses are known, e.g., from the Atlas Mountains and Scotland. Defense, however, never wholly accounts for observed phenomena and may also be symbolic, as has been suggested for the Pueblo buildings. The survival of an archaic defensive form in some areas and its disappearance in other adjacent regions show the complexity of the natural and cultural forces in operation (cf. Rapoport 1969: 31-33).

4.3.9.2. Marking and limiting of house:
Introducing his chapter on "The Sanctity of the Threshold" Raglan (1964: 25 ff.) remarked: "The rites described in the last chapter are clear evidence that cities, villages, temples, palaces and houses are, or are apt to be, islands of sanctity in a profane world". And he went on to state that the inhabitants of these sanctuaries must communicate with the outside world but that the gates and doors which enable them to get out at will also give enemies an opportunity to come in. "Gates and doors mark the division between the sacred and the profane world, and so do thresholds, but precautions taken at the latter are far more numerous and widespread than at gateways, and at doors and doorways as distinct from thresholds. It seems not to matter how you go through a gateway, but in most parts of the world you must not go through a doorway without observing the threshold ritual" (cf. also Knapp 1952; Rapoport 1968).

Here, as in many other cases, one cannot resist wondering if sanctity and taboo formulations are not just special, cultural manifestations for marking and giving importance to behavioural territories. Rapoport (1969: 80) thinks so, stating: "The sanctity of the threshold is also probably related to this constant need to define territory, but the specific manner in which it is defined varies in different cultures and periods, and constitutes the element of change. Not only do devices for defining threshold vary, but the threshold itself occurs at different points in the total space. The compound in India, or the Mexican or Moslem house, put the threshold further forward than the Western house does, and the fence of the English house puts it further forward than the open lawn of the American suburb".

In any case, the outer walls of the house are of particular importance. "Through the walls a private space is cut out from the common one, and thus an inner space is separated from an outer. Man – according to Simmel characterized by his ability to both put up and cross boundaries – carries out this limiting most visibly in the walls of his house. This duality of inner and outer space is fundamental to the further building up of experienced spaces, not to say of human life altogether" (Bollnow 1963: 130).

Not seldom is the wall of the house complemented by a particular outside wall-construction. Thus it is for instance said in connection with the cities of China: "The wall is the most conspicuous example of Chinese monumental architecture. Its ubiquity and persistence may be taken as evidence of the civilization's fundamental need for defence, control and definition. Even the garden, the freest form of Chinese architecture, is often encircled by an incongruously massive rampart. The house is walled in. The charm of trees and courtyards lies entirely inside. To the world outside the house presents an austere blank" (Tuan 1968: 239-240). And concerning Japan it was said: "one feature of the division between the public and private spheres of urban development – the use of walls – has helped give visual form to the Japanese city. Even large private buildings have walls or at least bamboo fences setting the structures off from the streets" (Meyerson 1963: 95).

4.3.9.3. Ground delimitation:

Thus the human settlement is in most cases not restricted just to the house but involves a lesser or larger piece of earth too. In the urban context this is realized in different ways, and the loss of it is strongly noticed. "When one's territory begins at the door and no buffer zone exists in the form of a garden in front of and behind the house, one becomes particularly guarded and contact inhibitions appear" (Oeter 1974: 8; cf. p. 146).

From the squatter settlements of Lusaka it is reported: "Although none of the property legally belongs to the residents, there is no doubt in anybody's mind about the *de facto* ownership of each piece of ground. Ask a householder where his ground ends and his neighbour's begins and he will be able to show you. With a stick he will delineate exactly the boundary line in a flat dusty piece of ground. There is neither post nor stones nor hedge since there is no need of them; the forces of nature have arrived at a state of equilibrium. A challenge of the neighbour's property has been made, discussion and even argument have been held, and the matter settled" (R. J. Martin 1969).

There are other places where stones are felt to be necessary, for instance, a plot that used to be roughly square has been divided into two plots, which are, as a result, long and thin. At the extreme ends, which seem to be a long way from the house and to which the owner doesn't seem to have any real right, you find a row of stones. Often there will be something more emphatic, such as a fence. And if you look round the compound with a new eye you will notice that a fence is used only in two circumstances. Either it establishes a boundary which might otherwise be in dispute, because the plot is a 'false' shape, or it acts as a security measure. "A certain amount of ground is felt to be necessary for human dignity and living; this is the fundamental ingredient of territory". (op. cit.).

In the Cuevas settlements of Lima, Peru, the great majority of people preferred the illegal alternative of squatting if the prospects of obtaining *de facto* possession were good, even though very considerable sacrifices had to be made to get a plot of land and to build. The wage-earning family that could not afford tolerable accommodation or that desperately needed the security

of home-ownership might also be forced to squat if there was no other alternative. It was further said that in terms of space, sunlight, and unpolluted air,
their squatter shacks were a vast improvement over the dark, unventilated,
and crowded rooms on narrow, smelly and noisy slum courts (Turner 1971:
72-74):

"As the security provided by the possession of a home-site is the settlers'
first concern, top priority is given to action that will consolidate tenure. If
there is no way of obtaining title legally and at short notice, and if the pre-
cedents show that, once settled, land of low value is rarely reclaimed, then the
surest way of ensuring permanent tenancy is to settle firmly on the land. The
squatter associations therefore demand that their members build as soon as
they take possession of their allocated plots, so all who can do so, even if it is
only to place some foundations. . . .

Where there is little or no rainfall, as in Lima, it may be more appropriate to
enclose the plot with a perimeter wall than to build two or three rooms with
permanent roofs. The perimeter wall provides privacy and an improved
microclimate in which the discomforts of a shack are greatly reduced; the
family is no longer pestered by neighbours' dogs and children, it is more
secure against pilfering, and has, in effect a spacious living area, even if the
rooms are temporary shacks". Without doubt these squatter studies represent
some of the best contributions to the knowledge of what behavioural territoriality really is and how it functions.

4.3.9.4. Single house and flat:
There seems to be great unanimity about what represents the best habitation of man. "Without doubt, the detached one-family house with garden is
the ideal solution. From a spatial point of view the distances are here so
measured that individual and family life can take place in the necessary
seclusion" (Heuer and Lowinski 1955: 31). Among more than 5,000 persons
interviewed in the cities of Bayern, Germany, 31.2 percent preferred a
detached one-family villa with garden, 17.2 percent a one-family house in
row with garden, 17.2 percent a two-family house, 24.5 percent a three-storey
apartment house and 9.9 percent an even higher apartment house (op. cit.
p. 51).

In an interesting question study of about 500 persons in Münster,
Germany, it was found that 29 percent associated earth and ground with
house (with or without garden) or private home, 27 percent with security,
property, capital etc., 20 percent with agriculture and economic gardening, 15
percent with building and plans, 3 percent with garden and work therein, 3

percent with home and place trust and 3 percent with nature and recreation (Schäfer 1968: 46). "Another factor of the greatest importance is stress on the freestanding house in its own clearly defined plot of land facing an ordinary road, expressing anonymity and avoiding any form of grouping. This, I think, explains the general nonacceptance of cluster housing. . . . The popular house is based on the ideal that one's home is indeed one's castle, and on a belief in independence. The house is to be as private and isolated as possible, with a moatlike separation; even children who have always lived in tall London apartment blocks draw houses in this way" (Rapoport 1969: 134).

Thus: "What every normal man wants for himself and his family is a detached house in an adequate garden, with neighbours close enough to be found if needed or one feels like a social call, yet far away to be avoided at other times. What we see instead is the cancerous growth of the huge blocks of flats of so-called satellite cities creeping out into the countryside, and very soon we shall reach the point where individuals simply cannot any longer be allowed to acquire a piece of land of their own and erect a single family house in it: in the interest of the Common Good the block of flats will have to become compulsory. Our civilization is marching with banners flying from battery hen to battery consumer" (Leyhausen 1965b:32).

Certain of the dilemmas of *High Living* are summarized in an Australian book with this title where it was said that some provision must be made to compensate for the loss of backyard or "growing-space". The areas of gardens and lawns on the estate do not provide this compensation because they belong to everybody and therefore belong to nobody. They are useful but with obvious limitations as a play-area for children. The open nature of the ground makes it almost impossible for tenants to identify themselves with any particular area. There can certainly be no privacy for anyone who wishes to sit on the lawns. Perhaps if more low-level painting was done or if the buildings themselves were used to break up ground-space, such space could then be put to fuller use by the tenants (cf. Stevenson, Martin and O'Neill 1967: 146).

As to the wellknown house-flat controversy, it is evident that in most countries flats are unpopular among large sections of the community, particularly in families with children. It has been suggested that the principal reason for this is that living in owned houses with private gardens means better possibilities to supervise children. But considerable proportions of the population are not members of families with children, and here one might expect a preference for flats, particularly among aged and single-living persons (cf. *Design of Dwellings* 1944: 12-13).

It is interesting to note that a detailed study of the population of

Manchester, Great Britain, disclosed that "*approximately 66 percent of all dwellings should be designed for families with no young children, while only 34 percent of all dwellings would be designated for families with children...*" (Orlans 1953: 106-107). At the same time it was reported that out of 1,100 British people, mainly housewives, interviewed in 1941-1942, no less than 90 percent unequivocally preferred a house to a flat. In spite of bias of the sample in this investigation it seems to be very probable that, independent of categories, there is a general preference for living in an owned or at least single house, and territorial feelings could here be of great influence. Not unexpectedly, Le Corbusier opposed such reasoning, claiming that this so-called family house will never merit its title but will drag society into the universal waste-land of garden-cities'.

The complications do not, however, only depend on the flat or single house character of the habitation but on its magnitude and structure as well. "Space is probably the most important single factor, short of a certain minimum of firmness, in the quality of a dwelling, particularly an urban dwelling. The amount of space per house, both inside and out, plays a determining part not only in the convenience and adequacy of the interior arrangements, but also in light, air, ventilation, outlook, health, cleanliness, quiet, privacy, and recreational facilities. It is not true *ad infinitum*, that the more space there is, the better is the dwelling.... But there is a definite point in urban housing below which it is true, that the less space the worse dwelling" (Bauer 1934: 17).

It was reported from the cities of Great Britain in the 19th century that houses with a basement area of just 12 square meters were not rare, and they were built so close that there could be 50 to 60 houses on one acre, that is, on 4,046.71 square meters (Berlepsch-Valendàs 1912: 28-29). It is likewise known from the squatter settlements of Dehli, India, that most building plots are 12 to 25 square meters in size (Payne 1974: 64). Against this it could be stated that in the garden city of München-Perlach, Germany, at the beginning of this century, 21 houses were erected on 8,040 square meters (Berlepsch-Valendás and Hansen 1910:66), which equals the usual magnitude of small villa ground in Western societies but which, of course, could be doubled several times in more exclusive districts.

Minimum hygienic demands were stated by H. Peters (1954:43) to be between 12.8 and 20 square meters per person depending on magnitude of family, and the *Revised Cologne Recommendations* (1971:46) advised 35 square meters as a minimum for a one-person dwelling. From recent investigations it is known that there are in comfortable flats in France 30, in normal flats in France 15, in normal flats in Dakar, Senegal 10 and in shantytown huts in Dakar 6 square meters per inhabitant (Dr. E. Giroult of the W. H. O. Regional Office for Europe in a letter of March 13, 1974).

In the very valuable but also much criticized (cf., e.g., Altman 1975: 116) book *Defensible Space*, Oscar Newman (1972: 51-77) showed how the detailed limiting and structuring of the space outside and inside American apartment buildings have a far-reaching influence on the functional economics and desirability of the houses. The bigger and more unform the projects are, the worse for their inhabitants, while the remedies seem to be subdivision and territorial identification. "These mechanisms succeed in providing both resident and outsider with a perceptible statement of individual and group concern over areas of buildings and grounds. More importantly, in so doing, they allow occupants to develop a heightened sense of responsibility toward care of the environment and control of its penetration by outsiders" (op. cit. p. 53).

Thus the house with adjacent ground in different forms and structures corresponds to the demands of behavioural territoriality, certainly best as a single, one-family habitation with garden but still also as a private flat in a multi-storey building with thousands of rooms. This last unit will next be investigated from a territorial point of view.

4.3.10. Room

4.3.10.1. Requirements of rooms:
It has been suggested that "there are three basic physical spatial qualities used to indicate the kind of social interaction to be expected in the space. They are position, distance and symbolic decoration, and these three work together to define a fourth quality – territory". These factors are thus responsible for the organization and use of the room to provide cues for interaction through territoriality, zoning, and personal orientation (Joiner 1971: 11-13).

In a concrete way the basic demands are formulated thus: "(1) The dwelling room must give an impression of seclusion; (2) The size is vital, and large rooms seem to be unpleasant; and (3) Particularly important is the way in which the furniture is arranged, as empty rooms appear cold" (Bollnow 1963: 150-151).

So the magnitude, delimitation and structuring of space is of utmost importance in connection with rooms and undoubtedly commands their territorial value in relation to the inhabitants. That this value can be great is evident already from the fact that people often strongly keep to their rooms. It was for instance stated from a home for the aged that "residents almost never change their rooms once they have been admitted", and "the possibility that residents choose or change their rooms in order to be closer to their friends can be ruled out; . . ." (E. P. Friedman 1966: 568).

About black youths in a crowded district of Boston it was said: "Their own room was very important to those who were afforded such space", and it was added that the number of persons per room not only indicates the relative degree of crowding but also conveys some information about territoriality, the physical proximity of family members and the availability of personal space in a household (cf. Ladd 1972: 110). Interesting experiments about control dynamics between residents and visitors in students' dormitory rooms indicated that territory residents experienced more passive control and found, not unexpectedly, their territories more private and pleasant than visitors did. (Edney 1975).

"One room for every human" (Doxiadis 1974) is, however, still a luxury for a main part of the population in most countries. It is thus reported that there were recently 3.1 persons to a room in Malaysia and 3.4 in the Central African Republic against 0.6 to a room in British houses (Goldsmith 1973: 466). But it should be remembered that Lord Shaftesbury, who worked for a bettering of the habitation conditions in Britain one-and-a-half century ago, not seldom personally found up to 16 inhabitants per room in London (Berlepsch-Valendàs 1912: 35). In the single-room tenements of Bombay around 1950 there were an overall average of 7 persons in a room while 10 persons in an area of 10 by 15 feet was common; in Singapore families of 6 to 8 members lived in rooms of 7 by 10 feet and in Hongkong 5 to 6 humans shared cubicles measuring 40 square feet. From Jamaica it was not long ago reported that 9 persons occupied huts of 6 by 10 feet, and in Panama 20 humans lived in huts of 15 by 15 feet, in which cases sleeping had to be done in relays (Abrams 1964: 6).

As a basis of comparison for these figures, it has been prescribed that, medically-speaking, the minimum permissible dimensions for the normal room plus its auxiliaries (bath, kitchen, storage) are 18 sq. m. with a height of 2.40 m. The maximum dimensions of the normal room are 46 sq.m. with the auxiliaries. These figures do not include the open and connecting spaces corresponding to each room. This space cannot be measured on a global basis, because factors such as climate, culture, habits, location, type of inhabitants, etc., are involved. These figures have to be decided by each country and specific case, and become parts of special regulations. To this, five needs of quality are added, namely that for isolation ranging from protection from noise to complete security, that of opening up the room by means of doors, windows etc., the need for ownership, the need to separate the room definitely from places which are controlled by machines and the need for optimal relationship between humans and the city (Doxiadis 1974: 150-151).

"Concerning space division man has remained close to animals. Perhaps people think that it is a cultural acquisition to divide up houses into bedrooms, dining-rooms, sitting-rooms and kitchens. But where there is a lack of space we can also find even within one room a similar partition, to which man adheres with animal tenacity. The bond with special spheres of activity is so self-evident to man that it is observed only when it is lacking. This is the case with certain mentally abnormal people who have lost their system of spatial binding and show complete confusion as to the choice of activity places" (Holzapfel-Meyer 1943: 28).

4.3.10.2 The major space:
Whether temples were the first buildings or not, it is of interest that "The Major Space" (Rowan 1965) of contemporary churches has long been territorially subdivided and marked out into compartments according to religious, social and other parameters. Joiner (1971: 11) described a Danish countryside church where the priest conducting his service is provided with a richly carved pulpit, raised above the level of the congregation, as well as with a font and an altar, secreted away behind the arched opening. But slightly higher than the pulpit there is a box for the local lord and his family, decorated with gilt panelling, coat of arms and canopy. Not only are the places for these important people set aside physically from those of the ordinary visitors, but the form and decoration further emphasizes the differences. They also dominate the nave of the church, where the seating is divided into territories for the smaller social groups of families by gates at the ends of the pews, distinguished by the use of symbolic decorations.

Courtrooms (cf., e.g., Hazard 1962) and many other more or less official major spaces have similar territorial divisions, and to take quite another example, professional musicians as a rule are spatially isolated from the audience in the dance-hall. They are mostly placed on a platform, which, being more or less inaccessible to the public, provides a physical barrier that prevents any direct interaction. "This isolation is welcomed because the audience, being made up of squares, is felt to be potentially dangerous. The musicians fear that direct contact with the audience can lead only to interference with the musical performance. Therefore, it is safer to be isolated and have nothing to do with them" (H. S. Becker 1951-1952: 142). Where such isolation is not automatically provided, the musicians often effectively segregate themselves by means of instruments, etc.

Very disclosing were studies made at Sampson Air Force base in the United States with three quite open and three "closed" cubicle barracks, each housing 60 recruits. In both cases bunks were segregated into units of six, and the only difference was that the "closed" barracks had walls enclosing each unit of six bunks but with the entrance between them quite open without door. Nevertheless the walls evidently brought about a strong group territory feeling. The effect was that the "closed" cubicles significantly increased relationships between inhabitants in the same unit and reduced them with those in other units (Blake, Rhead, Wedge and Mouton 1956; cf. also Blood and Livant 1957).

4.3.10.3. Offices:
Lately there has been a growing interest in the spatial problems of offices. "The word territoriality is relevant in office design in reference to proper spacing and orientation of work stations or desks in order to protect against overexploitation that part of the environment belonging to each clerk. It has been mentioned that individual requirements for privacy are the least considered element of design in existing office environments. This viewpoint is made with regard to a noticeably strong cultural requirement for territorial definition in the Australian society. With few exceptions, Australian house properties are fenced along their entire perimeter; in much the same way within the office environment, desks are considered 'private territory'. The requirement for privacy from external noise and visual activity plague some clerks in their attempt to conduct their business routine. They use charts and equipment, such as typewriters, to define and protect their territory" (Sloan 1972: 362-363).

A detailed investigation was made by Joiner (1971) of seating orientations and furniture arrangements in single-person office rooms of different commercial, government and academic institutions in Britain and Sweden. First it was found that the rooms, by means of desks and other equipment, were effectively divided into two zones, a private zone for the occupant and a public one for visitors and that this phenomenon was "closely related to the social behavioural concepts of territoriality and interaction distance" (p. 12). Further the results showed that the academics generally sat sideways to their

commercial and government occupants, who predominantly sat facing their

cussions their dominant role was sustained by maintaining social distance across desk tops.

Room layout in commercial offices seemed to be very much contingent upon occupant status, with those of higher executives showing stronger territorial definition than those of lower status. Even in the *bürolandschaft*-type offices, where the pinning up of pictures and postcards was officially forbidden, they were still appearing. It was found likely that here, lacking wall space, these small display elements were of utmost importance for marking out territories. Position, distance and zoning are probably of special significance in these situations, and corner sites were, e.g., generally occupied by senior staff (op. cit.).

Let us take one office example of the consequences for the personnel of some rather small structure changes (Richards and Dobyns 1957, cited after Stea 1965: 15-16): "(1) The territory was slightly reduced in size; (2) the protective file-cabinet barrier was removed, allowing an external supervisor visual access into the territorial interior; (3) access to the outside corridor was removed; (4) disposition of their territorial property was taken out of their control; and (5) arrangement of territorial units within the cluster was altered".

The result was an increased regimentation, a loss of the primary status symbol and inevitably, greatly decreased morale and a nearly catastrophic reduction in work efficiency. Thus, as the external boundaries of the territory became increasingly permeable, this miniature social system lost its autonomy. Psychological stress resulted from a reduction in the number of alternative behaviours available to the members, restrictions in freedom of movement and a loss of overt behavior symbols of in-group uniqueness. In other words, with the alteration in the shape, size, boundedness and differentiation of the territorial cluster and of the territorial units came marked alteration in the behavior of the individual members.

4.3.10.4. Territorial furniture:
As indicated above too little but also too much space is disorganizing for territorial urges in habitable rooms. In fact the same is true for the structuring of such spaces as underlined by Donaldson (1969: 73) in a chapter with the suitable name "Little Boxes", illustrated by the verses of the well-known territorial song by Malvina Reynolds: "The precious breathing space of the

house leaks out of its pores under the pressure of forces from within and without – from the outside the crushing weight of confinement by a skimpy lot and looming neighbors, from the inside the cancerous growth of household equipment. Steadily, the suburbanite fills every inch of available space with the 'latest' in furnishings and equipment, and the overall impression is one of cramped clutter. He forgets that 'Pure space, or, as we glibly call it, useless space is something of a necessity for man to keep sane and to live a dignified life. It is the unoccupied space which makes a room inhabitable, says Lin Yutang. Unfortunately, the implications are largely lost upon us' ".

Furniture, as already demonstrated for offices, cannot only produce territorial demarcations but even function as territory itself, particularly chairs and tables. "As long as man must live in a world of walls, furniture, doors, and fences, there is good reason to study how they influence his behavior" (Sommer 1959: 258; cf. also Sommer 1974: 81-101).

Concerning chairs it should first be remembered that their use since ancient times has been a symbol of power, exemplified by the tripod of the Delphic prophetess, the throne of kings and other rulers and the seats of judges and chairmen of various kinds (cf. Winick and Holt 1961: 171-174). And "In private homes, in clubs, in pubs and in university senior common rooms, it is common for specific chairs to be regularly used by the same people, and for furniture arrangements to be unchanged. The pattern is not confined to leisure time; the same people tend to sit next to one another in buses and trains; and I have noticed, as a lecturer, that students in lectures, seminars and tutorials invariably sit in the same, or similar, positions each week" (Lipman 1967a: 564).

Alan Lipman (op. cit.) also reported very interesting observations from a British old people's home; the title of his paper, "Chairs as territory", was particularly relevant. This depended on the very great proportion of waking hours which residents spent in their chairs, namely about twelve, arising only for meals, brief journeys to the toilet and, for a minority, short strolls. The seating arrangement in the communal sitting-room was fixed and regular, chairs being placed in shoulder-to-shoulder ranks along the perimeter walls and back-to-back in central rows. Residents occupied the same chairs in the same positions day after day, the physical and social limitations of this order of things being apparent. These conditions were the more remarkable as the official policy of the welfare department as well as of the staff of the Home was that no chair should "belong" to any particular resident but that all should be available to everyone.

"Despite the formal rule, and the positions of the residents in the authority hierarchies of the Homes, the informal norm was that seats *were* stably held by specific individuals. The research records are littered with instances in which residents defended, by, among other means, verbal invective and physical attacks, 'their' chairs in the face of occupation, or attempted occupation, by newcomers and/or fellow residents suffering from senile dementia. In spite of the expectations contained in the rule the staffs recognised the informal norm, as the researcher was forced to do in the course of field work" (Lipman 1968: 94).

In fact there was 100 percent occupation by a single resident in 3 of the 27 chairs in one community room and the others would have had almost the same percentage of occupation, if it were not for special intervening such as illness. This room was also divided by the central rows of chairs into two hostile groups and social territories. Thus "The chairs are not mere repositories for bodies: it would seem no extravagance to assume that profound psychic and emotional significance is attached to the objects in which overwhelming proportions of the residents' waking hours are spent. And certainly social relationships are linked with and symbolised in, chair ownership" (Lipman 1967a: 566; cf. also Lipman 1967b).

4.3.10.5. Seating arrangements:
There is already a long series of observational and experimental investigations concerning seating arrangements, above all in lecture rooms. Even though most concentrate on items like leadership, interaction and participation, they often give results with territorial implications. If we look at one of the many valuable papers by Robert Sommer (1967), called "Classroom Ecology", it is at once evident that the initial choice of seats is far from random. When the rooms are first opened in a library study area, individual tables are occupied until there are no free ones left. Then newcomers must sit at tables already occupied and typically they use a "distant" or catercornered arrangement so that they do not face or sit alongside the earlier occupant. In other reading areas the general results obtained for the total user group showed that only "a single strong influence is at play, that for sole possession of a table" (Eastman and Harper 1971: 427).

DeLong studied in a series of papers the dominance-territory relations in a small group seated at a rectangular seminar table. He first saw that there were two psychologically and territorially demarcated subgroups, one on each side of the table. Further he got an indication of a proximity-based relationship, in

180 TERRITORY IN MAN

which the members' nearness in the hierarchical structure of the group is reflected in their psychical contiguity within the spatial ecology of the room (cf. DeLong 1970: 184-190).

Later on DeLong found that some members of the group selected territories commensurate with previously acquired hierarchical stature, while others gave priority just to staking out territories, being content to have their positions territorially determined. Still others seemed to be patently unconcerned about the degree of correspondence between their hierarchical and territorial position and some were, finally, in a state of flux, adjusting their hierarchical and territorial claims diachronically in accordance with what other group members were doing. It was thus found that dominance and territoriality do not always compete with each other (cf. DeLong 1971: 260-264).

In a third paper (DeLong 1973: 61-62) the author reported that regardless of where a member stakes out his territorial claim the degree to which he is found consistently occupying the immediate vicinity around it is functionally related to his ultimate position within the dominance hierarchy (cf. also Blood and Livant 1957).

Not only the occupation of lecture rooms but also of restaurants has been studied: "Have you ever observed how a pub fills up in the afternoon? If there are no special attractions in the centre, the 'cosy corners' are first occupied. When they are filled, the customers sit down at the tables along the walls. When all the chairs are taken up which have some kind of protection in some direction, people occupy the unprotected chairs in the middle of the pub, which are objects of attraction to all eyes. The idea of choosing a table in the centre of a quite empty restaurant hardly ever occurs to any human being" (Kleemann 1963: 77-78).

All these problems connected with hierarchy and territoriality at right angle structures were evidently acknowledged as well by recent organizers of political and other conferences as by ancient kings: "The importance of the circular seating arrangement as a symbol of equality can be clearly seen in the legend of King Arthur; the Round Table was a sign of the equality of the 150 knights who sat around ('about') it" (Winick and Holt 1961: 173).

On many different levels behavioural territoriality has shown itself to be manifest within rooms of various magnitude, design and use, and a fast growing number of studies are being made in this area which, together with the next, are perhaps the only ones where our actual knowledge is more than fragmentary.

4.3.11. Confinement settings

4.3.11.1. Isolation and the nervous system:

It must first be emphasized that the term confinement settings here denotes closed institutions into which humans enter voluntarily or involuntarily. General features are, of course, the barriers which separate these restricted environments from the outside world, which are difficult to pass and inside which people are compelled, in varying degree, to stay for a limited or unlimited period of time (cf. Ellenberger 1971: 188-192).

Confinement settings thus reduce the freedom of movement that the individual normally enjoys, but they do not always involve isolation, which is the result of the removal of individuals from their accustomed milieu, above all from their companions. However, there are most often combinations between the two in a variety of more or less stressful situations, the reactions to which are throughout very similar. In short, one can interpret the human behaviour in confinement and isolation as an attempt to maintain some level of arousal (cf. Burns and Kimura 1963: 170, 178).

Grey Walter (1953) stressed that the nervous system requires constant sensory input to function normally and efficiently; it could be added that this input must be meaningful (Davis, McCourt, Solomon and Solomon 1959-1960). Success in meeting most of life's basic needs involves becoming responsive to appropriate cues from the physical and social milieu in which we live. This can only be done through the sensory apparatus in the form of complex perceptions. Such perceptions remain with us through life at various levels of recall, aiding us with our primary task of survival.

"To be alone, cut off from familiar things and other people, is an experience that is both sought and feared, depending upon what expectancies, values, and goals one imputes to the situation. Some can be terribly disturbed by the stress-laden condition of loneliness; others, as we shall see, seek it out intentionally, finding in it comfort or the secret to a new integration of the personality" (Brownfield 1965: 10). In any case it is indubitable that as the length and severity of the confinement-isolation period increases, the behaviour of the individual is quite likely to change towards the abnormal.

Sometimes all such phenomena, that is, the confinement to a limited space, the separation from particular persons, places or things, the removal from the total environment by the monotonizing, reduction or elimination of stimulation, are analyzed under the concept of isolation (op. cit. p. 10-12). It should be remembered, however, that confinement is predominantly characterized by monotony and boredom, that separation in this sense equals what was earlier defined as isolation, and that removal from the total environment is still not possible although it is aimed at in experiments. (cf. Walther-Büel 1958: 196; Poulton 1970: 62-67; *Man in Isolation and Confinement* 1973).

In connection with our treatise on children's territories reference was briefly made to hospitalism through lack of adequate personal and perhaps also spatial conditions and its not seldom mortal influence in very small infants (p. 58). Without doubt hospitalism depends on a special form of sensory deprivation during a crucial period for development and imprinting of the nervous system. It has, however, long been known that even adults who are in different ways isolated for long periods may suffer from mental abnormalities.

Experimentally it has been shown that sensory deprivation can be attained by means of reduced patterning, reduced absolute levels and imposed structuring of stimuli, the last of which involves a narrowing down of the variety of sensory and perceptual experience to an invariant level. Observations have shown the following human reactions in such cases: "intense desire for extrinsic sensory stimuli and bodily motion, increased suggestibility, impairment of organized thinking, oppression and depression, and, in extreme cases, hallucinations, delusions, and confusion" (Solomon, Leiderman, Mendelson and Wexler 1957-1958: 362-363; cf. also Kubzansky and Leiderman 1961). In fact acute hallucinatory melancholia occurs rarely in freedom and, like acute hallucinatory paranoia, is a characteristic psychosis of solitary confinement (cf. Nitsche and Wilmanns 1970: 74).

In the 5th century A.D. monasteries of the West were afflicted by a widespread epidemic of a peculiar neurosis called acedia. It was a consuming boredom associated with doubts about one's religious vocation, and *horror loci*, which here means repulsion for the monastery cell. Also in the Middle Ages and later there have been cases and epidemics of acedia and other forms of mental disorder in monasteries. It seems reasonable to assume that territorial confinement and destructuring has contributed to these phenomena (Ellenberger 1960: 136), which might also be related to claustrophobia (cf. Burton 1964: 298).

4.3.11.2. Experimental confinement:
The territorial behaviour in confinement indubitably differs with changing psychological conditions and varying degrees of restriction. Our treatment starts with the most voluntary form, the experimental. It must be underlined that the reaction of a person who can at any moment withdraw from the stressful situation should not be compared with the behaviour in real, serious

experience. "However, it is likely that the more immobilizing confinement conditions are made, the stronger will be the stress effects. At some point a perceptual isolation experiment might be turned into a pain endurance experiment. Experiments which allow the S to move about within the isolation room, should be less stressful than experiments where the S is confined to his bed" (Zuckerman 1964: 265-266).

As early as 1950 investigations were made in which a number of often paid subjects had, for instance, to stay in closed-off beds with a very restricted extrinsic sensory input, which they could not tolerate more than two or three days (cf. R. Cooper 1968). Ten years later the first large-scale experiment was undertaken, as reported in "Psychological and Social Adjustment in a Simulated Shelter" (Altman, Smith, Meyers, McKenna and Bryson 1961). After three short pilot studies four groups of 30 persons each were chosen, containing people of both sexes and between 7 and 72 years of age. Three groups stayed one week and the fourth two weeks with 11 adults joining, coming in during the last 20 hours in the closed shelter. It was found that the amount of space available to shelterers, 8 square and 58 cubic feet per person, was adequate for good individual adjustment and a satisfactory level of group organization and morale. This assumed a high degree of flexibility in converting three-tier bunking space into sitting and recreation space. Included was storage, food preparation and lavatory space but not space for ventilation and auxiliary power equipment.

Neither crowding nor lack of privacy resulting from this experiment was a problem sufficiently serious to suggest that more space is absolutely required for such a period as long as adequate ventilation and temperature conditions can be maintained. As a comparison it was said that different American and Swedish authorities had recommended shelters with 10 to 12 square feet per person in civil defense protection service. And a German experiment with healthy males between 16 and 47 years of age during five days in a shelter containing just 5.5 square feet per occupant had showed that this was adequate, "but only in the most minimum sense" (op. cit. p. 21).

In a later study 18 American navy recruits with as many controls were run in dyads, living and working in a small room for ten days with minimum outside contact. "That the stress was not trivial for isolated Ss is indicated by the fact that two of the nine isolated dyads aborted – asked to be released from isolation – before the ten-day period had elapsed. In addition, two of the remaining seven displayed serious overt hostility toward each other" (Haythorn, Altman and Myers 1966: 303).

The isolated subjects first established bed territoriality, followed by side of table and finally by chair territoriality. Perhaps two factors associated with beds led to this rapidly-begun and persistent behaviour. First, beds possess a high degree of personal character connected with olfactory cues, body contact, amount of time spent there and general cultural practices regarding the inviolability and sanctity of a person's bed, bedding and pillow. Second, beds are located in a fixed geographical region.

The next order of territoriality occurred for areas around the table, which became pronounced by the second three-day block. Red and green chair preferences then grew strong and reached their peak during the final days of isolation. Side of table territoriality may have developed more rapidly because it entailed a fixed geographical area, while chair territoriality involved movable objects. Furthermore, sides of the table may have assumed importance because of unique cues associated with a specific geographical position, such as wall arrangements, lighting, visual configurations and so on.

"To summarize, the present experiment indicated that a condition of social isolation, in which pairs of men were isolated from society for ten days, led to a gradual increase in territorial behavior with respect to areas and objects in the environment and to a general pattern of social withdrawal" (Altman and Haythorn 1967: 181).

A third study involved different combinations, yielding eight isolation conditions ranging from a short 4-day, private, stimulated environment to a 20-day, non-stimulated, non-private environment. In the last milieu a large proportion of groups, 53 percent, were unable to complete the isolation period and aborted. "They reported more feelings of stress and anxiety,... performed less effectively on team tasks, had perceptual changes involving greater stimulus boundedness and lower ideational activity and imaginative capacity....

Most important, they showed a characteristic pattern of territorial behavior, social activity and bed usage as they approached their abort day. Aborters, typically, showed *lower* territorial behavior early in isolation, compared with completers, and *higher* territorial behavior later.... If one views territorial behavior as an adaptive response, important to individual and group integrity and identity, especially in an isolated and confined situation, then the manifestation of such behavior early in a relationship could be taken as a sign that the group members had begun behaving so as to create a viable relationship with one another" (Altman 1971: 296-297; cf. also S. Smith 1969).

4.3.11.3. Psychiatric hospitals:

Going over to the mental hospital, we arrive in a normally closed institution where admission is in most cases, and departure nearly always, involuntary. As a complement to general evidence presented in the section on territories of the mentally abnormal (4.1.3.) we here give some reports which seem to be particularly dependent on confinement in psychiatric institutions.

In the U.S.A. schizophrenic males from a research ward were studied as to territoriality, rank order and other behavioural phenomena by means of investigations in a dayroom, marked with tape into three feet square grids (Esser, Chamberlain, Chapple and Kline 1964). A first paper was built on 330 location observations each of all the 22 patients during 16 weeks, and the dominance hierarchy was determined according to interaction contacts. If a person was found in a certain place during at least 25 percent of the observations, the crucial square or group of squares was called his territory (for one individual 273 of the 330 observations were made in one spot). The results were that only half of the patients made use of the available space and half occupied specific territories, that the highest and lowest in rank did not show territorial behaviour – in the first case because of total freedom to go unimpeded and in the second because of total domination by others everywhere – and that with non-established position in the hierarchy the chances for aggressive incidents increased.

After three years there was a new intense study over six weeks, when territory was determined for places with at least 15 percent of the total number of location observations for every single person. The results were now i.a. that patients high in rank dominated the lower ranked in 65 percent of encounters outside territories and in 87.5 percent of encounters within their territories (Esser 1970).

Without doubt "Patient space too is comprised of a variety of 'territories'. The restrooms, beds, and night stands represent a few of the more common areas ordinarily reserved for patient use, but none, ordinarily, are inviolably private areas. In practice, patients at any level of retardation seek out areas of relative privacy. For the profoundly retarded, whose capacity for mobility through space is limited, one finds a not infrequent positioning in spots of relative privacy, i.e., under their bed, in the same chair or corner day after day, or similar unoccupied spots where 'squatter's rights' are open. Higher-grade retardates, being generally more mobile, often make rather sophisticated and extended use of space. Working patients 'take over' storage space in their work places. Over the years, employees yield informal 'ownership' or 'title' to this space and possessiveness on the 'owner's' part is speedily conveyed to any and all intruders" (Cleland and Dingman 1970: 156).

An interesting observation from a psychiatric ward was that only in six-bed and larger rooms was more than one patient likely to occupy the space at a given time. In smaller rooms, the most probable number of occupants was one. As long as possible, the patients seemed to treat all bedrooms, regardless of size, as if they were single rooms. Their remarkable success in achieving this goal suggested a tacit arrangement among them to leave each other alone in the bedrooms. "Whether this represents a mutual respect for each other's privacy, the dominance of one patient, who stakes out the room as his territory, or some other social process cannot be determined from our data" (Ittelson, Proshansky and Rivlin 1970: 438).

A lot of evidence about territoriality in the mental hospital was offered by Goffman (1973: 227-248) in his book *Asylums*. He first divided the space available into such that was off limits or out of license for the patients, into what he called surveillance space that is, areas where the patients were allowed to be but where they were subject to the authority and restrictions of the establishment and, finally, into more or less non-surveillance space or free places like toilets, cafeterias, disused sub-basements, small woods adjacent to the buildings and so on. In some cases a group of patients added to their access to a free place the proprietary right to keep out all other patients except when properly invited. Such group territories as well as individual ones were found, e.g., in the recreation buildings, guardhouses, porches and even corners in day rooms, segregated by chairs.

On neglected wards a special pecking order of a sort was in practice, with vocal patients in good contact taking favorite chairs and benches from those not in contact. This was in a known instance carried to a point where one patient forced a mute one off a footrest, leaving the vocal patient with a chair and a footrest, and the mute patient with nothing at all – a difference that is not negligible considering the fact that except for breaks at mealtime, some patients spent the whole of the day on these wards doing nothing but sitting or standing in one place. Perhaps the minimum space that was built into a personal territory was that provided by a blanket. In some wards, a few patients would carry their blankets around with them during the whole day. In an act thought to be highly regressive, each of them would curl up on the floor with his blanket completely covering him. Within this covered space the patient had some margin of control.

"Every patient, no matter how sick he is, needs some privacy and a place he can call his own where he may store his personal possessions. After all, man, like other animals, has territorial instincts, and those we ignore to his peril.

Even a comatose patient needs a closet where his clothing can hang to confirm the optimism underlying our therapeutic endeavors. Deteriorated schizophrenics and severely retarded patients quickly learn to use this private space and to enjoy it. To the relatives of the patients, the provision of this private space means that we are treating each patient as a somebody who has human needs that matter, and not as a nobody who has lost humanity" (R. Barton 1966: 336).

4.3.11.4 "Nestling" patients:
There is, however, also quite another reaction of territorial character in asylums of different kinds, known above all from mental hospitals and prisons. It was studied in France by Daumézon (1946-1947), who treated mental patients who had recovered but "taken root" in the hospital so that they tried to escape discharge or to return when discharged, just as captive animals often come back to their cages after escape. We may interpret such cases by saying that these patients have succeeded in acquiring a new territory in the mental hospital, where they have often stayed for a very long time. Some people will perhaps object that the comparison is inaccurate, because the animal from the zoo has in most cases no real choice, whereas the "nestling" patient has a choice but prefers captivity to freedom.

However, there is often less difference than one could imagine, because the "nestling" patient mostly is a person without his own home, who has created a territory for himself in the mental hospital. When discharged he is like an escaped lion with no place to seek protection except in the cage. The "nestling" process has been investigated mostly in patients who have recovered spontaneously. Among non-recovered patients it is much more difficult to recognize. But it could be rewarding to try to ascertain to what extent the "nestling" contributes to making the disease chronic by hampering recovery in certain cases, or, on the contrary, to try to ascertain whether the inability to "nestle" does not increase the suffering of certain mental patients (cf. Gatto and Dean 1955; Ellenberger 1960).

But the "nestling" patients are without doubt exceptions. The majority of inmates cannot feel at home in the hospital and give various expressions to their lack of adequate territories. Very disclosing here are the few comparisons which have been made of the behaviour of the same person in the hospital and at home. Particularly striking was the case of one man, who behaved in a wholly bizarre way in the hospital but quite normally in his house, and it was suggested that the explanation is territorial. In summary: "I found that the physical home setting, the peculiar arrangement of family life space, was a most valuable aid in understanding the form of the couple's adjustment. The couples in which one or both members appeared emotionally disturbed *away from home* had rigid, constricted, yet personally significant home environments which seemed to be an important factor in maintaining the family equilibrium" (Colman 1968: 465).

Thus space comprises a powerful aspect of the institutional value system. It enters importantly into the daily lives of patients and employees at nearly every rank and carries such weight that any reduction amounts literally to diminished status for the person who loses 'ground' (Cleland and Dingman 1970: 158; cf. also Sommer and Osmond 1961). "Hospital rooms, as currently designed, take into account virtually everything except the psychological influence of size, proportions, and outside view on the patient" (E. T. Hall 1963: 432).

In the United States, however, Osmond (e.g., 1961) has suggested a design that will allow the patient a small place to be away from the suffering of others, a place where he can "pull himself together" from time to time. This means a hospital in which very small spaces radiate in a circle from slightly larger rooms, in which two to four people can interact. These, in turn, are placed around a community day room, in which larger groups can meet. In France, Sivadon, first at Neuilly-sur-Marne and later in the Château de la Verrière at Le Mesnil-St. Denis, actually used space as a therapeutic agent, arranging the hospital in the form of small "villages" in a hierarchy from single to complex units. He concentrated on open spaces rather than on fences and walls, designing internal space so that room size can be altered by opening and closing sliding sections of the walls according to Japanese practice (cf., e.g., Baker, Davies and Sivadon 1959; Sivadon 1973).

4.3.11.5. Prison and prisoners:
Kurt Lewin (1936: 42-43) made the self-evident remark: "An example of a very limited space of free movement is the life space of a prisoner". Without doubt the dimensions of cells are in most cases the alpha and omega of prison life. The standard spatial amount supposed to be available in American prison cells is 38.5 square feet per person, but jails in Washington, D.C. have actually only about 19 square feet per person (Freedman 1975: 4).

As contrasts the conditions in two internment camps during the Second World War should be reported: in one Japanese camp for Americans the space for every person was estimated at 62 square feet and 437 cubic feet and in the strongly disreputable German concentration camp of Belsen there was in one barrack just 3 square feet and 22 cubic feet per person (Biderman 1967:

244). No wonder that hallucinations and other symptoms of the "barbed wire disease" (Vischer 1918) were frequent under such conditions.

One can easily assume that under prison conditions the drive for personal territory should be strong. As an example we will first cite one German description from a Soviet camp for prisoners of war: "A middle-class concept of property was caricatured by an individual who limited his place in the bunk by means of nailing pieces of board and of putting up strings. As with normal life, the man in prison was soon a slave of his customs while the process of inner petrifying proceeded without interruption" (Hassenstein 1950: 7; cf. also Leyhausen 1973a: 105).

In fact there are different kinds of territories even in a prison. "Geographical boundaries and prison regulations thereby define multiple home 'territories' within the penitentiary. Indeed, most of the inmates refer to their cell or dorm as their 'home'. Which of these home 'territories' a man lives in is largely a matter or his own choice. Some men prefer privacy; others find single cells confining and so prefer to live in dormitories. Though initially on entering the prison most men are assigned to dormitories, they are soon permitted to petition civilian clerks to live in other quarters. Moves are frequent, averaging two to three moves per man per year. Living assignments, in the main, reflect inmate preference though, occasionally, violent inmates may be separated from one another by officials" (L. H. Roth 1971: 511).

One particular American case involved 1,220 male prisoners, 107 of whom were homosexuals mostly preferring to live in cell blocks. This was especially so among 14 aggressive homosexuals, known by other inmates as "rapists". Only two of them lived together in the same area or home territory; the other twelve were apart from one another. Thus, on the average, one homosexual "rapist" lived in company with three or four other men in his territory who were known to engage in homosexual activity. "In other words, the prison contains multiple 'territories' in which one predator roams, unchallenged by other predators, surrounded by the 'prey' of his species" (op. cit. p. 512).

Observations of general interest seem to be that in prison there is a significant association between dominance and territorial possession (Austin and Bates 1973-1974) and that a decline in territorial behaviour is followed by an increase of disruptive behaviour (Sundstrom and Altman 1974). Further, cellular confinement is more inducive of severe psychosis and emotional regression, while group life in prison is more indicative of anti-social behaviour (Ellenberger 1960: 136-137).

Admission into prison is not seldom followed by a short-lived state of furious agitation, probably a consequence of sudden territorial confinement

and known as *"Zuchthausknall"*. This behaviour is most often terribly violent: "When an inmate destroys all the furnishings of his cell by breaking,
tearing, ripping and burning, he is in a sense breaking his own home, where he
spends the larger part of his life, where he eats and sleeps and dreams, and
which he often takes great pains to make livable and to beautify. The inmate
thus sees the cell as an extension of himself; but at the same time the walls of
the cell represent confining authority. The cell thus becomes both a symbol of
himself, and of his deprivation, where authority, whether good or bad, is most
concrete and immediate. The cell is the penitentiary" (Cormier, Kennedy and
Sendbuehler 1967: 318).

Comparative measurements of the "body-buffer" zones of eight violent
and six non-violent prisoners showed that these zones were four times larger
in the first than in the second group. Among the violent prisoners the rear
zones were larger than the front zones, while this condition was opposite
among the non-violents. The large zones in the violent group might reflect a
pathological body image state, and the psychopathological complex might
include, among other factors, a marked disturbance of personal space (Kinzel
1970). Another investigation of 36 inmates generally confirmed these results
but found that both aggressives and non-aggressives had increased sensitivity
to approach from the rear (Hildreth, Derogatis and McCusker 1971). These
observations give important clues to the territorial background of aggressive,
pathological behaviour as well as to the diagnosis and treatment of violence.

Very interesting and far-reaching are those consequences of confinement
and isolation which constitute the prerequisites of brainwashing in prisoners
(cf. Hunter 1956). Some of the phenomena grouped in this term have long
been known, but they were actualized and properly named in connection with
the Moskva trials in the 1930s, the Mindszenty Affair in 1948-1949, the
Korean Conflict 1950-1953 and the "Thought Reform" in Chinese com-
munist prisons during later decades. It is certainly true that "the most important effect of the social isolation which existed was the consequent emotional
isolation which prevented a man from validating any of his beliefs, attitudes,
and values through meaningful interaction with other men at a time when
these were under heavy attack from many sources, and when no accurate
information was available" (Schein 1956: 155).

It seems, however, reasonable to assume that both the social and the territorial constraint in isolation and confinement are responsible for the fatal
human disintegration called brainwashing. But we must remember that the
severity of the confinement always depends on the special cultural and psychological view of the persons involved. This can be illustrated by adjacent

peoples of French West Africa. Imprisonment in one place "seems an adventure that has nothing dishonourable about it; in another, on the contrary, it is equivalent to being condemned to death. There are some Africans who, if you put them in prison, will become a sort of domestic servant, and end by regarding themselves as members of your family. But if you imprison a Fulani he will die" (Delavignette 1968: 86). It could be that "nestling" is psychologically and culturally possible in the first case, in the second not (cf. e.g. Boven 1943).

In any case admission to a total institution seems always to be a serious affair for the individual and the reasons are summarized below: "In the institution people live communally with a minimum of privacy, and yet their relationships with each other are slender. Many subsist in a kind of defensive shell of isolation. Their mobility is restricted, and they have little access to general society. Their social experiences are limited, and the staff lead a rather separate existence from them. They are subtly oriented towards a system in which they submit to orderly routine, lack creative occupation and cannot exercise much self- determination" (Townsend 1962: 328-329).

Further, as could be expected and as is here verified, total institutions, with their great confinement of space, evoke different, clear and striking expressions of behavioural territoriality. Next, probable connections between urban crime, mental disorder and territoriality will be discussed.

4.3.12. Urban pathology and territoriality

4.3.12.1. Cities and crime:
It has long been known that both the total amount and the types of deviant behaviour, exhibited by residents of different regions, vary considerably. This seems to be true of criminality as well as of what perhaps could be called pure mental disorders and not only as a consequence of the fact that laws and their application, psychiatric diagnosis and standards of hospitalization 'and imprisoning are not always equal inside, and never between, countries. Especially this is quite evident: "Different areas of the city are associated with different rates of deviant behaviour and with particular forms of deviance" (Timms 1971: 31).

Thus Shaw and McKay (Burgess 1942), after twenty years' study of twenty American cities, found not only that physical deterioration and social disorganization were greatest in the central, intermediate in the middle and least in the outer urban zones but also that juvenile delinquency rates regularly declined with progression from the innermost to the outermost zones.

According to the National Commission on the Causes and Prevention of Violence in the United States, crime is "primarily a phenomenon of large cities". It was reported that per 100,000 people in the country there are yearly 1,070 crimes in rural areas, 2,376 in the suburbs, 3,430 in cities of 50,000 to 100,000 persons and 5,307 in cities with over a quarter of a million people. Six cities with more than a million persons have 10 percent of the country's population but 30 percent of its major violent crimes (cf. Ehrlich and Freedman 1971: 11). It is, however, not astonishing that a detailed analysis has in some cases shown that this urban centrifugal diminishment of crime is not without exceptions and not quite so simple as earlier thought (cf., e.g., Lander 1954: 84-88). With the centres of population-increase moving towards the suburbs, there has sometimes been a greater crime augmentation here than in the cores.

If, then, in most countries there is a growing criminality predominantly in parallel with increasing population density from small towns to big cities (e.g., Reckless 1964: 30) as well as from the outskirts toward the urban core, there is, as yet, hardly any consensus as to the causality of this phenomenon. For instance it has been said: "The higher crime rates of urban centers, especially those of crimes against property, are too consistent, and of too world-wide prevalence, to make sense in terms of either biological or economic theory except as the idea of social influences ('learning by association') is given a high order of priority in the scheme of explanation" (Vold 1958: 189). Surely such a statement is dubious, while in particular the general character, the wide distribution and the strong frequency of these phenomena speak for some kind of common innate background.

Of course there are many factors which tend to be associated with high population and high density, e.g., poverty, bad housing, alcoholism, heterogeneity and mobility of the inhabitants, etc. (*A Systematic Source Book in Rural Sociology* 1931: 297; Ehrlich and Freedman 1971: 11). It is also theoretically possible but not very probable that hereditary factors for pathological behaviour are coupled with such factors for crowded habitation aptitude (cf. Zlutnick and Altman 1972). In any case: "No city of a million or more people anywhere in the world today is free from juvenile delinquency and crime. This is the case in old cities and new cities, in cities with an ancient Christian tradition, in cities in India, and in cities that have developed within the Islamic tradition. Perhaps the most discouraging city from this point of view is Tel Aviv, because this was intended to be a new, young, moral, good city. In Tel Aviv, planners started a new, without having to deal with the sense of ages of sin that seems to hang over so many old cities in the Middle East and the Orient. But there is juvenile delinquency in Tel Aviv, just as there is juvenile delinquency in other large cities – in Copenhagen, or New York, or Taipei. There seems to be something about the size of the unit that is unmanageable at present, that makes it very difficult to care for children responsibly" (Mead 1964-1965: 29).

4.3.12.2 Urban mental disorder:

Leaving the constellation cities and crime we now have an interesting opportunity to trace the historic development of urbanization and mental disease in Belgium. Thus in the community of Geel all psychiatric patients from several Belgian cities in a unique way have been recieved and cared for in private families without any hospitalization since medieval times. Particularly for the years 1795-1855 and 1860-1970 it has been possible to calculate general figures for the magnitude of the population, the degree of urbanization and the number of the mentally diseased. For instance it was shown that between 1810 and 1846 the population of Brussels increased by 61 percent, while the number of the mentally disordered in the city tripled.

After a critical analysis of possible sources of error, the authors in this case find the causal relations indubitable. "Above all the enormous percentage of patients from cities cannot go unnoticed. It seems impossible to deny the decisive influence of the urban environment in combination with industrialization as sure factors behind mental abnormality. The statistics from the colony of Geel are striking proof of this. What the development in Brussels between the years 1800 and 1850 anticipated was confirmed between 1860 and 1965 for the whole of Belgium. Urbanization and mental abnormality are constant companions" (DeBont and Veraghtert 1974: 13, by courtesy of Professor Sven-Ulric Palme, Uppsala, Sweden).

Faris and Dunham (1939: IX-XX, 193), in their study of 34,864 cases of mental disease in Chicago 1922-1934, showed that the total insanity rate followed the ecological structure of the city, being highest in the central areas of social disorganization and steadily declining towards the periphery of the city, and that this was particularly evident for schizophrenia. In this connection it should be remembered that "Privacy, a space of one's own, is one of the most important aids in the treatment of schizophrenics. Improvement is noted immediately when patients have a cubicle, into which they can invite some, and from which they can exclude other people" (Rosenberg 1960: 425).

Faris (1948: 227) was still more outspoken when he maintained: "By far the greatest and most revealing contrasts of rates of mental disorders have been found in the various sections of large industrial cities. Here the contrasts are not a matter of high rates being merely three times greater than low rates; the contrasts are on the order of ten to one or greater. Furthermore, the study of variations in urban districts whose characteristics are already well known yields far more meaningful information than does the cruder contrast between urban and rural areas". As to this later antithesis Hare (1952: 586) in his prize-winning work on "The Ecology of Mental Disease" concluded: "It has long been known that the incidence of vice, crime, suicide and mental disease is higher in urban than in rural areas, and the evidence for this is now overwhelming".

But new critics of the presumed over-representative pathology of urban areas continually appear, concentrating on different possible bias, not the least an alleged old antagonism toward the city. Thus, e.g., Srole (1972) did not believe that there were real differences of mental disease between urban and rural districts. And even though Weinberg (1967: 25) admitted: "In general, ecological distributions are significant in showing the communities where the varied disorders are concentrated and where the disorders are sparse". But he stated: "Perhaps there is no single general inference to be made concerning the influence of the community on disorders, especially schizophrenia".

Maybe the truth is that in certain areas the urbanization of the countryside has gone so far that eventual discrepancies have disappeared. But scrutinizing a number of seemingly unbiased studies of psychiatric disorders from different parts of the world, every one made by the same investigator in both urban and rural setting, Dohrenwend and Dohrenwend (1973: 1369) stressed: "On the basis of this evidence – and it is the best we have available – there seems to be a tendency for total rates of psychiatric disorder to be higher in urban than in rural areas, due at least in part to an excess of neurosis and personality disorder in the urban areas".

Of special interest is that Malzberg (1940: 111-113) not only found in New York State a lower incidence of mental disease among the rural than among the urban population but on the whole a steady progression of disease with increasing size of population in communities. The same was reported by Hyde and Kingsley (1944). They personally examined 60,000 American army recruits and after measures to eliminate the effects of original family nationality and socio-economic level got rejection rates for mental disease from 7.5 percent unsuited for military service where the population density was 500-1,000 per square mile, up to 14 percent unsuited, where it was over 20,000 per square mile.

Very valuable were studies made of mental health and habitation standards in Paris. It was found among deviant children, for instance, that in a control group of the left-handed there were 1.9 persons per room, in a group with troubled behaviour 2.3, in a group with psycho-motorical retardation there were 2.7 persons per room and among the mentally-retarded 3.4 (Chombart de Lauwe 1959a: 80). Still more interesting perhaps was the finding that if the habitation number of square meters per person was 12-14 a critical threshold was attained, below which healthy mental conditions were not sure. And if there were not more than 8-10 square meters per person a pathological threshold was implied under which the chances for physical and mental troubles were seriously increased (Chombart de Lauwe 1959b: 121-122). This does not, of course, necessarily mean that crowded habitation conditions cause pathological behaviour in the youth. It might be so, e.g., that deviant children have deviant parents with miserable social and economic possibilities, who cannot procure spatial habitation. Nevertheless, these studies are of great territorial interest and probably it is so that spatial constriction is the releaser of pathological predispositions.

4.3.12.3. Explanations of urban pathology:
Going more deeply into the causality question we start by listening to Hare (1952: 592): "We can say, firstly, that at the present time the conditions of modern Western civilization are becoming increasingly important in the aetiology of mental disease; and, secondly, that the principal causative factor in these conditions is lack of the sense of security and worth which an individual must derive from a social group", and, we would add, from a space of social importance.

In any case there seems to be a rather common consensus about the social deficiency of the urban environment. "There are two schools of thought about why this should be so: the first argues that social factors, including 'social isolation' breed mental illness; the second maintains that central areas attract unstable people who seek the anonymity and lack of social constraints found there. . . . However, it should be noted that most practitioners schooled in biological psychiatry question the possibility of establishing a correlation between the prevalence and incidence of mental disorders and the social factors which some sociologists suspect of causing them" (*Human Settlements* 1974: 46-47).

As to migration and mental disease, it has been said that immigrants, both foreign- and native-born, stand greater risk of being affected by psychiatric disorder than other groups, but this should probably rather be put in connection with homesickness and lack of new adequate territories than with selective migration to the cities by the mentally insane. Certainly of great importance is the hypothesis supported by data that the "general incidence of emotional disorder in children parallels mobility rate, and that greater community mobility and poor integration has a more disturbing effect particularly upon the emotional adjustment of boys" (Gordon and Gordon 1959: 96). Concerning adults it is concluded that "the surest way to induce pathological responses in people through environmental manipulation is to force their move from a neighborhood which is congruent with their life styles without either a substitute life style desired on their part or a physically acceptable neighborhood open for their mass relocation" (Michelson 1970: 166).

Even though immigration and mobility are important characteristics of urban areas, it seems, however, not probable that they *per se* are solely responsible for the urban overweight of mental deficiency, particularly as this phenomenon has also been a reality when migration was not part of the picture. But if movement phenomena are not decisive, it is necessary to look at the total urban environment. G. Simmel (1957: 635-636) already at the turn of the century stressed the psychological consequences of urban intensification of the nervous stimulation and the eventual consequent blasé attitude – which can develop into withdrawal and pathological symptoms in connection with this mental strain (Plant 1939: 227-228; cf. also Malmberg 1971: 11).

The search for the factors involved in urban mental disorder has more and more been concentrated on specific aspects of the city. Once it was thought that housing conditions could be relevant and the great slum reconstructions were a consequence of this hypothesis. Without doubt physical health sometimes increased following such interferences, but the social pathologies did not lessen appreciably (Wilner, Walkley, Pinkerton and Tayback 1962: 241-252; Schorr 1963: 7-33).

However, two phenomena of a territorial character remain, which with great probability could be involved in the pathology of the city, namely, overcrowding – here defined as many persons per room – and high density – equal to many persons per areal unit. At least the first one is thought to have effects in the context as demonstrated for Paris. But when R. C. Schmitt (1966) was able to test the two factors against each other in Honolulu, Hawaii, he found high density to be the more important one, quite opposite to the findings of Jacobs (1962: 200-221) and others. It should be stressed that the term crowding is mostly used in order to denote the psychological phenomena which can be the consequence of dense population. In certain cases relations have become evident after density has been dissolved into its four components: (a) the number of persons per room; (b) the number of rooms per housing unit; (c) the number of housing units per structure; and (d) the number of residential structures per acre. Here it was shown that the most important component was number of persons per room and next came housing units per structure. It was maintained that overcrowding can affect mortality, fertility, ineffectual parental care, juvenile delinquency and psychiatric disorder (cf. Galle, Gove and McPherson 1972).

Great numbers of humans per unit of area are, however, not invariably associated with pathologies, which was likewise shown by R. C. Schmitt (1963) for Hongkong. Thirteen census tracts in this city have over 2,000 persons per acre of ground, while the highest densities in the U.S.A. are just 450 in Boston and New York. Yet, Hongkong is anything but a "behavioural sink" (sensu Calhoun 1962a) with the rates for all cases of serious crime less than half the American figures and the hospitalizations for psychiatric disorders less than one tenth of the number reported for United States.

"The effects of crowding thus cannot be evaluated solely in terms of population density. They depend on social organization and on the nature of relationships between individual people. Holland and Hongkong are among the most crowded areas of the world yet their populations enjoy good physical and mental health. Centuries of experience with crowding have forced them to develop patterns of human relationships that minimize social conflicts and allow people to retain a large measure of individual freedom despite lack of privacy. This does not mean that man can indefinitely increase the density of his populations but only that the safe limits have not been determined" (Dubos 1970: 171; as to recent critical discussion of the constellation crowding and mental disorder see Lawrence 1974; Stokols 1976; Choi, Mirjafari and Weaver 1976).

Indubitably, disruption to the individual and his psyche in a particular environment is very much dependent on the definitions and rules specified for him by the cultural system and by his relations within the social system (cf. Michelson 1970: 157). In the cited cases the secret could be, as suggested that, e.g., some Eastern peoples have adapted well to great number and close living. This in turn might have been possible through means of a superior capacity for adequately structuring and manipulating miniature space, which is evident both from housing, gardening and agriculture in China and Japan (cf. R. C. Schmitt 1963: 216; Canter and Canter 1971; R. A. Smith 1971). For "It is not the number of people per acre but rather the nature of separation of these people from each other and from nonresidential land uses that comprises the physical agent of health or pathology" (Michelson 1970: 157).

Finally we can say that in principle "Urbanization is deterritorialization in the classic sense of denial of land. But perhaps there may be conceptual substitutes or symbolic channels that will preserve our biological sanity. We may be sure, however, that we must somehow preserve NO TRESPASSING signs" (Ardrey 1972: 227-228). How people feel about giant agglomerations is best indicated by their headlong effort to escape them. The bigger the city, the higher the cost of space, but the more the level of living rises, the more people are willing to pay for low-density habitation. Nevertheless, as urbanized areas expand and collide, life in low-density surroundings becomes more and more difficult to attain, areally and economically, for the great majority of city people (cf. K. Davis 1965: 53).

The stress of urban life is not always thought to have yet had any extreme and catastrophic effects on common people. But what is nowadays considered normal urban behaviour is by some said to be strikingly like traits of schizophrenia. It is also marked by extreme withdrawal from stress, and this has led to an unrealistic belief in the self- sufficiency of individuals. This individualism is very different from healthy democratic respect for the single person's rights. Where contact with others reaches very high proportions – beyond the capacity of the individual organism – the human being is forced to shut these contacts out, and therefore to maintain an unreal belief in his own powers of self-sufficiency (cf. C. Alexander 1968: 78-79).

Thus a wealth of facts and conditions make it difficult to escape the conclusion that behavioural territoriality, even though the proper term is not much used in the context, constitutes a most important factor in urban pathology. It remains to look for some special forms of territory.

4.4. Special territories

4.4.1. Tombs

4.4.1.1. Interment and cemetery:
One remarkable and interesting fact is that territories do not just belong to living humans. They are namely still found among the dead in the form of tombs of various kinds. It could, of course, be stated: "The earth is one vast burial ground" (Puckle 1926: 129). But the spatial problems are mostly knitted to the special, collective interment areas, called cemeteries, which are found not the least in the urban context.

"As a result of population increase and urban centralization, one further demand for land, unfortunately a cumulative one, must be noted: the expansion of urban cemeteries in all cultures that maintain, as most 'Christian' nations do, the Paleolithic habit of earth burial. This has resulted in the migration of the burying ground from the center to the outskirts of metropolitan areas, where vast cemeteries serve, indeed, as temporary suburban parks, until they become a wilderness of stone monuments. Unless the custom of periodically emptying out these cemeteries, as was done in London and Paris with the bones in old churchyards, takes hold, or until cremation replaces burial, the demand for open spaces for the dead threatens to crowd the quarters of the living on a scale impossible to conceive in earlier urban cultures" (Mumford 1956: 394-395).

In old times burial took place either singly or in collective cemeteries near the settlements, more rarely inside habitated areas or even in houses, occasionally in sites, chosen for special reasons, including tomb chambers and churches. The tombs may have been lined with matting, bricks, etc., and marked by memorials, varying from a simple stone or wooden board to sumptuous mausoleums. Interment is probably the oldest method of burial, practised at least from the Middle Paleolithic. And cremation is not much younger, known from the Neolithic.

4.4.1.2. Tomb as house and home:
Tombs were originally often conceived of as houses for the dead in the form of tomb chambers and house-shaped sarcophagi. Urns, too, could be given the shape of a house, as among the Etruscans. In fact prehistoric tomb barrows were generally built around an actual round hut, in which the body was placed, along with tools and other personal effects (cf. Deffontaines 1948: 43-67, 178-193).

Already during the Stone Age tombs were sometimes surrounded and thus limited by large stones, as in the Ertebølle culture, or covered by spectacular marks in the form of dolmens, as in the Megalithic period. In Egypt the original sand mound over the tomb became a rectangular stone mastaba, and the superimposition on each other of mastabas of decreasing size finally produced the pyramid. Both in Mesopotamia and on Cyprus circular stone burial structures have been found, often in groups enclosed by dry-stone walls and roofed with corbeled vaults, thus producing the wellknown "beehive tomb", where people could be buried over several generations. And in Rome there were along Via Appia lines of tombs varying in type: mausoleum, tumulus, columbarium and others, mostly marked by epitaphs with biographical information (cf. Werblowsky 1964). "In very old times the tomb was part of the family property and was found in the middle of the settlement not far from the door" (Fustel de Coulanges 1920: 34-35).

In medieval Christian thought the tomb was considered an earthly prototype and symbol of a heavenly home, a concept which had already been evidenced in the Roman catacombs. The church building itself functioned as a tomb, and it was quite common to intern bodies in churches, chapels and monasteries with depictions of important deceased in carved or painted plaques or life-size "*gîsants*", i.e. sculptured figures of the dead, lying on their backs, placed above. But since the Renaissance the idea of the tomb as a home has disappeared with time (cf. Gowans 1964: 283), at least in Christian cultures.

In Moslem countries the situation is quite another. Particularly from Egypt we know that cemeteries serve as 'villegiature cities', that is recreation places on Thursday evening and Friday." Following the oldest Egyptian tradition, each well-to-do family possesses an '*arafa*' or House of the Dead which is occupied by old servants, the wet-nurses still alive, and by the families of undertakers. The City of the Dead in Cairo was also the hideout of outlaws and smugglers, and the theater of spectacles not quite inciting to virtue..." (Benet 1963-1964: 16).

According to detailed descriptions deceased persons are thought to occupy their tomb territories temporarily: "On Thursdays the dead watch our kind actions for them from their tombs and are pleased by them. The nocturnal prayer makes amends for the sins, and God descends in the night to forgive the supplicant. From early times females have also had the tendency to pass the night in the cemetery from Thursday to Friday. We have the same old custom that night when the destiny for the year is decided but with the aggravation that both men and women are observed together during this Nisf Sha'ban" (Massignon 1958: 30).

4.4.1.3. Marking and defending territories of the dead:
When comparing the settlement patterns of the living and the dead, Mumford (1961: 7) made the interesting reflection: "Mid the uneasy wanderings of paleolithic man, the dead were the first to have a permanent dwelling: a cavern, a mound marked by a cairn, a collective barrow. These were landmarks to which the living probably returned at intervals, to commune with or placate the ancestral spirits.... The city of the dead antedates the city of the living. In one sense, indeed, the city of the dead is the forerunner, almost the core, of every living city".

A general tendency is still to delimit the separate graves of the cemetery, wherever they are located. We give just one example: "In Norway a space is sometimes enclosed over the grave, about three yards square, surrounded by a low iron railing, in the centre of which a seat is placed to hold two or three people. Here, at Christmas and on other special occasions, the relatives meet and discuss family affairs and matters of local interest for some hours, in order that the dead may be kept posted with what is going on in the world in which they once played their part" (Puckle 1926: 145-146). Even though this particular formulation seems to be somewhat fanciful, customs of similar kind are well known in the Scandinavian countries.

Revealing are also the jurisdictional sides of the matter. "The right of the Englishman to burial in the parish churchyard was akin to his right to occupy his pew during church services" (P. E. Jackson 1964: 133), a right which was very fixed according to status as priest, noble or common person. Once a body is buried, laws in most countries guard the grave against unwarranted intrusions. Earlier it was often so, as we know, that the magnitude, bounding and marking of the tomb advertised the economic and social status of the dead citizen. Today regulations are mostly in favour of equal conditions for the living and the dead, the last perhaps most evident in the thousands of miniature graves in the cemeteries from the world wars. Even here, however, the integrity of every single unit is observed as far as possible.

The characteristic limiting, marking and defending of tombs make it very probable that behavioural territoriality, manifested by survivors, plays a role even after death. It will now be seen if it also makes sense in play and games.

4.4.2. Play and game territories

4.4.2.1. Meaning of play:

It is a fact easy to verify that animals play. A sizeable monograph on the matter was published by Groos (1896), who some few years later added a still more voluminous book on the play of man (Groos 1899). In spite of much research since that time covering both the purely zoological and the anthropological side of the phenomenon, the nature and causal background of play is still controversial.

However, it is evident that there are great similarities between usual, instinctive behaviour and play, for instance, in the form of "vacuum, substitute and displacement activity, incomplete instinctive behaviour, exploratory and appetitive behaviour. . . . As a final result we can state that play is an activity which uses acts of allochtonous origin but has a special motivation of its own, the general non-specific activity drive, i.e., a tendency to be active in any way whatsoever" (Meyer-Holzapfel 1956: 460-461).

As to dissimilarities, comparisons between playful and non-play behaviour have shown that "Differences between the two are shown to consist of the economy with which the pattern is performed, or the efficiency in terms of its function in its original context. Lack of economy arises in several ways, amongst them exaggeration, repetition, reordering of the sequence, and breaking up of the sequence by insertion of apparently unrelated acivities" (Loizos 1966: 1).

If we concentrate on exploratory behaviour it seems to be self-evident that it must be useful for the animal as well as for man when it is directed towards the environment. Play very often implies exploration of the milieu which is at the same time the background for territorial attribution. "We know that a dog gets information about his territory during hunting play. But we do not know if this is attained as an extra gain from the play with the hunted prey or if the situation has a particularly territorial side. Still less is our cognition about what, e.g., ungulates with their advanced social be- haviour can learn from play. Indeed it is suggested that the territorial field in this way could get a lot of additional characteristics, could develop new action patterns and could be emotionally divided" (Bally 1945: 54; cf. also Hutt 1966).

Certainly in some situations social and solitary forms of play appear to be reciprocally related, in that as social stimulation decreases, the amount of play with objects will increase. And in a perceptually restricted environment the length of bouts of social play becomes extended. The role of play in establishing and maintaining social relations is probably very important. "Far from being a 'spare-time', superfluous activity in either human or sub- human primate, it may be that play at certain crucial early stages is necessary for the ocurrence and success of all later social activity within one's own species" (Loizos 1967: 214).

4.4.2.2. Territorial plays and games:

One very common and striking experience which without much doubt should be labeled as a form of play territoriality is that formulated by Heymann (1943: 12): "When the little child of four or five years begins to make 'houles' with the help of table and chairs, hanging tablecloths and other suitable things and to creep into his "house," it is easy to see in this a need for some kind of territorial security. This demand is so manifest and evident that grown-up people can easily understand it" (cf. also Seiss 1969: 31).

There are very often game ingredients in the play behaviour of children (Redl 1959), and such games quite regularly have territorial components of some kind as demonstrated i.a. by Opie and Opie (1969). One game described by these authors is even called "Territories" and is played by two boys in a ground circle, divided by a line in two equal parts. The boys throw in turn a knife into each other's territory, and if one of them succeeds in sticking the knife into the counterpart sector, a new line is drawn through that point in the direction indicated by the position of the knife. This means a diminishing of one area and an augmenting of the other because the old line is rubbed out and the boys take position on each side of the new line. In this way the game goes on until one of the competitors has too little ground to stand on and thus becomes the loser, while the territorial usurper becomes the winner (op. cit. p. 221).

Other territorial play and games were reported by Seiss (1969: 30-31) who, concerning that game played by two parties and called "In and Out", remarked: "A place, designated as 'Free' is the centre of a particular territory. It is limited by a circle-line, denoting the farthest distance from the centre you can attain within a certain time. Anybody who is seen by the antagonists within the circle after this period is excluded. But anyone who can attain the 'Free spot' unseen belongs to the winners as a successful intruder into the territory of the ruling party. But this victory does not satisfy the territorial demands, and so next time the earlier winners are defenders of the 'Free' spot. Without doubt both the outsiders' secret encroachment and the keepers' proprietary defense belongs to territorial behaviour."

4.4.2.3. Football and other areal games:
It is no wonder if the same tendencies are found in games performed also by grown-up people. Some of the oldest and most popular ones are basically contests over ground, where success is marked by the scoring of goals. "To the psychologist the sight of two teams of footballers fighting a symbolic battle over the respective halves of a football ground is like a fight for the possession of territory. The game is to enter the opponents' country and to carry or to kick or head the ball, which is the weapon and the symbol of potency and mastery, right into their goal, which is like the very doorway of their strong-

hold. The side which can do this most often in the prescribed time and under the prescribed rules and laws of play is the winner – they have conquered the opponents' territory" (Pickford 1940-1941: 285).

The great importance of the off-side problem in "soccer" emphasizes the territorial aspects of the game, because it is a problem about how and when a player can be said to have an unfair territorial advantage. The same kind of territorial symbolism finds its way also into other games, such as golf, where the player who can lodge his ball in the final hole, after making it take the lesser number of leaps across the intervening territory, is the winner. It is also found in cricket, where the enemy is sent chasing the symbol of potency across the field, while the batsmen run for possession of territory as often as they can from one wicket to the other (cf. loc. cit.).

A very interesting fact in football as in other similar games is that the home team most often wins the match. It seems to be difficult to find another explanation for this than that of territoriality. As to baseball: "It is not only the presence of the hometown fans that makes the difference, but also a player's intimate knowledge of the special characteristics of the environment – every little mound on the diamond, the height and location of fences and guardrails, the likelihood of hitting home runs, and so on. Minnesota Fats, the poolhall genius, emphasized how a man had to be a real expert to travel from town to town and still win: 'You really have to be a good player to beat a man in his hometown'" (Sommer 1969: 14). And Tiger (1969: 122) summarized: "The fact that, other things being equal, teams play better on their home ground presumably has to do with the comfort of numbers and possibly some vaguely formulated but real territorial affiliation" (cf. also Altman 1975: 137).

That territorial drives with a strong emotional load are brought to bear in such cases cannot be denied by anyone who has witnessed some crucial competitions, e.g., in football. "When England plays Scotland it is like one of the historical battles fought over again. . . . It must be said that social psychologists look upon the spread of organized international sports and games with the greatest possible satisfaction. They believe that a very large number of human territorial and other battles could be fought out harmlessly and constructively in the form of games" (Pickford 1940-1941: 285; cf. also Vogt 1964: 127-131).

Unfortunately, it does not always function like that: "The widespread incidence of spectator violence surrounding team sports is presumably an indication of the mimetic interactions involved in spectator sports. Thus, in a generalized way, sports reflect and interpret quite primitive patterns of activity and affiliation" (Tiger 1969: 122). A strong, instinctive territoriality is clearly awakened, not only among the active players but also in the passive public through watching the contest. And it cannot be physically released by the spectators in a proper way under the crowded conditions in the stands.

The result is not seldom overt aggression, vandalism and sometimes disaster during or after the match, of which there are recent, tragic examples. To cite one: "More than 300 persons were killed and about 500 injured in events that followed an unpopular ruling by the referee in a soccer match between Peru and Argentina" (New York Times, May 25, 1964, cited after Zimbardo 1969: 245). And this is far from a novelty. "So great, indeed, was the violence of the games in the 18th century that other historians report that broken shins, broken heads, torn coats and lost hats were among the minor casualties, and that a Frenchman watching a game at Derby exclaimed that if Englishmen called this playing it would be impossible to say what they would call fighting" (Montague 1964: 566).

4.4.2.4. Chess:
As complements to the many indoor and outdoor areal games, where special forms of ground and floor space are contested for, there are as many where the play field is movable and thus still more symbolic (cf. Murray 1952). Among these we will here just list chess, "the royal game", which probably originated in India sometime before the 7th century A.D. (Murray 1913: 25-50). It could be vindicated that there is a double territorial fight involved in chess. First, every square is the defended and often conquered territory of just one piece. Second and most important, the whole board is a contested territory, attacked from each side by the two players with sixteen pieces each. It is characteristic that the end desired is that the foreign king is checkmated, that is, threatened with capture without chance to escape to any unattacked square. This means that one's winning team conquers the board and consequently the territory. Murray (loc. cit.) introduced his magnificent monograph in this way: "Historically chess must be classed as a game of war". And the well-known great popularity of chess in Soviet Russia is of particular interest in view of the restricted possibility for claiming and defense of real ground territory in a communistic country (cf. also p. 89–90).

Without doubt even play and game territories with their often strong emotional components must be taken seriously, not the least as an important source of release for dammed up territorial instincts. Maybe vehicles also might have such functions, which we will look for next.

4.4.3. Territorial vehicles

4.4.3.1. Boats:

In a way it could be said that man takes his territory with him wherever he goes as a very limited "Personal Space" (Sommer 1969). But he has also been able to construct vehicles, which can function as mobile territories. Thus the two otherwise mostly conflicting drives of exploration and nuclear territoriality, of centrifugal and centripetal tendencies, could be joined quite satisfactorily.

Without doubt boats were the first vehicles made, and the wide-spread custom of using ship-formed tombs or coffins and of sending the dead out to sea in a canoe might suggest a territorial desire. On the whole it is remarkable how people in ancient times dared to investigate vast unknown waters in small boats, and the explanation is perhaps to be found in the sense of security offered by the well-known territorial environment on board.

But if alone, the seaman faced the risk of sensory deprivation in face of monotonous milieus of the open sea. And if he had companions, territorial competition could be a serious problem, particularly under stress. Tiira (1954: 127-136) reported from his experiences with one comrade on a life raft during a month in the Indian Ocean that the territorial urge of the exhausted men was so pronounced that he could not even take their only torch from his companion, who was too weak to use it but refused to part with it. Maybe this very condition brought it about that only Tiira survived.

Larger boats were in the past structured in such a way that they left room for individual territorial claims. A good example from an American frigate in the 19th century was given by Herman Melville (1925: 302-303): "Notwithstanding the domestic communism to which the seamen in a man-of-war are condemned, and the publicity in which actions the most diffident and retiring in their nature must be performed, there is yet an odd corner or two where you may sometimes steal away, and, for a few moments, almost be private. Chief among these places is the chains, to which I would sometimes hie during our pleasant homeward-bound glide over those pensive tropical latitudes. ... The chains designates the small platform outside of the hull, at the base of the large shrouds leading down from the three mast-heads to the bulwarks, ... The huge blocks and lanyards forming the pedestals of the shrouds divide the chains into numerous little chapels, alcoves, niches, and altars, where you lazily lounge – outside of the ship, though on board".

Under the title "Jurisdiction: An Ecological Concept" Roos (1968) described territorial conditions on another American man-of-war in 1961. The crew was divided horizontally by rank and vertically by a complex division of labour. "Each such shipboard work group typically has a territory in the form of a room (a 'space') where most group members do much of their work.... Other members of the crew, whether officers or enlisted men, do not enter the territory except on business or by invitation from one of the work group. Intruders on business stand and generally leave when their business is concluded even though lower ranking members of the work group may remain seated. This is only the most obvious way in which a group controls its territory" (p. 75). Other common focuses of territorial behaviour on board included locked doors, asking introducers to state their business, using the space to store personal belongings and even on occasion asking intruders to leave.

It could be thought that submarines would represent extreme conditions, where territoriality should be striking. And without doubt it is the question of a very restricted spatial environment, when, e.g., it is known that there are about 5 cubic yards of space for every crew member of a nuclear submarine. Contrary to popular opinion the literature on the subject contains, however, very few references to claustrophobic or other strong territorial reactions. It is true that 20 percent of 331 sailors asked indicated "confinement" to be the most disliked aspect of submarine life and that 7 percent of a group of 186 submariners were disqualified after six months of duty because of "extreme dislike for crowded conditions", but this may not say very much. The explanation, suggested i.a. by medical officers, is rather that persons prone to claustrophobia and marked territoriality do not enlist for this kind of service or are eliminated by virtue of the training in recompression chambers prior to acceptance for service (Weybrew 1963: 92-93 and here cited literature).

Not unexpectedly, the reports of the most crowded human situations known come from slave-ships on the route from Africa to America. In one case it was stated that a group of women and girls were packed in such a way that each had just 1.1 square and 1.3 cubic feet, that is, hardly the displacement of an adult male, at her disposal. For comparison it can be noted that in New York City a subway car loaded to the legal maximum provides at least 2.2 square and 20.8 cubic feet per person (Biderman, Louria and Bacchus 1963: 7, 10). The slave traders had, of course, an economic interest in getting their cargo to the destination alive. Decent human considerations aside it is in fact astonishing that such extreme crowding could be consistent with minima for personal space needs and thus with profits. It is, however, known that there was a very great mortality on the slave ships.

4.4.3.2. Vertically moving vehicles:
Not far from the very crowded conditions in some boats are those in elevators during rush times. An investigator "suggests that the seeking of a defensible niche establishes standard priorities: first entrant takes up the corner near the controls or one of the rear corners; the next entrant is likely to take up the corner diagonally across from the taken one. The third and fourth passengers take up the remaining corners, the fifth the middle of the rear wall, the sixth the centre of the car. Members of withs [groups] however, tend to stay together, retaining an ecological expression of their status even though eyes are front. Gueldner also suggests that there is a point of crowding when effort to maintain space is rather suddenly given up and something approaching indiscriminate packing occurs" (John Gueldner: Behavior in Elevators 1965, unpublished, cited after Goffman 1972: 55).

When speaking of vertical transportation we will mention that even an airplane, of course, functions as a moving territory. The distance from physical ground is, however, considerable and this is perhaps at least part of the explanation for the fact that in American jet aviators a clearly defined phenomenon emerged which they described as a condition of spatial disorientation in which the pilot conceived himself to be isolated, detached, and physically separated from the earth, and no longer in contact with it (Bennett 1961: 169).

"The designers of space capsules have observed that the technical problems of providing food and air and other physical necessities are trivial beside the problem of keeping the capsule's inhabitants human. The greatest difficulty seems to be the stress of confinement. The totally man-made character of the capsule environment and the inability to escape appear to produce unbearable nervous stress" (Chermayeff and Alexander 1963: 46-47; cf. also Hanna and Gaito 1960). No wonder therefore that NASA recently decided that each crew member aboard Skylab should have a private sleeping compartment, which could satisfy "each person's need for privacy and personal territory" (Ford 1971: 45).

4.4.3.3. Trains and automobiles:
Different kinds of terrestrial vehicles have been used for thousands of years, mostly with horses. But only the railway trains and the automobiles of our own time have been so numerous and so popular that they should be treated in this context. As to trains there is a detailed and valuable investigation of territorial conditions in the subway of New York City (Fried and DeFazio 1974: 57).

"The observation of behavior in the subway car suggests that spacing behaviors are manifested even in the most inhospitable contexts. The popular
assumption that subway riders place a premium on 'getting a seat' does not
seem valid. Motivation for subterritories, for clearly demarcated spaces, for
increased personal distance and less vulnerable personal space appear to be
more viable factors in understanding passenger behavior. Of course, sitting
down does give a person possession of a space, but except for a few clearly
demarcated areas, the boundaries of most spaces are continually in doubt. In
the subway car spacing tendencies are most effectively satisfied by the occupation of areas which minimize boundary conflicts and the need to continually avoid contact with strangers. It is understandable, then, that certain
standing territories are preferred over available seats" (p. 57).

Between 1958 and 1968 the number of motor vehicles in the world increased
from 112 to 216 million, representing an average annual growth rate of about
4.5 percent. Indubitably no other form of transport equipment offers the
same degree of personal mobility as the motor car, provided that the traffic
system functions.

But the amount of road space needed to move an average of 1.5 persons per
car on heavily used routes is excessive both in comparison with other modes
of transport and in relation to other urban functions. In central Los Angeles,
e.g., more than 60 percent of the land area is occupied by streets, freeways and
parking lots. The demands of the motor car are increasingly dictating the
layout of urban areas, where the rising ratio of cars to people is inevitably
leading authorities to consider to what extent cars can be allowed the freedom
of the cities (cf. *Human Settlements* 1974: 158-161).

Thus the success of the automobile is both remarkable and terrifying, and
the reasons behind the motorization must be strong and with great probability instinctive. Regarding automobile critics, one defender said that
these facts have been reported innumerable times by those who draw from
them the conclusion that mass transit, being more economical, is morally
preferable to the private automobile. Those who preach this have probably
in no other case relied on economy to carry their point, it was charged. On
other subjects, they demand that a solution be chosen for its quality, not
its cost:

"The standard of comfort in the automobile, with its private space, freedom to smoke, a profusion of scenic variety, leg room, fresh air or air conditioning, and radio entertainment, is so seductive to the American citizen
that one has about as much chance to lure him away from it into the bus or
subway on the grounds of economy as one would have to lure guests from the

Waldorf Astoria to the YMCA by telling them how much money they might save" (Starr 1966: 189).

But the critics still have no lack of arguments stressing that any vehicle when not moving is ineffectual. The larger proportion of a car's life is spent in immobility. The stationary car is not only inefficient and uneconomic, it is said, it is indecent. Any transportation system for city populations will be effective only if every vehicle is constantly moving. An average car requires some four hundred square feet of paved space, the equivalent of 25 percent of the floor area now provided for the average American family's house. But the sales prices themselves do not tell us the true costs of the car. Its true cost is that it causes the sacrifice of other means of transportation:

"There is nothing wrong with the car *per se*. What is wrong is the exaggerated use we make of it. Essentially a private convenience, it violates public interest in too many places. The immense investment of public money in roads, bridges, garages and parking prevents the development of all the other forms of transportation that would be more appropriate to different purposes and scales. It even prevents walking" (Chermayeff and Alexander 1966: 86-87).

Edward T. Hall (1969: 163-166), the pioneer of human territorial research, gave in a chapter called "The Automobile Syndrome" some special arguments complementing the usual ones from the economic. planning, esthetic, health and environmental realms: "In modern American cars the kinesthetic sense of space is absent. Kinesthetic space and visual space are insulated from each other and are no longer mutually reinforcing. Soft springs, soft cushions, soft tires, power steering, and monotonously smooth pavements create an unreal experience of the earth. One manufacturer has even gone so far as to advertise his product by showing a car full of happy people *floating on a cloud above the road!* Automobiles insulate man not only from the environment but from human contact as well. They permit only the most limited types of interaction, usually competitive, aggressive, and destructive. If people are to be brought together again, given a chance to get acquainted with each other and involved in nature, some fundamental solutions must be found to the problems posed by the automobile".

Yet, in spite of all these and other critical arguments people value their cars so much that these sometimes seem to be more essential for them than their homes. The attitude of some young Americans, communicated by Bloch and Niederhoffer (1958: 185), is probably not quite unfamiliar even for their parents. The young person "can thus displace his anxiety by the strategic retreat to the insulated world of the auto. No longer does he expose himself to the stigma of cowardice, either by the accusations of his comrades or by his internal awareness. In this new situation which is now under his control, the weight of an oppressive society is relieved. By this conjunction of a seemingly universal adolescent need with the ubiquitous vehicle with which satisfaction may be obtained, both on the symbolic and realistic plane, we suggest an explanation for the overpowering affinity of the adolescent to the auto- mobile" (cf. also Kleemann 1963: 68-76).

4.4.3.4. The car as territory:

A car seems to act much like a dangerous weapon in the hands of many drivers, a weapon that can destroy many of our controls and inhibitions. The reason for this is obscure, but some psychologists have theorized that at least part of it is due to the extension of our personal territories when we are in a car. Our own zones of privacy expand and the zone of privacy of the car becomes much greater and our reaction to any intrusion on that zone is greater still (cf. Fast 1973: 44).

Thus it seems probable that the car functions as a movable and most effec- tive territory, joining the otherwise irreconcilable drives towards home on one side and migration on the other. Most interesting is the development in the direction of larger and larger cars, station wagons to sleep in and finally trailers, the movable home. Already in 1960 it was said: "Three million Americans now call 1.2 million trailers their permanent homes. Every tenth house built today is of this type" (Higbee 1960: 137). And Europe follows, at least as to second homes, of which 16 percent were recently said to be caravans in England and Wales (Bielckus, Rogers and Wibberley 1972: 50-65; cf. also A. Wilson 1959-1960). We can also easily "turn the family car into a house, and when the child, together with the cat and the dog and familiar toys, is moved to a strange place, the car will still be a familiar home" (Mead 1972: 246).

But if the two urges could now really be tested against each other, the odds are that fixed territory as home would win. And this is hardly astonishing. "We now have not only trailers, but trailer camps, and trailer camps have tended to become in the last few years subdivisions rather than camps. The average length of time that a trailer has remained in one location has grad- ually lengthened until now it is about two years – no more turnover than apartments in Oakland. So there is a serious question about the extent of mobility or the frequency of mobility. Actually, the trailer is being used as a house. But it is still potentially, if not actually, movable" (Cramer 1960: 49).

Summarizing the phenomenon of the car as territory Ardrey (1972: 244) reported: "The ambiguity of the automobile in urban life bears fascinated if morbid inspection. It is a mobile territory without doubt, confirmed by the readiness to defend it emotionally on the part of both the driver and the dog beside him. The territorial boundaries of bumpers and fenders likewise separate proprietors so that even in a standstill traffic jam one confronts a territorial mosaic in which proprietors, aside from fleeting rage, acknowledge not at all each other's existence. Perhaps the car is a tender subconscious keepsake from a time when we walked beneath trees that were our own. Yet in urban life the car is a monstrosity. While it provides for the proprietor a tiny area of spatial privacy and a carpet on which to fly away, still in the city it exposes him to human density at its worst. As a territorial prize worth gaining, the car could not exist. Only its value as a symbol of status converts the urban automobile from prison to prize", a statement which, however, seems to underestimate the territorial ingredient.

So the movable expressions of behavioural territoriality seem to be both common and striking, and they will be kept in mind when we now go over to a final type of special territory, this time a symbolic, portable one.

4.4.4. Jews and symbolic territory

4.4.4.1. The promised land:
The various forms of territory marking can be imagined as symbols of the owner, as "*Pars pro toto*" (Bilz 1940). Here we will take up just one interesting case of a physical, portable symbolization of a well-known national territory, that of the Jews.

The general background is the following. When a cultural-territorial system has been disrupted, that is, when a group has been separated from its territory – if such a separation is survived at all – a different culture-territory system may develop in the course of time, based in another support area. If this is radically different from the original one, then institutions and social relations will change totally in adaptation to the new environment. A displaced group that fails to find a new territorial base will eventually lose its identity, usually by absorption into other cultures. No politically-organized group has been known to exist any length of time without its own territory (cf. Maier 1975: 18).

"Jewish difficulties with territory, it seems, began a very long time ago, when God promised Abraham, leader of some wandering pastoral tribes, title to a most unremarkable piece of real estate on the Mediterranean littoral. No people ever took a promise harder. They managed to gain it, and to settle down, but they were such a quarrelsome, rebellious lot that somebody was always carting them off into slavery. First it was Egypt, where they made out very well but still dreamed of nothing but the Promised Land. After some hair-raising experiences they managed to regain their territory, but then it was the Chaldeans. Nebuchadnezzar hauled most of them away to Babylon. Later it was the Roman Empire that found itself unequal to Jewish argument and so dispersed them by force to a variety of Western destinations. For almost 2000 years the Jew of the West and the Jew of the East had one thing in common: they never saw their Promised Land again" (Ardrey 1967: 306).

As a consequence of this it is often said that the Jewish people differs from all other nations of the world in that their sense of unity is not based on territory but on faith and long and continuous tradition. And the mobile as well as resistant qualities of their nationalism have enabled the Jews to do another unparalleled thing, namely to make a peaceful and deep penetration into a lot of other territorial nations without losing their identity (cf. Keith 1948: 375-378). To this add the fact that the Jews in the "diaspora" – their dispersal all over the world – were not only denied a common social territory. As foreigners they were most often forbidden even to own private ground, making it the more remarkable that the deterritorialized Jews could preserve their group-feeling over thousands of years in exile. One wonders if they at least had some surrogate and should for this reason go to history.

Prior to returning to the Promised Land from Egypt, the people of Israel travelled through the desert under the leadership of Moses, who instructed them in the ways of the Law, which, received directly from God, was carried in a portable ark. During periods of rest the ark was housed in a tent at the core of the encampment, and the people gathered about the temporary territory, identified by the symbol of the new nationhood. The subsequent history became that of a territory-defending nation and thus did not differ much from that of the neighbours around.

4.4.4.2. Torah as territory:
Power and identification based on real territory weakened the spiritual hold of the Law – to the lament of the prophets – until it was nearly forgotten. In the form of handwritten parchment scrolls, called the Torah, the Law was now installed in the first temple of Jerusalem, where it was "miraculously rediscovered" in connection with the Babylonian captivity, during which the Israelites were sustained by the treasured possession of the Torah. After the destruction of the second temple in 69 A.D. the Jews scattered into the

Diaspora with the Torah as their most precious belonging, more valuable than life itself (cf. Maier 1975: 22).

The central theme of the Torah is its feminine gender and its nature as "Mother Earth". If this symbol, arising from the soul of the people, can stir the beholding Israelites, it seems to perform the function of territory. "Standing upon which the people, like Antaeus, are constantly renewing their strength. This kind of symbolic territory gave rise to the social and political structure of the ghetto, so typically internalized and isolated from the political reality of the outside world.... The Talmud (i.e., the Torah and commentaries) gave the landless and persecuted Jew of the diaspora another world into which he could escape and survive when the vicissitudes of the real world had become too great to bear" (Maier 1975: 20-22). It was also verbally stated that "It gave him a fatherland, which he could carry about with him when his own land was lost" (C. Roth 1953: 132).

In the late nineteenth century one witnessed, however, a beginning of the dissolving of the ghettos in many countries. New scientific methods seemed to provide answers to the problems that confronted man, and Jews were increasingly integrated into the social structure of the nations in which they lived. Emancipated Jewish intellectuals looked upon the study of Talmud and the mystical traditions as sterile scholasticism. Thus the spiritual hold of the Torah as a substitute for territory was weakened. But at the same time as the assimilation of the Jews finally gained momentum, political Zionism was born. The founders of this movement instinctively felt that only a return to the Promised Land could save the identity of the people. War and persecution hastened the realization of the national territory in a region of the world that was sanctified from ancient times (cf. Maier 1975: 22).

Thus it should not be be surprising that modern Israel is a secular state and that the identification of Israelians is with land. The Torah does not dominate the life of the people as before, although there are many orthodox Jews who, like the ancient prophets, accuse the government of having neglected the teaching of the holy documents. Apparently real territory is better suited to rally the people than the movable one which, however, did well enough for nearly two thousand years. And this development has, of course, been exaggerated through the hostility and fighting against the surrounding Arab countries (cf. Ardrey 1967: 308-309).

"The Palestinians claim their territory in what is now Israel, which contains their ancient blood and place ties. Israel's intrusion upsets their collective mind's order which is derived partly from these territorial images. The Arab cause utilizes these images for political purposes, an example of man's inappropriate use of his animal-type images for socio-cultural purposes. The human use of man's animal images may erupt into virulent social pollution for which, in the case of this hijacking, there is no reasonable antidote and no technical solution" (Esser 1971a: 13).

Probably the Babylonians as well as the Romans meant to destroy the irritating Jews through their removal, knowing that no people can exist definitely without a land. But they did not succeed, for it appears that the people were not without territory after all. They had taken the land with them in the form of a portable symbolic territory, the Torah, just as when they came upon the Promised Land three thousand years ago (cf. Maier 1975: 23).

The case of Palestine and its probable representation in the holy Torah of the synagogues and in the hearts of the dispersed Jews gives a view of the very strong need for national territory even in symbolic form during times when the country itself is not available for the people.

With this example of a movable symbolic territory we have rendered account of territories in many different realms and contexts and now proceed to a few generalizing and causative chapters, first to a survey of some common features of behavioural territoriality.

4.5. Fundamental facts of behavioural territoriality

4.5.1. Environment – behaviour basis

Since a large part of the input into our nervous system, from the day of birth, comes from the perception of our environment, it seems very improbable that surroundings should not have a great deal to do with the development of our mental patterns and powers. "The presence and importance of such influences emanating from the milieu is borne out by all evidence available from studies of animals under controlled conditions, from human experiments with artificial sensory deprivations, from psychiatric experience, and from psychological, pedagogic and sociological observations of human behavior" (Parr 1965: 14). Likewise it looks uncontestable that "Man's response to his physical environment is a complex, multifaceted and multi-layered affair, and not to be adequately understood in terms of a restricted causal chain or functional relationship linking particular stimuli or variables of stimulation to particular responses" (Kates and Wohlwill 1966: 18; cf. also Altman 1973).

The two major kinds of scientific approach to the environment, the purely objective and the phenomenological, are, of course, both necessary for an understanding of the environmental situation. Such an understanding should require at least a study of how this environment comes into being, the process by which the individual perceives, cognizes and "creates" it, and more critically, the role played by the physical environment in all these processes. Clearly, a major task of any attempt to conceptualize the human environment must include the relationship between a person's physical world and the world he constructs from it, as well as the connections between the latter and human behaviour and experience (cf. Proshansky, Ittelson and Rivlin 1970b: 28).

Among thirteen assumptions concerning behaviour and milieu which the editors of *Environmental Psychology* (1970) have found clear evidence for and support, the following should be named: Human behaviour in relation to a physical setting is enduring and consistent over time and situation and so the characteristic patterns of behaviour for that setting can be identified, but it reveals diversity over space at any given moment and continuous variability in any given space over time. The physical setting that defines and structures any concrete situation is not a closed system and even behaviour in relation to a physical setting is dynamically organized. Changes in the characteristic behaviour pattern of a physical setting can be induced by changing the physical, social or administrative structures which define that setting. The environment is an active and continuing process and is unique at any given time and place. The editors conclude:

"Perhaps the greatest value of many of the assumptions lies in the warning they give against environmental research that fails to recognize the complexity of the phenomena studied. Most, if not all, of the assumptions point to the need for investigations that are willing to discard the relatively simple cause-and-effect paradigm that typifies some of the more laboratory-oriented behavioral science research. Many of the assumptions make it clear that such an approach, at least at the present stage of knowledge about behavior in relation to space, provides useless information. Others bring us back to a point we have made frequently: the total environmental process can and should be studied from different vantage points and at different levels of analysis. This means, of course, that only a multidisciplinary approach can lead to a viable theory of, and a fruitful body of knowledge in, environmental psychology" (Proshansky, Ittelson and Rivlin 1970b: 37).

The detection, isolation and structuring of environmental problems grow, further, out of an analysis of human behaviour systems. Their design is restricted by the physiological and psychological characteristics of the population under analysis. They are also constrained by the cultural system within which participating humans must operate. Thus it is "only after a behavior system has been conceptualized – in response to the organization's purpose(s), goals and subgoals – that the very existence of a physical problem can be determined. Without a proper behavioral analysis we are not only likely to misstructure physical problems, but may also misclassify them as well. That is, we often see a problem as physical when it is another aspect of the environment which is causing behavioral dissonance. A physical problem exists if and only if there is disequilibrium between requisite behaviors and the designed environment.... For example, dissonance may be relieved by re-structuring and/or delineating certain territorial boundaries..." (Studer 1969: 186, 193).

It would be spurious to try to establish an absolute hierarchy between space and time, which are so closely correlated to each other that they can no longer be separated. Modern physics has synthesized them into a single concept, and what actually unifies them is movement. In the case of the adult it is an individual history which is constantly confronted with a new situation composed of collective images, the product of a certain culture and therefore of a social history. This is why the historic, and thus the temporal aspect of the personality seems to be so important.

"But if, by an effort of phenomenological reduction in Husserl's sense, we manage to return to this 'world before knowledge' which is certainly that of the child and of the animal, and seems also to be that in which the mentally sick and regressed individual lives, it becomes clear that the 'situation' is no longer the encounter between an individual history and a social history, but simply of a living organism and a world which derives its meaning from essentially spatial relationships rather than cultural layers" (Sivadon 1970: 410).

And in this living human organism we will now try to trace the biological background of behavioural territoriality.

4.5.2. Biological background

4.5.2.1. Territorial instinct:
If we suggest that this "world before knowledge" is also part of the basic mental constitution of normal man we are not far from the concept of instinct, some general aspects of which were discussed earlier (2.4.). Even as to the grounds for behavioural territoriality the controversy over this concept is rather heated. It was for instance stated by the psychiatrist Horowitz (1968: 31): "Clinical observation of these and other patients tells us something more

important about spatial behavior; it is highly individual in its nuances of meaning, and it is not an imperative or innate factor present in this or that way throughout a group. The personal and idiosyncratic determinants are in complex relationship with cultural patterns of spatial usage and group phenomenon. . . . This is in contrast and disagreement with Ardrey's statements about the imperative or instinctive nature of human territoriality. . .".

To this it should be said that the conclusions were based on observed interpersonal distances between 25 mental patients of three categories, schizophrenics, depressives and neurotics, and under such circumstances it is hardly astonishing that a uniform instinctive reaction was not discerned. Incidentally, individual nuances or modifications are, of course, wholly consistent with instinctual theory, which cannot in any way be nullified by either cultural variants neither by "idiosyncratic determinants". From most observations and investigations of the mentally abnormal, earlier referred to, it is quite evident that the general uniformity, rigidity and strength of the "territorial imperative" seems to be quite impossible to explain without instinctive, genetic components.

The anthropologist Keiter (1966: 213) maintained the following view: "One should not convey the whole idea of territoriality in a specific instinct but in a very general tendency, namely the need for an undisturbed free space for one's own movements." The conclusion would be the opposite if one – which seems reasonable – equated the general tendency for undisturbed free movement in space with some kind of territorial instinct.

Among the many critical comments on instinctive behavioural territoriality discussed in the book *Man and Aggression* we find this dubious statement by the ethologist Crook (1970c: 171): "Certainly our modern appreciation of the important role of learning and tradition in the maintenance of non-human primate societies would lead us to emphasise this kind of historical change rather than the possible development of a territorial instinct of the type Ardrey requires" (cf. also Elms 1972). Here we will only refer back to our treatment of primates (3.2.4.-3.2.6.) and stress that there are today "probably few who would disagree that most human social behaviors are an *interaction* of cultural-environmental and biological influences" (Altman 1975: 111).

Many a one like the architect Jan C. Rowan (1965: 145) put the whole case in this straightforward way: "I think people have an instinct for space". The zoologist Etkin (1963: 305) vindicated without hesitation that "man's motivational organization is basically innate, that is to say he shares with other vertebrates such drives as territory, status, sexuality, socialization and learning" (cf. also Fabricius 1971: 71). And the geographer Maier (1975: 18) took the full consequences: "Association with, and defense of, territory resulted in an inherited behavior pattern as thoroughly genetically determined as is physical structure", an opinion which we share.

4.5.2.2. Hereditary differences:
In this connection facts about a hereditary character of territoriality should, of course, be of greatest interest, and some evidence is beginning to show up as verifications of Ardrey's (1967: 116) thesis: "The territorial nature of man is genetic and ineradicable". Thus it was reported by Money (1965: 15): "Sex differences in the androgen-estrogen ratio may conceivably account for some of the differences between men and women in their thresholds for erotically related behavior and activity. In the male, for instance, there is typically a greater expenditure of energy in the service of sexual searching, pursuit, and consummation. This energy expenditure extends also to adventurous, exploratory roaming, to assertiveness and aggression, and to the defense of territorial rights". Corinne Hutt (1973: 93-94) in her valuable survey *Males & Females* asserted that males excel in spatial ability, that there is evidence of male superiority in this respect as early as at three or four years of age and that spatiality develops under the control of the sex hormones, which, of course, have hereditary fixation.

Working with the differences in spatial ability and throwing accuracy between the two sexes Kolakowski and Malina (1974) made the following basic comments on the presumed sexual division of labour during the 99 percent of human history that men have been hunters. "Certainly, directional orientation and memory for visual landmarks must have been required for a man to find his way back to the group. If, in addition, spatial ability were positively correlated with judgment of distance and throwing accuracy in males (for example, as regards such weapons as stones and spears), this could presumably have allowed them to hit game at greater distances, thereby making hunting less hazardous and resulting in longer lived hunters as well as more meat".

We think thus that this reasoning can be applied to our theme, too, for there is much evidence for sexual difference as to territoriality, involving i.a. that males are more inclined to keep and defend territories than females, even though the investigators themselves do not always interpret their results in this way (cf., e.g., Leibman 1970; Ehrlich and Freedman 1971 and further p. 60, 89). It should also be added that, e.g., Cheyne and Efran (1972: 485) have shown sexually mixed pairs to be more successful in defending territories than two females.

4.5.2.3. Neural location:

If, as we have found it most probable, there is an instinctive, genetic base for territoriality, a crucial question is, of course, its neural location. But "The discovery of the *unconscious* sources of much of our behavior and the discrepancies between our conscious acts and unconscious motives could not be reconciled with our knowledge of the Central Nervous System until the contrasting functions of the neocortical and the limbic systems were conceptualized" (Esser 1971a: 14). The limbic system of the brain is generally related to the organism's feeding behaviour and thus to the struggle for survival. Together with the hypothalamus this system is also responsible for other important instinctive behaviours and emotions, more specifically the control of biological rhythms, sexuality, fear, rage and motivation (cf. Ganong 1971: 173-185).

The following statements are of special interest: "It lies close at hand that oral behaviour (Amygdaloid-circle) and sexual behaviour (Septum-circle) should belong to different anatomical-neurophysiological function systems. But in fact they are connected by means of the brain organization in such a way that they could be integrated agonistically as well as antagonistically. Thus it is understandable why oral behaviour, attack, flight and sexual behaviour are frequently activated together. The development of instincts is thus related to many inner and outer factors which influence the pattern of the final behaviour. This cooperation becomes doubtless more complicated in the course of the phylogenetic series. However, one must remember that the limbic system compared to younger telencephalic structures is very conservative. It remains therefore comparatively primitive even in man" (Ploog 1964: 388-389). To this could be added: "The concept of limbic integration of social communication gives rise to the hypothesis that a selection mechanism triggers, from the many innate motor patterns, that social signal which is both the expression of the animal's disposition and the appropriate message for the partner" (Ploog 1973: 1436).

So it seems very reasonable to assume that territoriality should be placed within the limbic system. These basal parts of the brain are old and unchanged enough to be responsible for a phenomenon common to all groups of vertebrates. The near connections with centres of sexual import could further explain that territories are most strongly held during reproduction time and by mixed pairs, and the closeness to centres of aggression could be responsible for the sometimes violent expressions of territorial defense. Recent experiments with rats even suggested that spatial memory is located within the hippocampus, part of the limbic system (Olton 1977). And at least some mental patients showing extreme territorial behaviour suffered from diseases or damages which could be referred to the limbic system (cf. e.g. Pontius 1967).

Here it should also be mentioned that the right cerebral hemisphere may act more in tune with the elaboration of subcortical, that is, brainstem and limbic system processes, and the left cerebral hemisphere as a transformer of physical and social space into more abstract, verbal, higher-order processes. The inherent conflicts caused by different levels of cognition and by the dichotomy with which the hemispheres process information "may explain much of our confusion in discussing human spatial behavior" (Esser 1976: 119).

4.5.3. Territory characteristics

4.5.3.1. Territorial systems:

Topophilia is the name of a recent book, the theme of which is defined as "the affective bond between people and place or setting" (Tuan 1974: 4). This is one of many examples that territoriality is now being approached from all directions, often, as in this example, without use of the proper name. That the emotional side is underlined seems to be in accordance with a location of instincts and affections close to each other in the limbic system of the brain. In fact this emotional bond is an absolute prerequisite, without which neither the high frequency nor the obvious strength of behavioural territoriality would be possible.

It was further stressed by the mammalogist Burt (1943: 346): "The behavioristic trait manifested by a display of property ownership – a defense of certain positions or things – reaches its highest development in the human species", and in this case it might be allowed to equate property and territory. And Leyhausen (1971a: 30) maintained: "The evidence for absolute social hierarchy in humans is so abundant that I need not produce examples, but the tendency to establish oneself as a kind of territory-owner is equally obvious if one only looks for it".

The more astonishing is this statement: "Man is the most seriously overlooked species in this respect" (Stokes 1974: 237). Maybe it has something to do with another proposition: "Man is thus territorial in a number of senses. He has a personal space halo, notions of property in land, a willingness to defend areas of ground, and limits to the range of his daily, yearly, and lifetime wanderings" (Peterson 1975: 63). It looks as if many people cannot see the forest because of all the different trees.

Edward T. Hall (1963: 422) proposed the term *proxemics* for "The Study of

Man's Spatial Relations" as a science complementary to territorology or the study of space-related behaviour in animals, the latter term being presented in 1961 by Hediger (1970b: 34). It was said in the context, however: "It is convenient now to make a terminological distinction – although a time may come when human behavior and animal behavior can be included under the same rubric" (E. T. Hall 1963: 422). In our opinion this time is already here, particularly as the author himself admitted: "The hypothesis behind the proxemic classification system is this: it is in the nature of animals, including man, to exhibit behavior which we call territoriality" (E. T. Hall 1969: 120).

It should, however, also be stressed that proxemics, as suggested by the name and according to definition, primarily must study the isolating mechanisms between human beings, described with increasing interval as intimate, personal, social and public distance (op. cit. p. 107-122), the terms personal and social distance being earlier also used in a special sociological meaning (e.g., Poole Jr. 1926-1927). Most often being moving and changing spaces without other limitation than display, these distance zones could also be summarized as portable territories.

Some other systems of territory classification should be briefly mentioned here. David Stea (1965: 14) first discerned stationary and moving territory, then individual (personal space, territorial unit) and collective (some territorial clusters and territorial complexes) and finally formal (professional) and informal (social) territories on the collective level. All these spaces were said to possess certain properties in common, such as shape, size, number of units, extensiveness and types of boundary, differentiation (detail), relatedness, etc.

Lyman and Scott (1967-1968: 236) recognized: "Territoriality, or the attempt to control space, is conceived as a fundamental human activity". They distinguished four types of territory, viz., public, home, interactional and body territories, three types of territorial encroachment, viz., violation, invasion and contamination, three forms of reaction to encroachment, viz., turf defense, insulation and linguistic collusion and three kinds of exploitation of body territories, viz., manipulation, adornment and penetration.

And Suttles (1973: 165-166) described four forms explicitly identified as territorial. "First, there are exclusive territorial groups which are relatively autonomous and not further divided within themselves. This seems a rather rare form among humans, very concentrated among primitive peoples, and directly comparable to the defended and exclusive territories found among some nonhumans. Second, we find populations in which territorial groups roughly similar to the ones mentioned above can be drawn together in a series of shifting alliances as each group selects sides in an oppositional structure. A third, and similar form, is one where alliances between groups are pyramided into increasingly inclusive units in some fixed order of combination while remaining in opposition to equivalent territorial combinations. ... A fourth form is the administrative pyramid which draws a series of subunits into increasingly inclusive units until they finally combine in a single territorial unit".

Finally, Altman (1975: 120), using the criteria of degree of control, use by occupants and relative duration of users' claim to the space, made the following distinctions: "Primary territories are usually under relatively total control of occupants for long periods of time. In addition, they are usually quite central to the life of the occupant. Secondary territories also have a durable quality of ownership, but it is not wholly continuous or permanent and there is some access by others, so that occupancy is not totally exclusive. Public territories are relatively temporary and occupancy is public, as long as users follow some social rules and norms".

4.5.3.2. Individual and social territories:
Here we will give some general comments about the two main categories of individual and social territories. Perhaps it could be said that the human body is the first and smallest as well as the most private form of individual territory, and it is known how even the right to touch it is greatly restricted, how it is marked out by scars, cuts, burns, tattoos, etc., in addition to clothing. The free exercise of the territory surrounded by the skin is a most useful one and may be a necessary compensation for lack of or difficulty in staking out and keeping other territories (Lyman and Scott 1967-1968: 241-243). However, we concentrate in this survey on external physical spaces, outside of and larger than the body.

We have, then, first to keep count of personal space, which "is conceived as an expanding and contracting ring or bubble surrounding the individual which defines the physical separation he requires in relation to others with respect to specific activities and defined relationships. Although personal space may be conceptualized as a special form of territoriality, it is unique in that it moves with the individual, is highly elastic and rapidly altered, and is not ordinarily linked to permanent physical referents in the environment" (Leibman 1970: 209; for an actual survey of personal space see Evans and Howard 1973).

It is a central feature of individual territories that legitimate claims to them vary greatly according to the accountings available in the setting and that the

bases for these change, sometimes continuously. "The very notion of an egocentric territory suggests that the body is not only a preserve but also a central
marker of various preserves.... The prototypical territorial offence occurs
when one individual encroaches on the preserve claimed by and for another
individual, the first thereby functioning as an impediment to the second's
claim" (Goffman 1972: 67, 74).

Without doubt "The most logical extension of the *territory* concept is to
define it as an area controlled by an individual, family, or other face-to-face
collectivity" (Sommer 1966: 61). It was laconically emphasized by C. G. Jung
(Carol 1965: 2): "Each person should possess his own piece of land, then the
old instincts would flourish again". But the area surrounding an individual,
anywhere within which an entering by others is possible, causes him to feel
encroached upon, leading him to show displeasure and sometimes to withdraw (cf. Goffman 1972: 52). This should be stressed: "If there is a true human
territorial factor, it appears that implied physical threat and implicit threat in
the form of status are among the most likely social releasers of territorial
behavior" (Bailey, Hartnett and Gibson 1972).

"Society is made up of individuals spatially separated, territorially distributed, and capable of independent locomotion" (Park and Burgess 1929:
508). However, man is not only surrounded by fixed and portable individual
territories "but is also encased in a series of larger socially-based territorial
bubbles to which each individual devotes varying degrees of attention, identity, and feelings of exclusiveness. The family is probably still the strongest of
all, although it has been declining in importance for many centuries. In addition to the family, however, there are several varieties of local communities
and neighborhoods, larger scale urban, metropolitan, and regional societies,
the nation-state, and occasionally still larger units.... The key distinction is
between those societies in which there is a social definition of territory and
those in which there is a territorial definition of society" (Soja 1971: 33-52).

It is significant that we use such originally spatial terms as social position,
social distance and social mobility in talking about societies, for the social
order is always closely related to spatial arrangements. In fact social rank and
territorial behaviour are at least as characteristic of man as of other vertebrates. The geographical expression of human territoriality is most striking
in the division of the world into units of political organization, each sovereign
and capable both of peaceable and warlike interaction (cf. Wagner 1960:
51-58).

Biologically speaking, man usually lives in a colonial nesting system with
homes on territories. His activities are mostly carried out in groups meeting

daily at special sites. Full time association in single groups is rare, but some family territories include both nesting and harvesting space, e.g., farms. Man builds shelters for his families or other groups but also expends considerable resources to create, inside, a seemingly very inefficient spacing system, which, however, suits his nature. Each person has, if possible, his own bed, preferably in a separate room that is treated as highly personal territory with restrictions on entry (cf. McBride 1971: 64).

Marriage and other pair constellations involve a decisive narrowing of the individual's space of free movement and personal territory, all the more because an all-embracing love means a stronger territorial encroachment than most other group memberships. Not a few marital problems have their roots in the difficulty of permanent close contact between individuals with pronounced territoriality (cf. Lewin 1948: 94-95). But most often the effect of marriage predominantly is a marked pair and family territory, which is not easily violated against the will of the defenders. Probably commitment to a long-term relationship is necessary before a co-residing couple develops more outspoken territorial behaviour and hence married couples were shown to have stronger territoriality than unmarried pairs living together (Rosenblatt and Budd 1975). Single individuals are particularly reluctant to intrude upon group-shared space (cf. Cheyne and Efran 1972: 477).

All societies have, of course, a spatial dimension, but it has often been maintained that only a few revolve around territorially-defined groups. This should, however, not be interpreted as meaning that territoriality does not exist except in these few societies. "All comprehensive social systems with recognizable political organization and some autonomous authority over an area have some form of territoriality in that there exist certain points, lines, or areas which elicit group identities and engender a sense of group exclusiveness against outsiders. This is the essence of human territoriality at both the individual and societal levels" (Soja 1971: 33).

Here we will remember the fundamental notion of Peterson (1975: 62) concerning Australian aborigines but undoubtedly of general relevance to mankind: "Once a person or party has been through a rite of entry, however, they have equal access with the hosts to the everyday resources of the territory. Greeting ceremonies are thus functionally analogous to boundary defense, in that they prevent unregulated movement between territories and control access to food resources through ceremonies that frequently incorporate agonistic displays and controlled aggression between males. In this way, rites of entry insure that people are encapsulated in groups and do not wander from one area of abundance to another: they help create and maintain local groups".

Without doubt territoriality is more complicated, diffuse and discontinuous in some parts of the actual community e.g. of the city. "But the existence of recognized and named neighborhoods; areas of homogeneous and segregated residential patterns and ethnic, religious, and occupational composition; and pronounced barriers and boundaries to human interaction which are not solely based on physical features all attest to the continuing operation of powerful local territorial mechanisms in the modern urban context" (Soja 1971: 36). It could be added that increasing knowledge of man's structuring of his territorial space suggests that this is as vital to humans as it is to other animals (cf. O. M. Watson 1970: 114).

The very structuring is one of the weighty factors behind territorial variability, which now comes to the fore.

4.5.4. Territorial variability

4.5.4.1. Cultural variations:
We recently summarized facts about the biological background of territoriality. It was vindicated not only that this phenomenon is of instinctive, genetic character but also that there are inherited differences between the sexes. Probably we have individual degrees of territorial aptitude, too. But most variations of territorial behaviour are certainly of cultural origin. It has been said for instance that: "Man has elaborated *territoriality* to such a degree that it is hardly recognizable as such". However, even though territorial patterns vary, we still find that each culture makes allocations for a place to work and play for each member of the society, a territory reserved exclusively for men and for women, and distinct areas for each social unit, beginning with the family and ending with the largest political unit, such as the nation state (E. T. Hall 1961: 71).

However, "Culture transcends man in both time and space; i.e., it is 'supra-organic', which tends to divert attention from the fact that culture, on the individual, behavioral, objective, or manifest level, is also rooted in, or can be traced back to, biological activities. Man's cultural elaborations of his handling of space illustrate this point. However, man has so developed his use of space in any given culture, as well as the great diversity of space patterns between cultures, that it is fruitful to consider lower life forms as a means of clarifying the phylogenetic base" (E. T. Hall 1963: 424.)

Here we will mention just a few studies on cultural variation, which, however, are centred mostly on interactional distance (e.g., Engebretson 1973). E.

T. Hall (1969: 12) tried to draw up the lines for a general anthropology of space and denoted about his own people: "according to European standards, Americans use space in a wasteful way and seldom plan adequately for public needs. In fact, it would seem that Americans feel that people have no needs associated with space at all". And he proceeded to describe the Germans with their sense of order in space, their dislike of intrusions and their guarding of the private sphere, making further interesting remarks with territorial implications about the English, the French, the Japanese and the Arabs.

A special investigation on the proxemics, here defined as "the study of how man structures microspace", of Arab and American college students was undertaken by Watson and Graves (1966), showing as expected that the former interacted closer to each other than the latter (cf. also O. M. Watson 1970: 101-108). In two papers (Aiello and Jones 1971; Jones and Aiello 1973) the proxemic behaviour of 6 to 10 year old school children of black, Puerto Rican and white origin were compared. As in earlier studies with adults, the authors found differences concerning distances held between members of the subcultures named, the representatives of the first two standing closer to each other than those of the third. At least among whites there were also sex dissimilarities, in that girls stood closer than boys, an observation also confirmed for 11 to 12 year old American whites (Guardo 1969). All the differences decreased with age and the conclusion drawn by the authors were i.a. that proxemic patterns are learned early in life, that variations shown are rooted in social class rather than in culture *per se* and that some behaviours are more basic to subcultural group membership and remain intact, while others may be subject to change. These results seem, however, to be explained as well or better on the basis of innate spatial aptitudes, the territorial expressions of which are later modified by experience and culture.

One of the many basic differences between cultures is that they extend different anatomical and behavioural features of the human organism. Whenever there is cross-cultural borrowing, the borrowed items have to be adapted. Otherwise the new and the old do not match, and in some instances, the two patterns are completely contradictory. Le Corbusier's great buildings at Chandigarh, capital of Punjab, had to be modified by the residents to make them habitable. The Indians walled up Corbusier's balconies, converting them into kitchens! Similarly, Arabs coming to the United States find that their own internalized fixed-feature patterns do not fit American housing. Arabs feel oppressed by it – the ceilings are too low, the rooms too small, privacy from the outside inadequate, and views non-existent.

Indubitably it is so that what is fixed-feature space in one culture may be semifixed in another, and vice versa. In Japan, for example, walls are movable, opening and closing as the day's activities change. In the United States, people move from room to room or from one part of a room to another for each different activity, such as eating, sleeping, working or socializing with relatives. It should not be thought, however, that incongruity between internalized and externalized patterns occurs only between cultures. As our own technology explodes, air conditioning, fluorescent lighting, and soundproofing make it possible to design houses and offices without regard to traditional patterns of windows and doors. The new inventions sometimes result in great barnlike rooms where the territory of employees in a "bull pen" is ambiguous (cf. E. T. Hall 1969: 100-101).

4.5.4.2. Social variations:

The increasing spatial differentiation of the modern community has got one of its most characteristic features in the separation of house and work and thus in the splintering of territorial areas. "Sixty years ago the orbits of men and women were also essentially the same. Automobile transportation has greatly increased the mobility of both, but has also separated the orbits of housewives from those of husbands and of women workers in business, industry, government and the professions. This reduction of urban experience shared in common by men, women and children also reduces their ability to communicate with each other" (Parr 1967: 4). However, there are in this respect great differences between the social classes.

At one extreme the professional elite is a primary group not based on kinship, ethnicity, nationality or place. Rather it is a voluntary association of men joined by shared interests and values. "As men who trade in information and ideas, they must necessarily maintain intensive communication with other members of their spatially dispersed, *non-place* communites. ... These folk approximate the true cosmopolites for whom territorial distance is a minor barrier to interaction and whose professional social communities are the least shaped by territorialism. ... The life spaces of these highly-specialized professional types are multidimensional and supraterritorial, being scaled against measures of social rank, generation, age, stage of the life cycle, educational attainment, and, almost incidentally, geographic distance" (Webber 1964a: 60). This does not mean, of course, that these persons cannot in other contexts be strongly territorial, e.g., at home, and even their business relations might fit into a spider-web territorial system.

For the working class the street becomes an extension of the house, itself a place where people live and where much of the social interaction takes place.

In striking contrast to middle-class groups, social organization is here territorially equal to neighborhood place. "Just outside the few blocks that surround the resident's apartment lies foreign territory. Even though it too may be inhabited by families having apparently identical demographic and cultural characteristics, there is typically no way into its close-knit network of family ties and neighbor associations; and its residents may therefore be seen as strangers and regarded with suspicion and hostility. . . .

One's conception of himself and of his place in society is thus subtly merged with his conceptions of the spatially limited territory of limited social interaction. . . . But more important than that, and in marked contrast with contemporary intellectual elites, the underlying conceptions of order and the protocols of social propriety among working-class groups seem to demand clean boundaries and clearly-articulated structure. . . . However rich in subtleties of interpersonal associations, life in the working class tends to be concrete and particularistic. One typically knows where he stands, whether in the social hierarchy of his family and friends or in the territorial domain of his physical world" (Webber 1964a: 62-63).

When persons come into another's immediate local presence, they become accessible to each other in unique ways, and the possibilities for physical as well as psychical disturbance arise tremendously, e.g., in connection with "transgressing certain territories of the self of the other. . ." (Goffman 1964: 269). It is then of great interest that, as earlier noted, the personal space generally is greater in some violent criminals and in schizophrenics than in other groups (p. 191) and it has even been noted that very disturbed patients did not allow the therapist any territory at all (cf. Horowitz 1963: 236). Thus the size, shape and penetrability of the in this case portable territory would depend on immediate interpersonal events as well as on the current ego and motivational state of the individual (Horowitz, Duff and Stratton 1964), and this gives clues as to the treatment and rehabilitation of mentally disordered persons and to a bettering of the professional working environment.

Doubtless we are here approaching the functions and effects of behavioural territoriality, which will now be discussed.

4.6. Effect and functions of behavioural territoriality

4.6.1. The causative aspect

4.6.1.1. Behavioural meaning and territorial need:

Before entering into the intricate matter of territory causation the very nature of behavioural meaning should be touched upon.

"So far we have spoken as though the function of every behavioural system is so obvious that it can be taken for granted. No one bothers to ask what the function of eating is – or that of brooding or migration. Nevertheless, there are a number of long-recognized behavioural systems the functions of which remain obscure. A notable one is the territorial behaviour of many species of bird and mammal. No one doubts that such behaviour falls into the general class we are calling instinctive, yet the exact advantage (or advantages) that it confers on a species often remains unclear. Nevertheless it is characteristic of contemporary biological thought that any instinctive behaviour is confidently presumed to have some particular function (or functions) that aids species survival, even though the nature of that function is not yet agreed by students of the subject" (Bowlby 1971: 170).

It seems, however, to be quite possible to give plausible reasons for human behavioural territoriality, like other systems signified by order, constraint and communication. Maybe it could be maintained that spatial order is a purpose *per se*. But territoriality particularly involves restrictions on totally unselective movement, draws a line between members and non-members and assumes some form of individual or group recognition (cf. Suttles 1973: 144-145). For among vertebrates a highly developed social organization is always, as mentioned before, based on individual, personal acquaintance (cf. Leyhausen 1969a: 514). Thus human territories function within the frame of an information-ecology, which has long been neglected but which becomes more and more valued as a necessary complement to the well-known energetics-ecology (cf. Count 1969: 77).

Most often "the need for a territory is thought to be universal" (Lipman 1970: 68). Or to put it otherwise: "In a very general way, all higher living beings, practically all the vertebrates, exhibit a double need, analogous and related to the need to eat and reproduce: the need to maintain a territory, and to keep some distance from other beings" (Sivadon 1970: 413). In fact "The individual needs more than the minimum space that guarantees that others will not touch him and that allows him to breathe, move, and carry on in recurrent transient situations. He must be able to move freely within and between physical settings to satisfy not only his hunger, thirst, sex, and other biological drives, but also his needs for affiliation, achievement, success, and other complex social motives. In this sense, then, and under given circumstances, the individual may have to define a large enough space for himself to permit the satisfaction of these drives and motives, including those that are sociospatial in nature" (Proshansky, Ittelson and Rivlin 1970a: 179).

4.6.1.2. Territory as information:

According to the laws of cybernetics territory represents both information and action and is thus both symbol and physical phenomenon. Man develops models of the world based on the recognition of similarities and differences. This is necessary in order to give us a survey of changing situations and in order to make possible the fast reactions which are prerequisites for survival. Without doubt territory is thus a semiotic phenomenon.

"An information-ecology is concerned first with the organism's efforts after meaning. As students of organism, we are concerned primarily, not secondarily, with the semeion of message. When an organism utters, it is saying something. What it is saying expresses its space-time organizing. What the utterance means to the auditor is a function in turn of its space-time organizing. The system which is capable of an utterance output is a system to which some other individual's output generates an input. What goes on inside the organism is nodal. All the foregoing is the rationale for the attempt to comprehend communication first from what happens to an input. Here is where the coding begins" (Count 1969: 88-89).

From this it will be clear that the environment is much more than the source of stimuli, arranged in series or flows. Rather it is so that our milieu presents programs and controls for the regulation of input in relation to the demands of environmental systems and the behaviour arsenal. The meaning is also that the same environment unit can give different inputs to different persons as well as to the same person according to rhythm and mood. A consequence will even be that the environmental program will change with changing ecological conditions, if, for example, the population decreases or increases (cf. Barker 1965: 12).

"Ecology, I claim, is the study of systems at a level in which individuals or whole organisms may be considered elements of interaction, either among themselves, or with a loosely organized environmental matrix. . . . The success of life springs from miniaturization. It depends on the packing, in a small space, of a prodigious number of overlapping mechanisms, wonderfully persistent by virtue of built-in regulatory circuits and sufficiently open to carry into the future a promise of new developments" (Margalef 1968: 3-4).

Even though this packing self-evidently has its limits it is the background i.a. of cognitive mapping, a process composed of a series of psychological transformations by which an individual acquires, codes, stores, recalls, and decodes information about the relative locations and attributes of phenomena in his everyday spatial environment. Thus "*human spatial behavior is dependent on the individual's cognitive map of the spatial environment"* (Downs and Stea 1973: 9).

In his book *The Meaning of Information* Nauta (1972: 138-139) gave an explanation that seems to fit well to the communicative aspects of a territorial instinct: "Biology, especially biocybernetics, ecology and ethology, offers an abundance of instances which illustrate how goal-directed behavior is made possible by a complex organizational structure (involving a set of inner states) in which the vital environmental constraints are reflected; and this in the sense that an adequate behavior mechanism is aroused by specific signal patterns. The specific input patterns in question are 'decoded' by this organizational structure as to their VITAL MEANING, and as a consequence the corresponding adequate response mechanism is triggered and effectuated. The point is that decoding and responding have been fixed once and for all, according to a preformed plan or program", e.g. a territorial instinct.

4.6.1.3. Overstimulation and understimulation:
Most stressful encounters are avoided through spatial segregation. The orbits in which people travel tend to remove them from contact with those whom they dislike or disagree with. Avoidance is the first line of defense against interpersonal stress, but when this is not possible or effective, an individual develops alternate methods. Limiting the range of visual contact through social conventions or using actual physical barriers are other possibilities (cf. Sommer 1965: 347). This leads us to the fact that among the functions of territoriality Robert Ardrey (1967: 170) mentioned stimulation. The present author (Malmberg 1972: 11) also suggested territory as a source of appropriate sensory input to the nervous system. Without doubt the need for adequate stimulation is a most basic one, even though its level is a matter of discussion, and its most important dimensions are said to be those of intensity, novelty, complexity and temporal change or variation (cf. Wohlwill 1966: 32; as to critics of the stimulation theory see Evans and Eichelman 1976).

Concerning the understimulation earlier referred to it needs only be said that "early sensory deprivation prevents the formation of adequate models and strategies for dealing with the environment and that later sensory deprivation in normal adults disrupts the vital evaluation process by which one constantly monitors and corrects the models and strategies one has learned to employ in dealing with the environment" (Bruner 1961: 207). On the other hand: "Studies of sensory overload reveal that there are limits to the amount of information that can be accepted by an organism. Beyond this limit, stress is caused, which may take many forms. Studies carried out at the Eastern

Psychiatric Hospital in Philadelphia show that many people confronted with sensory overload respond by 'filtering out' the overload to such a degree that they suffer hallucinations as a result of sensory *underload*. The physical environment of the city is generally so chaotic that people have to 'filter out' in order to survive, but if there is too little for them to grasp, they finally filter too much and become understimulated" (McHarg 1966: 64-65). Sometimes an underload of information input is called a lack stress instead of sensory deprivation, but the term stress is normally reserved for consequences of an excess or overload of stimulation (cf. J. G. Miller 1961). Mostly stress is viewed as "one of many intraorganismic variables moderating the relationship between environmental stimuli and behavioral responses" (Sells 1970: 173; cf. also Appley and Trumbull 1967).

Hypothetically it is thus proposed that one primary object of territorial behaviour is to prevent understimulation as well as overstimulation of the limbic system, which is non-discriminatory as to external and internal stimuli and reacts in a diffuse and persistently lasting way, perhaps accountable for some part of psycho-somatic disease (cf. Pontius 1967).

4.6.1.4. Demands for room:
Beyond the essential physical needs there are, as we have seen, some other less obvious, but deepseated, biological demands that man shares with other animals. These needs – for personal space, for territorial room, for contact with other animals and with plants, for social interaction within small clans and family groups and for diversity in surroundings – all derive from our pre-human origin. Maybe these general aspects of territorial causation become most concrete from an application to the urban context:

"In recent years, perhaps the outstanding example of disregard for human needs has been the attempt to house low-income families in high-rise apartment complexes fringed in places with a useless border of clipped green lawn. The social deterioration resulting from this attempt is now well known and has been demonstrated in American cities from New York to San Francisco. The inhabitants of these cages lack contact with soil and nature, and without territory or safe travelways they are at the mercy of human predators whose traits have developed in the behavioral sink of the dying city. Children at play on the ground are isolated from mothers aloft, all sense of community is lost, and regulations prove worse than useless" (Stearns 1972: 272-274).

Thus it could be maintained that a certain amount of ground and room is felt to be necessary for human dignity and living and that this is a fundamental ingredient of territory. For "the biological impulse to establish a territory... with its strong association of the person with a unique situation, probably exerts a stronger hold on people than any other factor in housing" (R. J. Martin 1969: 214). It should be added that the artificial habitation represents a territorial innovation of an utmost, maybe decisive importance for the life and development of mankind.

The maximum freedom to impose control is accorded to the individual and the family group at home. Rather less control is permitted to other groups, which, while recognizable and exclusive, are less tightly knit, as the church, the club or the school. The territorial rights of the rather loosely knit social group known as the general public are more severely restricted, as demonstrated in the street, at the bus terminal or in the library. Territories with free occupancy cannot retain their character if restrictions are placed upon freedom of action that go beyond the limits of generally accepted social behavior (cf. Brower 1965: 9).

Home and site attachment could be equated with the centripetal tendencies of nucleated territoriality stressing the centre of the territory, while centrifugal forces are characteristic of exploratory behaviour in territorial areas far from the home-base. So an adequate territorial supply of some magnitude can in a way, like territorial vehicles, satisfy both these two basic needs. "To have a territory is to have one of the essential components of life; to lack one is one of the most precarious of all conditions" (E. T. Hall 1959: 69).

Already stimulation phenomena suggest: "The vertebrate biogram is diphasic" (Count 1958: 1065). Looking more deeply into some psychological needs we will now examine identity, privacy and security with their opposing anonymity, sociality and anxiety in their respective relevance to territoriality.

4.6.2. Psychological needs

4.6.2.1. Identity and anonymity:
First among the three basic psychological needs, thought to be involved in territoriality, comes identity. "Since the dawn of time, man has searched in various ways to answer the question, who am I? This quest for a personal sense of identity seems to be a fundamental aspect of man's nature and is certainly a fundamental tenet of modern psychology which is becoming increasingly concerned with this question" (Kira 1970: 272).

The term identity can, however, express both a persistent sameness within oneself and likewise a persistent sharing of some kind of essential character with others. In this first sense, even called ego identity as opposed to group identity (cf. Erikson 1956: 56-57), it means that every human being demands to be sure of his self-constancy or integrity. "A basic theoretical assumption which is implicit in this formulation is that any adult human must have some sort of viable role and identity which permits him to organize his own behavior and make meaningful contact with others in his social environment. One may conjecture that this assumption is but an extension of a general principle in psychology which is receiving increasing support – namely, that the nervous system functions in such a manner as to organize the perceptual world; i.e., that random stimulation is intolerable (produces basic anxiety) and either must be organized by the nervous system itself or avoided by the organism" (Schein 1961: 223).

Concerning the opposite of identity it has been stated that anonymity is part of a continuous spectrum ranging from total anonymity to full acquaintance, and it may well be that measurement of the precise degrees of anonymity in cities and towns would help to explain the quality of life in each. Conditions of full acquaintance offer security and familiarity but may also be stifling, because the individual is caught in a web of established relationships. By contrast, conditions of complete anonymity provide freedom from routinized social ties but may also create feelings of alienation and detachment (cf. Milgram 1970: 1464).

And "where social conditions of life destroy individual identity by making people feel anonymous, then what will follow is the deindividuated types of behaviors outlined previously. Assaultive aggression, senseless acts of destruction, motiveless murders, great expenditure of energy and effort directed toward shattering traditional forms and institutionalized structures become our dependent variables. Vandalism is the prototype of this behavior and represents a social problem which will soon reach epidemic proportions" (Zimbardo 1969: 282-283).

That there are not only social prerequisites for identity is stressed, e.g., by Joiner (1971: 14), saying that objects are used to express some aspects of the occupant's identity and that the place in which objects are situated becomes associated with that person. Among the three central ingredients of societal territoriality Soja (1971: 34) placed first "*a sense of spatial identity*, which in many ways represents an extension of personal space into a larger sociospatial sphere and is usually manifested in the development of a territorial symbolism or iconography (flags, imagery, insignia, certain physical structures or locations, etc.). Very rare is the individual who does not share in

common with other individuals a sense of belonging to a particular place or
area, even when he may not actually be residing there".

Particularly the loss of a residential area brings to the fore the importance
of the local spatial region and alerts us to the greater generality of spatial
conceptions as determinants of behaviour. "In fact, we might say that a *sense
of spatial identity* is fundamental to human functioning" (Fried 1963: 156),
representing an integration of important experiences concerning environmental arrangements and contacts in relation to the individual's conception
of his own body in space. This sense is based on spatial memories, spatial
imagery and the spatial framework of current activity, as well as on implicit
spatial components of ideals and aspirations.

It is further underlined: "The old family home is a place to escape from the
outer public, as well as contributory in other ways to identity" (Laufer,
Proshansky and Wolfe 1973: 364). And it is summarized: "Territory is space,
a part of the world space which is for personal occupation and control.
Territory is identity" (R. J. Martin 1969: 214).

4.6.2.2. Privacy and sociality:

Privacy approaches and complements identity to such a degree that removal
of it has demonstrable effects on the personality, effects which in some cases
may be quite serious (cf. Kira 1970: 272). However, it is not easy to define this
complex concept. "Privacy is not one thing but many things. It can be described as a psychological phenomenon, a social phenomenon, a political
phenomenon, and, indirectly, even as a economic phenomenon" (Laufer,
Proshansky and Wolfe 1973: 353). From a territorial point of view this is of
interest: "Privacy is the exclusive access of a person (or other legal entity) to a
realm of his own. The right to privacy entitles one to exclude others from (a)
watching, (b) utilizing, (c) invading (intruding upon, or in other ways affecting) his private realm" (Haag 1971: 149).

Among the many terms related to privacy only solitude (loneliness) should
be mentioned here. The difference between the two concepts is often formulated like this: "*Privacy is freedom from social contact and observation when
these are not desired*, and *Solitude is the lack of desired social contact*. . . . In our
modern mass-society complete physical isolation is rare, particularly in urban
life, there being numerous opportunities for physical togetherness without
interpersonal, affective relations, that is, without social contacts in the nar-
rower and more appropriate sense of the word" (Halmos 1952: 102-103). This
is the reason behind the statement, "Civilization, then, has not only failed to

dispel our anxiety of loneliness, it has served to magnify it" (Brownfield 1965: 31).

Basic facts are further, that "the modern claim to privacy derives first from man's animal origins and is shared, in quite real terms, by men and women living in primitive societies" and that the functions privacy perform for individuals in democratic societies can "be grouped conveniently under four headings – personal autonomy, emotional release, self-evaluation, and limited and protected communication" (Westin 1968: 7, 32). It was also said: "In order for the individual to function effectively, over time, there must be a reasonable balance between interaction and privacy" (Laufer, Proshansky and Wolfe 1973: 356).

In fact, no society can completely obliterate all privacy. There are walls which separate buildings, fences, hedges, blinds, and doors which offer some protection to the privacy of families. Even though much life is lived in the open, there are some barriers, physical or social, that restrict the observability of life. "The separateness of places, the impenetrability of their physical boundaries, the limited curiosity of equals, and the limited powers of rulers, and indifference, have been the main bulwarks of that privacy which human beings have possessed or desired to possess through most of history. Changes in any of these affect the magnitude of the privacy that a society enjoys" (Shils 1966: 288; cf. also Pastalan 1970).

Self-evidently space, then, is here sensible. It has meaning according to the purpose for which it is sought and the circumstances under which it is experienced. In the context of 'life quality' it is quite clear that it is not functional economic space that is being sought but rather the space that provides for privacy, isolation or freedom whatever one finds distasteful in the environment (cf. Sonnenfeld 1966: 74). The psychological need for privacy seems also to vary during the course of life, systematically growing among persons not in institutions, regardless of background. Although most of this change occurs between the ages of 20 and 40 years, it is suggested that the need for privacy generally increases with age (cf. Lawton and Bader 1970; Lawton 1972). Nearly three-quarters of the new residents in a home for old people said that they would prefer to live in single bedrooms, although only a fifth in fact had one, and many long-stay residents maintained a tenacious hold on their individuality and on hopes for eventual return to a home of their own (cf. Townsend 1962: 369-370). In another similar connection the general comment was: "Everyone has to have his own privacy, especially when he gets old" (Vivrett 1960: 554; see further the valuable book *Spatial Behavior of Older People* 1970).

"Privacy is most urgently needed and most critical in the place where people live, be it house, apartment, or any other dwelling. The dwelling is the little environment into which all the stresses and strains of the large world are today intruding, in one way or another, ever more deeply.... It is our further contention that to contain this kind of dwelling, and to develop both privacy *and* the true advantages of living in a community, an entirely new anatomy of urbanism is needed, built of many hierarchies of clearly articulated domains.... Only when the habitat of urbanizing man is given such an order shall we perhaps restore to urban life a fruitful balance between community and privacy" (Chermayeff and Alexander 1963: 37).

No wonder, then, that the characteristics of bad housing are usually defined in terms of lack of privacy, overcrowding of interior space, land congestion, poor maintenance and deterioration (cf. Loring 1956: 161). "Very likely the best means for producing an urban environment that inhibits the build-up of violent conflict are provided by an elaboration of designs for privacy" (Meier 1966: 12).

Certainly it is so that the chances of privacy diminish roughly and unevenly as crowding increases, and an augmenting population ineluctably intensifies crowding. "Traffic necessarily abridges the privacy of participants and that of everyone affected by the noise and the fumes. Thus, even though urban residences can be built so as to protect privacy almost as well as rural residences might (walls can be thickened, for example) privacy actually cannot be preserved in urban life. The urban resident must join streams of traffic as soon as he leaves his residence. Moreover space, and thick walls, are quite costly; an apartment or house protected from noise is a luxury few can afford.... Individual relations and mutual toleration of individuality require comparative permanence, shared objects, and a feeling of singularity and nonrecurrence. Under crowded conditions people are less likely to become significant to one another; each person relates to the crowd. The effect is isolation, a 'lonely crowd' of people who have few ties to one another, and whose ties come too easily undone" (Haag 1971: 162-163).

As to extreme cases it is a truism that "Neither the prisoner of war nor the forced laborer is ever alone. All the time he is crowded in with strangers, he cannot find a quiet corner, he has no privacy. He never enjoys that seclusion from other people that cultured man needs.... The loss of privacy, of individuality, is felt as an extreme form of humiliation, as a social degradation" (Meerlo 1946: 117).

Without doubt islands of privacy exist in all establishments and throughout even the most intimate household. These islands are protected by an intricate set of rules. When these rules are violated secret places are sought after, discovered, and employed as facilities for private action. These places and their permeability constitute one type of maps of interpersonal relationships and reveal the nature of the selves participating in them (Schwartz 1967-1968: 750). Thus it can be summarized: "The crucial role of privacy in any attempt to understand man's relationship to a manmade world is not to be disputed" (Proshansky, Ittelson and Rivlin 1970a: 176).

The territoriality background of privacy is thus most often clear, even though not always verbally mentioned. Concerning old age homes it is, e.g., said that the territorial behaviour so common in this setting undoubtedly serves partially to substitute for the privacy which is unattainable where one has a roommate and limited mobility. One may defend better and feel more confident about personal autonomy in an area which one has staked out as one's own. It remains for future investigation to determine further characteristics of those who need spatial privacy and to study the natural history of alternative modes of attaining this in environmental situations which preclude a true satisfaction of the need (cf. Lawton and Bader 1970: 54), e.g., by means of structuring and compartmentalization.

The counterpart of privacy is sociality, and we need here just question the theory, often accepted without discussion, of man as an unreservedly social animal. An interesting fact is first that the word "social" is Latin in origin and has no equivalent in Greek language and thought. Further Aristotle's "*Zoon politikon*" was wrongly translated by Seneca and Thomas Aquinas as "*homo est naturaliter politicus, id est socialis*" (man is by nature political, that is, social), which has had immense influence on later thinking (Arendt 1959: 22-24). Today there are, however, authors who directly state, e.g., that "Unlike the ants and bees, man is not biologically a social animal equipped by heredity with prepotent capacities for complex associative life, but in every individual case must be bent and broken to group living through the arduous process of socialisation and be kept in the paths of conformity through the imposition of social controls" (Murdock 1965, cited after Goldsmith 1976: 47). The present author (Malmberg 1972: 13) proposed "a classification of the human animal as semi-social", and all this gives a still more pronounced picture of the demand for privacy and territory in man, notwithstanding that there are also social territories.

Malinowski (1961, cited after Goldsmith 1976: 47) vindicated: "Very often it is assumed by anthropologists that humanity developed from a gregarious simian species and that man inherited from his animal ancestors the so-called 'herd-instincts'. Now this hypothesis is entirely incompatible with the view here taken that common sociability develops by extension of the family bonds and from no other sources".

Of course it is difficult for man to live long alone, as shown under natural conditions, e.g., by Ishi, the last Yahi-indian (Kroeber 1962: 3-10). But we also know that mankind lived for about 98 percent of its time on earth in small, probably rather loose flocks of let us say 25 to 50 persons. "Thus we know from many prehistoric and other studies that the original group size of human societies was small. Many things in our social behaviour of today which seem objectionable depend on the fact that man did not evolve for the conditions of the mass society and that our behavioural system therefore revolts against it" (Leyhausen 1968: 89).

So it was brought out clearly: "We live in a continual competition with society over the ownership of our selves. Society continues to lay claim to them. Society makes demands upon us, involving our obligations as good citizens. But we maintain that each of us has the right to be his own man. In the course of this competition, a territory gets to be staked out that is peculiarly our own. Its boundaries may be crossed by others only when we expressly invite them. Within these boundaries our own interests are sovereign, all initiative is ours, we are free to do our thing, insulated against outside influence and observation. This condition of insulation is what we call privacy" (A. Simmel 1971: 72; for a recent survey of the concept of privacy, see Altman 1976).

4.6.2.3. Security and anxiety:

Both identity and privacy can, of course, be threatened and are thus always related to defense and to security, which is needed by man in its physical as well as in its psychical meaning. "There is a demand for some sense of stability in the midst of the forces that surround him, a desire for the assured repeatability and preservation of basic satisfactions already experienced; the demand for some kind of form which seems to have reality and from which flow and development can occur in order to avoid a feeling of personal chaos or social anarchy" (Cantril 1963: 212). It is even vindicated that "the actions of all individuals in all places and at all times can be viewed in the scheme of security theory. This does not mean that security is to be considered a panacea for all the world's ills, or as a new form of religion. It is a system of psychology which meets the criteria of being both comprehensive and consistent.... Security is a state of mind in which one is willing to accept the consequences of one's behaviour" (Blatz 1966: 112).

As to children it is doubtless so that the constant presence of familiar things makes it easier to maintain a minimum level of safety-feeling (cf. Sandler 1960: 355). For instance it was said that "To kibbutz children, then, basic security is provided not by their parents but the kibbutz" (Bettelheim 1969: 71). And from America it was reported: "Another guess which we hazard with respect to the Hopi child is that he has a strong feeling of social security. His is a world which he knows intimately and which accepts him completely. A Hopi is never driven from his village; he is never an outcast; he never starves when others have food; he never lacks a place in which to sleep. He lives in a social world in which he has an indubitable place" (Dennis 1943: 634).

The opposite to security is anxiety, a concept which is allied to that of fear. These two states of mind also have, of course, fundamental psychological importance. "The biological state basic to anxiety is one of a general readiness for action" (Shands 1970: 144), and in this connection the two extremes of reaction are called defense and flight (cf. Forel 1942). Concerning the crime situation in the modern city it was for instance stated that all the different elements which combine to make a defensible space have a common goal – an environment in which latent territoriality and sense of community in the inhabitants can be translated into responsibility for ensuring a safe, pro-ductive, and well-maintained living space:

"The public areas of a multi-family residential environment devoid of de-fensible space can make the act of going from street to apartment equivalent to running the gauntlet. The fear and uncertainty generated by living in such an environment can slowly eat away and eventually destroy the security and sanctity of the apartment unit itself. On the other hand, by grouping dwelling units to reinforce associations of mutual benefit; by delineating paths of movement; by defining areas of activity for particular users through their juxtaposition with internal living areas; and by providing for natural oppor-tunities for visual surveillance, architects can create a clear understanding of the function of a space, and who its users are and ought to be. This, in turn, can lead residents of all income levels to adopt extremely potent territorial attitudes and policing measures, which act as strong deterrents to potential criminals. . . .

The essential ingredient of our proposal is territorial definition coupled with improvements to the capacity of the territorial occupants to survey their newly defined realm. Territorial definition may appear to be the antithesis of the open society, and surveillance a further restriction on its freedom. Territory and surveillance have after all traditionally been understood as the devices of the propertied classes and their agents or police authority. We, however, are advocating territorial definition and the creation of surveillance opportunities to allow the *citizen* of the open society to achieve control of his environment for the activities he wishes to pursue within it – to make him instrumental in curtailing others from destroying his habitat. whether the others are criminals or a reactionary authority" (Newman 1972: 3-4, 204).

Because the psychiatrists nearly always find extensive elements of insecurity in maladjusted and abnormal individuals, they have generally stated that feelings of security – as well as of identity and privacy – are necessary for mental health (cf. Plant 1939: 95). Under such conditions it is self-evident that the ward housing the mentally deficient must be such that the patients feel secure. This feeling is the first prerequisite for the re-establishment of the patient's normal relations with his environment (Baker, Davies and Sivadon 1959: 24). Experiments with severely disturbed neuropsychiatric patients have shown that there was a significant reduction of anxiety when the need for personal space diminished (cf. Booraem and Flowers 1972).

"The fact that changes in clinical behavioral symptomatology appear to have their correlates in changes in territorial behavior does not mean that changes in specific behavior exclusively *cause* changes in territorial behavior or that changes in the capacity to establish territories *cause* changes in specific behaviors. Improved capacity for communication of intentions, for example, makes territorial ownership easier; the security afforded by territorial ownership reduces anxiety . . . and makes communication easier. Thus, territorial behavior interrelates with other parameters of overall psychological functioning in the institutionalized individual" (Paluck and Esser 1971b: 289).

Consequently, there is some minimum need for security, without doubt, since lacking sufficient satisfaction we are consumed and immobilized by anxiety (Ardrey 1967: 338). "Dominance and possession of territory make us *feel* secure and it is hard for man to deny his animal past" (Esser 1971a: 13). Thus it seems to be quite clear that behavioural territoriality is involved in all the three basic human needs just treated. And it can be summarized: "It is quite possible that frustration of the sense of territoriality that man shares with most of the higher animals may contribute far more importantly to the psychological problems of our age than we now have adequate reason to suspect" (Parr 1965: 18).

The relations of territory to the still more decisive population regulation problems will finally also be taken up for discussion.

4.6.3. Population regulation

4.6.3.1. Distribution and increase of human population:
The psychological needs for identity, privacy and security probably do not represent final causes themselves. It should here be examined whether they, together with earlier mentioned functions of territoriality, could be parts of a biological system for the dispersal and above all regulation of human numbers, as suggested for corresponding phenomena in non-human animals. In this connection we have first to look briefly at the populations of man.

In spite of the fact that no substantial historical data are available on which to base estimates of the world population before A.D. 1500, such estimations have been made by means of different kinds of archaeological and anthropological evidence, e.g., the magnitude of excavated habitations and cemeteries. Calculating the increase of settlement and population size since the inception of agriculture Max Pettersson (1960) assumed that the inhabitants of earth at 10,000 B.C. numbered between 1 and 10 million and that the doubling time up to this point had been at least 75,000 years. From 10,000 B.C. to A.D. 1500, when a fairly firm estimate of about 350 million persons could be deduced, the doubling time should be about 1,730 years and between 1500 and 1950 about 164 years, the latter year with a world population of about 2,500 million people. In another investigation, Ehrlich and Ehrlich (1972: 6) proposed that in 8,000 B.C. there were on our planet about 5 million humans, in A.D. 1650 circa 500 million, in 1850 round 1,000 million, in 1930 very close to 2,000 million and that in 1975 there should have been 4,000 million inhabitants, with the doubling times between these points being 1,500, 200, 80 and 45 years respectively.

Still more detailed were the assumptions of Deevey (1960), saying that 1,000,000 years ago we had 125,000 humans on earth, 300,000 years ago 1 million, 25,000 years ago 3.3 million and 10,000 years ago 5.3 million people. Then came the agricultural revolution and 6,000 years ago there should have been 86.5 million, 2,000 years ago 133 million, after the beginning of the industrial revolution 310 years ago 545 million, 210 years ago 728 million, 160 years ago 906 million, 60 years ago 1,610 million, and 10 years ago 2,400 million inhabitants. The density was estimated to have been 0.004 persons per square kilometer one million years ago and 16.4 ten years ago (cf. also Brass 1970).

It is supposed that between 60 and 100 billion humans have lived on this planet, of which the now existing 3.7 billion make up between 4 and 5 percent (cf. Ehrlich and Ehrlich 1972: 5). Further it is quite clear that there is now an exponential increase of the population. "The extraordinary proliferation of the human species which is going on in the world at present is part of a trend which began about two centuries ago and which has been gathering momentum since the beginning of the present century. This cannot fail to be recognized as one of the principal features of modern world history. In historical perspective, it appears as a unique episode in the growth of the species since its origin; it has no parallel in previous history or prehistory for the speed and magnitude of expansion of numbers, and it seems highly unlikely that a comparable expansion would occur again in the future after the present trend has run its course" (Durand 1971: 37).

The inhabited regions of the earth extend over an area of some 52 million square miles. According to this and an estimation of approximately 3.3 billion people in total some few years ago the general world population density would be 63 persons per square mile. If the dispersion of people over all inhabitable ground was random, the average distance between a given person and the nearest other one would be approximately 590 feet. But this is certainly not the case. "The probability that at any given time a given square foot of habitable ground on earth is occupied by an individual is certainly quite low, in fact, one in 500,000. But once we have located one individual, we will almost certainly find another within a few yards. It is a rather safe assumption that the average distance between a given individual and the nearest other person is today less than ten yards" (Zajonc 1971: 143). It is presupposed that man's physical body occupies somewhere between two and four cubic feet of space (cf. Sears 1969: 83-84).

Among the continents Europe is most densely populated with 142 persons per square mile, as against Asia with 78, North America with 23, South America with 19, Africa with 17 and Australia with 3 persons per square mile. More interesting are, however, figures for different regions within continents, and it is well known that some of the most densely populated ones are found in Asia. As to the population density among different subsistence categories it was stated (Harrison, Weiner, Tanner and Barnicot 1964: 494) that in food-gatherers there were up to 2 persons per square mile, in higher hunters and fishers up to 20, in simple cultivators during early centuries up to 150 heads per square mile. The actual overall density on the world's entire land area today was given by Doxiadis (1965: 200) as 0.21 person per hectare and as 0.74 in inhabited areas. It was highest, 2.0 to 4.0 in the Netherlands, Belgium, the United Kingdom, Western Germany, Taiwan, Korea and Japan and lowest, 0.003 to 0.007 persons per hectare in S. W. Africa, Mauritania, Libya, Mongolia and French Guiana.

In settlements the residential densities may range from as low as 1 person per hectare in some garden suburbs to 7,500 in parts of Hongkong, the normal maximum being 200 to 300 persons per hectare without and 300 to 400 with multistorey buildings. It can be added that ancient Rome and Paris in the 16th century are thought to have had 700 persons, and the densest district in Paris housed 800 persons per hectare in 1959 (Carlestam 1970: 140; cf. also 4.3.12.3.).

"In mid-1974 the world population was estimated at 4061 million, with an annual growth rate of 2.2 percent. The rate of growth is conspicuously uneven in different parts of the world. Several rich countries are now very close to zero growth (births and deaths are balanced) and in virtually all European countries the growth rate is below 1 percent a year" (Owen 1976: 3). Nevertheless, with a general picture of long and fast increasing numbers of people on earth the first reaction must be that we are running out of space, that the population density is becoming dangerously high. Particularly important to note is that human population growth now world-wide shows a positive correlation with density and that thus no effective density-dependent control seems to be in function (cf. Odum 1971: 514).

4.6.3.2. Crowding and its symptoms:

High density of population is therefore a common condition in many parts of the world, particularly in urban areas. And two notable traits of humans in close association are a heightening of emotionality and a lowering of responsibility. "The crowd-situation seems to allow a release to motives which are otherwise controlled, even if conscious, or to motives of which the actor may be unaware" (Sprott 1958: 162). Griffith and Veitch (1971: 96-97) investigated students of both sexes and found that under conditions of high temperature and high population density both personal-affective, social-affective and nonsocial-affective responses were significantly more negative than under conditions of comfortable temperature and low population density. And it was noted that males respond still more negatively to high density than females (cf., e.g., Freedman, Levy, Buchanan and Price 1972).

Summarizing extensive studies of kindergarten children Kälin (1972: 87, 92) made the following two conclusions: "Our hypothetical assumption that an increasing density of population within a limited space is accompanied by an augmentation of aggression manifestations has been confirmed with great significance; and our presupposition that increasing density of population within a limited space brings about a diminishment of interactions between individuals in spite of the theoretically expected augmentation is also very significantly confirmed."

It is of certain interest in this connection that "studies of attempted suicide have shown that the most important social correlate is overcrowding. Typically, the person who makes a non-fatal suicidal gesture has been harassed beyond endurance by recurrent friction within the domestic group, in cramped and overcrowded premises" (Carstairs 1969: 758).

In his paper on "Mental Health and Overpopulation" Marmor (1972: 131, 133) vindicated that "under conditions of overcrowding there is inevitably a lack of privacy, which also can become a source of stress. The fundamental factor involved in both excessive noise and lack of privacy is the amount of sensory input with which the human nervous system has to deal. Under conditions of extreme crowding there is a constant sensory input of high intensity. When that input goes beyond a certain optimum level, stress reactions tend to develop in human beings, with evidencies of anxiety, irritability, and, ultimately, psycho-somatic disorders...". And he summarized: "I trust, however, that I have been able to demonstrate to you that the problem of overpopulation is highly relevant to questions of mental health. If we ignore it, we endanger not only our physical comfort and our biological health, but also, in the final analysis, our basic emotional well-being".

It has been simply proposed that "crowding is experienced as a syndrome of stress resulting from the disparity between one's supply of and demand for space" (Stokols, Rall, Pinner and Schopler 1973: 89). And it was even maintained: "As population density increases, spatial constraints become more acute until, finally, they eventuate in social disorganization and physiological pathology. Situations of crowding, then, are characterized both by the element of spatial restriction and by the manifestation of its deleterious effects on organisms over time" (Stokols 1972: 74).

A valuable survey of the territorial implications of crowding was published by Proshansky, Ittelson and Rivlin (1970b). First they stressed that crowds are ubiquitous phenomena of the urban setting, which may severely limit the control of territories but which not always signify social problems. Their conceptualization as both a cause and a consequence of modern urban life goes beyond the question of the number of persons in a given space. How a space is organized, for what purpose it is designated, and what kinds of activities are involved – all are factors that contribute to crowding phenomenology.

"Crowding as a psychological phenomenon, then, is only indirectly related to mere numbers or densities of people. It is possible to feel crowded in the presence of few people or not crowded in the presence of many. The significant element appears to be frustration in the achievement of some purpose because of the presence of others. Crowding is thus directly related to privacy and territoriality. Crowding occurs when the number of people an individual is in contact with is sufficient to prevent him from carrying out specific behavior and thereby restricts his freedom of choice" (op. cit. p. 182; cf. also Russell and Russell 1968: 206-252). We have thus clearly to distinguish between the physical condition (density) and the psychological experience (crowding), terms which are, however, not always used in these meanings (cf. p. 197-198).

We must admit that little is known about the density of population or the intensity of stimulation that is optimum in the long run for the physical and psychical well-being of man, and we know that crowding is a relative term. But "The biological significance of population density must be evaluated in the light of the past experience of the group concerned, because this experience conditions the manner in which each of its members responds to the others as well as to environmental stimuli and trauma. Laying claim to a territory and maintaining a certain distance from one's fellow are probably as real biological needs in man as they are in animals, but their expressions are culturally conditioned" (Dubos 1965b: 109).

In any case we should remember a statement by Raymond Pearl (1939: 249) in his well-known book *The Natural History of Population*: "The major problems of population are primarily and fundamentally biological in nature, because the size and other characteristics of populations rest upon the operation of the fundamental biological principles of individual survival, reproduction, variability, and their mutual interactions and integrations with the environment". With these words in mind we will now look at the regulation of populations.

4.6.3.3. Regulation of populations:
Here we have to remember first that the normal fluctuations of animal populations are thought to be regulated by the varying influence and interaction of density-dependent factors like food supply, enemies, parasites and diseases. These fluctuations are, of course, made possible by means of the reproductive capacity of the species but are mostly restricted to a very limited range around a certain mean, according to the environment-organism characteristics of the system. Even though it is rather generally agreed that food should be the ultimate decisive factor, it is most often found that the total carrying capacity of the habitat is hardly ever exploited (cf. Lack 1967: 275-278). Thus "The

popular Malthusian notion that the number surviving from year to year is determined by the current supply of food, with the excess dying from starvation, is no longer supported by any student of natural populations" (Stott 1962: 356).

Instead, animal species have evolved devices by which they can escape the danger of eating their offspring out of a living and which have presumably been brought about by the operation of natural selection. Populations which fail to produce effective devices of this kind will eliminate themselves from the scene, so that only those which evolve a successful control can persist. This depends essentially on some method by which the effective population density can be assessed, and the animals' reproductive behaviour modified accordingly.

"The devices employed are found nearly always to involve many elements which are basically conventional, in the sense that their importance is not intrinsic (as it is with actual food), but depends on the social organisation of the population. For instance, the amount of space available to a population is usually determined as being some rather arbitrary 'territory', which the population 'owns'. Within this space individuals compete, not so much for actual food, but for some conventionally accepted status symbol. The competition for these status symbols is usually not so much by actual fighting but rather by some form of display or conventional competition. Such displays are technically known as 'epideictic' displays, in contrast to 'epigamic' displays, which are concerned solely with winning mates" (Waddington 1972: 266-267).

The regulation of population density this way, depending on processes that are automatic and self-contained within the population concerned, is a typical form of homeostasis. Its operation is not necessarily perfect, and, especially where the habitat is violently or repeatedly disturbed, as happens under most regimes of human land-use, numbers tend to get out of hand and pest conditions are generated. "Social organizations appear to have evolved as entities in their own right, each with its characteristic structures, codes and adaptations. They have been improved and perfected by natural selection, discriminating in favour of efficient systems which preserve the balance between population and environment without detriment to resources or prejudice to what the future brings. Less efficient systems are eliminated because they lead either to overpopulation and cumulative damage, or to the attenuation and extinction of the group" (Wynne-Edwards 1965: 177-178). Even though these theories, particularly as to group selection, are still not generally agreed upon, they seem to be of great interest and probably contain some fundamental truth.

A dynamic stability depending on some kind of natural control has indubitably always characterized and still characterizes the populations of "primitive" man as long as they, by means of selective devices, are balanced against the permanent carrying capacity of their habitats. In early man the traditional or customary element in achieving population homeostasis had developed as complements to innate control. Social competition ceased to have a direct phsyiological effect on fertility, when traditional codes of behaviour took over the population regulation.

"Local tribes had their own hunting territories, and corresponding systems of land tenure were developed by pastoral and later by agricultural peoples, down to historic times. Customary restrictions were placed on fertility in the place of physiological ones, and so far as we know all primitive peoples practised family limitation in some form. The four commonest methods were by the determent of marriage for ten years or more beyond puberty, by compulsory abstention from intercourse which resulted in births being widely spaced, by abortion, and by infanticide. One or more of these was found in every stone-age race that survived into modern times" (Wynne-Edwards 1972: 63; cf. also Carr-Saunders 1922: 197-242; Harrison, Weiner, Tanner and Barnicot 1964: 495-506).

Mary Douglas (1972) in her interesting paper "Population Control in Primitive Groups" gave some detailed examples, summarized in this way: "To conclude, it seems that population homeostasis does occur in human groups. The kind of relation to resources that is sought is more often a relation to limited social advantages than to resources crucial to survival ...". It is evidently true that social behaviour in the form of customs, rites and taboos are often further developments of the instinctive behaviour already found in animals. Thus all these factors have certainly not developed, as Wynne-Edwards (1972: 63) put it, "at the expense of automatic, innate controls" but as complements and superstructures to basic instincts. The relations of such inborn behaviour to the proximate causes of population regulation are very clear in most of the examples mentioned by Douglas.

"Gradually, with the spread of the agricultural revolution, which tended to concentrate the population at high densities on fertile soils and led by degrees to the rise of the town, the craftsman, and the merchant, the old customs and taboos must have been forsaken. The means of population control would have been inherited originally from man's subhuman ancestors, and among stone age peoples their real function was probably not even dimly discerned except perhaps by a few individuals of exceptional brilliance and insight. The continually expanding horizons and skills of modern man rendered intrinsic limitation of numbers unnecessary, and for 5,000 or 10,000 years the advanced peoples of the Western world and Asia have increased without appearing to harm the world about them or endanger its productivity. But the underlying principles are the same as they have always been. It becomes obvious, at last, that we are getting very near the global carrying capacity of our habitat, and that we ought swiftly to impose some new, effective, homeostatic regime before we overwhelm it,..." (Wynne-Edwards 1969: 111).

The enormous human population growth during later centuries is, of course, first of all, the direct consequence of a decreasing death rate due to improved health standards and medical practices. In a very general way we can say that the agricultural and industrial revolution has enormously augmented the temporary capacity of the environment to hold human bodies. Unlike animal populations, which have a rather fixed amount of food and space at their disposal, the human stock lives in a world in which the capacity of the environment to hold people has continually gone up. And in doing so it has allowed human populations to explode (cf. Holling 1969: 138-140).

But still there are many questions: "Why is modern man unique among the animals in seemingly being unable to control his numbers? Has the unchecked growth of human population signalled the beginning of physiological and social catastrophes as a 'natural' reaction against overpopulation? Are the ecological disasters generated by a crowded world an inevitable outgrowth of spiraling population numbers?" (Soja 1971: 31). As a provisory answer we will again underline that most populations of "primitive" man seem to be under as good a natural control as those of animals but that the agricultural and still more the industrial revolution by overexploitation of the permanent carrying capacity of the habitats has strongly increased the material resources, which seem to be the ultimate factors of population regulation. Because the exploitable resources are limited, and the proximate regulating factors in the long run cannot function without support of the ultimate ones, the recent, rapid increase of mankind cannot go much farther without fatal consequences (as to the terms proximate and ultimate factor, see J. R. Baker 1938; Lack 1967: 5).

4.6.3.4. The population crisis and behavioural territoriality:
It remains to give behavioural territoriality its definitive place in the context as a very important device of constraint in the society, which, however, has not been able to function effectively for the prevention of overpopulation in modern man. Coon (1961: 427) said in his opening remarks to a symposium on crowding, stress and natural selection: "As the population of the world

grows at compound interest every year, we need to know what happens to animals, including *Homo sapiens*, when their territories become overpopulated.... Anthropologists seeking to explain the evolution of man are coming to realize that it was not only the acquisition of tool-making and speech that made our ancestors human, but also their ability to tolerate each other's presence. There can be little doubt that our ancestors were genetically changed by natural selection so that they could live in increasingly larger and more complexly organized social aggregations".

The simple fact seems, however, to be that "phylogeny has left us with a set human nature, with a basic construction of the species, which cannot be altered at will and needs enormous periods of time for harmonious evolution" (Leyhausen 1965a: 261). It is then not very probable that man in relatively late times was genetically altered so that he is able to live for long under the present complex, social and crowded conditions. On the contrary there is, as recently mentioned, much evidence suggesting that man is still, zoologically speaking, in most cases not very social. It was also recognized by Coon (1961: 427): "Now that the rate of human population increase has itself increased to unparalleled proportions, the problems of food supply and standing room become insignificant and academic compared to the problem of increasing stress and decreasing sanity...".

Thus the proximate factors of behavioural territoriality, long lacking support from the ultimate regulating ones of food and other fundamental provisions, have probably, at least from the beginning of the agricultural revolution onwards, been unable to stop the population increase. Surely this does not mean that these brakes have not functioned at all, only that their effect in the long run has been insufficient. "As nations expand, their borders push against those of their neighbors, and individuals fence their territorial lines. International conflicts occur, national boundaries change, and the defeated masses migrate into new habitats to begin anew the cycle of national expansion. With time, however, the amount and the quality of the unused habitat depreciates and the existing space becomes saturated with people and their by-products. As man again strives to space out his kind, he finds no new lands to tread upon and thus aggression can no longer play a positive role. Man is at the crossroads – either he limits his numbers by reducing human births or he allows aggression to assume the negative role of genocide" (Sorenson 1974: 28).

Without doubt the great adaptability of territoriality, manifested i.a. in various dividing, marking and structuring techniques has long been able to respond to the cited psychological and spatial needs of permanently increasing populations by means of a still more worked-out compartmentalization and decoration, particularly in urban settings. By virtue of symbols and taboos man has partly been able to suppress or canalize different instincts that are incompatible with or at least undesirable for society as a whole under existing socialization. "Current interest in the stress phenomenon stems in part from the fact that the genetic (biological) programme of the Stone Age is not properly suited to a civilized being who is supposed to act socially" (Carlestam 1971: 140).

It must, however, be taken for granted that territorial and hierarchical patterns of behaviour still have great adaptive value for the populations of man (cf. Dubos 1965b: 300). Territoriality or as Leyhausen terms it "relative ranking order" restricts the spatial compatibility of individuals of the same species more than absolute ranking does and therefore sets drastic limits on acceptable density. At the same time it reserves places and spheres for the individual where it can remain independent of the various absolute ranking orders within the community, where indeed it is superior to all others regardless of how low its absolute ranking may be. "If for some reason relative hierarchy becomes too prominent in a society, it is no longer possible to solve great communal problems. Conversely, if individual liberty is reduced too far absolute social hierarchy develops into tyranny" (Leyhausen 1973c: 236).

Certainly, the territorial limitation which is of prime interest here is the tolerance limit between humans. It seems strange that until recently almost nobody was aware of such a boundary. It was therefore thought that all population problems could be solved by stepping up production so that the ever-growing numbers of people in the world could be amply supplied not only with food and shelter but also with all other goods, and that only physical factors could set a limit to population growth. "It is impossible to speak of human ecology without first and last considering the impact numbers, densities and density-dependent stressors have on the social behaviour of individuals, groups and whole societies, and in what way and to what extent they change human behaviour towards the rest of the environment" (Leyhausen 1971b: 248).

Thus if behavioural territoriality, in spite of its indubitable character as fundamental, constraining, proximate factor with many-sided effects, has not been able to stop the rapid and steady increase of the human population during historical time, this seems to have two grounds. One is that the ultimate factor behind them, namely available resources of food and other goods necessary for human life, have all the time increased by means of still more pronounced cultivation, exploitation and transport, violating the permanent carrying capacity of the earth (cf. Berghe 1974: 785). The other is the great density-dependent adaptability of territoriality, demonstrated as the compartmentalization and structuring above all of settlements and habitations. The physical and psychical evils of our time suggest that both these factors are now in many parts of the world pressed to their utmost possible limits or have already gone out of function.

The more necessary it is, then, to put behavioural territoriality in an evolutionary perspective, involving the past, the present and the future.

4.7. Behavioural territoriality in the past, the present and the future

4.7.1. Genetic stability and environmental imprint

It is a truism that we have "an unmistakable continuity in the flow of evolution, a profound relationship between past, present, and future events" (Bigelow 1972: 44). Maybe this statement is also obvious: "Until recently it had seemed self-evident that the biological survival of the evolutionary experiment called man was assured" (Freedman and Roe 1961: 455). Further it could be maintained that "the struggle for existence is predominantly a struggle for space" (Sölch 1929: 111). And it can hardly be denied that behavioural territoriality has a most important place in this struggle for existence as a weighty part of the man-environment system, with great probability an evolutionary adaptation (for critics of this view, see Williams 1966: 239-246).

As earlier underlined it seems evident that the genetic endowment of *Homo sapiens* has changed only in minor details since the Stone Age and that there are not any great chances that it can be significantly modified in the foreseeable future. This hereditary stability defines the potentialities and requirements of man's nature and determines the physiological limits beyond which human life cannot be safely altered by technological and other innovations. The frontiers of technology are in the final analysis less important for the life of man than his own frontiers, which are fixed by the genetic constitution (cf. Dubos 1973: 200).

In this connection it should be stressed that contrary to popular belief genes do not determine the traits of a person but his response to the physical and social environment. Furthermore, not all the genes are active all the time. Through complex mechanisms environmental stimuli decide which parts of the genetic equipment are being repressed or are being activated. Thus each individual person is perhaps as much the product of his environment as of his hereditary endowment. Human beings perceive the world and respond to it, not through the whole spectrum of their potentialities, but only through the areas of this spectrum that have been made functional by environmental stimulation. The long-term life experiences decide what parts of the genetic equipment should be converted into functional attributes by means of a permanent feedback between environment and genes (cf. Dubos 1968: 16-18).

"Thus, the qualitative functions must, to a considerable degree, be regarded as a kind of integrated imprint of all the ecological factors which prevailed over geologically extended periods of time during the evolution of the species in question. In other words, their development during the ontogeny of the individual is secured by information received and stored in the genetic code prior to the individual's existence. What evolved as a consequence of environmental demands on the ancestors is now demanded by the individual from the environment: the individual can live and stay healthy only if its particular environment offers, within the limits detailed below, those same conditions which helped select its genes. These demands or requirements of the individual from its environment are unconditional and unalterable as long as the species remains virtually unchanged by further evolution, and they pertain to the whole of the environment, inanimate, animate and most especially social" (Leyhausen 1973b: 337-338).

Two main characteristics of man are, however, also his versatility and his capacity for innovation under certain conditions. Exercising these related gifts he has in recent millennia extended the environments in which he is capable of living and breeding to include extremes of natural conditions. Not only this, but he has also, more or less deliberately, changed these surroundings so as to create a series of entirely new man-made biotopes. These modifications are at least partly responsible for the spectacular increase of the world population of the species (cf. Bowlby 1971: 85).

"Paradoxically the dangers of overpopulation will be increased by the extreme adaptability of the human race. Human beings can become adapted to almost anything – polluted air, treeless avenues, starless skies, aggressive behavior, the rat-race of overcompetitive societies, even life in concentration camps. But in one way or another, we have to pay later for the adjustment we make to undesirable conditions" (Dubos 1968: 21). And it should be stressed that an extreme adaptability can easily lead to overspecialization. In two independent papers presented at the 1961-1962 meeting of the American Association for the Advancement of Science it was maintained that all biological species as well as human tribes that have earlier become extinct have been lost for one single reason – overspecialization (Buckminster Fuller 1964: 237).

"In brief, it is obvious that the technological factors, such as supplies of food, power, or natural resources, that are required for the operation of the body machine and of the industrial establishment are not the only factors to be considered in determining optimum population size. Just as important for maintaining *human* life is an environment in which it is possible to satisfy the longing for quiet, privacy, independence, initiative and open space. These are not frills or luxuries but constitute real biological necessities. They will be in short supply long before there is a critical shortage of the sources of energy and materials that keep the human machine going and industry expanding" (Dubos 1968: 22).

Without doubt the range of habitats in which man now lives and breeds is enormous, and the speed at which man's environment has been diversified, especially in recent centuries of man-made change, has far outstripped the pace at which natural selection is able to work. We can therefore be fairly sure that none of the environments in which civilized, or even half-civilized, man lives today conforms to the environment in which his environmentally stable behavioural systems were evolved and to which they are intrinsically adapted. Thus the only relevant criterion by which to consider the natural adaptedness of any particular part of present-day man's behavioural equipment is the degree to which and the way in which it might contribute to population survival in his primeval environment (cf. Bowlby 1971: 86-87).

4.7.2. Territory and human evolution

It seems very probable that, in anthropoid apes as in other social or semisocial vertebrates, in addition to dispersal functions, "Territorial behavior is designed to prevent the loss of contact among reproducing units. Within the territory, the specific 'social distances' act effectively against any dissolution of the group. Aggressions, and indications thereof, or threats, prevent any dangerous crowding of territories. . . . Thus, territorial behavior of a group insures the right degree of distance and contact within the biotope; and social distance, the right degree of distance and contact between the individuals within their territory" (Hediger 1970b: 37, 55).

It would appear that this primate tendency to maintain territoriality should be closely bound up with the differentiation of races and varieties, and perhaps even of species, by selection and inbreeding. It may be necessary to postulate some such innate habit of relative immobility within a narrow environmental range to account for the early differentiation of the very distinct physical varieties or races of man (cf. Hooton 1946: 331-332).

What is known or suggested about early men affirms the presence of some kind of territoriality, and a bulk of evidence of the same kind comes from "primitive" societies. Many anthropologists still hold the opinion that the original grouping of mankind was by kinship, and that it was only when such groups settled on land that the demarcation became territorial. Keith (1948: 5, 16) and others think, however, that the territorial group was primary and regarded the territorial sense "as a highly important factor in human evolution. Every such territory serves as an evolutionary cradle".

Thus it is assumed that in the primeval world human groups were rooted in the soil, but that they also had a migratory, dynamic urge within them, which from time to time compelled them to pull up their roots and, with or without conquest, win a new abode. For progressive evolutionary change both moods are needed, and it is presupposed that the original small territorial groups under certain conditions could develop into tribes, nations and races. Speaking of the eviction of natives in Kenya caused by gold mining, Keith (1948: 32-33) asserted: "Here, then, in a modern instance, we have brought home to us the part played by territory in securing the independent and continued existence of a tribal group; without territory a separate community could not work out its evolutionary destiny.... I have been placing before my readers the grounds for believing that the primal world, inhabited by evolving mankind, was a chequerboard of territories on which the great game of evolution was played".

The unique attributes of man include kinship, exogamy and incest taboo. These behavioural elements are closely interwoven and reflect a fundamental adaptation of primitive social organization. If hominid hunting cultures were territorial, which was evidently the case, an exchange of women between neighbouring groups may have been a means of maintaining friendly relations between two groups while yet retaining their individual integrity. To prevent early attachments from forming between related men and women a ritualized prevention of sexual relations could account for the prevalent prohibition of incest in almost all human legal systems. In order to determine with whom sexual right could be established, some form of reckoning relationship or kinship system became mandatory. Thus with this hypothesis one can account for the almost simultaneous occurrence of the phenomena of kinship, incest taboo, and exogamy (cf. Eisenberg 1966: 76).

"Man began to develop his humanness when he emerged from his shelter in the forest into the luminous and open horizons of the African savanna. Ever since, he has retained a biological and psychological need both for protective enclosures and also fairly large, open vistas.... Modern man still has a biological need to be part of a group and probably to be identified with a place. He tends to suffer from loneliness not only when he does not belong but also when the society or the place in which he functions is too large for his comprehension. Industrial societies will therefore have to find some way to reverse the trend toward larger and larger agglomerations and to recreate units small enough so that they can develop a social identity and a spirit of place" (Dubos 1973: 200-202).

The landscape is not just our supply depot but also our *oikos*, home, in which we live. It was the emergence of agriculture which made the permanent home obligatory. Only then could individuals acquire immovable possessions and, above all, really own land. Then only could relative social hierarchy become more prominent in the social structure of human communities than it is with our living relatives, the monkeys and apes. And thus man alone was able to develop that combination of exceptional individualisation with smoothly functioning organisation of complex and far-reaching communal enterprises which is characteristic of today's mankind. In this way agriculture led to increased territorial ownership and defense, to decreased spatial tolerance both within and between groups, to family, village and tribal feuds and eventually to national war (cf. Leyhausen 1973c: 238).

"Nothing in animal example or primate precedent offers any but the conclusion that territory is conservative, that it is invariably defensive, that the biological nation is the supreme natural mechanism for the security of a social group, and that when intrusion becomes maladaptive and no longer of selective value to a species, the territorial imperative will itself command its abandonment" (Ardrey 1967: 253). The group must present to all its unequal members equal opportunities to develop their genetic potential. In return the individual must by consent or coercion sacrifice any right to produce young in greater number than the society can tolerate, or the fulfilment of the individual must be suffocated by indiscriminate numbers. So, following the social contract, we proceed towards a guarantee demanding that spatial arrangements must be such that minimum distortion, psychological or physiological, may inhibit or divert the development of society (cf. Ardrey 1972: 220).

"Urban concentration must be approached with utmost care by the evolutionist. It is a challenge of a central sort in the contemporary condition. In that grand tradition of the modern human being, we oppose nature, master our environment, and, victims of nature's tricks, we are threatened by the urban environment which we in our hubris have created. The evolutionist's comments on the city must be limited to his comments on man" (op. cit. p. 219-229). It seems, however, to be quite clear that the urban dilemma is at least partly, probably predominantly, a territorial one. For even adaptability has its limits and the consequences are evident. Stress syndromes, atheros-clerosis and other cardiovascular diseases, schizophrenia and other psychotic and neurotic mental abnormalities as well as juvenile delinquency and other forms of social pathology have been shown to be of higher incidence in congested urban areas than in more spacious surrounding (cf. Hoagland 1964 as well as 4.3.12.).

4.7.3. Overpopulation and territoriality

Looking around we find that "After a short period of belief in the mechan-isms of automatic progress, we have now reached a stage when the world is perceived by many as increasingly chaotic. The opinion is spreading that if mankind shall have a future at all, we need to be able not only to forecast coming events but consciously and purposely to invent this very future". And in this context "it is not likely that the spatial aspects are given much atten-tion. One may well use the mode of expression that events take place but that does not mean that time and space co-ordinates are given much explanatory weight.... All this seems to indicate that the spatial condition of human existence has been taken too light-heartedly in study and in practice" (Hägerstrand 1970: 1-5).

A great number of population projections for the future have been made. The later they have appeared, the more pessimistic they have been, in general. No one really knows what total number of people we can expect before the net reproduction rate of one can be achieved. "Some authors are more hopeful, looking at the fact that in not less than 56 of 66 nations from which we have decently reliable statistics, a decrease in fertility has already been observed. Others are less hopeful, concentrating their attention on the improbability of a technological breakthrough in so called 'family planning' methods. And nor does anyone seem to know how many people the world can feed, the size of the 'final population carrying capacity' of the globe, if we are to maintain a long-run ecological equilibrium" (Adler-Karlsson 1973: 199).

Although the future size of the world's population will to a considerable extent be determined by current demographic features – recent levels and patterns of mortality and fertility, together with the age structure – much will depend on how these characteristics change. Mortality is already fairly low and is likely to decline further, barring major and persistent catastrophes. Fertility is still rather high, being more than twice the level that would ultimately result in a nongrowing population, and even though it declines, the decrease is likely to be small and gradual.

The age structure of the world's population is highly favorable to growth, because just a small proportion, fewer than 6 percent, is over 65 years old and a large female proportion is in the childbearing ages. Still more important is that very great numbers of women will enter the childbearing ages in the coming decades, since about 37 percent of the total world population is under 15 years of age. Moreover, at least during the 1970's, generations of comparable size are likely to be born and to survive, judging from current fertility and mortality levels and patterns (cf. Frejka 1973). Under such circumstances it seems very probable that this statement from the United Nations in the World Population Year of 1974 will be shown to be quite correct: "World population growth cannot possibly stop before at least a century" (cf. "A Startling Picture a Century from Today" 1974).

"As it is well-known that crowding, or rather the behavior associated with crowding leads to a decrease in reproductive capacity, it may be appropriate to comment briefly on the possible implications of crowding for future population growth, a problem that is of world-wide concern at the moment. The relevance of this question stems from the universal trend towards urban, i.e., crowded habitation. In analogy with the findings of animal research, there would seem to be reason to believe that the generally observed lower rates of population growth in urban as compared with rural areas are a reflection of a higher degree of nervous tension. . . . In the developed or industrial countries more or less complete urbanization is within sight. This means that tomorrow's parents will all come from an urban environment, a new experience in human history. As there is some question about the ability of any truly urban population to reproduce itself over any length of time, it would seem to introduce a new and so far neglected element into the present concern about future population growth" (Olin 1971: 209-210).

G. Morgan (1971: 213-214) long tried to find any population which was able to survive more than a few generations of urban living. It was suggested to him that the Parsees of Bombay should be such an example, but a detailed investigation showed that to be wrong. "This is representative of what we have been able to find of urban populations all over the world. The cities are places of exploitation of human resources, accumulated in generations of healthy rural living". If these rural population reserves are emptied out, it will, of course, influence the whole demographic and urban development, and even evolutionary consequences might begin to show up. "Evolution is what controls both the level of responses to stress and the occurrence of factors which are socially stressful" (R. D. Martin 1970: 1086).

In summary, it seems that overpopulation only aggravates the widespread threat to social stability for people who are basically unsure of their personal future and who have lost confidence in their chances of ever attaining a secure place in the community. It is imperative that we recognize the gravity of this threat, because mankind today commands such destructive powers that we cannot afford to risk outbreaks of mass violence, and yet the lesson of history points to just such disasters. "Unless the masses of our city poor can be persuaded that there is a future for them too in the Great Society, their morale is likely to crumble until vast human communities degenerate into the semblance of concentration camp inmates, if not even to that of Zuckerman's pathologically belligerent apes" (Carstairs 1969: 763).

It is without doubt characteristic that the Committee on Violence of the Department of Psychiatry of the Stanford University School of Medicine presented the following as a first and foremost guideline for social and political programs: "Respect human 'territoriality' and avoid overcrowding" (Rosenthal and Ilfeld 1970: 393). And Leyhausen (1973b: 345) put it this way: "Unless we succeed not only in stopping population growth everywhere on this planet but also in reducing numbers in many areas, and most especially in the overpopulated, overdeveloped countries like our own nothing will save us".

Self-evidently this makes the prospect of the human species not very hopeful, even though a lack in the capacity of urban populations to reproduce themselves would provide some relief. Already today it is said that we face identical problems in all fields of action belonging to human settlements, and we can never handle them easily because humanity has lost the ability to organize its needs in a territorial sense. Man has often passed through comparable phases of confusion and then has found the answer through territorial organization. This is how tribes avoided conflicts and how villages, towns and cities were organized (cf. *Human Health and Human Settlements* 1974: 159).

There is certainly some truth in the phrase stating that "when everyone possesses an individual territory, the reasons for one man to dominate another will disappear" (Sommer 1971: 282). A true recognition of the territorial demands in man at home and at work will therefore hopefully make it possible in the future not only to provide normal individuals and groups with adequate room but also to take care of the special spatial needs in, e.g., violent criminals and the mentally deficient. By means of better marking and structuring the most important qualitative aspects of territoriality, often neglected in different contexts, could be satisfied.

4.7.4. Territory, conceptual space and human freedom

In his paper "Space and the Strategy of Life" John B. Calhoun (1971) gave a new and stimulating explanation for the development of mammal populations in time and space with special relevance to the human population explosion. He concluded: "Man stands unique among animals in learning how to bypass the strictures placed by limitation of physical space on further population growth. He has made this escape by discovering how to create conceptual space, the total information pool generated by man from which rules, codes and theories may be condensed which permit more effective coping with the physical and social environment. In particular, this process of increasing conceptual space as population increases permits each individual on the average to become involved in the same number of social interactions per day as held true in the earlier times, when life was primarily confined to experiences within a hunter-gatherer band of 12 adults and their associated children. To continue enlarging conceptual space requires involving more and more individuals in a common communication network. Such union will continue until the entire world population becomes incorporated into a single network" (op. cit. p. 365-366).

Irrespective of whether we do or do not accept this fascinating theory it seems indubitable that even conceptual space cannot wholly and forever compensate still more people for lack of real territories. When all comes to all physical territory is an absolute prerequisite for healthy man as well as for a sound society. Territoriality is perhaps also the only natural phenomenon which motivates and gives some hope for individual freedom and right in the future. For in a vertebrate community that is not solely governed by absolute hierarchy the individual, as earlier noted, not only acquires personality through his territory, he also has some place there, some preserve where he is superior to all other members of the community. No matter how big or small the territory may be, and no matter what the ranking of the individual is in the various absolute hierarchies of the community – as territory owner he is equal among his equals. "In this capacity, and in this capacity alone, the human individual is able to enter, as a responsible, participating, cooperating, independent, self-respecting, and self-supporting citizen, the type of communal organization we call a democracy" (Leyhausen 1973d: 141). Thus.

territoriality is not at all, as is sometimes maintained, a reactionary device, an antithesis to the open society. Instead, it offers the maybe only natural and so the only solid basis for the two cornerstones of a democracy: freedom and equality.

5. References

References are, if possible, cited in their original context, the first year of publication given within parentheses. Different publications by the same author are listed after first letters in heading. Books compiled by an editor are presented under title. First figure after journal or book name means volume, figure after colon designs heft number and figures after comma indicate pages. Works preceded by an asterisk seem to be of particular interest for the study of human territoriality.

"A Startling Picture a Century from Today". 1974. *The Unesco Courier* 27: July-August, 15-19.

A Systematic Source Book in Rural Sociology 1-3. 1930-1932. P. A. Sorokin, C. C. Zimmerman and C. J. Galpin, eds. Minneapolis: The University of Minnesota Press.

Abler, R., Adams, J. S. and Gould, P. 1972. *Spatial Organization. The Geographer's View of the World*. London: Prentice-Hall International, Inc.

Abrams, C. 1964. *Man's Struggle for Shelter in an Urbanized World*. Cambridge, Mass.: The Massachusetts Institute of Technology Press.

Abrams, C. 1965. "The Uses of Land in Cities". *Scientific American* 213:3, 151-160.

*Acheson, J. M. 1972. "Territories of the Lobstermen". *Natural History* 81, 60-69.

Acheson, J. M. 1975. "The Lobster Fiefs: Economic and Ecological Effects of Territoriality in the Maine Lobster Industry". *Human Ecology* 3, 183-207.

Adams, R. M. 1960. "The Origin of Cities". *Scientific American* 203:3, 153-168.

Adler-Karlsson, G. 1973. "Some Roads to Humanicide". *Instant Research on Peace and Violence* 4, 198-210.

*Aiello, J. R. and Aiello, T. D. C. 1974. "The Development of Personal Space: Proxemic Behavior of Children 6 Through 16". *Human Ecology* 2, 177-189.

Aiello, J. R. and Jones, S. E. 1971. "Field Study of Proxemic Behavior of Young School Children in Three Subcultural Groups". *Journal of Personality and Social Psychology* 19, 351-356.

Alexander, C. 1968. "The City as a Mechanism for Sustaining Human Contact". In: *Environment for Man. The next Fifty Years*. W. R. Ewald Jr. ed. Bloomington-London: Indiana University Press. P. 60-109.

Alexander, T. 1973. *Human Development in an Urban Age*. Englewood Cliffs, N.J.: Prentice Hall, Inc.

Allesch, G. J. v. 1937. "Die Beziehungen zwischen tierpsychologischen und menschenpsychologischen Tatbeständen". *Zeitschrift für Tierpsychologie* 1, 128-139.

Altman, I. 1971. "Ecological Aspects of Interpersonal Functioning". In: *Behavior and Environment. The Use of Space by Animals and Men*. A. H. Esser, ed. New York-London: Plenum Press. P. 291-306.

Altman, I. 1976. "Privacy. A Conceptual Analysis". *Environment and Behavior* 8, 7-29.

Altman, I. 1973. "Some Perspectives on the Study of Man-Environment Phenomena". *Representative Research in Social Psychology* 4, 109-126.

*Altman, I. 1975. *The Environment and Social Behavior*. Monterey, Cal.: Brooks/Cole Publishing Company.

Altman, I. and Haythorn, W. W. 1967. "The Ecology of Isolated Groups". *Behavioral Science* 12, 169-182

*Altman J. W., Smith, R. W., Meyers, R. L., McKenna, F. S. and Bryson, S. 1961. *Psychological and Social Adjustment in a Simulated Shelter. A Research Report.* Washington: American Institute for Research.

Alverdes, F. 1935. "The Behavior of Mammalian Herds and Packs". In: *A Handbook of Social Psychology.* C. Murchison, ed. Worcester, Mass.: Clark University Press. P. 185-203.

Anderson, N. 1963. "Aspects of the Rural and Urban". *Sociologia Ruralis* 3, 8-22

Anderson, P. K. and Hill, J. L. 1965. "Mus musculus: Experimental Induction of Territory Formation". *Science* 148, 1753-1755.

Anderson, T. R. and Egeland, J. A. 1961. "Spatial Aspects of Social Area Analysis". *American Sociological Review* 26, 392-398.

Andersson, C. J. 1856. *Lake Ngami; or, Explorations and Discoveries, during Four Years' Wanderings in the Wilds of South Western Africa.* London: Hurst and Blackett.

Andreski, S. 1964. "Origin of Wars". In: *The Natural History of Aggression.* J. D. Carthy and F. J. Ebling, eds. Institute of Biology Symposia 13. London-New York: Academic Press. P. 129-136.

Appley, M. H. and Trumbull, R. 1967. "On the Concept of Psychological Stress". In: *Psychological Stress. Issues in Research.* H. M. Appley and R. Trumbell, eds. New York: Appleton-Century-Crofts. P. 1-13.

*Appleyard, D. and Lintell, M. 1972. "The Environmental Quality of City Streets: The Residents' Viewpoint". *Journal of the American Institute of Planners* 38, 84-101.

*Ardrey, R. 1972. (1970) *The Social Contract. A Personal Inquiry into the Evolutionary Sources of Order and Disorder.* London: Collins.

*Ardrey, R. 1967 (1966). *The Territorial Imperative. A Personal Inquiry into the Animal Origins of Property and Nations.* London: Collins.

Arendt, H. 1959 (1958). *The Human Condition.* Chicago: The University of Chicago Press.

Aronson, E. 1976 (1972). *The Social Animal.* 2nd ed. San Francisco: W. H. Freeman and Company.

Assem, J. v. d. 1967. "Territory in the Three-spined Stickleback Gasterosteus aculeatus L., An Experimental Study in Intra-specific Competition". *Behaviour.* Supplement 16, 2-4, 44-52, 81-83, 90-93, 144-153, 158-159.

Atz, J. W. 1970. "The Application of the Idea of Homology to Behaviour". In: *Development and Evolution of Behavior. Essays in Memory of T. C. Schneirla.* L. R. Aronson, E. Tobach, D. S. Lehrman and J. S. Rosenblatt, eds. San Francisco: W. H. Freeman and Company. P. 53-74.

*Austin, W. T. and Bates, F. L. 1973-1974. "Ethological Indicators of Dominance and Territory in a Human Captive Population". *Social Forces* 52, 447-455.

Avis, H. H. 1974. "The Neuropharmacology of Aggression: A Critical Review". *Psychological Bulletin* 81, 47-63.

Bailey, K. G., Hartnett, J. J. and Gibson, F. W. 1972. "Implied Threat and the Territorial Factor in Personal Space". *Psychological Reports* 30, 263-270.

Baker, A., Davies, R. L. and Sivadon, P. 1959. "Psychiatric Services and Architecture". *World Health Organization Public Health Papers* 1. Geneva: World Health Organization.

Baker, J. R. 1938. "The Evolution of Breeding Seasons". In: *Evolution. Essays on Aspects of Evolutionary Biology presented to Professor E. S. Goodrich on his Seventieth Birthday.* G. R. de Beer, ed. Oxford: At the Clarendon Press. P. 161-177.

*Bakker, C. B. and Bakker-Rabdau, M. K. 1973. *No Trespassing! Explorations in Human Territoriality.* San Francisco: Chandler and Sharp Publishers. Inc.

Bally, G. 1945. *Vom Ursprung und von den Grenzen der Freiheit. Eine Deutung des Spiels bei Tier und Mensch.* Basel: Benno Schwabe & Co.

Bandura, A. 1973. *Aggression. A Social Learning Analysis.* Englewood Cliffs, N.J.: Prentice-Hall Inc.

Bargheer, 1930-1931. "Grumus merdae". In: *Handwörterbuch des Deutschen Aberglaubens* 3. E. Hoffman-Krayer and H. Bachtold-Stäubli, eds. Berlin-Leipzig: Walter de Gruyter & Co. Column 1178-1180.

Bargheer, 1932-1933. "Kot". In: *Handwörterbuch des Deutschen Aberglaubens* 5. E. Hoffman-Krayer and H. Bachtold-Stäubli, eds. Berlin-Leipzig: Walter de Gruyter & Co. Column 330-350.

Barker, R. G. 1968. *Ecological Psychology*. Stanford: Stanford University Press.

Barker, R. G. 1965. "Explorations in Ecological Psychology". *American Psychologist* 20, 1-14.

Barnett, S. A. 1967. "Attack and Defense in Animal Societies". In: *Aggression and Defense. Neural Mechanisms and Social Patterns*. Brain Function 5. UCLA Forum in Medical Sciences 7. Berkeley-Los Angeles: University of California Press. P. 35-56.

Barnett, S. A. 1962. "Attitudes to Childhood". In: *Lessons from Animal Behaviour for the Clinician*. S. A. Barnett, ed. Little Club Clinics in Developmental Medicine 7. London: William Heinemann, P. 1-9.

Barnett, S. A. 1973. "Biological Myths". *New Society:* 12.4.1973, 68-69.

Barnett, S. A. 1969. *Instinct and Intelligence*. Englewood Cliffs, N.J.: Prentice-Hall, Inc.

Barnett, S. A. 1964. "Social Stress". In: *Viewpoints in Biology* 3. J. D. Carthy and C. L. Duddington, eds. London: Butterworths. P. 170-218.

Barnett, S. A. and Evans, C. S. 1965. "Questions on the Social Dynamics of Rodents". *Symposia of the Zoological Society of London* 14, 233-248.

Barrows, H. H. 1923. "Geography as Human Ecology". *Annals of the Association of American Geographers* 13, 1-14.

Bartholomew, G. A. and Birdsell, J. B. 1953. "Ecology and the Protohominids". *American Anthropologist* 55, 481-498.

Barton, R. 1966. "The Patient's Personal Territory". *Hospital & Community Psychiatry* 17, 336.

Barton, R. F. 1949. *The Kalingas. Their Institutions and Custom Law*. Chicago: The University of Chicago Press.

Bass, M. H. and Weinstein, M. S. 1971. "Early Development of Interpersonal Distance in Children". *Canadian Journal of Behavioural Science* 3, 368-376.

Bates, M. 1953. "Human Ecology". In: *Anthropology Today. An Encyclopedic Inventory*. Prepared under the Chairmanship of A. L. Kroeber. Chicago: The University of Chicago Press. P. 700-713.

Bates, M. 1955. *The Prevalence of People*. New York: Charles Scribner's Sons.

Bateson, G. and Jackson, D. D. 1964. "Some Varieties of Pathogenic Organization". *Association for Research in Nervous and Mental Disease. Research Publications* 42, 270-290.

Bauer, C. 1934. *Modern Housing*. Boston-New York: Houghton Mifflin Company.

Bausinger, H., Braun, M., and Schwedt, H. 1959. *Neue Siedlungen. Volkskundlich-soziologische Untersuchungen des Ludwig-Uhland-Instituts Tübingen*. Stuttgart: W. Kohlhammer.

Beach, F. A. 1955. "The Descent of Instinct". *Psychological Review* 62, 401-410.

Beaglehole, E. 1931. *Property. A Study in Social Psychology*. Studies in Political Science & Sociology 1. London: George Allen & Unwin Ltd.

Beaujeu-Garnier, J. and Chabot, G. 1967. *Urban Geography*. London: Longmans.

Beck, R. 1967. "Spatial Meaning, and the Properties of the Environment". In: Environmental Perception and Behavior. D. Lowenthal, ed. *University of Chicago. Department of Geography. Research Paper* 109, 18–41.

Becker, E. 1964. *The Revolution in Psychiatry. The New Understanding of Man*. London: The Free Press of Glencoe and Collier-McMillan Limited.

*Becker, F. D. 1973. "Study of Spatial Markers". *Journal of Personality and Social Psychology* 26, 439-445.

*Becker, F. D. and Mayo, C. 1971. "Delineating Personal Distance and Territoriality". *Environment and Behavior* 3, 375-381.

Becker, H. S. 1951-1952. "The Professional Dance Musician and his Audience". *American Journal of Sociology* 57, 136-144.

*Behavior and Environment. 1971. The Use of Space by Animals and Men. Proceedings of an International Symposium held at the 1968 Meeting of the American Association for the Advancement of Science in Dallas, Texas. A. H. Esser, ed. New York-London: Plenum Press.

Behaviour Studies in Psychiatry. 1970. Based on the Proceedings of a Symposium held at The Human Development Research Unit, Park Hospital for Children, Oxford, July 1968. S. J. Hutt and C. Hutt, eds. Oxford-New York-Toronto-etc.: Pergamon Press.

Benet, F. 1963-1964. "Sociology Uncertain: The Ideology of the Rural-urban Continuum". Comparative Studies in Society and History 6, 1-23.

Bennett, A. M. A. 1961. "Sensory Deprivation in Aviation". In: Sensory Deprivation. A Symposium held at Harvard Medical School. P. Solomon, P. E. Kubzansky, P. H. Leiderman, J. H. Mendelson, R. Trumbull and D. Wexler, eds. Cambridge, Mass.: Harvard University Press. P. 161-173.

Berghahn, W. 1965. "In der Fremde, in der Enge". In: Die Kunst zu Hause zu sein. München: R. Piper & Co. P. 103-117.

*Berghe, P. L. v. d. 1974. "Bringing Beasts back in: Toward a Biosocial Theory of Aggression". American Sociological Review 39, 777-788.

Berkowitz, L. 1962. Aggression: A Social Psychological Analysis. New York-Toronto-London-San Francisco: McGraw-Hill Book Company, Inc.

Berkowitz, L. 1969. "Simple Views of Aggression. An Essay Review". American Scientist 57, 372-383.

Berlepsch-Valendàs, B. D. A. 1912. Die Gartenstadtbewegung in England, ihre Entwickelung und ihr jetziger Stand. Die Kultur des modernen England in Einzeldarstellungen 3. E. Sieper, ed. München-Berlin: R. Oldenbourg.

Berlepsch-Valendàs, B. D. A. and Hansen. 1910. Die Garten-Stadt München-Perlach. München: E. Reinhardt.

Bernard, L. L. 1942. An Introduction to Sociology. A Naturalistic Account of Man's Adjustment to his World. New York: Thomas Y. Crowell Company.

Bernard, L. L. 1924. Instinct. A Study in Social Psychology. London: George Allen & Unwin Ltd.

Bernatzky, A. 1974. "Die Bedeutung des Gartens für Freizeit und Umwelt". Der Siedler-Berater 21, 15-23.

Bernfeld, S. 1925. Psychologie des Säuglings. Wien: Julius Springer.

Berry, B. J. L. et al. 1974. "Land Use, Urban Form and Environmental Quality". University of Chicago. Department of Geography. Research Paper 155, 1-440.

Berry, B. J. L. and Horton, F. E. 1970. Geographic Perspectives on Urban Systems with Integrated Readings. Englewood Cliffs, N.J.: Prentice-Hall, Inc.

Bettelheim, B. 1969. The Children of the Dream. London: Collier-McMillan Ltd.

Bettelheim, B. 1955. Truants from Life. The Rehabilitation of Emotionally Disturbed Children. Glencoe, Ill.: The Free Press.

Bews. J. W. 1935. Human Ecology. London: Oxford University Press-Humphrey Milford.

Biderman, A. D. 1967. "Life and Death in Extreme Captivity Situations". In: Psychological Stress. Issues in Research. M. H. Appley and R. Trumbull, eds. New York: Appleton-Century-Crofts. P. 242-277.

Biderman, A. D., Louria, M. and Bacchus, J. 1963. Historical Incidents of Extreme Overcrowding. Washington D.C.: Bureau of Social Science Research, Inc.

Bielckus, C. L., Rogers, A. W. and Wibberley, G. P. 1972. Second Homes in England and Wales. A Study of the Distribution and Use of Rural Properties taken over as Second Residences. Studies in Rural Land Use 11. London: Wye College, School of Rural Economics and Related Studies, Countryside Planning Unit.

Bigelow, R. 1972. "The Evolution of Cooperation, Aggression, and Self-Control". Nebraska Symposium on Motivation 1972, 1-57.

Bilz, R. 1967. "Menschliche Aggressivität, Versuch einer verhaltensphysiologischen Differenzierung". Zeitschrift für Psychotherapie und Medizinische Psychologie 17, 157-202.

Bilz, R. 1940. *Pars pro toto. Ein Beitrag zur Pathologie menschlicher Affekte und Organfunktionen.* Schriftenreihe zur Deutschen Medizinischen Wochenschrift 5. Leipzig: Georg Thieme.

Birdsell, J. B. 1966. "Some Environmental and Cultural Factors influencing the Structuring of Australian Aboriginal Populations". In: *Human Ecology. Collective Readings.* J. B. Bresler, ed. Reading, Mass.: Addison-Wesley. P. 51-90.

Blake, R. R., Rhead, C. C., Wedge, B. and Mouton, J. S. 1956. "Housing Architecture and Social Interaction". *Sociometry* 19, 133-139.

Blatz, W. E. 1966. *Human Security. Some Reflections.* Toronto: University of Toronto Press.

Blaut, J. M. 1961. "Space and Process". *The Professional Geographer* 13, 1-7.

Bloch, H. A. and Niederhoffer, A. 1958. *The Gang. A Study in Adolescent Behavior.* New York: Philosophical Library.

Blomqvist, R. 1951. *Lunds historia 1. Medeltiden.* Lund: C. W. K. Gleerup.

*Blood, R. O. and Livant, W. P. 1957. "The Use of Space within the Cabin Group". *The Journal of Social Issues* 13, 47-53.

Blumenfeld, H. 1967. "The Modern Metropolis". In: *Cities, A 'Scientific American' Book.* Harmondsworth: Penguin Books. P. 49-66.

Blumenfeld, H. 1964. "The Urban Pattern". *The Annals of the American Academy of Political and Social Science* 351: March, 74-83.

Boette, 1930-1931. "Heimweh". In: *Handwörterbuch des Deutschen Aberglaubens* 3. E. Hoffman-Krayer and H. Bachtold-Stäubli, ed. Berlin-Leipzig: Walter de Gruyter & Co. Column 1687-1691.

Boggs, S. W. 1940. *International Boundaries. A Study of Boundary Functions and Problems.* New York: Columbia University Press.

Bohannan, P. 1964. *Africa and Africans.* Garden City, N.Y.: The Natural History Press.

Bolk, L. 1926. *Das Problem der Menschwerdung.* Jena: Gustav Fischer.

Bollnow, O. F. 1963. *Mensch und Raum.* Stuttgart: W. Kohlhammer.

Bonwick, J. 1967 (1870). *Daily Life and Origin of the Tasmanians.* New York: Johnson Reprint Corporation.

Bookwalter, J. W. 1911. *Rural versus Urban. Their Conflict and its Causes. A Study of the Conditions affecting their Natural and Artificial Relations.* New York: The Knickerbocker Press.

Booraem, C. D. and Flowers, J. V. 1972. "Reduction of Anxiety and Personal Space as a Function of Assertion Training with Severely Disturbed Neuropsychiatric Inpatients". *Pscyhological Reports* 30, 923-929.

Borrie, W. D. 1970. *The Growth and Control of World Population.* London: Weidenfeld and Nicholson.

Bourlière, F. 1952. "Le territorialisme dans l'organisation sociale des Vertébrés". In: *Structure et Physiologie des Sociétés Animales.* P. P. Grassé, ed. Colloques Internationaux du Centre National de la Recherche Scientifique 34. Paris: Centre National de la Recherche Scientifique. P. 199-206.

Bourlière, F. 1951. *Vie et Moeurs des Mammifères.* Paris: Payot.

Bourne, P. G. 1970. *Men, Stress and Vietnam.* Boston: Little, Brown and Company.

Boven, W. 1943. "D'un prisonnier par vocation". *Revue Médicale de la Suisse Romande* 63, 859-865.

Bowlby, J. 1971 (1969). *Attachment. Attachment and Loss* 1. The International Psycho-Analytical Library 79. Harmondsworth: Penguin Books Ltd.

Brass, W. 1970. "The Growth of World Population". In: *Population Control.* A. Allison, ed. Harmondsworth: Penguin Books. P. 131-151.

Brepohl, W. 1952. "Die Heimat als Beziehungsfeld. Entwurf einer soziologischen Theorie der Heimat". *Soziale Welt* 4, 12-22.

Briault, E. W. H. and Hubbard, J. H. 1963 (1957). *An Introduction to Advanced Geography.* London: Longmans.

Brier, M. A. 1970. *Les résidences secondaires*. Biarritz: Dunod Actualité.

Brody, S. and Axelrad, S. 1971. "Maternal Stimulation and Social Responsiveness of Infants", In: *The Origins of Human Social Relations*. H. R. Schaffer, ed. London-New York: Academic Press. P. 195-215.

Bronson, G. W. 1971. "Fear of the Unfamiliar in Human Infants". In: *The Origins of Human Social Relations*. H. R. Schaffer, ed. London-New York: Academic Press. P. 59-66.

*Brookfield, H. C. and Brown, P. 1963. *Struggle for Land, Agriculture and Group Territories among the Chimbu of the New Guinea Highlands*. Melbourne: Oxford University Press.

*Brower, S. N. 1965. "Territoriality. The Exterior Spaces, The Signs we Learn to Read". *Landscape* 15:1, 9-12.

Brown, J. L. 1969. "Territorial Behavior and Population Regulation in Birds. A Review and Re-evaluation". *The Wilson Bulletin* 81, 293-329.

Brown, J. L. 1964. "The Evolution of Diversity in Avian Territorial Systems". *The Wilson Bulletin* 76, 160-169.

Brown, J. L. and Orians, G. H. 1970. "Spacing Patterns in Mobile Animals". *Annual Review of Ecology and Systematics* 1, 239-262.

Brown, L. E. 1966. "Home Range and Movement of Small Animals". In: *Play, Exploration and Territory in Mammals*. P. A. Jewell and C. Loizos, eds. Symposia of the Zoological Society of London 18, 111-142.

Brownfield, C. A. 1965. *Isolation. Clinical and Experimental Approaches*. New York: Random House.

Bruhn, J. G. 1970. "Human Ecology in Medicine". *Environmental Research* 3, 37-53.

Bruner, J. S. 1961. "The Cognitive Consequences of Early Sensory Deprivation". In: *Sensory Deprivation. A Symposium held at Harvard Medical School*. P. Solomon, P. E. Kubzansky, P. H. Leiderman, J. H. Mendelson, R. Trumbull and D. Wexler, eds. Cambridge, Mass.: Harvard University Press. P. 195-207.

Brunner, H. 1957. "Zum Raumbegriff der Ägypter". *Studium Generale* 10, 612-620.

Buckminster Fuller, R., 1964. "The Prospects of Humanity: 1965-1985". *Ekistics* 18, 232-242.

Bühler, K. 1922 (1918). *Die geistige Entwicklung des Kindes*. 3rd edition. Jena: Gustav Fischer.

Bühler, K. 1926. "Die Instinkte des Menschen". *Bericht über den IX Kongress für experimentelle Psychologie 1925*. Jena: Gustav Fischer. P. 3-23.

Burgess, E. W. 1942. "Introduction". In: Shaw, C. R. and McKay, H. D. *Juvenile-Delinquency and Urban Areas. A Study of Delinquents in Relation to Differential Characteristics of Local Communities in American Cities*. Chicago: The University of Chicago Press. P. IX-XIII.

Burns, N. M. and Kimura, D. 1963. "Isolation and Sensory Deprivation". In: *Unusual Environments and Human Behavior*. N. M. Burns, R. M. Chambers and E. Hendler, eds. London: The Free Press of Glencoe. P. 167-192.

Burt, W. H. 1949. "Territoriality". *Journal of Mammalogy* 30, 25-27.

Burt, W. H. 1943. "Territoriality and Home Range Concepts as applied to Mammals". *Journal of Mammalogy* 24, 346-352.

*Burton, A. 1964. "Time, Space and Ascensionism". *Journal of Existential Psychology* 4, 289-300.

Buttimer, A. 1969. "Social Space in Interdisciplinary Perspective". *The Geographical Review* 59, 417-426.

Cain. S. A. 1967. "Man and his Environment". *Ekistics* 23. 203-205.

Calhoun, J. B. 1962a. "A 'Behavioral sink'". In: *Roots of Behavior. Genetics, Instinct, and Socialization in Animal Behavior*. E. L. Bliss, ed. New York: Harper & Brothers. P. 295-315.

Calhoun, J. B. 1956. "A Comparative Study of the Social Behavior of Two Inbred Strains of House Mice". *Ecological Monographs* 26, 81-103.

Calhoun, J. B. 1973. "From Mice to Men". *Transactions and Studies of the College of Physicians of Philadelphia*. 4 Series 41:2, 92-118.

Calhoun, J. B. 1962b. "Population Density and Social Pathology". *Scientific American* 206:2, 139-148.

Calhoun, J. B. 1968. "Space and the Strategy of Life". American Association for the Advancement of Science, 135 Annual Meeting (mimeographed).

Calhoun, J. B. 1971. "Space and the Strategy of Life". In: *Behavior and Environment, The Use of Space by Animals and Men*. A. H. Esser, ed. New York-London: Plenum Press. P. 329-387.

Callan, H. 1970. *Ethology and Society. Towards an Anthropological View*. Oxford: Clarendon Press.

Canter, D. and Canter, S. 1971. "Close together in Tokyo". *Design and Environment* 2, 60-63.

Cantril, H. 1963. "The Individual's Demand on Society". In: *The Dilemma of Organizational Society*. H. M. Ruitenbeek, ed. New York: E. P. Dutton & Co. Inc. P. 207-224.

Carlestam, G. 1971. "The Individual, the City and Stress". In: *Society, Stress and Disease 1. The Psychosocial Environment and Psychosomatic Diseases*. L. Levi, ed. London-New York-Toronto: Oxford University Press. P. 134-147.

Carol, H. 1965. "C. G. Jung, and the Need for Roots". *Landscape* 14:3, 2.

Carpenter, C. R. 1941. "A Field Study in Siam of the Behavior and Social Relations of the Gibbon (Hylobates lar)". *Comparative Psychology Monographs* 16:5, 1-212.

Carpenter, C. R. 1934. "A Field Study of the Behavior and Social Relations of Howling Monkeys". *Comparative Psychology Monographs* 10:2, 1-168.

Carpenter, C. R. 1935. "Behavior of the Red Spider Monkeys in Panama". *Journal of Mammalogy* 16, 171-180.

Carpenter, C. R. 1952. "Social Behavior of Non-human Primates". In: *Structure et Physiologie des Sociétés Animales*. P.-P. Grassé, ed. Colloques Internationaux du Centre National de la Recherche Scientifique 34. Paris: Centre National de la Recherche Scientifique. P. 227-245.

Carpenter, C. R. 1961 (1958). "Territoriality: A Review of Concepts and Problems". In: *Behavior and Evolution*. A. Roe and G. G. Simpson, eds. New Haven: Yale University Press. P. 224-250.

Carpenter, N. 1931. *The Sociology of City Life*. New York-London-Toronto: Longmans, Green and Co.

Carr, H. A. 1966 (1935). *An Introduction to Space Perception*. New York-London: Hafner Publishing Company.

Carr-Saunders, A. M. 1922. *The Population Problem. A Study in Human Evolution*. Oxford: At the Clarendon Press.

Carstairs, G. M. 1969. "Overcrowding and Human Aggression". In: *The History of Violence in America*. H. D. Graham and T. R. Gurr, eds. New York: F. A. Praeger. P. 751-764.

Carthy, J. D. and Ebling, F. J. 1964. Prologue and Epilogue. In: *The Natural History of Aggression*. J. D. Carthy and F. J. Ebling, eds. Institute of Biology Symposia 13. London-New York: Academic Press. P. 1-5.

Cassirer, E. 1957. *The Philosophy of Symbolic Forms 3. The Phenomenology of Knowledge*. New Haven: Yale University Press. P. 142-161.

Cathrein, V. 1892. *Das Privatgrundeigenthum und seine Gegner*. Die Soziale Frage beleuchtet durch die "Stimmen aus Maria-Laach" 5. Freiburg im Breisgau: Herder'sche Verlagshandlung.

Champion, Y. 1958. *Essai de synthèse des recherches en matière d'épidémiologie et de pathologie mentales concernant la mobilité géographique des populations (Psychiatrie médico-sociale des migrations et transplantations)*. Faculté de Médecine de Paris 226. Paris: Librairie Arnette.

Chance, M. R. A. 1967. "Open Groups in Hominid Evolution". *Man* 2, 130-131.

Charles-Dominique, P. 1974. "Aggression and Territoriality in Nocturnal Prosimians". In: *Primate Aggression, Territoriality and Xenophobia. A Comparative Perspective*. R. L. Holloway, ed. New York-London: Academic Press. P. 31-48.

Chermayeff, S. and Alexander, C. 1966. *Community and Privacy. Toward a New Architecture of Humanism*. Harmondsworth: Penguin Books.

*Cheyne, J. A. and Efran, M. G. 1972. "The Effect of Spatial and Interpersonal Variables on the Invasion of Group Controlled Territories". *Sociometry* 35, 477-489.

Childe, V. G. 1948 (1936). *Man Makes Himself*. The Thinker's Library 87. London: Watts & Co.

Childe, V. G. 1958. *The Prehistory of European Society*. Harmondsworth: Penguin Books.

Childe, V. G. 1950. "The Urban Revolution". *Town Planning Review* 21, 3-17.

Choi, S. C., Mirjafari, A. and Weaver, H. B. 1976. "The Concept of Crowding. A Critical Review and Proposal of an Alternative Approach". *Environment and Behavior* 8, 345-362.

Chombart de Lauwe, P. H., Antoine, S., Couvreur, L. and Gauthier, J. 1952. *Paris et l'agglomération parisienne. I. L'espace social dans une grande cité*. Paris: Presses Universitaires de France.

Chombart de Lauwe, Y. M.-J. 1959a. "Dégradation du logement et ses conséquences". In: Chombart de Lauwe, P. et le Groupe d'Ethnologie Sociale. *Famille et habitation. 1. Sciences humaine et conceptions de l'habitation*. Paris: Centre National de la Recherche Scientifique. P. 103-124.

Chombart de Lauwe, Y. M.-J. 1959b. *Psychopathologie sociale de l'enfant inadapté. Essai de sélection des variables du milieu et de l'hérédité dans l'étude des troubles du comportement*. Paris: Centre National de la Recherche Scientifique.

Christaller, W. 1933. *Die zentralen Orten in Süddeutschland*. Jena: Gustav Fischer.

Christian, J. J. 1963. "The Pathology of Overpopulation". *Military Medicine* 128, 571-603.

Christoffel, H. 1934. "Zur Biologie der Enuresis". *Zeitschrift für Kinderpsychiatrie* 1, 13-24, 49-58, 76-86, 105-115.

Clark, J. D. 1960. "Human Ecology during Pleistocene and Later Times in Africa south of the Sahara". *Current Anthropology* 1, 307-324.

Clawson, M. 1970. "Open (uncovered) Space as a New Urban Resource". In: *The Quality of the Urban Environment. Essays on "New Resources in an Urban Age"*. H. S. Perloff, ed. Washington D.C.: Resources for the Future Inc. P. 139-176.

Cleland, C. C. and Dingman, H. F. 1970. "Dimensions of Institutional Life: Social Organizations, Possessions, Time and Space". In: *Residential Facilities for the Mentally Retarded*. Baumeister, A. and Butterfield, E., eds. Chicago: Aldine Publishing Company. P. 138-162.

Clout, H. D. 1972. *Rural Geography. An Introductory Survey*. Oxford-New York-Toronto-etc.: Pergamon Press.

Clout, H. D. 1974. "The Growth of Second-Home Ownership: An Example of Seasonal Suburbanization". In: *Suburban Growth. Geographical Processes at the Edge of the Western City*. J. H. Johnson, ed. London-New York-Sidney-Toronto: John Wiley & Sons. P. 121-127.

Collias, N. E. 1944. Aggressive Behaviour among Vertebrate Animals. *Physiological Zoölogy* 17, 83-123.

*Colman, A. D. 1968. "Territoriality in Man. A Comparison of Behavior in Home and Hospital". *American Journal of Orthopsychiatry* 38, 464-468.

Coon, C. S. 1961. "Chairman's Opening Remarks. Symposium on Crowding, Stress, and Natural Selection". *Proceedings of the National Academy of Sciences* 47, 427.

Coon, C. S. 1971. *The Hunting Peoples*. Boston-Toronto: Little, Brown and Company.

Cooper, J. M. 1939. "Is the Algonquian Family Hunting Ground System Pre-Columbian?" *American Anthropologist* 41, 66-90.

Cooper, R. 1968. "The Psychology of Boredom". *Science Journal* 4, 38-42.

Cormier, B. M., Kennedy, M. and Sendbuehler, M. 1967. "Cell Breakage and Gate Fever. A Study of Two Syndromes Found in the Deprivation of Liberty". *The British Journal of Criminology* 7, 317-324.

Count, E. W. 1969. "Animal Communication in Man-Science: An Essay in Perspective". In: *Approaches to Animal Communication*. T. A. Sebeok and A. Ramsay, eds. Approaches to Semiotics 1. The Hague-Paris: Mouton. P. 71-130.

Count, E. W. 1958. "The Biological Basis of Human Sociality". *American Anthropologist* 60, 1049-1085.

Cox, B. A. 1968. "Conflict in the Conflict Theories: Ethological and Social Arguments". *Anthropologica* 10, 179-191.

Cox, K. R. 1972. *Man, Location, and Behavior: An Introduction to Human Geography.* New York-London-Sidney-Toronto: John Wiley & Sons, Inc.

Craig, W. 1918. "Appetites and Aversions as Constituents of Instincts". *Woods Hole Marine Biological Laboratory. Biological Bulletin* 34, 91-107.

Cramer, R. D. 1960. "Images of Home". *Journal of the American Institute of Architects* 34:3, 40-49.

Crawford, M. P. 1939. "The Social Psychology of the Vertebrates". *Psychological Bulletin* 36, 407-446.

Crook, J. H. 1970a. "Introduction – Social Behavior and Ethology". In: *Social Behavior in Birds and Mammals. Essays on the Social Ethology of Animals and Man.* J. H. Crook, ed. London-New York: Academic Press. P. XXI-XL.

Crook, J. H. 1970b. "Social Organization and the Environment: Aspects of Contemporary Social Ethology". *Animal Behaviour* 18, 197-209.

*Crook, J. H. 1970c (1968). "The Nature and Function of Territorial Aggression". In: *Man and Aggression.* M. F. Ashley Montagu, ed. London-Oxford-New York: Oxford University Press. P. 141-178.

Curl, J. S. 1970. *European Cities and Society. A Study of the Influence of Political Climate on Town Design.* London: Leonard Hill.

Darwin, C. 1871. *The Descent of Man, and Selection in Relation to Sex* 1. London: John Murray.

Darwin, C. 1963 (1859). *The Origin of Species by Means of Natural Selection or the Preservation of Favoured Races in the Struggle for Life.* New York: The New American Library of World Literature, Inc.

Daumézon, G. 1946-1947. "L'enracinement des malades guéris à l'asile". *L'Hygiène Mentale (Supplement de L'Encéphale)* 36, 57-71.

Davis, D. E. 1949. "An Animal's Home is its Castle". *The Scientific Monthly* 69, 249-254.

Davis, D. E. 1962. "An Inquiry into the Phylogeny of Gangs". In: *Roots of Behavior. Genetics, Instinct and Socialization in Animal Behavior.* E. L. Bliss, ed. New York: Harper and Brothers. P. 316-320.

Davis, D. E. 1952. "Social Behavior and Reproduction". *The Auk* 69, 171-182.

Davis, D. E. 1941. "The Relation of Abundance to Territorialism in Tropical Birds". *Bird-Banding* 12, 93-97.

Davis, H. 1956. "Space and Time in the Central Nervous System". *Electroencephalography and Clinical Neurophysiology* 8, 185-191.

Davis, J. M., McCourt, W. F., Solomon, S. I. and Solomon, P. 1959-1960. "The Effect of Visual Stimulation on Hallucinations and other Mental Experiences during Sensory Deprivation". *The American Journal of Psychiatry* 116, 889-892.

Davis, K. 1974. "The Migrations of Human Populations". *Scientific American* 231:3, 93-105.

Davis, K. 1955. "The Origin and Growth of Urbanization in the World". *The American Journal of Sociology* 60, 429-445.

Davis, K. 1965. "The Urbanization of the Human Population". *Scientific American* 213:3, 41-53.

Dawson, J. 1881. *Australian Aborigines. The Languages and Customs of several Tribes of Aborigines in the western District of Victoria, Australia.* Melbourne-Sidney-Adelaide: George Robertson.

Dayton, N. A. 1940. *New Facts on Mental Disorders. Study of 89,190 Cases.* Springfield, Ill. - Baltimore, Md.: Charles Thomas.

Debont, M. and Veraghtert, K. 1974. "Incidence de l'urbanisation sur les maladies mentales". *Sixième Congrès International d'Histoire Economique. Copenhague 19-23 août 1974. Thème 3: Environment et urbanisation* (mimeographed).

Deevey, E. S. Jr. 1960. "The Human Population". *Scientific American* 203:3, 195-204.

Deffontaines, P. 1948. *Géograqhie et Religions*. 2nd edition. Géographie Humaine 21. Paris: Gallimard.

Delavignette, R. 1968. *Freedom and Authority in French West Africa*. London-Edinburgh: Frank Cass & Co. Ltd.

Dellenbaugh, F. S. 1901. *The North-Americans of Yesterday. A Comparative Study of North-American Indian Life Customs, and Products, on the Theory of the Ethnic Unity of the Race.* New York-London: G. P. Putnam's Sons-The Knickerbocker Press.

*DeLong, A. J. 1971. "Dominance-Territorial Criteria and Small Group Structure". *Comparative Group Studies* 2, 235-266.

*DeLong, A. J. 1970. "Dominance-Territorial Relations in a Small Group". *Environment and Behavior* 2, 170-191.

*DeLong, A. J. 1973. "Territorial Stability and Hierarchical Formation". *Small Group Behavior* 4, 55-63.

Demaret, A. 1971. "La psychose maniaco-dépressive envisagée dans une perspective étholo-gique". *Acta Psychiatrica Belgica* 71, 429-448.

Dennis, W. 1943. "The Hopi Child". In: *Child Behavior and Development. A Course of Representative Studies.* R. G. Barker, J. S. Kounin and H. F. Wright, eds. New York-London: McGraw-Hill Book Company Inc. P. 621-636.

Design of Dwellings. 1944. London: His Majesty's Stationary Office.

De Vore, I. 1971. "The Evolution of Human Society". In: *Man and Beast: Comparative Social Behavior.* J. F. Eisenberg and W. S. Dillon, eds. Smithsonian Annual III. Washington: Smithsonian Institution Press. P. 297-311.

Diamond, A. S. 1935. *Primitive Law.* London-New York-Toronto: Longmans, Green and Co.

Diamond, S. 1971. "Gestation of the Instinct Concept". *Journal of the History of the Behavioral Sciences* 7, 323-336.

Dice, L. R. 1952. *Natural Communities.* Ann. Arbor: The University of Michigan Press.

Dickinson, R. E. 1964. *City and Region. A Geographical Interpretation.* London: Routledge & Kegan Paul Ltd.

Dickinson, R. E. 1967. *The City Region in Western Europe.* London: Routledge & Kegan Paul Ltd.

Die Strassen der Tiere. 1967. H. Hediger, ed. Die Wissenschaft 125. Braunschweig: Friedr. Vieweg & Sohn.

Dobriner, W. M. 1958. "Theory and Research in the Sociology of the Suburbs". In: *The Suburban Community.* W. M. Dobriner, ed. New York: G. P. Putnam's Sons. P. XIII-XXVIII.

Dobzhansky, T. 1963. "Cultural Direction of Human Evolution – A Summation". *Human Biology* 35, 311-316.

Doherty, J. M. 1969. "Developments in Behavioural Geography". *London School of Economics and Political Science. Graduate Geography Department. Discussion Paper* 35, 1-17.

Dohrenwend, B. P. and Dohrenwend, B. S. 1973. "The Prevalence of Psychiatric Disorders in Urban versus Rural Settings". In: *Psychiatry. Proceedings of the V. World Congress of Psychiatry. Mexico D.F. 25 Nov.-4 Dec., 1971.* Part 2. Amsterdam: Excerpta Medica. P. 1365-1373.

Dolhinow, P. 1972. "Primate Patterns". In: *Primate Patterns.* P. Dolhinow, ed. New York-Chicago-San Francisco: Holt, Rinehart & Winston, Inc. P. 352-392.

Donaldson, S. 1969. *The Suburban Myth.* New York-London: Columbia University Press.

Dorst, J. 1962 (1956). *The Migration of Birds.* London-Melbourne-Toronto: Heinemann.

Douglas, M. 1972. "Population Control in Primitive Groups". In: *Population Crisis. An Interdisciplinary Perspective.* S. T. Reid and D. L. Lyon, eds. Glenview, Ill. - London: Scott, Foresman and Company. P. 49-55.

Downs, R. M. and Stea, D. 1973. "Cognitive Maps and Spatial Behavior: Process and Products". In: *Image and Environment. Cognitive Mapping and Spatial Behavior.* R. M. Downs and D. Stea, eds. Chicago: Aldine Publishing Company.

Doxiadis, C. A. 1968a. "A City for Human Development". *Ekistics* 25, 374-394.

Doxiadis, C. A. 1966. "Anthropocosmos: The World of Man". *Ekistics* 22, 311-318.

Doxiadis, C. A. 1965. "Densities in Human Settlements. *Ekistics* 20, 199-205.

Doxiadis, C. A. 1968b. *Ekistics. An Introduction to the Science of Human Settlements*. London: Hutchinson.

Doxiadis, C. A. 1968c. "Man and the Space around him". *Saturday Review* 1968: December 14, 21-23.

Doxiadis, C. A. 1974. "One Room for every Human". *Ekistics* 38, 149-152.

Drever, J. 1921 (1917). *Instinct in Man. A Contribution to the Psychology of Education*. 2nd Edition. Cambridge: At the University Press.

Dubos, R. 1965a. "Humanistic Biology". *American Scientist* 53, 4-19.

Dubos, R. 1965b. *Man Adapting*. New Haven-London: Yale University Press.

Dubos, R. 1968 (1967). "Man Adapting: His Limitations and Potentialities". In: *Environment for Man. The next Fifty Years*. W. R. Ewald Jr., ed. Bloomington-London: Indiana University Press. P. 11-26.

Dubos, R. 1973. "The Biological Basis of Urban Design". *Ekistics* 35, 199-204.

Dubos, R. 1970. "The Human Environment". *Ekistics* 30, 170-173.

Dumont, L. 1970. *Homo hierarchicus. An Essay on the Caste System*. Chicago: The University of Chicago Press.

Duncan, O. D. 1957. "Population Distribution and Community Structure". In: *Population Studies: Animal Ecology and Demography*. Cold Spring Harbor Symposia on Quantitative Biology 22, 357-371.

Duncan, O. D. and Schnore, L. F. 1959-1960. "Cultural, Behavioral, and Ecological Perspectives in the Study of Social Organization". *The American Journal of Sociology* 65, 132-153.

Durand, J. D. 1971. "The Modern Expansion of World Population". In: *Man's Impact on Environment*. J. Yates and D. Dunham, eds. New York-St. Louis-San Francisco-etc.: McGraw-Hill Book Company. P. 36-49.

Durbin, E. F. M. and Bowlby, J. 1950 (1939). *Personal Aggressiveness and War*. London: Routledge & Kegan Paul Ltd.

*Eastman, C. M. and Harper, J. 1971. "A Study of Proxemic Behavior. Toward a Predictive Model". *Environment and Behavior* 3, 418-437.

Ebermann, H. and Möllhoff, G. 1957. "Psychiatrische Beobachtungen an heimatvertriebenen Donaudeutschen". *Der Nervenartzt* 28, 399-405.

*Edney, J. J. 1974. "Human Territoriality". *Psychological Bulletin* 81, 959-975.

*Edney, J. J. 1976. "Human Territories. Comment on Functional Properties". *Environment and Behavior*. 8, 31-47.

Edney, J. J. 1972a. "Place and Space: The Effect of Experience with a Physical Locale". *Journal of Experimental Social Psychology* 8, 124-135.

*Edney, J. J. 1972b. "Property, Possession and Permanence: A Field Study in Human Territoriality". *Journal of Applied Social Psychology* 2, 275-282.

*Edney, J. J. 1975. "Territoriality and Control: A Field Experiment". *Journal of Personality and Social Psychology* 31, 1108-1115.

*Edney, J. J. and Jordan-Edney, N. L. 1974. "Territorial Spacing on a Beach". *Sociometry* 37, 92-104.

Efran, M. G. and Cheyne, J. A. 1973. "Shared Space: the Co-operative Control of Spatial Areas by two Interacting Individuals". *Canadian Journal of Behavioural Science* 5, 201-210.

Ehrlich, P. R. and Ehrlich, A. H. 1972 (1970). *Population, Resources, Environment. Issues in Human Ecology*. 2nd ed. San Francisco: W. H. Freeman and Company.

Ehrlich, P. and Freedman, J. 1971. "Population, Crowding and Human Behaviour". *New Scientist and Science Journal* 50:745, 10-14.

Eibl-Eibesfeldt, I. 1966. "Ethologie. Die Biologie des Verhaltens". In: *Handbuch der Biologie* 2. F. Gessner, ed. Frankfurt am Main: Akademische Verlagsgesellschaft Athenaion. P. 341-559.

Eibl-Eibesfeldt, I. 1970. *Ethology. The Biology of Behavior*. New York-Chicago-San Francisco-etc.: Holt, Rinehart & Winston.

Eibl-Eibesfeldt, I. 1961. "The Fighting Behavior of Animals". *Scientific American* 205:6, 112-122.

*Eibl-Eibesfeldt, I. 1974. "The Myth of the Aggression-Free Hunter and Gatherer Society". In: *Primate Aggression, Territoriality, and Xenophobia. A Comparative Perspective*. R. L. Holloway, ed. New York-London: Academic Press. P. 435-457.

Eickstedt, E. v. 1949. "Vom Wesen der Anthropologie". *Homo* 1, 1-13.

Eigentum und Freiheit. Zeugnisse aus der Geschichte. 1972. F. Forwick, ed.. München: Deutscher Taschenbuch.

Einstein, A. 1969 (1954). "Foreword". In: Jammer, M. *Concepts of Space. The History of Theories of Space in Physics*. 2nd ed. Cambridge, Mass.: Harvard University Press. P. XI-XV.

Einstein, A. and Freud, S. 1933. "Pourquoi la guerre?" *Correspondance* 2, 11-63.

Eisenberg, J. F. 1967. "Nagetier-Territorien und -Wechsel". In: *Die Strassen der Tiere*. H. Hediger, ed. Braunschweig: Friedr. Vieweg & Sohn. P. 83-101.

Eisenberg, J. F. 1966. "The Social Organization of Mammals". In: *Handbuch der Zoologie* 8:39. J.-G. Helmcke, H. v. Lengerken, D. Starck and H. Wermuth, eds. Berlin: Walter de Gruyter & Co. P. 1-92.

Elkins, T. H. 1973. *The Urban Explosion*. London-Basingstoke: MacMillan.

Ellefson, J. O. 1968. "Territorial Behavior in the Common White-Handed Gibbon, Hylobates lar Linn.". In: *Primates. Studies in Adaptation and Variability*. P. C. Jay, ed. New York-Chicago-San Francisco-etc: Holt, Rinehart & Winston. P. 180-199.

Ellenberger, H. F. 1971. "Behavior under Involuntary Confinement". In: *Behavior and Environment. The Use of Space by Animals and Men*, A. H. Esser, ed. New York-London: Plenum Press. P. 188-203.

Ellenberger, H. F. 1960. "Zoological Garden and Mental Hospital". *Canadian Psychiatric Association Journal* 5, 136-149.

Elliott, H. W. 1886. *An Arctic Province. Alaska and the Seal Islands*. London.

Elms, A. C. 1972. "Some People read Newspaper Horoscopes to find out why Human Beings behave the Way they do; other People read the Works of Robert Ardrey". *Psychology Today* 6: 5, 36-44, 126-127.

Emlen, J. T. Jr. 1957. "Defended Area? A Critique of the Territory Concept and of Conventional Thinking". *The Ibis* 99, 352.

Engebretson, D. 1973. "Interactional Distance: A Definition of Relationship". In: *Focus on Classroom Behavior. Readings and Research*. W. Scott McDonald and G. Tanabe, eds. Springfield Ill.: Charles C. Thomas. P. 31-35.

Engels, F. 1966 (1884). "Der Ursprung der Familie, des Privateigentums und des Staats". In: *Karl Marx and Friedrich Engels. Ausgewählte Schriften in zwei Bänden*. II. Berlin: Dietz. P. 155-301.

Ennen, E. 1953. *Frühgeschichte der Europäischen Stadt*. Bonn: Ludwig Röhrscheid Verlag.

Environmental Psychology: Man and his Physical Setting. 1970. H. M. Proshansky, W. H. Ittelson & L. G. Rivlin, eds. New York-Chicago-San Francisco-etc.: Holt, Rinehart & Winston.

Erikson, E. H. 1956. "The Problem of Ego Identity". *Journal of the American Psychoanalytic Association* 4, 56-121.

Errington, P. 1946. "Predation and Vertebrate Populations". *The Quarterly Review of Biology* 21, 144-177, 221-245.

*Esser, A. H. 1973. "Cottage Fourteen. Dominance and Territoriality in a Group of Industrialized Boys". *Small Group Behavior* 4, 131-146.

Esser, A. H. 1968. "Dominance Hierarchy and Clinical Course of Psychiatrically Hospitalized Boys". *Child Development* 39, 147-157.

*Esser, A. H. 1970. "Interactional Hierarchy and Power Structure on a Psychiatric Ward.

Ethological Studies of Dominance Behavior in a Total Institution". In: *Behaviour Studies in Psychiatry*. Based on the Proceedings of a Symposium held at The Human Development Research Unit, Park Hospital for Children, Oxford, July 1968. S. J. Hutt and C. Hutt, eds. Oxford-New York-Toronto-etc.: Pergamon Press. P. 25-59.

Esser A. H. 1971a. "Social Pollution". *Social Education* 35, 10-18.

Esser, A. H. 1971b. "The Importance of Defining Spatial Behavioral Parameters". In: *Behavior and Environment. The Use of Space by Animals and Men*. A. H. Esser, ed. New York-London: Plenum Press. P. 1-8.

*Esser, A. H. 1976. "Theoretical and Empirical Issues with Regard to Privacy, Territoriality, Personal Space and Crowding". *Environment and Behavior* 8, 117-124.

*Esser, A. H., Chamberlain, A. S., Chapple, E. D. and Kline, N. S. 1964. "Territoriality of Patients on a Research Ward". *Recent Advances in Biological Psychiatry* 7, 37-44.

Estvan, F. J. and Estvan, E. W. 1959. *The Child's World: His Social Perception*. New York: G. P. Putnam's Sons.

Etkin, W. 1964a. "Co-operation and Competition in Social Behavior". In: *Social Behavior and Organization among Vertebrates*. W. Etkin, ed. Chicago-London: The University of Chicago Press. P. 1-34.

Etkin, W. 1963. "Social Behavioral Factors in the Emergence of Man". *Human Biology* 35, 299-310.

Etkin, W. 1964b. "Theories of Socialization and Communication". In: *Social Behavior and Organization among Vertebrates*. W. Etkin, ed. Chicago-London: The University of Chicago Press. P. 167-205.

Evans, G. W. and Eichelman, W. 1976. "Preliminary Models of Conceptual Linkages among Proxemic Variables". *Environment and Behavior* 8, 87-116.

Evans, G. W. and Howard, R. B. 1973. "Personal Space". *Psychological Bulletin* 80, 334-344.

*Eyles, J. 1971. "Space, Territory and Conflict". *University of Reading. Department of Geography. Geographical Paper* 1, 1-15.

Eyre, E. J. 1845. *Journals of Expeditions of Discovery into Central Australia and over land from Adelaide to King George's Sound, in the years 1840-1841: sent by the Colonists of South Australia, with the Sanction and Support of the Government: including an Account of the Manners and Customs of the Aborigines and the State of their Relations with Europeans* 2. London: T. and W. Boone.

Fabricius, E. 1971. "Ethological Evidence of Genetically Determined Behaviour Patterns, and Conflicts between these Patterns and Changed Environmental Conditions". In: *Society, Stress and Disease* 1. L. Levi, ed. London-New York-Toronto: Oxford University Press. P. 71-78.

Fabricius, E. 1975. "Etologiska aspekter på aggressionen". *Societas Scientiarum Fennica. Arsbok* LI B 1974, 1-27.

Faris, R. E. L. 1944. "Ecological Factors in Human Behavior". In: *Personality and the Behavior Disorders* 1-2. J. Mc V. Hunt, ed. New York: The Ronald Press Company. P. 736-757.

Faris, R. E. L. 1948. *Social Disorganization*. New York: The Ronald Press Company.

Faris, R. E. L. 1966. "The Discipline of Sociology". In: *Handbook of Modern Sociology*. R. E. L. Faris, ed. Chicago: Rand McNally & Company. P. 1-35.

Faris, R. E. L. and Dunham, H. W. 1939. *Mental Disorders in Urban Areas. An Ecological Study of Schizophrenia and other Psychoses*. Chicago, Ill.: The University of Chicago Press.

Fast, J. 1973 (1970). *Body Language*. New York: Pocket Books.

*Felipe, N. J. and Sommer, R. 1967. "Invasions of Personal Space". *Social Problems* 14, 206-214.

Fischer, F. 1971. "Ten Phases of the Animal Path: Behavior in Familiar Situations". In: *Behavior and Environment. The Use of Space by Animals and Men*. A. H. Esser, ed. New York-London: Plenum Press. P. 9-21.

Fletcher, J. M. 1932. "The Verdict of Psychologists on War Instincts". *The Scientific Monthly* 35, 142-145.

Fletcher, R. 1957. *Instinct in Man in the Light of Recent Work in Comparative Psychology*. London: George Allen & Unwin Ltd.

Fleure, H. J. 1936. "The Historic City in Western and Central Europe with Diagrams". *Bulletin of the John Rylands Library* 20, 3-22.

Flint, B. M. 1966. *The Child and the Institution. -A Study of Deprivation and Recovery*. Toronto: University of Toronto Press.

Flugel, D. L. 1955 (1945). *Man, Moral and Society. A Psycho-Analytical Study*. Harmondsworth: Penguin Books.

Foley, D. L. 1964. "An Approach to Metropolitan Spatial Structure". In: Webber, M. M., Dyckman, J. W., Foley, D. L., Guttenberg, A. Z., Wheaton, L. C. and Wurster, C. B. *Explorations into Urban Structure*. Philadelphia: University of Pennsylvania Press. P. 21-77.

Ford, B. 1971. "Making the Spaceship Fit the Man". *Design and Environment* 2, 43-45.

Forde, C. D. 1934. *Habitat, Economy and Society. A Geographical Introduction to Ethnology*. London: Methuen & Co. Ltd.

Forel, O. 1942. "Psychologie de l'insécurité". *Schweizerische Zeitschrift für Psychologie* 1, 66-74, 189-198.

Forsyth, W. D. 1942. *The Myth of Open Spaces. Australian, British and World Trends of Population and Migration*. Melbourne-London: Melbourne University Press.

Fox, M. W. C. 1968. "Ethology: An Overview". In: *Abnormal Behavior in Animals*. M. W. Fox, ed. Philadelphia-London-Toronto: W. B. Saunders Company. P. 21-43.

Fox, R. 1971. "The Cultural Animal". In: *Man and Beast: Comparative Social Behavior*. J. F. Eisenberg and W. S. Dillon, eds. Smithsonian Annual III. Washington: Smithsonian Institution Press. P. 273-296.

Frank, L. K. 1943. "Man's Multidimensional Environment". *The Scientific Monthly* 56, 344-357.

Fraser, D. 1968. *Village Planning in the Primitive World*. New York-London: Braziller and Studio Vista.

Freedman, J. L. 1975. *Crowding and Behavior*. San Francisco: W. H. Freeman and Company.

Freedman, J. L., Levy, A. S., Buchanan, R. W. and Price, J. 1972. "Crowding and Human Aggressiveness". *Journal of Experimental Social Psychology* 8, 528-548.

Freedman, L. Z. and Roe, A. 1961 (1958). "Evolution and Human Behavior". In: *Behavior and Evolution*. A. Roe and G. G. Simpson, eds. New Haven: Yale University Press. P. 455-479.

Freeman, D. 1971. "Aggression: Instinct or Symptom". *Australian and New Zealand Journal of Psychiatry* 5, 66-76.

Freeman, D. 1964. "Human Aggression in Anthropological Perspective". In: *The Natural History of Aggression*. J. D. Carthy and F. J. Ebling, eds. Institute of Biology Symposia 13. London-New York: Academic Press. P. 109-119.

Frejka, T. 1973. "The Prospects for a Stationary World Population". *Scientific American* 228: 3, 15-23.

Fretwell, S. D. 1969. "On Territorial Behavior and other Factors influencing Habitat Distribution in Birds. III. Breeding Success in a local Population of Field Sparrows (Spizella pusilla Wils.)". *Acta Biotheoretica* 19, 45-52.

Fretwell, S. D. and Calver, J. S. 1969. "On Territorial Behavior and other Factors influencing Habitat Distribution in Birds. II. Sex Ratio Variation in the Dickcissel (Spiza americana Gmel.)". *Acta Biotheoretica* 19, 37-44.

Fretwell, S. D. and Lucas, H. L. Jr. 1969. "On Territorial Behavior and other Factors influencing Habitat Distribution in Birds. I. Theoretical Development". *Acta Biotheoretica* 19, 16-36.

Freund, W. 1910. "Über den 'Hospitalismus' der Säuglinge". *Ergebnisse der Inneren Medizin und Kinderheilkunde* 6, 333-368.

Fried, M. 1963. "Grieving for a Lost Home". In: *The Urban Condition. People and Policy in the Metropolis*. L. J. Duhl, ed. New York-London: Basic Books, Inc. P. 151-171.

*Fried, M. and Gleicher, P. 1961. "Some Sources of Residential Satisfaction in an Urban Slum". *Journal of the American Institute of Planners* 27, 305-315.

Fried, M. H. 1967. *The Evolution of Political Society. An Essay in Political Anthropology*. New York: Random House.

*Fried, M. L. and DeFazio, V. J. 1974. "Territoriality and Boundary Conflicts in the Subway". *Psychiatry* 37, 47-59.

Friedman, A. B. 1968. "The Scatological Rites of Burglars". *Western Folklore* 27, 171-179.

Friedman, E. P. 1966. "Spatial Proximity and Social Interaction in a Home for the Aged". *Journal of Gerontology* 21, 566-570.

Friedmann, J. and Miller, J. 1965. "The Urban Field". *Journal of the American Institute of Planners* 31, 312-320.

Friholt, O. 1974. *Leva i slum. En berättelse om indisk vardag.* Stockholm: SIDA.

Fromm, E. 1973. *The Anatomy of Human Destructiveness*. New York-Chicago-San Francisco: Holt, Rinehart & Winston.

Frost, I. 1938. "Home-Sickness and Immigrant Psychoses. Austrian and German Domestic Servants the Basis of Study". *The Journal of Mental Science* 84, 801-847.

Fuller, J. L. and Waller, M. B. 1962. "Is early Experience different?" In: *Roots of Behavior. Genetics, Instinct, and Socialization in Animal Behavior*. E. L. Bliss, ed. New York: Harper and Brothers. P. 235-245.

Fustel de Coulanges, M. 1920. *La cité antique. Étude sur le culte, le droit, les institutions de la Grèce et de Rome*. 26th edition. Paris: Librairie Hachette.

Fustel de Coulanges, M. 1889. "Le problème des origines de la propriété foncière". *Revue des Questions Historiques* 45, 349-439.

Galle, O. R., Gove, W. R. and Miller McPherson, J. 1972. "Population Density and Pathology: What are the Relations for Man?" *Science* 176, 23-30.

Gallion, A. B. 1950. *The Urban Pattern. City Planning and Design*. London-New York-Toronto: D. van Nostrand Company, Inc.

Ganong, W. F. 1971 (1963). *Review of Medical Physiology*. Los Altos, Cal.: Lange Medical Publications.

Gans, H. J. 1963. "Effects of the Move from City to Suburb". In: *The Urban Condition, People and Policy in the Metropolis*. L. J. Duhl, ed. New York-London: Basic Books, Inc. P. 184-198.

Gardiner, S. J. 1898. "The Natives of Rotuma". *The Journal of the Anthropological Institute of Great Britain and Ireland* 27, 396-435.

Gartlan, J. S. and Brain, C. K. 1968. "Ecology and Social Variability in Cercopithecus aethiops and C. mitis". In: *Primates. Studies in Adaptation and Variability*. P. C. Jay, ed. New York-Chicago-San Francisco-etc.: Holt, Rinehart & Winston. P. 253-292.

Gatto, L. E. and Dean, H. L. 1955. "The 'Nestling' Military Patient". *Military Medicine* 117, 1-26.

Geddes, P. 1949 (1915). *Cities in Evolution*. The Outlook Tower Association, Edinburgh, and The Association for Planning and Regional Reconstruction, ed. New and revised edition. London: Williams and Norgate Ltd.

Gerard, R. W. 1957. "Units and Concepts of Biology". *Science* 125, 429-433.

Gesell, A., Ilg, F. L. and Bullis, G. E. 1949. *Vision. Its Development in Infant and Child*. New York: Paul B. Hoeber, Inc.

Gibb, J. A. 1961. "Bird Populations". In: *Biology and Comparative Physiology of Birds* 2. A. J. Marshall, ed. New York-London: Academic Press. P. 413-446.

Gibson, J. J. 1950. *The Perception of the Visual World*. Cambridge, Mass.: The Riverside Press.

Ginsberg, A. 1952. "A Reconstructive Analysis of the Concept 'Instinct'". *The Journal of Psychology* 33, 235-277.

Glanzmann, E. 1934. "Zur Psychopathologie der Enkopresis". *Zeitschrift für Kinderpsychiatrie* 1, 69-76.

Gleichmann, P. 1963. *Sozialwissenschaftliche Aspekte der Grünplanung in der Grosstadt*. Stuttgart: Ferdinand Enke.

Glover, E. and Ginsberg, M. 1934. "A Symposium on the Psychology of Peace and War". *British Journal of Medical Psychology* 14, 274-293.

Goffman, E. 1973 (1961). *Asylums. Essays on the Social Situation of Mental Patients and other Inmates.* Harmondsworth: Penguin Books.

Goffman, E. 1964. "Mental Symptoms and Public Order". *Association for Research in Nervous and Mental Disease. Research Publications* 42, 262-269.

Goffman, E. 1972 (1971). *Relations in Public. Microstudies of the Public Order.* Harmondsworth: Penguin Books.

"Gold in Kenya and Native Reserves". 1933. *Nature* 131, 37-39.

Goldfinger, E. 1941. "The Sensation of Space". *Architectural Review* 89-90, 262-269.

Goldsmith, E. 1973. "Does building Houses increase Homelessness?" *The Ecologist* 3, 462-467.

Goldsmith, E. 1974, "The Ecology of War". *The Ecologist* 4, 124-135.

Goldsmith, E. 1976. 'The Family Basis of Social Structure". *The Ecologist* 6, 14-19, 46-53.

Goodey, B. 1973 (1974). *Perception of the Environment. An Introduction to the Literature.* Centre for Urban and Regional Studies. Occasional Paper 17. Birmingham: The University of Birmingham.

Goodman, M. 1968. "Phylogeny and Taxonomy of the Catarrhine Primates from Immunodiffusion Data". In: *Taxonomy and Phylogeny of Old World Primates with Reference to the Origin of Man.* B. Chiarelli, ed. Turin: Rosenberg & Seller. P. 95-107.

Goody, J. 1962. *Death, Property and the Ancestors. A Study of the Mortuary Customs of the Lodagaa of West Africa.* Stanford, Cal.: Stanford University Press.

Gordon, R. E. and Gordon, K. K. 1959. "Emotional Disorders of Children in a rapidly growing Suburb". *The International Journal of Social Psychiatry* 4, 85-97.

Gottman, J. 1966a. *Essais sur l'aménagement de l'espace habité.* Paris-La Haye: Mouton & Co.

Gottman, J. 1966b (1961). *Megalopolis. The Urbanized Northeastern Seaboard of the United States.* Cambridge, Mass.-London: The Massachusetts Institute of Technology Press.

Gottman, J. 1969. *The Renewal of the Geographic Environment.* An Inaugural Lecture delivered before the University of Oxford on 11 February 1969. Oxford: At the Clarendon Press.

Gowans, A. 1964. "Tomb". In: *Encyclopaedia Britannica* 22. Chicago-London-Toronto-etc.: Encyclopaedia Britannica, Inc. P. 283.

Grant, E. C. 1965. "The Contribution of Ethology to Child Psychiatry". In: *Modern Perspectives in Child Psychiatry.* J. G. Howells, ed. Edinburgh-London: Oliver & Boyd. P. 20-37.

Gras, N. S. B. 1926. "The Rise of the Metropolitan Community". In: *The Urban Community.* E. W. Burgess, ed. Chicago: The University of Chicago Press. P. 184-191.

Graves, W. 1974. "Denmark, Field of the Danes". *National Geographic Magazine* 145, 245-275.

Gray, P. 1958. "Theory and Evidence of Imprinting in Human Infants". *The Journal of Psychology* 46, 155-166.

*Greverus, I.-M. 1972. *Der territoriale Mensch. Ein literaturanthropologischer Versuch zum Heimatphänomen.* Frankfurt am Main: Athenäum.

Grey Walter, W. 1953. *The living Brain.* London: Gerald Duckworth & Co. Ltd.

Griffith, W. and Veitch, R. 1971. "Hot and Crowded. Influences of Population Density and Temperature on Interpersonal Affective Behavior". *Journal of Personality and Social Psychology* 17, 92-98.

Groos, K. 1899. *Die Spiele der Menschen.* Jena: Gustav Fischer.

Groos, K. 1896. *Die Spiele der Thiere.* Jena: Gustav Fischer.

Group Processes. 1955-1959. Transactions of the Conference 1-5. B. Schaffner, ed. New York: Josiah Macy Jr. Foundation.

Guardo, C. J. 1969. "Personal Space in Children". *Child Development* 40, 143-151.

Guest, A. M. 1973. "Urban Growth and Population Densities". *Demography* 10, 53-69.

Gutkind, E. A. 1953. *The Expanding Environment. The End of Cities – The Rise of Communities.* London: Freedom Press.

Haag, E. v.d. 1971. "On Privacy". In: *Privacy*. R. J. Pennock and J. W. Chapman, eds. Nomos 13. New York: Atherton Press. P. 149-168.

Haartman, L. v. 1957. "Adaptation in Hole-Nesting Birds". *Evolution* 11, 339-347.

Haberland, E. 1957. "Naturvölkische Raumvorstellungen". *Studium Generale* 10, 583-589.

Hägerstrand, T. 1967 (1953). *Innovation Diffusion as a Spatial Process*. Chicago-London: The University of Chicago Press.

Hägerstrand, T. 1957. "Migration and Area. Survey of a Sample of Swedish Migration Fields and Hypothetical Considerations on their Genesis". In: *Migration in Sweden. A Symposium*. D. Hannerberg, T. Hägerstrand and B. Odeving, eds. Lund Studies in Geography. Ser B. Human Geography 13. P. 27-158.

Hägerstrand, T. 1970. "Regional Forecasting and Social Engineering". In: *Regional Forecasting*. M. Chisholm, A. E. Frey and P. Haggett, eds. Colston Papers 22. London: Butterworths. P. 1-7.

Hagget, P. 1975 (1979). *Geography: A Modern Synthetis*. 2nd edition New York-Evanston-San Francisco-London: Harper & Row.

Haldane, J. B. S. 1956. "The Argument from Animals to Men: An Examination of its Validity for Anthropology". *Journal of the Anthropological Institute* 86, 1-14.

Hall, E. T. 1971. "Environmental Communication". In: *Behavior and Environment. The Use of Space by Animals and Men*. A. H. Esser, ed. New York-London: Plenum Press. P. 247-256.

*Hall, E. T. 1968. "Proxemics". *Current Anthropology* 9, 83-108.

Hall, E. T. 1963. "Proxemics. The Study of Man's Spatial Relations". In: *Man's Image in Medicine and Anthropology*. I. Gladstone, ed. Institute of Social and Historical Medicine 4. New York: International Universities Press. P. 422-445.

*Hall, E. T. 1969 (1966). *The Hidden Dimension. Man's Use of Space in Public and Private*. London-Sydney-Toronto: The Bodley Head.

Hall, E. T. 1961. "The Language of Space". *Journal of the American Institute of Architects* 35, 71-74.

Hall, E. T. 1959. *The Silent Language*, Garden City, N.Y.: Doubleday & Company, Inc.

Hall, G. S. 1897. "Some Aspects of Early Sense of Self". *The American Journal of Psychology* 9, 351-395.

Hall, K. R. L. 1968. "Behaviour and Ecology of the Wild Patas Monkey, Erythrocebus patas, in Uganda". In: *Primates. Studies in Adaptation and Variability*. P. C. Jay, ed. New York-Chicago-San Francisco-etc.: Holt, Rinehart & Winston. P. 32-119.

Hallowell, A. I. 1955. *Culture and Experience*. Philadelphia: University of Pennsylvania Press.

Hallowell, A. I. 1970 (1961). "The Protocultural Foundations of Human Adaptation". In: *Social Life of Early Man*. S. L. Washburn, ed. Chicago: Aldine Publishing Company. P. 236-255.

*Hallowell, A. I. 1949. "The Size of Algonkian Hunting Territories: A Function of Ecological Adjustment". *American Anthropologist* 51, 35-45.

Halmos, P. 1952. *Solitude and Privacy. A Study of Social Isolation, its Causes and Therapy*. London: Routledge & Kegan Paul Limited.

Hamblin, D. J. 1973. *The First Cities. The Emergence of Man*. The Netherlands: Time-Life International.

Handbook of American Indians North of Mexico 1-2. 1907-1910. F. W. Hodge, ed. Bureau of American Ethnology. Bulletin 30. Washington: Smithsonian Institute.

Hanna, T. D. and Gaito, J. 1960. "Performance and Habitability Aspects of Extended Confinement in Sealed Cabins". *Aerospace Medicine* 31, 399-406.

*Hansen, W. B. and Altman, I. 1976. "Decorating Personal Places. A Descriptive Analysis". *Environment and Behavior* 8, 491-504.

Hare, E. H. 1952. "The Ecology of Mental Disease. A Dissertation on the Influence of Environmental Factors in the Distribution, Development and Variation of Mental Disease". *The Journal of Mental Science* 98, 579-594.

Harris, C. D. and Ullman, E. L. 1945. "The Nature of Cities". *The Annals of the American Academy of Political and Social Science* 242, 7-17.

Harrison, G. A., Weiner, J. S., Tanner, J. M. and Barnicot, N. A. 1964. *Human Biology. An Introduction to Human Evolution, Variation and Growth.* Oxford: At the Clarendon Press.

Hart, R. A. and Moore, G. T. 1973. "The Development of Spatial Cognition: A Review". In: *Image and Environment. Cognitive Mapping and Spatial Behavior.* R. M. Downs and D. Stea, eds. Chicago: Aldine Publishing Company. P. 246-288.

Hassenstein, F. 1950. "Der Mensch in der Gefangenschaft". *Studium Generale* 3, 5-8.

Hatt, G. 1937. *Landbrug i Danmarks Oldtid.* Köbenhavn: G. E. C. Gad.

Hawley, A. H. 1950. *Human Ecology.* New York: The Ronald Press.

Haythorn, W. W., Altman, I. and Myers, T. I. 1966. "Emotional Symptomatology and Subjective Stress in Isolated Pairs of Men". *Journal of Experimental Research in Personality* 1, 290-305.

Hazard, J. N. 1962. "Furniture Arrangement as a Symbol of Judicial Roles". *ETC. A Review of General Semantics* 19, 181-188.

Heape, W. 1931. *Emigration, Immigration and Nomadism.* Cambridge: W. Heffer & Sons Ltd.

Hebb, D. O. and Thompson, W. R. 1954. "The Social Significance of Animal Studies". In: *Handbook of Social Psychology 1. Theory and Method.* G. Lindzey, ed. Cambridge, Mass.: Addison-Wesley Publishing Company, Inc. P. 532-561.

Hediger, H. 1946. "Bemerkungen zum Raum-Zeit-System der Tiere. Ein kleiner Beitrag zur vergleichenden Psychologie". *Schweizerische Zeitschrift für Psychologie* 5, 241-269.

Hediger, H. 1941. "Biologische Gesetzmässigkeiten im Verhalten von Wirbeltieren". *Mitteilungen der Naturforschenden Gesellschaft in Bern* 1940, 37-55.

Hediger, H. 1944. "Die Bedeutung von Miktion und Defäkation bei Wildtieren". *Schweizerische Zeitschrift für Psychologie* 3, 170-182.

Hediger, H. 1965. "Environmental Factors influencing the reproduction of Zoo Animals". In: *Sex and Behavior.* F. A. Beach, ed. New York-London-Sidney: John Wiley & Sons, Inc. P. 319-354.

Hediger, H. 1956. "Instinkt und Territorium". In: *L'instinct dans le comportement des animaux et de l'homme.* P. P. Grassé, ed. Paris: Masson et Cie. P. 521-545.

Hediger, H. 1949. "Säugetier-Territorien und ihre Markierung". *Bijdragen tot de Dierkunde* 28, 172-184.

Hediger, H. 1955. *Studies of the Psychology and Behaviour of Captive Animals in Zoos and Circuses.* London: Butterworths Scientific Publications.

Hediger, H. 1970a. "The Development of the Presentation and the Viewing of Animals in Zoological Gardens". In: *Development and Evolution of Behavior. Essays in Memory of T. C. Schneirla.* L. R. Aronson, E. Tobach, D. S. Lehrman and J. S. Rosenblatt, eds. San Francisco: W. H. Freeman and Company. P. 519-528.

*Hediger, H. 1970b (1961). "The Evolution of Territorial Behavior". In: *Social Life of Early Man.* S. L. Washburn, ed. Chicago: Aldine Publishing Company. P. 34-57.

Hediger, H. 1942. *Wildtiere in Gefangenschaft. Ein Grundriss der Tiergartenbiologie.* Basel: Benno Schwabe & Co.

Hediger, H. 1940. "Über die Angleichungstendenz bei Tier und Mensch". *Die Naturwissenschaften* 28, 313-315.

Heinroth, O. 1910. "Beiträge zur Biologie, namentlich Ethologie und Psychologie der Anatiden". In: *Verhandlungen des V. Internationalen Ornithologen-Kongresses in Berlin 30. Mai bis 4. Juni 1910.* Berlin: Deutsche Ornithologen-Gesellschaft. P. 589-702.

*Heinz, H. J. 1972. "Territoriality among the Bushmen in General and the !ko in Particular". *Anthropos* 67, 405-416.

Helle, H. J. 1965. *Squatters in Hamburg. Eine empirisch-soziologische Untersuchung des Kleingartenwesens im Hamburgischen Staate.* 2nd edition. Hamburg: Seminar für Sozialwissenschaften der Universität.

Hellwig, A. 1914. "Zum Brauch des Grumus Merdae". *Schweizerisches Archiv für Volkskunde* 18, 186-187.

*Helm, J. 1968. "The Nature of Dogrib Socioterritorial Groups". In: *Man the Hunter*. R. B. Lee and I. DeVore, eds. Chicago: Aldine Publishing Company. P. 118-125.

*Hereford, S. M., Cleland, C. C. and Fellner, M. 1973. "Territoriality and Scent-Marking: A Study of Profoundly Retarded Enuretics and Encopretics". *American Journal of Mental Deficiency* 77, 426-430.

Herron, R. E. 1971. "Mapping Human Movement with the Aid of a Computer". In: *Behavior and Environment. The Use of Space by Animals and Men*. A. H. Esser, ed. New York-London: Plenum Press. P. 115-117.

Herskovits, M. J. 1949. *Man and his Works*. New York: Alfred A. Knopf.

Herskovits, M. J. 1940. *The Economic Life of Primitive Peoples*. New York-London: Alfred A. Knopf.

Hess, E. H. 1962. "Ethology. An Approach toward the Complete Analysis of Behavior". *New Directions in Psychology* 1, 157-266.

Hessing, F. J. 1958. "Die wirtschaftliche und soziale Bedeutung des Kleingartenwesens". *Sonderdruck des Instituts für Siedlungs- und Wohnungswesen der Universität Münster* 20, 1-94.

Heuer, J. and Lowinski, L. 1955. *Das Eigenheim. Eine soziologische und volkswirtschaftliche Analyse. Beiträge und Untersuchungen*. Köln-Braunsfeld: Rudolf Müller.

Heymann, K. 1943. *Seelische Frühformen. Beiträge zur Psychologie der Kindheit*. Psychologische Praxis I. Basel: S. Karger.

Hiatt, L. R. 1961-1962. "Local Organization among the Australian Aborigines". *Oceania* 32, 267-286.

Hiatt, L. R. 1968. "Ownership and Use of Land among the Australian Aborigines". In: *Man the Hunter*. R. B. Lee and I. DeVore, eds. Chicago: Aldine Publishing Company. P. 99-102.

Higbee, E. 1960. *The Squeeze. Cities without Space*. New York: William Morrow & Company.

Hildreth, A. M., Derogatis, L. R. and McCusker, K. 1971. "Body-Buffer Zone and Violence. A Reassessment and Confirmation". *American Journal of Psychiatry* 127, 1641-1645.

Hilzheimer, M. 1926-1927. "Historisches und Kritisches zu Bolks Problem der Menschwerdung". *Anatomischer Anzeiger* 62, 110-121.

Hinde, R. A. 1956. "The Biological Significance of Territories of Birds". *The Ibis* 98, 340-369.

Hinsche, G. 1944. "Zur Genese der Stereotypien und Manieren 1. Wege-Riten". *Psychiatrisch-Neurologische Wochenschrift* 46, 233-239.

Hoagland, H. 1964. "Mechanisms of Population Control". *Daedalus* 93, 814-829.

Hobhouse, L. T., Wheeler, G. C. and Ginsberg, M. 1930. *The Material Culture and Social Institutions of the Simpler Peoples*. London: Chapman & Hall.

Hobley, C. W. 1910. *Ethnology of A-Kamba and other East African Tribes*. Cambridge: At the University Press.

Hockett, C. F. 1973. *Man's Place in Nature*. New York-San Francisco-St. Louis-etc.: McGraw-Hill Book Company.

Hockett, C. F. and Ascher, R. 1964. "The Human Revolution". *Current Anthropology* 5, 135-168.

Hoebel, E. A. 1949. *Man in the Primitive World*. New York-Toronto-London: McGraw-Hill Book Company.

Hofer, H. and Altner, G. 1972. *Die Sonderstellung des Menschen. Naturwissenschaftliche und geisteswissenschaftliche Aspekte*. Stuttgart: Gustav Fischer.

Holling, C. S. 1969. "Stability in Ecological and Social Systems". In: *Diversity and Stability in Ecological Systems*. Brookhaven Symposia in Biology 22, 128-141.

Holzapfel, M. 1940. "Triebbedingte Ruhezustände als Ziel von Appetenzhandlungen". *Die Naturwissenschaften* 28, 273-280.

Holzapfel-Meyer, M. 1943. "Affektive Grundlagen tierischen Verhaltens". *Schweizerische Zeitschrift für Psychologie* 2, 19-42.

Hooton, E. 1946. *Man's Poor Relations*. Garden City, N.Y.: Doubleday and Company.

Hoppe, R. A., Greene, M. S. and Kenny, J. W. 1972. "Territorial Markers: Additional Findings". *The Journal of Social Psychology* 88, 305-306.

Horowitz, M. J. 1963. "A Study of Interaction Painting with Schizophrenics". *American Journal of Psychotherapy* 17, 230-239.

Horowitz, M. J. 1965. "Human Spatial Behavior". *American Journal of Psychotherapy* 19, 20-28.

Horowitz, M. J. 1968. "Spatial Behavior and Psychopathology". *The Journal of Nervous and Mental Disease* 146, 24-35.

*Horowitz, M. J., Duff, D. F. and Stratton, L. O. 1964. "Body-Buffer Zone". *Archives of General Psychiatry* 11, 651-656.

Hose, C. 1926. *Natural Man. A Record from Borneo*. London: Macmillan and Co. Limited.

Howard, E. 1948 (1920). *Territory in Bird Life*. New Edition. London: Collins.

Howard, Eb. 1946 (1902). *Garden Cities of To-morrow*. London: Faber & Faber.

Hoyt, H. and Pickard, J. P. 1969. "The World's Million-Population Metropolises". *Urban Land* 23, 2, 7-10.

Hsu, F. L. K. 1964. "Rethinking the Concept 'Primitive'". *Current Anthropology* 5, 169-178.

"Human Health and Human Settlements". 1974. *Ekistics* 37, 158-159.

Human Settlements. The Environmental Challenge. 1974. A Compendium of United Nations Papers Prepared for the Stockholm Conference on the Human Environment 1972. London-Basingstoke: Macmillan.

Hunter, E. 1956. *Brainwashing. The Story of Men who Defied it*. New York: Farrer, Straus & Cudahy.

Hurd, R. M. 1924 (1903). *Principles of City Land Values*. New York: The Record and Guide.

Hutt, C. 1966. "Exploration and Play in Children". *Symposia of the Zoological Society of London* 18, 61-81.

Hutt, C. 1973. *Males & Females*. Harmondsworth: Penguin Education.

Hutt, C. and Vaizey, M. J. 1966. "Differential Effects of Group Density on Social Behaviour". *Nature* 209, 1371-1372.

Hutt, S. J. and Hutt, C. 1970. *Direct Observation and Measurement of Behaviour*. Springfield, Ill.: Charles C. Thomas.

Hutton, G. 1972. "Assertions, Barriers and Objects: a Conceptual Scheme for the Personal Implications of Environmental Texture". *Journal for the Theory of Social Behaviour* 2, 83-98.

Huxley, J. S. 1934. "A Natural Experiment on the Territorial Instinct". *British Birds* 27, 270-277.

Huxley, J. S. 1948 (1927). *Man in the Modern World*. New York: The New American Library of World Literature, Inc.

Huxley, T. H. 1864. *Evidence as to Man's Place in Nature*. London: Williams and Norgate.

Hyde, R. W. and Chisholm, R. M. 1944. "The Relation of Mental Disorders to Race and Nationality". Studies in Medical Sociology 3. *The New England Journal of Medicine* 231, 612-618.

Hyde, R. W. and Kingsley, L. V. 1944. "The Relation of Mental Disorders to Population Density". Studies in Medical Sociology 2. *The New England Journal of Medicine* 231, 571-577.

Iersel, J. J. A. v. 1953. "An Analysis of the Parental Behaviour of the Male Three-Spined Stickleback". *Behaviour*. Supplement 3, 1-159.

Imanishi, K. 1957-1958. "Social Behavior in Japanese Monkeys, Macaca fuscata". *Psychologia* 1, 47-54.

Immenroth, W. 1933. *Kultur und Umwelt der Kleinwüchsigen in Afrika*. Studien für Völkerkunde 6. Leipzig: Druckerei der Werkgemeinschaft Leipzig C 1.

Ittelson, W. H. 1960. *Visual Space Perception*. New York: Springer Publishing Company, Inc.

Ittelson, W. H., Proshansky, H. M. and Rivlin, L. G. 1970. "The Environmental Psychology of the Psychiatric Ward". In: *Environmental Psychology: Man and his Physical Setting*. H. M. Proshansky, W. H. Ittelson and L. G. Rivlin, eds. New York-Chicago-San Francisco-etc.: Holt, Rinehart & Winston Inc. P. 419-438.

Jackson, J. B. 1969. "A New Kind of Space". *Landscape* 18: 1, 33-35.

Jackson, P. E. 1964. "Death (Legal Aspects): Burial". *Encylopaedia Britannica* 7. Chicago-London-Toronto-etc: Encyclopaedia Britannica, Inc. P. 133-134.

Jacobs, J. 1962 (1961). *The Death and Life of Great American Cities.* London: Jonathan Cape.

James, W. 1892. *Text-Book of Psychology.* London: Macmillan and Co.

Jaspers, K. 1909. *Heimweh und Verbrechen.* Leipzig: F. C. W. Vogel.

Jay, P. 1963. "The Indian Langur Monkey (Presbytis entellus)". In: *Primate Social Behavior.* C. H. Southwick, ed. Princeton, N.J.-Toronto-London-New York: D. van Nostrand Company, Inc. P. 114-123.

Jelínek, J. 1973. *Den stora boken om människans forntid.* Stockholm: Folket i Bild.

Jenkins, D. W. 1944. "Territory as a Result of Despotism and Social Organization in Geese". *The Auk* 61, 30-47.

Johnson, J. H. 1967. *Urban Geography. An Introductory Analysis.* Oxford-London-Edinburgh-etc.: Pergamon Press.

Johnson, R. P. 1973. "Scent Marking in Mammals". *Animal Behaviour* 21, 521-535.

Joiner, D. 1971. "Social Ritual and Architectural Space". *Architectural Research and Teaching* 1, 11-22.

Jolly, A. 1972. *The Evolution of Primate Behavior.* New York-London: The MacMillan Company and Collier-MacMillan Limited.

Jones, A. H. M. 1954. "The Cities of the Roman Empire". *Recueils de la Société Jean Bodin* 6, 135-176.

Jones, E. 1966. *Towns and Cities.* Opus 13. London-New York-Toronto: Oxford University Press.

Jones, F. W. 1929. *Man's Place among the Mammals.* London: Edward Arnold & Co.

Jones, G. I. 1949. "Ibo Land Tenure". *Africa* 19, 309-323.

Jones, S. E. and Aiello, J. R. 1973. "Proxemic Behavior of Black and White First-, Third-, and Fifth-Grade Children". *Journal of Personality and Social Psychology* 25, 21-27.

Jones, S. N. B. 1959. "Boundary Concepts in the Setting of Place and Time". *Annals of the Association of American Geographers* 49, 241-255.

Jonge, J. de. 1967-1968. "Applied Hodology". *Landscape* 17: 2, 10-11.

Joyant, E. 1934 (1923). *Traité d'urbanisme.* 1. Paris: Librairie de l'enseignement technique.

Junker, C. A. 1971. "Suburban Design". In: *The Growth of Cities.* D. Lewis, ed. Architects' Year Book 13. London. P. 48-63.

Juppenlatz, M. 1970. *Cities in Transformation. The Urban Squatter Problem of the Developing World.* St. Lucia: University of Queensland Press.

Kalela, O. 1954. "Über den Revierbesitz bei Vögeln und Säugetieren als populationsökologischer Faktor". *Annales Zoologici Societatis Zoologicae Botanicae Fennicae 'Vanamo'* 16: 2, 1-48.

*Kälin, K. 1972. *Populationsdichte und soziales Verhalten.* Europäische Hochschulschriften. Reihe 6: Psychologie 5. Bern-Frankfurt/M.: Herbert Land & Peter Lang.

Kant, E. 1957. "Suburbanization, Urban Sprawl and Commutation. Examples from Sweden". In: *Migration in Sweden. A Symposium.* D. Hannerberg, T. Hägerstrand and B. Odeving, eds. Lund Studies in Geography, Ser. B. Human Geography 13. P. 244-309.

Kantor, J. R. 1920. A Functional Interpretation of Human Instincts. Psychological Review 27, 50-72.

Kates, R. W. and Wohlwill, J. F. 1966. "Man's Response to the Physical Environment". *The Journal of Social Issues* 22: 4, 15-20.

Katz, D. 1953. (1937). *Animals and Men. A Psychologist looks at Human Beings and other Animals, and discusses the Processes that lie behind Behaviour.* Melbourne-London-Baltimore: Penguin Books.

Kaufmann, H. 1970. *Aggression and Altruism. A Psychological Analysis.* New York-Chicago-San Francisco-etc.: Holt, Rinehart & Winston, Inc.

Kaufmann, J. H. 1971. "Is Territoriality Definable?" In: *Behavior and Environment. The Use of Space by Animals and Men*. A. H. Esser, ed. New York-London: Plenum Press. P. 36-40.

Keiter, F. 1966. *Verhaltensbiologie des Menschen auf kulturanthropologischer Grundlage*. München-Basel: Ernst Reinhardt.

*Keith, A. 1948. *A new Theory of Human Evolution*. London: Watts & Co.

Kellett, J. M. 1973. "Evolutionary Theory for the Dichotomy of the functional Psychoses". *The Lancet* 7808, 860-863.

Kendeigh, S. C. 1961. *Animal Ecology*. Englewood Cliffs, N.J.: Prentice Hall Inc.

Kennedy, J. S. 1954. "Is Modern Ethology Objective?" *The British Journal of Animal Behaviour* 2, 12-19.

Kenyatta, K. 1959 (1938). *Facing Mount Kenya. The Tribal Life of the Gikuyu*. London: Secker Warburg.

King, M. G. 1966. "Interpersonal Relations in Preschool Children and Average Approach Distance". *The Journal of Genetic Psychology* 109, 109-116.

*Kinzel, A. F. 1970. "Body-Buffer Zone in Violent Prisoners". *The American Journal of Psychiatry* 127, 59-64.

Kira, A. 1970. "Privacy and Bathroom". In: *Environmental Psychology: Man and his Physical Setting*. H. M. Proshansky, W. H. Ittelson and L. G. Rivlin, eds. New York-Chicago-San Francisco-etc.: Holt, Rinehart & Winston. P. 269-275.

Kleemann, G. 1963. *Zeitgenosse Urmensch. Verhaltensweise, die uns angeboren sind*. Stuttgart: Franck'sche Verlagshandlung.

Klima, B. 1962. "The First Ground-Plan of an Upper Paleolithic Loess Settlement in Middle Europe and its Meaning". In: *Courses toward Urban Life. Archeological Considerations of some Cultural Alternates*. R. J. Braidwood and G. R. Willey, eds. Viking Fund Publications in Anthropology 32, 193-210.

Kline, L. W. 1898. "The Migratory Impulse vs. Love of Home". *The American Journal of Psychology* 10, 1-81.

Klopfer, P. H. 1968. "From Ardrey to Altruism: A Discourse on the Biological Basis of Human Behavior". *Behavioral Science* 13, 399-401.

Klopfer, P. H. 1969. *Habitats and Territories. A Study of the Use of Space by Animals*. New York-London: Basic Books, Inc.

Knapp, W. 1952. "Haus und Hof. Anregung zur Begründung einer Bauphilosophie zum Phänomen der Grenze". *Studium Generale* 5, 627-635.

Koffka, K. 1935. *Principles of Gestalt Psychology*. London: Routledge and Kegan Paul Ltd.

Kohl-Larsen, L. 1937. "Issansu-Märchen". *Baessler-Archiv* 20, 1-68.

Köhler, W. 1947. *Gestalt Psychology. An Introduction to New Concepts in Modern Psychology*. New York-Toronto-London: The New American Library and The New English Library Limited.

Kojima, R. 1974. "Development of the Ideas of the Great Leap Forward after the Cultural Revolution". *Ekistics* 38, 209-216.

Kolakowski, D. and Malina, R. M. 1974. "Spatial Ability, throwing Accuracy and Man's Hunting Heritage". *Nature* 251, 410-412.

Korn, A. 1953. *History builds the Town*. London: Lund Humphries.

Kramer, G. 1950. "Über individuell und anonym gebundene Gemeinschaften der Tiere und Menschen". *Studium Generale* 3, 565-572.

Kramer, S. N. 1958. "Love, Hate, and Fear. Psychological Aspects of Sumerian Culture". *Eretz-Israel* 5, 66-74.

Kristof, L. K. D. 1959. "The Nature of Frontiers and Boundaries". *Annals of the Association of American Geographers* 49, 269-282.

Kroeber, T. 1962. *Ishi in two Worlds. A Biography of the last Wild Indian in North America*. Berkeley-Los Angeles: University of California Press.

Kubzansky, P. E. and Leiderman, P. H. 1961. "Sensory Deprivation: An Overview". In: *Sensory*

Deprivation. A Symposium Held at Harvard Medical School. P. Solomon, P. E. Kubzansky, P. H. Leiderman, J. H. Mendelson, R. Trumbull and D. Wexler, eds. Cambridge, Mass.: Harvard University Press. P. 221-238.

Kuhn, M. 1968. "Researches in Human Space". *Ekistics* 25, 395-398.

*Kummer, H. 1971. "Spacing Mechanisms in Social Behavior". In: *Man and Beast: Comparative Social Behavior*. J. F. Eisenberg and W. S. Dillon, eds. Smithsonian Annual III, 220-234.

*Kurtzberg, R. L. 1973. "Territorial Identification, perceived Threat and Aggression in Young Children". *Dissertation Abstracts International* 33, 5000-B.

Lack, D. 1967 (1954). *The Natural Regulation of Animal Numbers*. Oxford: At the Clarendon Press.

Lack, D. and Lack, L. 1933-1934. "Territory reviewed". *British Birds* 27, 179-199.

Ladd, F. C. 1972. "Black Youths view their Environments: Some Views of Housing". *Journal of the American Institute of Planners* 38, 108-116.

Lander, B. 1954. *Toward an Understanding of Juvenile Delinquency. A Study of 8,464 Cases of Juvenile Delinquency in Baltimore*. New York: Columbia University Press.

Laufer, R. S., Proshansky, H. M. and Wolfe, M. 1973. "Some Analytic Dimensions of Privacy". In: *Architectural Psychology*. Proceedings of the Lund Conference. R. Küller, ed. Lund-Stroudsburg: Studentlitteratur and Dowden, Hutchinson & Ross. P. 353-372.

Laughlin, W. S. 1968. "Hunting: An Integrating Biobehavior System and its Evolutionary Importance". In: *Man the Hunter*. R. B. Lee and I. DeVore, eds. Chicago: Aldine Publishing Company. P. 304-320.

Lavedan, P. 1926. *Histoire de l'urbanisme* [1]. Antiquité – Moyen Age. Paris: Henri Laurens.

Lawick-Goodall, J. v. 1968. "A Preliminary Report on Expressive Movements and Communication in the Gombe Stream Chimpanzees". In: *Primates. Studies in Adaptation and Variability*. P. C. Jay, ed. New York-Chicago-San Francisco-etc: Holt, Rinehart & Winston. P. 313-374.

Lawrence, J. E. S. 1974. "Science and Sentiment: Overview of Research on Crowding and Human Behavior". *Psychological Bulletin* 81, 712-720.

Lawton, M. P. 1972. "Some Beginnings of an Ecological Psychology of Old Age". In: *Environment and the Social Sciences: Perspectives and Applications*. J. F. Wohlwill and D. H. Carson, eds. Washington, D.C.: American Psychological Association. P. 114-122.

Lawton, M. P. and Bader, J. 1970. "Wish for Privacy by Young and Old". *Journal of Gerontology* 25, 48-54.

Leacock, E. 1954. "The Montagnais 'Hunting Territory' and the Fur Trade." American Anthropological Association Memoir 78. *American Anthropologist* 56: 5, Part 2, 1-59.

Leakey, L. S. B., Tobias, P. V. and Napier, J. R. 1964. "A New Species of the Genus Homo from Olduvai Gorge". *Nature* 202, 7-9

Lee, E. S. 1966. "A Theory of Migration". *Demography* 3, 47-57.

Lee, T. 1968. "Urban Neighbourhood as a Socio-Spatial Schema". *Human Relations* 21, 241-267.

Lehrman, D. S. 1953. "A Critique of Konrad Lorenz's Theory of Instinctive Behavior". *The Quarterly Review of Biology* 28, 337-363.

Lehrman, D. S. 1970. "Semantic and Conceptual Issues in the Nature-Nurture Problem". In: *Development and Evolution of Behavior. Essays in Memory of T. C. Schneirla*. L. R. Aronson, E. Tobach, D. S. Lehrman and J. S. Rosenblatt, eds. San Francisco: W. H. Freeman and Company. P. 17-52.

*Leibman, M. 1970. "The Effects of Sex and Race Norms on Personal Space". *Environment and Behavior* 2, 208-246.

*Lerup, L. 1972. "Environmental and Behavioral Congruence as a Measure of Goodness in Public Space: the Case of Stockholm". *Ekistics* 34, 341-358.

Lévi-Strauss, C. 1968. "The Concept of Primitiveness'. In: *Man the Hunter*. R. B. Lee and I. DeVore, eds. Chicago: Aldine Publishing Company. P. 349-352.

Lewin, K. 1935. *A Dynamic Theory of Personality. Selected Papers*. New York-London: McGraw-Hill Book Company, Inc.

Lewin, K. 1936. *Principles of Topological Psychology*. New York-London: McGraw-Hill Book Company, Inc.

Lewin, K. 1948. *Resolving Social Conflicts*. New York: Harper & Brothers Publishers.

Lévy-Bruhl, L. 1922. *La mentalité primitive*. Paris: Librairie Félix Alcan.

Lévy-Bruhl, L. 1927. *L'âme primitive*. Paris: Librairie Félix Alcan.

*Leyhausen, P. 1973a (1954). "A Comparison between Territoriality in Animals and the Need for Space in Humans". In: Lorenz, K. and Leyhausen, P. *Motivation of Human and Animal Behaviour. An Ethological View*. New York-Cincinnati-Toronto-etc.: Van Nostrand Reinhold Company. P. 98-109.

Leyhausen, P. 1971a. "Dominance and Territoriality as Complements in Mammalian Social Structure". In: *Behavior and Environment*. A. H. Esser, ed. New York-London: Plenum Press. P. 22-33.

Leyhausen, P. 1973b. "Ecology, Behaviour, Quality of Life and the Method of Quantification". In: *Systems Approaches and Environmental Problems*. H. W. Gottinger, ed. Göttingen: Vandenhoeck & Ruprecht. P. 333-349.

Leyhausen, P. 1973c. "Ethological Aspects of Human Behaviour". In: *Atti del colloquio internazionale sul tema: L'origine dell'uomo indetto in occasione del primo centenario della publicazione dell'opera di Darwin "The Descent of Man" (Roma 28-30 ottobre 1971)*. Roma: Accademia Nazionale dei Lincei. P. 219-241.

Leyhausen. P. 1969a. "Human Nature and Modern Society". *Social Research* 36, 510-529.

*Leyhausen, P. 1973d. "Social Organization and Density Tolerance in Mammals". In: Lorenz, K. and Leyhausen, P. *Motivation of Human and Animal Behavior. An Ethological View*. New York-Cincinnati-Toronto-etc.: Van Nostrand Reinhold Company. P. 120-143.

Leyhausen, P. 1969b. "Säugetierkunde und Verhaltensforschung am Menschen". In: *Verhaltensforschung im Rahmen der Wissenschaft vom Menschen*. F. Keiter, ed. Göttingen: Musterschmidt. P. 71-89.

Leyhausen, P. 1974. "The Biological Basis of Ethics and Morality". *Science, Medicine & Man* 1, 215-235.

Leyhausen, P. 1964. "The Communal Organisation of Solitary Mammals". *Animal Behaviour* 12, 394.

Leyhausen, P. 1965a. "The Communal Organization of Solitary Mammals". *Symposium of the Zoological Society of London* 14, 249-263.

Leyhausen, P. 1965b. "The Sane Community – a Density Problem". *Discovery* 26: 9, 27-33.

Leyhausen, P. 1971b. "The Scope of Human Ecology". In: *Proceedings of the Fourth International Conference "Science and Society" on Science, Man and his Environment. Yugoslavia*. P. 243-255.

Leyhausen, P. 1968. "Von den Grenzen menschlicher Anpassungsfähigkeit". In: *Was ist das – der Mensch?* München: R Piper & Co. P. 83-92.

[Linnaeus, C.] 1956 (1758). *Caroli Linnaei Systema Naturae*. A Photographic Facsimile of the First Volume of the Tenth Edition. Regnum Animale. London: British Museum (Natural History).

L'instinct dans le comportement des animaux et de l'homme. 1956. P. P. Grassé, ed. Paris: Masson et Cie Éditeurs.

Linton, R. 1964 (1936). *The Study of Man. An Introduction*. Student's Edition. New York: Appleton-Century-Crofts.

Lipman, A. 1968. "A Socio-Architectural View of Life in Three Homes for Old People". *Gerontologia Clinica* 10, 88-101.

*Lipman, A. 1967a. "Chairs as Territory". *New Society* 20: 20 April, 564-566.

Lipman, A. 1967b. "Old People's Homes: Sitting and Neighbourhood Integration". *The Sociological Review* 15, 323-338.

*Lipman, A. 1970. "Territoriality: Useful Architectural Concept?" *Royal Institute of British Architects Journal:* February 1970, 68-70.

Loizos, C. 1967. "Play Behaviour in Higher Primates: A Review". In: *Primate Ethology*. D. Morris, ed. London: Weidenfeld and Nicolson. P. 176-218.

Loizos, C. 1966. "Play in Mammals". *Symposium of the Zoological Society of London* 18, 1-9.

Lopez, R. S. 1966 (1963). "The Crossroads within the Wall". In: *The Historian and the City*. O. Handlin and J. Burchard, eds. Cambridge, Mass.-London: The Massachusetts Institute of Technology Press. P. 27-43.

Lorenz, K. 1974. "Analogy as a Source of Knowledge". *Science* 185, 229-234.

Lorenz, K. 1965 (1963). *Das sogenannte Böse. Zur Naturgeschichte der Aggression*. 7-11th edition. Wien: Dr. G. Borothra-Schoeler.

Lorenz, K. 1935. "Der Kumpan in der Umwelt des Vogels". *Journal für Ornithologie* 83, 137-213, 289-413.

Lorenz, K. 1973 (1965). *Evolution and Modification of Behavior*. Chicago-London: The University of Chicago Press.

Lorenz, K. 1956. "Plays and Vacuum Activities". In: *L'instinct dans le comportement des animaux et de l'homme*. P. P. Grassé, ed. Paris: Masson et Cie. P. 633-645.

Lorenz, K. 1950. "The Comparative Method in Studying Innate Behaviour Patterns". In: *Physiological Mechanisms in Animal Behaviour*. Symposium of the Society for Experimental Biology 4, 221-268.

Lorenz, K. 1951. "The Role of Gestalt Perception in Animal and Human Behaviour". In: *Aspects of Form*. W. F. Whyte, ed. London: Lund Humphries. P. 157-178.

Lorenz, K. 1939. "Vergleichende Verhaltensforschung". *Zoologischer Anzeiger. Supplement* 12, 69-102.

Lorenz, K. 1953. "Über angeborene Instinktformeln beim Menschen". *Deutsche Medizinische Wochenschrift* 78, 1566-1569, 1600-1604.

Lorenz, K. 1937. "Über die Bildung des Instinktbegriffes". *Die Naturwissenschaften* 25, 289-300, 307-318, 324-331.

Loring, W. C. Jr. 1956. "Housing Characteristics and Social Disorganization". *Social Problems* 3, 160-168.

Lowenthal, D. 1961. "Geography, Experience, and Imagination: Towards a Geographical Epistemology". *Annals of the Association of American Geographers* 51, 241-260.

Lowie, R. H. 1921. *Primitive Society*. London: George Routledge & Sons, Ltd.

Lowie, R. H. 1937. *The History of Ethnological Theory*. New York: Rinehart & Company.

Lowie, R. H. 1927. *The Origin of the State*. New York: Harcourt, Brace and Company, Inc.

Lumley, H. de 1969. "A Paleolithic Camp at Nice". *Scientific American* 220: 5, 42-50.

Lumley, H. de. 1966. "Les fouilles de Terra Amata à Nice". *Bulletin du Musée d'Anthropologie Préhistorique de Monaco* 13, 29-51.

*Lyman, S. M. and Scott, M. B. 1967-1968. "Territoriality: A Neglected Sociological Dimension". *Social Problems* 15, 236-249.

Lynch, K. 1965. "The City as Environment". *Scientific American* 213: 3, 209-219.

Lynch, K. 1954. "The Form of Cities". *Scientific American* 190: 4, 55-63.

Lynch, K. and Rivkin, M. 1958-1959. "A Walk around the Block". *Landscape* 8: 3, 24-34.

*Mack, R. W. 1953-1954. "Ecological Patterns in an Industrial Shop". *Social Forces* 32, 351-356.

Mackensen, R., Papalekas, J. C., Pfeil, E., Schütte, W. and Burckhardt, L. 1959. *Daseinsformen der Grosstadt. Typische Formen sozialer Existenz in Stadtmitte, Vorstadt und Gürtel der industriellen Grosstadt*. Industrielle Grosstadt 1. Tübingen: J. B. C. Mohr (Paul Siebeck).

Mackintosh, J. H. 1973. "Factors Affecting the Recognition of Territory Boundaries by Mice (Mus musculus)". *Animal Behaviour* 21, 464-470.

Mahler, M. S. 1969. *On Human Symbiosis and the Vicissitudes of Individuation 1. Infantile Psychosis*. The International Psycho-Analytic Library 83. London: The Hogarth Press and The Institute of Psycho-Analysis.

*Maier, E. 1975. "Torah as a Movable Territory". *Annals of the Assocation of American Geographers* 65, 18-23.

Malinowski, B. 1935. *Coral Gardens and their Magic. A Study of the Methods of tilling the Soil and of Agricultural Rites in the Trobriand Islands* 1. New York-Chicago: American Book Company.

Malinowski, B. 1945. *The Dynamics of Culture Change. An Inquiry into Race Relations in Africa.* New Haven: Yale University Press.

Malmberg, T. 1972. "Biological Man in Future Urban Europe". In: *Fears and Hopes for European Urbanization. Ten Prospective Papers and Three Evaluations.* Plan Europe 2000 published under the Auspices of the European Cultural Foundation. Project 3: Urbanization – Planning Human Environment in Europe 1. The Hague: Martinus Nijhoff. P. 1-18.

Malmberg, T. 1971. "Censuses of the Rook Corvus frugilegus L. in Scania, Sweden 1955-1970". *Ornis Scandinavica* 2, 89-117.

Malzberg, B. 1940. *Social and Biological Aspects of Mental Disease.* Utica, N.Y.: State Hospitals Press.

Man and Aggression. 1970 (1968). M. F. Ashley Montagu, ed. London-Oxford-New York: Oxford University Press.

Man in Isolation and Confinement. 1973. J. E. Rasmussen, ed. Chicago: Aldine Publishing Company.

Mangin, W. 1967. "Squatter Settlements". *Scientific American* 217: 4, 21-29.

Mangoldt, R. v. 1907. *Die städtische Bodenfrage. Eine Untersuchung über Tatsachen, Ursachen und Abhilfe. Die Wohnungsfrage und das Reich.* Eine Sammlung von Abhandlungen herausgegeben vom Deutschen Verein für Wohnungsreform 8. Göttingen: Vandenhoeck & Ruprecht.

Mann, P. H. 1970 (1968). *An Approach to Urban Sociology.* London: Routledge & Kegan Paul.

Marbe, K. 1925. "Über das Heimweh". *Archiv für die gesamte Psychologie* 50, 513-527.

Marcus, M. G. and Detwyler, T. R. 1972. "Urbanization and Environment in Perspective". In: Detwyler, T. R. and Marcus, M. G. *Urbanization and Environment. The Physical Geography of the City.* Belmont, Cal.: P. 3-25.

Margalef, R. 1968. *Perspectives in Ecological Theory.* Chicago-London: The University of Chicago Press.

Marler, P. 1976a. "On Animal Aggression. The Roles of Strangeness and Familiarity". *American Psychologist* 31, 239-246.

Marler, P. 1976b. "Social Organization, Communication and Graded Signals: the Chimpanzee and the Gorilla". In: *Growing Points in Ethology.* P. P. G. Bateson and R. A. Hinde, eds. Cambridge: Cambridge University Press. P. 239-280.

Marler, P. 1972. "Vocalizations of East African Monkeys 2. Black and White Colobus". *Behaviour* 42, 179-180.

Marmor, J. 1972. "Mental Health and Overpopulation". In: *Population Crisis. An Interdisciplinary Perspective.* S. T. Reid and D. L. Lyon, eds. Glenview, Ill.-London: Scott, Foresman and Company. P. 130-133.

Marmor, J. 1942. "The Role of Instinct in Human Behavior". *Psychiatry* 5, 509-516.

Martin, R. D. 1970. "Social Stress'. *New Society*: 17 December 1970, 1086-1088.

*Martin, R. J. 1969. "The Ecology of a Squatter Settlement". *Architectural Review* 145, 213-214.

Maslow, A. H. 1953-1954. "The Instinctoid Nature of Basic Needs". *Journal of Personality* 22, 326-347.

Mason, W. A. 1968. "Use of Space by Callicebus Groups". In: *Primates. Studies in Adaptation and Variability.* P. C. Jay, ed. New York-Chicago-San Francisco-etc.: Holt, Rinehart & Winston. P. 200-216.

Masotti, L. H. 1973. "Prologue: Suburbia Reconsidered – Myth and Counter-Myth". In: *The Urbanization of the Suburbs.* L. H. Masotti and J. K. Hadden, eds. Urban Affairs Annual Reviews 7, 15-22.

Masserman, J. H. 1946. *Behavior and Neurosis.* Chicago: The University of Chicago Press.

Masserman, J. H. 1973. "The Biodynamics of Concordance and Violence in Human Behavior". In: *Psychiatry. Proceedings of the V. World Congress of Psychiatry, Mexico, D.F. 25 Nov.-4 Dec. 1971.* Part 1. Amsterdam: Excerpta Medica. P. 131-137.

Massignon, L. 1958. "La cité des morts au Caire (Qarâfa-darb al-Ahmar)". *Bulletin de l'Institut Français d'Archéologie Orientale* 57, 25-79.

Maunier, R. 1927. "Zur Soziologie der Kabylen". *Jahrbuch für Soziologie* 3, 315-336.

Maurer, D. W. 1955. "Whiz mob. A Correlation of the Technical Argot of Pick-pocket with their Behavior Pattern". *Publications of the American Dialect Society* 24, 1-19

Maurer, G. L. v. 1854. *Einleitung zur Geschichte der Mark-, Hof-, Dorf- und Stadt- Verfassung und der öffentlichen Gewalt.* München: Christian Kaiser.

Maurer, K. 1852. *Beiträge zur Rechtsgeschichte des Germanischen Nordens. 1: Die Entstehung des Isländischen Staats und seiner Verfassung.* München: Christian Kaiser.

Mayr, E. 1935. "Bernard Altum and the Territory Theory". *Proceedings of the Linnean Society of New York* 1933-1934, 24-38.

McBride, G. 1964. "A General Theory of Social Organization and Behaviour". *University of Queensland Papers, Faculty of Veterinary Science* 1, 71-110.

McBride, G. 1971. "Theories of Animal Spacing: the Role of Flight, Fight and Social Distance". In: *Behavior and Environment. The Use of Space by Animals and Men.* A. H. Esser, ed. New York-London: Plenum Press. P. 53-68.

McCann, W. H. 1941. "Nostalgia: A Review of the Literature". *Psychological Bulletin* 38, 165-182.

McHarg, I. 1966. "The Ecology of the City. A Plea for Environmental Consciousness of the City's Physiological and Psychological Impacts". In: *The Architect and the City.* M. Whiffen, ed. Cambridge, Mass.-London: Massachusetts Institute of Technology. P. 53-65.

McKenzie, R. D. 1968. *On Human Ecology. Selected Writings.* Introduction by A. H. Hawley, ed. Chicago-London: University of Chicago Press.

Mead, M. 1972. "Neighbourhoods and Human Needs". In: *Human Identity in the Urban Environment.* G. Bell and J. Tyrwhitt, eds. Harmondsworth: Penguin Books. P. 245-251.

Mead, M. 1964-1965. "Special University Lectures in Architecture and Town Planning 1965". *Transactions of the Bartlett Society* 3, 8-41.

Medawar, P. B. 1976. "Does Ethology throw any Light on Human Behaviour?" In: *Growing Points in Ethology.* P. P. G. Bateson and R. A. Hinde, eds. Cambridge: Cambridge University Press. P. 497-506.

Meerlo, A. M. 1946. *Aftermath of Peace. Psychological Essays.* New York: International Universities Press.

Mehrabian, A. 1976. *Public Places and Private Spaces. The Psychology of Work, Play, and Living Environments.* New York: Basic Books Inc.

Meier, R. L. 1966. "Some Thoughts on Conflict and Violence in the Urban Setting". *American Behavioral Scientist* 10, 11-12.

Melville, H. 1925. *White-Jacket or, The World in a Man-of-war.* London: Jonathan Cape.

Mercer, D. C. 1970. "Urban Recreational Hinterland. A Review and Example". *The Professional Geographer* 22, 74-78.

*Meyer-Holzapfel, M. 1952. *Die Bedeutung des Besitzes bei Tier und Mensch. Ein psychologischer Vergleich.* Biel: Institut für Psycho-Hygiene.

Meyer-Holzapfel, M. 1964. "Tierpsychologie, Verhaltensforschung und Psychiatrie". *Bibliotheca Psychiatrica et Neurologica* 122, 253-294.

Meyer-Holzapfel, M. 1956. "Über die Bereitschaft zu Spiel- und Instinkthandlungen". *Zeitschrift für Tierpsychologie* 13, 442-462.

Meyerson, M. 1963. "Character and Urban Development". *Public Policy* 12.

Michelson, W. H. 1970. *Man and his Urban Environment: A Sociological Approach.* Menlo Park-London-Don Mills: Addison & Wesley Publishing Company.

Mikesell, M. P. 1967. "Geographic Perspectives in Anthropology". *Annals of the Association of American Geographers* 57, 617-634.

Milgram, S. 1970. "The Experience of Living in Cities". *Science* 67, 1461-1468.

*Miller, E. J. 1954. "Caste and Territory in Malabar". *American Anthropologist* 56, 410-420.

Miller, J. G. 1965. "Living Systems: Structure and Process". *Behavioral Science* 10, 337-379.
Miller, J. G. 1961. "Sensory Overloading". In: *Psychophysiological Aspects of Space Flight*. B. E. Flaherty, ed. New York: Columbia University Press. P. 215-224.
Mobility and Mental Health. 1965. M. B. Kantor, ed. Proceedings of the Fifth Annual Conference on Community Mental Health Research, Social Science Institute, Washington University 1963. Springfield, Ill.: Charles C. Thomas.
Moffat, C. B. 1903. "The Spring Rivalry of Birds. Some Views on the Limit to Multiplication". *The Irish Naturalist* 12, 152-166.
Money, J. 1965. "Psychosexual Differentiation". In: *Sex Research. New Developments*. J. Money, ed. New York-Chicago-San Francisco-etc.: Holt, Rinehart & Winston. P. 3-23.
Montague, L. 1964. "Football: Early History". In: *Encyclopaedia Britannica* 9. Chicago-London-Toronto-etc.: Encyclopaedia Britannica, Inc. P. 566-567.
Morgan, C. L. 1895. "Some Definitions of Instinct". *Natural Science* 6, 321-329.
Morgan, C. L., Baldwin, J. M., Gross, K. and Stout, G. F. 1901-1905. "Instinct". In: *Dictionary of Philosophy and Psychology*. New York-London: Macmillan & Co.
Morgan, G. 1971. "Discussion of Session III: Population Density and Crowding". In: *Behavior and Environment. The Use of Space by Animals and Men*. A. H. Esser, ed. New York-London: Plenum Press. P. 212-214, 216.
Morgan, L. H. 1878. *Ancient Society or Researches in the Lines of Human Progress from Savagery through Barbarism to Civilization*. New York: Holt & Co.
Morrill, R. L. 1965. *Migration and the Spread and Growth of Urban Settlement*. Lund Studies in Geography, Ser. B. Human Geography 26, 1-208.
Morris, D. 1969. *The Human Zoo*. London: Jonathan Cape.
Morris, R. N. 1971 (1968). *Urban Sociology*. Studies in Sociology 2. London: George Allen and Unwin Ltd.
Mühlmann, W. E. 1952. "Das Problem der Umwelt beim Menschen". *Zeitschrift für Morphologie und Anthropologie* 44, 153-181.
Müller, F. 1882. *Unter Tungusen und Jakuten. Erlebnisse und Ergebnisse der Olenék-Expedition der Kaiserlichen Russischen Geographischen Gesellschaft in St. Petersburg*. Leipzig: F. A. Brockhaus.
Mumford, L. 1963. "On the Origin of Cities". *Landscape* 12: 3, 14-16.
Mumford, L. 1961. *The City in History. Its Origins, its Transformations, and its Prospects*. London: Secker & Warburg.
Mumford, L. 1938. *The Culture of Cities*. New York: Harcourt, Brace and Company.
Mumford, L. 1946. "The Garden City Idea and Modern Planning". In: Howard, Eb. *Garden Cities of To-morrow*. London: Faber & Faber Ltd. P. 29-40.
Mumford, L. 1956. "The Natural History of Urbanization", In: *Man's Role in Changing the Face of the Earth*. W. L. Thomas, ed. Chicago, Ill.: The University of Chicago Press. P. 382-398.
Mumford, L. 1954. "The Neighbourhood and the Neighbourhood Unit". *Town Planning Review* 24, 256-270.
Mumford, L. 1960-1961. "The Social Function of Open Spaces". *Landscape* 10: 2, 1-6.
Munn, N. L. 1965 (1955). *The Evolution and Growth of Human Behavior*. London-Wellington-Bombay-Sydney: George G. Harrap & Co. Ltd.
Munroe, R. L. and Munroe, R. H. 1971. "Effect of Environmental Experience on Spatial Ability in an East African Society". *The Journal of Psychology* 83, 15-22.
Murphey, R. 1969. "Urbanization in Asia". In: *The City in Newly Developing Countries. Readings on Urbanism and Urbanization*. G. Breese, ed. Englewood Cliffs, N. J.: Prentice-Hall, Inc. P. 58-75.
Murphy, R. F. 1964. "Social Distance and the Veil". *American Anthropologist* 66, 1257-1274.
Murray, H. J. R. 1952. *A History of Board-Games other than Chess*. Oxford: At the Clarendon Press.

Murray, H. J. R. 1913. *A History of Chess*. Oxford: At the Clarendon Press.

Nagashima, C. 1974. "Some Definitions of Megalopolis in Japan". *Ekistics* 38, 163-169.
Nauta, D. 1972. *The Meaning of Information*. Approaches to Semiotics 20. The Hague-Paris: Mouton.
Nerlove, S. B., Munroe, R. H. and Munroe, R. L. 1971. "Effect of Environmental Experience on Spatial Ability: A Replication". *The Journal of Social Psychology* 84, 3-10.
*Newman, O. 1973. *Defensible Space. Crime Prevention through Urban Design*. New York: Collier Books.
Nice, M. M. 1941. "The Role of Territory in Bird Life". *The American Midland Naturalist* 26, 441-487.
Nice, M. M. 1933. "The Theory of Territorialism and its Development". In: *Fifty Years' Progress of American Ornithology 1883-1933*. Published by the American Ornithologists' Union on the Occasion of its Semi-centennial Anniversary, New York, N.Y., November 13-16, 1933. Revised edition. Lancaster, Pa: American Ornithologists' Union. P. 89-100.
Nicolai, G. F. 1917. *Die Biologie des Krieges. Betrachtungen eines Deutschen Naturforschers*. Zürich: Art. Institut Orell Füssli.
Nind, S. 1831. "Description of the Natives of King George's Sound (Swan River Colony) and adjoining Country". *The Journal of the Royal Geographical Society of London* 1, 2nd edition. 21-51.
Nippold, W. 1954. *Die Anfänge des Eigentums bei den Naturvölkern und die Entstehung des Privateigentums*. 's-Gravenhage: Mouton & Co.
Nitsche, P. and Wilmanns, K. 1970 (1912). *The History of the Prison Psychoses*. Nervous and Mental Disease Monograph Series 13. New York: Johnson Reprint Corporation.

Oakley, K. P. 1962. "A Definition of Man". In: *Culture and the Evolution of Man*. M. F. Ashley Montagu, ed. New York: Oxford University Press. P. 3-12.
O'Connor, N. 1971. "Children in Restricted Environments". *Psychiatria, Neurologia, Neurochirurgia* 74, 71-77.
Ödegaard, Ö. 1932. *Emigration and Insanity. A Study of Mental Disease among the Norwegianborn Population of Minnesota*. Acta Psychiatrica et Neurologica Supplementum IV, 1-206.
Odum, E. P. 1971 (1953). *Fundamentals of Ecology*. 3rd edition. Philadelphia-London-Toronto: W.B. Saunders Company.
Oeter, D. 1974. "Wohnen und Gesundheit". *Der Siedler-Berater* 21: 2, 1-14.
Offer, D. and Sabshin, M. 1966. *Normality. Theoretical and Clinical Concepts of Mental Health*. New York-London: Basic Books Inc.
Ogburn, W. F. and Duncan, O. D. 1964. "City Size as a Sociological Variable". In: *Contributions to Urban Sociology*. E. W. Burgess and D. J. Bogue, eds. Chicago-London: The University of Chicago Press. P. 129-147.
Olin, U. 1971. "Discussion of Session III: Population Density and Crowding". In: *Behavior and Environment. The Use of Space by Animals and Men*. A. H. Esser, ed. New York-London: Plenum Press. P. 209-211.
Oliver, J. H. 1953. "The Ruling Power. A Study of the Roman Empire in the Second Century after Christ through the Roman Oration of Aelius Aristides". *Transactions of the American Philosophical Society* 43, 871-1003.
Olton, D. S. 1977. "Spatial Memory". *Scientific American* 236: 6, 82-98.
O'Neill, S. M. and Paluck, R. J. 1973. "Altering Territoriality through Reinforcement." *Proceedings of the 81st Annual Convention of the American Psychological Association 8*. Montreal. American Psychological Association. P. 895-896.
Opie, I. and Opie, P. 1969. *Children's Games in Street and Playground*. Oxford: At the Clarendon Press.

Oppenheimer, R. 1956. "Analogy in Science". *The American Psychologist* 11, 127-135.

Orlans, H. *Utopia Ltd. The Story of the English New Town of Stevenage.* New Haven: Yale University Press.

Osmond, H. 1961 (1959). "The Relationship between Architect and Psychiatrist". In: *Psychiatric Architecture. A Review of Contemporary Developments in the Architecture of Mental Hospitals, Schools for the Mentally Retarded and Related Facilities.* C. E. Goshen, ed. Washington: American Psychiatric Association. P. 1-15.

Owen, D. F. 1976. "Human Inequality: An Ecologist's Point of View". *Oikos* 27, 2-8.

*Paluck, R. J. and Esser, A. H. 1971a. "Controlled Experimental Modification of Aggressive Behavior in Territorities of Severely Retarded Boys". *American Journal of Mental Deficiency* 76, 23-29.

*Paluck, R. J. and Esser, A. H. 1971b. "Territorial Behavior as an Indicator of Changes in Clinical Behavioral Conditions of Severely Retarded Boys". *American Journal of Mental Deficiency* 76, 284-290.

Park, R. E. 1952. *Human Communities: the City and Human Ecology.* Glencoe, Ill.: Free Press.

Park, R. E. 1927-1928. "Human Migration and the Marginal Man". *The American Journal of Sociology* 33, 881-893.

Park, R. E. and Burgess, E. W. 1929 (1924). *Introduction to the Science of Sociology.* 2nd edition. Chicago: The University of Chicago Press.

Parr, A. E. 1964-1965. "Environmental Design and Psychology". *Landscape* 14: 2, 15-18.

*Parr, A. E. 1965. "In Search of Theory VI". *Art and Architecture* 82, 14-15, 32.

Parr, A. E. 1967. "The Child in the City: Urbanity and the Urban Scene". *Landscape* 16: 3, 3-5.

Pastalan, L. A. 1970. "Privacy as an Expression of Human Territoriality". In: *Spatial Behavior of Older People.* L. A. Pastalan and D. H. Carson, eds. Ann Arbor: The University of Michigan. P. 88-101.

Paulsson, G. 1973 (1953). *Svensk stad 2. Från bruksby till trädgårdsstad.* Lund: Studentlitteratur.

Payne, G. K. 1974. "Functions of Informality: Squatter Settlements in Dehli". *Ekistics* 38, 63-66.

Pearl, R. 1939. *The Natural History of Population.* London: Humphrey Milford.

Peiper, A. 1961 (1949). *Die Eigenart der kindlichen Hirntätigkeit. 3* augmented and revised edition. Leipzig: VEB George Thieme.

Peters, D. S. 1962. "Gedanken zum Revierproblem". *Ornithologische Mitteilungen* 14, 161-171.

Peters, H. [1954] *Biologie einer Gross-Stadt.* I. Heidelberg: Dr. Johannes Hörning.

*Peterson, N. 1975. "Hunter-Gatherer Territoriality: The Perspective from Australia". *American Anthropologist* 77, 53-68.

Petter, J. J. 1970. " 'Domaine vital' et 'territoire' chez les lémuriens malgaches". In: *Territoire et domaine vital.* G. Richard, ed. Paris: Masson et Cie P. 107-114.

Pettersson, M. 1960. "Increase of Settlement Size and Population since the Inception of Agriculture". *Nature* 186, 870-872.

Pfeil, E. 1948. *Der Flüchtling. Gestalt einer Zeitenwende.* Hamburg: Hans von Hugo.

Pfister-Ammende, M. 1950. "Das Problem der Entwurzelung". *Schweizerische Medizinische Wochenschrift* 80, 151-158.

Pfister-Ammende, M. 1949. "Psychologische Erfahrungen mit sowjetrussischen Flüchtlingen". In: *Die Psychohygiene. Grundlagen und Ziele.* M. Pfister-Ammende, ed. Bern: Hans Huber. P. 231-264.

Piaget, J. and Inhelder, B. 1956 (1948). *The Child's Conception of Space.* London: Routledge & Kegan Paul.

Pickford, R. W. 1940-1941. "Aspects of the Psychology of Games and Sports." *The British Journal of Psychology. General Section* 31, 279-293.

Pilleri, G. 1971. "Instinktbewegungen des Menschen in biologischer und neuropathologischer Sicht". In: *Beiträge zur Verhaltensforschung.* R. Bilz and N. Petrilowitsch, eds. Aktuelle Fragen der Psychiatrie und Neurologie 11, 1-37.

Pitelka, F. A. 1959. "Numbers, Breeding Schedule, and Territoriality in Pectoral Sandpipers of Northern Alaska". *The Condor* 61, 233-264.

Plant, J. S. 1939 (1937). *Personality and the Cultural Patterns.* New York: The Commonwealth Fund.

Ploog, D. 1958. "Endogene Psychosen und Instinktverhalten". *Fortschritte der Neurologie, Psychiatrie und ihrer Grenzgebiete* 26, 83-98.

Ploog, D. 1973. "Social Communication in Squirrel monkeys: Analysis by Electrical Stimulation of Limbic Structures". In: *Psychiatry. Proceedings of the V. World Congress of Psychiatry, Mexico D.F. 25 November-4 December 1971.* Part 2. Amsterdam: Excerpta Medica. P. 1430-1437.

Ploog, D. 1964. "Verhaltensforschung und Psychiatrie". In: *Psychiatrie der Gegenwart. Forschung und Praxis.* H. W. Gruhle, R. Jung, W. Mayer-Gross and M. Müller, eds. I/1B. Berlin-Göttingen-Heidelberg: Springer. P. 291-443.

Pöhlmann, R. 1884. *Die Übervölkerung der antiken Grosstädte im Zusammenhange mit der Gesammtentwicklung städtischer Civilisation.* Preisschriften gekrönt und herausgegeben von der Fürstlich Jablonowski'schen Gesellschaft zu Leipzig 24. Leipzig: Bei S. Hirzel.

*Pontius, A. A. 1967. "Neuro-Psychiatric Hypothesis about Territorial Behavior". *Perceptual and Motor Skills* 24, 1232-1234.

Poole, W. C. Jr. 1926-1927. "Social Distance and Personal Distance". *Journal of Applied Sociology* 11, 114-120.

Porteous, J. D. 1971. "Design with People. The Quality of the Urban Environment". *Environment and Behavior* 3, 155-178.

Poulton, E. C. 1970. *Environment and Human Efficiency.* Springfield, Ill.: Charles C. Thomas.

Pounds, N. J. G. 1969. "The Urbanization of the Classical World". *Annals of the Association of American Geographers* 59, 135-157.

Potash, L. 1967. " 'On Aggression' in the Context of a Comparative Psychology". *The Cornell Journal of Social Relations* 2, 85-100.

Primates, Studies in Adaptation and Variability. 1968. P. C. Jay, ed. New York-Chicago-San Francisco-etc.: Holt, Rinehart & Winston.

Proceedings of the IGU Symposium in Urban Geography, Lund 1960. 1962. Lund Studies in Geography. Ser. B. Human Geography 24, 1-602.

Proshansky, H. M., Ittelson, W. H. and Rivlin, L. G. 1970a. "Freedom of Choice and Behavior in a Physical Setting." In: *Environmental Psychology: Man and his Physical Setting.* H. M. Proshansky, W. H. Ittelson and L. G. Rivlin, eds. New York-Chicago-San Francisco-etc.: Holt, Rinehart & Winston Inc. P. 173-183.

Proshansky, H. M., Ittelson, W. H. and Rivlin, L. G. 1970b. "The Influence of the Physical Environment on Behavior: Some Basic Assumptions." In: *Environmental Psychology: Man and his Physical Setting.* H. M. Proshansky, W. H. Ittelson and L. G. Rivlin, eds. New York-Chicago-San Francisco-etc.: Holt, Rinehart & Winston Inc. P. 27-37.

Prosser, C. L. 1969. "Principles and General Concepts of Adaptation". *Environmental Research* 2, 404-416.

Puckle, B. S. 1926. *Funeral Customs. Their Origin and Development.* London: T. Werner Laurie Ltd.

Racamier, P. C. 1957. "Introduction à une sociopathologie des schizophrènes hospitalisés". *L'Evolution Psychiatrique* 1957, 47-94.

Rachfahl, F. 1900. "Zur Geschichte des Grundeigentums". *Jahrbücher für Nationalökonomie und Statistik* 74, 1-33, 161-216.

Ragatz, R. L. 1970. "Vacation Housing: A missing Component in Urban and Regional Theory". *Land Economics* 46, 118-126.

Raglan, F. R. S. 1964. *The Temple and the House.* London: Routledge & Kegan Paul.

Rajecki, D. W. 1973. "Imprinting in Precocial Birds: Interpretation, Evidence, and Evaluation". *Psychological Bulletin* 79, 48-58.

Rapoport, A. 1969. *House Form and Culture.* Englewood Cliffs, N.J.: Prentice-Hall, Inc.

Rapoport, A. 1968. "Sacred Space in Primitive and Vernacular Architecture". *Liturgical Arts* 36: 2, 36-40.

Ratzel, F. 1912. *Anthropogeograqhie 2. Die geographische Verbreitung des Menschen.* Stuttgart: J. Engelhorns Nachf.

Reckless, W. C. 1964. *Die Kriminalität in den USA und ihre Behandlung.* Münsterische Beiträge zur Rechts- und Staatswissenschaft. 8. Rechts- und Staatswisenschaftliche Fakultät der Westfälischen Wilhelms-Universität in Münster, eds. Berlin: Walter de Gruyter & Co.

Redl, F. 1959. "The Impact of Game Ingredients on Children's Play Behavior". In: *Group Processes. Transactions of the Fourth Conference, October 13, 14, 15 and 16, 1957, Princeton, N.J.* B. Schaffner, ed. New York: Josiah Macy Jr. Foundation. P. 33-81.

Reichenbach, H. 1958 (1928). *The Philosophy of Space and Time.* New York: Dover Publications, Inc.

Reiss, A. J. Jr. 1957a. "The Spatial and Temporal Patterns of Cities". In: *Cities and Society. The Revised Reader in Urban Sociology.* P. K. Hatt and A. J. Reiss Jr., eds. 2nd edition. Glencoe, Ill.: The Free Press. P. 223-226.

Reiss, A. J. Jr. 1957b. "The Nature and Extent of Urbanization and Population Redistribution". In: *Cities and Society. The Revised Reader in Urban Sociology.* P. K. Hatt and A. J. Reiss Jr., eds. 2nd edition. Glencoe, Ill.: The Free Press. P. 79-82.

Revised Cologne Recommendations. 1971. Cahiers familles dans le monde. Luxembourg: Commission du logement familial de l'U.I.O.F.

Reynolds, V. 1966. "Open Groups in Hominid Evolution". *Man* 1, 441-452.

Rheingold, H. L. and Eckerman, C. O. 1971. "Departures from the Mother". In: *The Origins of Human Social Relations.* H. R. Schaffer, ed. London-New York: Academic Press. P. 73-82.

Richard, P.-B. 1970. "Le comportement territorial chez les vertébrés". In: *Territoire et domaine vital.* G. Richard, ed. Paris: Masson et Cie P. 2-19.

Riesen, A. H. 1958. "Plasticity of Behavior: Psychological Aspects". In: *Biological and Biochemical Bases of Behavior.* H. F. Harlow and C. N. Woolsey, eds. Madison: The University of Wisconsin Press. P. 425-450.

Ripley, S. 1967. "Intertroop Encounters among Ceylon Gray Langurs (Presbytis entellus)". In: *Social Communication among Primates.* S. A. Altmann, ed. Chicago-London: The University of Chicago Press. P. 237-253.

Rivers, W. H. R. 1922 (1920). *Instinct and the Unconscious. A Contribution to a Biological Theory of the Psycho-Neuroses.* 2nd edition. Cambridge: At the University Press.

Roe, A. and Simpson, G. G. 1961 (1958). "Evolution and Human Behavior". In: *Behavior and Evolution.* A. Roe and G. G. Simpson, eds. New Haven: Yale University Press. P. 417-419.

Rodman, P. S. 1973. "Population Composition and Adaptive Organisation among Orang-utans of the Kutai Reserve". In: *Comparative Ecology and Behavior of Primates. Proceedings of a Conference held at the Zoological Society, London November 1971.* R. P. Michael and J. H. Crook, eds. London-New York: Academic Press. P. 171-209.

Rohracher, H. 1960 (1946). *Einführung in die Psychologie,* 7th revised edition. Wien-Innsbruck: Urban & Schwarzenberg.

*Roos, P. D. 1968. "Jurisdiction: An Ecological Concept". *Human Relations* 21, 75-84.

Rose, H. M. 1970. "The Development of an Urban Subsystem: The Case of the Negro Ghetto". *Annals of the Association of American Geographers* 60, 1-17.

Rosenberg, G. 1960. "High Population Densities in Relation to Social Behaviour". *Ekistics* 25, 425-427.

*Rosenblatt, P. C. and Budd, L. G. 1975. "Territoriality and Privacy in Married and Unmarried Cohabiting Couples". *The Journal of Social Psychology* 97, 67-76.

Rosenthal, A. J. and Ilfeld, F. W. "Summary of Recommendations". In: *Violence and the Struggle for Existence.* Work of the Committee on Violence of the Department of Psychiatry,

Stanford University School of Medicine. D. N. Daniels, M. F. Gilula and F. M. Ochberg, eds. Boston: Little, Brown and Company. P. 391-403.

Roth, C. 1953 (1946). *A Short History of the Jewish People*. Revised and enlarged illustrated edition. London: East and West Library.

*Roth, L. H. 1971. "Territoriality and Homosexuality in Male Prison Population". *American Journal of Orthopsychiatry* 41, 510-513.

Rowan, J. C. 1965. "The Major Space". *Progressive Architecture* 46, 140-145.

Russell, C. and Russell, W. M. S. 1961. *Human Behaviour. A New Approach*. London: Andre Deutsch.

Russell, C. and Russell, W. M. S. 1968. *Violence, Monkeys and Man*. London-Melbourne-Toronto: Macmillan.

Rüstow, A. 1963. "Garten und Familie". In: *Sozialwissenschaft und Gesellschaftsgestaltung. Festschrift für Gerhard Weisser*. F. Karrenberg and H. Albert, eds. Berlin: Dunker & Humblot. P. 285-303.

Sahlins, M. D. 1959. "The Social Life of Monkeys, Apes and Primitive Man". In: *The Evolution of Man's Capacity for Culture*. J. N. Spuhler, ed. Detroit: Wayne State University Press. P. 54-73.

Sahlins, M. D. 1968. *Tribesmen*. Englewood Cliffs, N.J.: Prentice Hall, Inc.

Salzen, E. A. 1970. "Imprinting and Environmental Learning". In: *Development and Evolution of Behavior. Essays in Memory of T. C. Schneirla*. L. R. Aronson, E. Tobach, E. L. Lehrman and J. S. Rosenblatt, eds. San Francisco: W. H. Freeman and Company. P. 158-178.

Sandler, J. 1960. "The Background of Safety". *The International Journal of Psycho-Analysis* 41, 352-356.

Sarasin, P. and Sarasin, F. 1893. *Ergebnisse naturwissenschaftlicher Forschung auf Ceylon in den Jahren 1884-1886* III: 4-6. Wiesbaden: C. W. Kreidel's.

Sarvis, M. A. 1960. "Psychiatric Implication of Temporal Lobe Damage". *The Psychoanalytic Study of the Child* 15, 454-481.

Schachermeyer, F. 1952-1953. "The Genesis of the Greek Polis". *Diogenes* 1: 4, 17-30.

Schäfer, B. 1968. *Bodenbesitz und Bodennutzung in der Grosstadt. Eine empirisch-soziologische Untersuchung am Beispiel Münster*. Beiträge zur Raumplanung 4. Zentral-institut für Raumplanung der Universität Münster, eds. Bielefeld: Bertelsmann Universitätsverlag.

Schafer, E. H. 1963. "Cosmos in Miniature. The Tradition of the Chinese Garden". *Landscape* 12: 3, 24-26.

Schaller, G. B. 1972. "The Behavior of the Mountain Gorilla". In: *Primate Patterns*. P. Dohlinow, ed. New York-Chicago-San Francisco-etc.: Holt, Rinehart & Winston. P. 85-124.

Schaller, G. B. 1963. *The Mountain Gorilla. Ecology and Behavior*. Chicago, Ill.: The University of Chicago Press.

Schapera, I. 1956. *Government and Politics in Tribal Societies*. London: Watts.

*Scheflen, A. E. and Ashcraft, N. 1976. *Human Territories. How we behave in space-time*. Englewood-Cliffs, N.J.: Prentice-Hall, Inc.

Schein, E. H. 1961. *Coercive Persuasion. A Socio-psychological Analysis of the "Brainwashing" of American Civilian Prisoners by the Chinese Communists*. New York: W. W. Norton & Company, Inc.

Schein, E. H. 1956. "The Chinese Indoctrination Program for Prisoners of War. A Study of Attempted 'Brainwashing'" *Psychiatry* 19, 149-172.

Scheller, H. 1957. "Das Problem des Raumes in der Psychopathologie". *Studium Generale* 10, 563-574.

Schlatter, R. 1951. *Private Property. The History of an Idea*. London: George Allen & Unwin.

Schmidt, W. 1937, 1940. *Das Eigentum auf den ältesten Stufen der Menschheit. 1. Das Eigentum in den Urkulturen. 2. Das Eigentum im Primärkulturkreis der Herdenviehzüchter Asiens*. Münster in Westfalen: Aschendorfsche Verlagsbuchhandlung.

296

Schmidt, W. 1952. "Die Urkulturen: Ältere Jagd- und Sammelstufe". In: *Ein Handbuch der Weltgeschichte in Zehn Bänden I. Frühe Menschheit*. Bern: Francke Verlag. P. 375-501.

Schmitt, C. 1950. *Der Nomos der Erde im Völkerrecht des Jus Publicum Europaeum*. Köln: Greven.

Schmitt, R. C. 1966. "Density, Health, and Social Disorganization". *Journal of the American Institute of Planners* 32, 38-40.

Schmitt, R. C. 1963. "Implications of Density in Hong Kong". *Journal of the American Institute of Planners* 29, 210-217.

Schnore, L. F. 1957-1958. "Satellites and Suburbs". *Social Forces* 36, 121-127.

Schoener, T. W. 1968. "Sizes of Feeding Territories among Birds". *Ecology* 49, 123-141.

Schorr, A. L. 1963. *Slums and Social Insecurity. An Appraisal of the Effectiveness of Housing Policies in helping to eliminate Poverty in the United States*. U.S. Department of Health, Education and Welfare. Social Security Administration, Division of Research and Statistics, Research Report 1. Washington: U.S. Government Printing Office.

Schulman, S. 1967. "Latin American Shantytown". In: *Taming Megalopolis 2. How to Manage an Urbanized World*. H. Wentworth Eldredge, ed. Garden City, N.Y.: Doubleday & Company, Inc. P. 1004-1011.

Schultz, A. H. 1969. *The Life of Primates*. London: Weidenfeld and Nicholson.

Schurtz, H. 1900. "Die Anfänge des Landbesitzes". *Zeitschrift für Socialwissenschaft* 3, 245-255, 352-361.

Schwab, G. 1925. "Über Heimweh beim Kleinkind". *Jahrbuch für Kinderheilkunde* 108, 15-39.

Schwabedissen, H. 1962. "Northern Continental Europe". In: *Courses toward Urban Life. Archeological Considerations of some Cultural Alternates*. R. J. Braidwood and G. R. Willey, eds. Viking Fund Publications in Anthropology 32, 254-266.

Schwartz, B. 1967-1968. "The Social Psychology of Privacy". *The American Journal of Sociology* 73, 741-752.

Schwidetzky, I. 1959. *Das Menschenbild der Biologie. Ergebnisse und Probleme der naturwissenschaftlichen Anthropologie*. Stuttgart: Gustav Fischer.

Scott, J. P. 1958. *Aggression*. Chicago: The University of Chicago Press.

Scott, J. P. 1962. "Hostility and Aggression in Animals". In: *Roots of Behavior. Genetics, Instinct, and Socialization in Animal Behavior*. E. L. Bliss, ed. New York: Harper and Brothers Publishers. P. 167-178.

Scott, J. P. 1969 (1954). "The Social Psychology of Infrahuman Animals". In: *The Handbook of Social Psychology*. G. Lindzey and E. Aronson, eds. 4. Group Psychology and Phenomena of Interaction. Reading-Menlo Park-London-Don Mills: Addison-Wesley Publishing Company. P. 611-642.

Sears, P. B. 1969 (1958). "The Inexorable Problem of Space". In: *The Subversive Science. Essays toward an Ecology of Man*. P. Shepard and D. McKinley, eds. Boston: Houghton Mifflin Company. P. 77-92.

Seeley, I. H. 1973. *Outdoor Recreation and the Urban Environment*. London-Basingstoke: Macmillan.

Seiss, R. 1969. *Verhaltensforschung und Konfliktgeschehen. Eine biologisch-psychologische Studie*. Basel: Ernst Reinhardt.

Sells, S. B. 1970. "On the Nature of Stress". In: *Social and Psychological Factors in Stress*. J. E. McGrath, ed. New York: Holt, Rinehart and Winston. P. 134-176.

Senden, M. V. 1932. *Raum- und Gestaltauffassung von operierten Blindgeborenen*. Leipzig: J. A. Barth.

*Shaffer, D. S. and Sadowski, C. 1975. "This Table is Mine: Respect for Marked Barroom Tables as a Function of Gender of Spatial Marker and Desirability of Locale". *Sociometry* 38, 408-419.

Shands, H. C. 1970. *Semiotic Approaches to Psychiatry*. Approches to Semiotics 2. T. A. Sebeok, ed. The Hague-Paris: Mouton.

Sharp, T. 1932. *Town and Countryside. Some Aspects of Urban and Rural Development.* London: Humphrey Milford.

Sheehan, E. R. F. 1968. "Conversions with Konrad Lorenz". *Harper's Magazine* 236, 69-77.

Sherif, M. and Sherif, C. W. 1970. "Motivation and Intergroup Aggression: A Persistent Problem in Levels of Analysis". In: *Development and Evolution of Behavior. Essays in Memory of T. C. Schneirla.* L. R. Aronson, E. Tobach, D. S. Lehrman and J. S. Rosenblatt, eds. San Francisco: W. H. Freeman and Company. P. 563-579.

Shils, E. 1966. "Privacy: Its Constitution and Vicissitudes". *Law and Contemporary Problems* 31, 281-306.

Simmel, A. 1971. "Privacy is not an Isolated Freedom". In: *Privacy.* J. R. Pennock and J. W. Chapman, eds. Nomos 13. New York: Atherton Press. P. 71-87.

Simmel, G. 1908. *Soziologische Untersuchungen über die Formen der Vergesellschaftung.* Leipzig: Dunker & Humblot.

Simmel, G. 1957 (1950). "The Metropolis and Mental Life". In: *Cities and Society.* P. K. Hatt and A. J. Reiss Jr. eds. 2nd edition. Glencoe, Ill.: The Free Press. P. 635-646.

Simpson, G. G. 1961. "Behavior and Evolution". In: *Behavior and Evolution.* A. Roe and G. G. Simpson, eds. New Haven: Yale University Press. P. 507-535.

Simpson, G. G. 1966. "The Biological Nature of Man". *Science* 152, 472-478.

Sims, N. L. 1940 (1928). *Elements of Rural Sociology.* New York: Thomas Y. Crowell.

Singh, S. D. 1969. "Urban Monkeys". *Scientific American* 221: 1, 108-115.

Sirjamaki, J. *The Sociology of Cities.* New York: Random House.

Sivadon, P. 1973. "Influence du milieu humain sur la réadaptation des malades mentaux en institution". In: *Psychiatry. Proceedings of the V. World Congress of Psychiatry, Mexico D.F. 25 November-4 Decembre 1971.* Part 1. Amsterdam: Excerpta Medica. P. 292-296.

*Sivadon, P. 1965. "L'espace vécu. Incidences thérapeutiques". *L'Evolution Psychiatrique* 30, 477-499.

Sivadon, P. 1970. "Space as Experienced: Therapeutic Implications". In: *Environmental Psychology: Man and his Physical Setting.* H. M. Proshansky, W. H. Ittelson and L. G. Rivlin, eds. New York-Chicago-San Francisco-etc.: Holt, Rinehart & Winston. P. 409-419.

Sjoberg, G. 1960. *The Preindustrial City.* New York: The Free Press.

Sjoberg, G. 1964. "The Rise and Fall of Cities: A Theoretical Perspective". In: *Urbanism and Urbanization.* N. Anderson, ed. International Studies in Sociology and Social Anthropology 2. Leiden: E. J. Brill. P. 7-20.

*Sloan, S. A. 1972. "Clerks are People". *Ekistics* 34, 359-366.

Sluckin, W. 1972 (1964). *Imprinting and Early Learning.* London: Methuen & Co. Ltd.

Smailes, A. E. 1953. *The Geography of Towns.* London: Hutchinson's University Library.

Smith, G. J. W. 1962. "Process – A Biological Frame of Reference for the Study of Behaviour". *Psychological Research Bulletin* II: 7, 1-20.

Smith, N. W. 1975. "A note on Sumerian ki-ag and territoriality". *Journal of the History of the Behavioral Sciences* 11, 87.

Smith, R. A. 1971. "Crowding in the City: The Japanese Solution". *Landscape* 19: 1, 3-10.

Smith, S. 1969. "Studies of Small Groups in Confinement". In: *Sensory Deprivation: Fifteen Years of Research.* J. P. Zubek, ed. New York: Appleton-Century-Crofts. P. 374-403.

Snow, C. P. 1965 (1964). *The Two Cultures: And a Second Look. An Expanded Version of the Two Cultures and the Scientific Revolution.* Cambridge: At the University Press.

*Soja, E. J. 1971. "The Political Organization of Space". *Commission on College Geography. Resource Paper* 8. Washington: Association of American Geographers. P. 1-54.

Sölch, J. 1929. "Die Frage der zukünftigen Verteilung der Menschheit". *Geografiska Annaler* 11, 105-146.

Solomon, P., Leiderman, P. H., Mendelson, J. and Wexler, D. 1957-1958. "Sensory Deprivation. A Review". *The American Journal of Psychiatry* 114, 357-363.

Sombart, W. 1938. *Vom Menschen. Versuch einer geistwissenschaftlichen Anthropologie.* Berlin-Charlottenburg: Buchholz & Weisswange.

*Sommer, R. 1967. "Classroom Ecology". *The Journal of Applied Behavioral Science* 3, 489-503.

*Sommer, R. 1965. "Further Studies of Small Group Ecology". *Sociometry* 28, 337-348.

Sommer, R. 1966. "Man's Proximate Environment". *The Journal of Social Issues* 22: 4, 59-70.

*Sommer, R. 1969. *Personal Space. The Behavioral Basis of Design.* Englewood Cliffs, N.J.: Prentice-Hall, Inc.

Sommer, R. 1971. "Spatial Parameters in Naturalistic Social Research". In: *Behavior and Environment. The Use of Space by Animals and Men.* A. H. Esser, ed. New York-London: Plenum Press. P. 281-290.

*Sommer, R. 1959. "Studies in Personal Space". *Sociometry* 22, 247-260.

Sommer, R. 1974. *Tight Spaces. Hard Architecture and How to Humanize it.* Englewood Cliffs, N.J.: Prentice-Hall, Inc.

*Sommer, R. and Becker, F. D. 1969. "Territorial Defense and the Good Neighbor". *Journal of Personality and Social Psychology* 11, 85-92.

Sommer, R. and Osmond, H. 1961. "Symptoms of Institutional Care". *Social Problems* 8, 254-263.

Sonnenfeld, J. 1966. "Variable Values in Space and Landscape: An Inquiry into the Nature of Environmental Necessity". *The Journal of Social Issues* 22: 4, 71-82.

Sorensen, M. W. 1974. "A Review of Aggressive Behavior in the Tree Shrews". In: *Primate Aggression, Territoriality, and Xenophobia. A Comparative Perspective.* R. L. Holloway, ed. New York-London: Academic Press. 13-30.

Sorokin, P. A. 1943. *Sociocultural Causality, Space, Time.* Durham, N.C.: Duke University Press.

Spatial Behavior of Older People, 1970. L. A. Pastalan and D. H. Carson, eds. Ann Arbor: The University of Michigan – Wayne University.

Speck, F. G. 1922. *Beothuk and Micmac. Indian Notes and Monographs.* F. W. Hodge, ed. New York: Museum of the American Indian-Heye Foundation.

*Speck, F. G. 1915. *Family Hunting Territories and Social Life of Various Algonkian Bands of the Ottawa Valley.* Canada Department of Mines. Geological Survey Memoir 70. Ottawa: Government Printing Bureau.

*Speck, F. G. and Eiseley, L. C. 1939. "Significance of Hunting Territory Systems of the Algonkian in Social Theory". *American Anthropologist* 41, 269-280.

Spitz, R. A. 1945-1946. "Hospitalism. An Inquiry into the Genesis of Psychiatric Conditions in Early Childhood". *The Psychoanalytic Study of the Child* 1, 53-74.

Sprott, W. J. H. 1958. *Human Groups.* Harmondsworth: Penguin Books.

Srole, L. 1972. "Urbanization and Mental Health: Some Reformulations". *American Scientist* 60, 576-583.

*Staehelin, B. 1953. "Gesetzmässigkeiten im Gemeinschaftsleben schwer Geisteskranker". *Schweizerisches Archiv für Neurologie und Psychiatrie* 72, 277-298.

Staehelin, B. 1954. "Soziale Gesetzmässigkeiten im Gemeinschaftsleben Geisteskranker, verglichen mit tierpsychologischen Ergebnissen". *Homo* 5, 113-116.

*Stanner, W. E. H. 1965-1966. "Aboriginal Territorial Organization: Estate, Range, Domain and Regime". *Oceania* 36, 1-26.

Starr, R. 1966. *The Living End: The City and its Critics.* New York: Coward-McCann.

Stavenhagen, K. 1939. *Heimat als Grundlage menschlicher Existenz.* Göttingen: Vandenhoek & Ruprecht.

Stea, D. 1970. "Home Range and Use of Space". In: *Spatial Behavior of Older People.* L. A. Pastalan and D. H. Carson, eds. Ann Arbor: The University of Michigan – Wayne State University. P. 138-147.

*Stea, D. 1965. "Space, Territory and Human Movements". *Landscape* 15: 1, 13-16.

Stearns, F. 1972. "The City as Habitat for Wildlife and Man". In: T. R. Detwyler and M. G. Marcus. *Urbanization and Environment.* Belmont, Cal.: P. 261-277.

Stevenson, A., Martin, E. and O'Neill, J. 1967. *High Living. A Study of Family Life in Flats.* Melbourne: University Press.

Stewart, C. T. Jr. 1958. "The Size and Spacing of Cities". *The Geographical Review* 48, 222-245.

Stöber, G. 1964. *Das Standortgefüge der Grosstadtmitte. Ein Beitrag zur kommunalen Strukturforschung am Beispiel der City in Frankfurt am Main.* Frankfurt am Main: Europäische Verlagsanstalt.

Stokes, A. W. 1974. "Introduction" and "Editor's Comments on Papers." In: *Territory.* A. W. Stokes, ed. Benchmark Papers in Animal Behavior. Stroudsburg: Dowden, Hutchinson & Ross, Inc. P. 1-4, 6-8, 80-81, 114-118, 218-219, 236-237, 254-255, 296-297.

Stokols, D. 1972. "A Social-Psychological Model of Human Crowding Phenomena". *Journal of the American Institute of Planners* 38, 72-83.

Stokols, D. 1976. "The Experience of Crowding in Primary and Secondary Environments". *Environment and Behavior* 8, 49-86.

Stokols, D. Rall, M., Pinner, B. and Schopler, J. 1973. "Physical, Social, and Personal Determinants of the Perception of Crowding". *Environment and Behavior* 5, 87-115.

Stott, D. H. 1962. "Cultural and Natural Checks on Population-Growth". In: *Culture and the Evolution of Man.* M. F. Ashley Montagu, ed. New York: Oxford University Press. P. 355-376.

Strachey, A. 1957. *The Unconscious Motives of War. A Psycho-Analytic Contribution.* London: George Allen & Unwin Ltd.

Strehlow, T. G. H. 1965. "Culture, Social Structure, and Environment in Aboriginal Central Australia". In: *Aboriginal Man In Australia. Essays in Honour of Emeritus Professor A. P. Elkin.* R. M. Berndt and C. H. Berndt, eds. Sydney-London-Melbourne: Angus and Roberson. P. 121-145.

Studer, R. G. 1969. "The Dynamics of Behaviour-Contingent Physical Systems". In: *Design Methods in Architecture.* G. Broadbent and A. Ward, eds. Architectural Association 4. London: Lund Humphries. P. 55-70.

Sugiyama, Y. 1967. "Social Organization of Hanuman Langurs". In: *Social Communication among Primates.* S. A. Altmann, ed. Chicago-London: The University of Chicago Press. P. 221-236.

Sugiyama, Y. 1973. "The Social Structure of Wild Chimpanzees". In: *Comparative Ecology and Behaviour of Primates. Proceedings of a Conference held at the Zoological Society, London, November 1971.* R. P. Michael and J. H. Crook, eds. London-New York: Academic Press. P. 375-410.

*Sundstrom, E. and Altman, I. 1974. "Field Study of Territorial Behavior and Dominance". *Journal of Personality and Social Psychology* 30, 115-124.

Suttles, G. D. 1973 (1972). *The Social Construction of Communities.* Chicago-London: The University of Chicago Press.

*Suttles, G. D. 1968. *The Social Order of the Slum. Ethnicity and Territory in the Inner City.* Chicago-London: The University of Chicago Press.

Swanton, J. R. 1943. *Are Wars Inevitable?* Smithsonian Institution War Background Studies 12. Washington D.C.: Smithsonian Institution.

"Symposium on Psycho-Analysis and Ethology: 1960". *The International Journal of Psycho-Analysis* 41, 105-146.

Tankel, S. B. 1963. "The Importance of Open Space in the Urban Pattern". In: *Cities and Space. The Future Use of Urban Land. Essays from the Fourth RFF Forum.* L. Wingo Jr., ed. Baltimore: The John Hopkins Press. P. 57-71.

Taylor, G. 1949. *Urban Geography. A Study of Site, Evolution, Pattern and Classification in Villages, Towns and Cities.* London: Methuen & Co. Ltd.

Tessman, G. 1913. *Die Pangwe. Völkerkundliche Monographie eines westafrikanischen Negerstammes. Ergebnisse der Lübecker Pangwe-Expedition 1907-1909 und früherer Forschungen 1904-1907* 2. Berlin: Ernst Wasmuth A.G.

Thakurdesai, S. G. 1972. "Sense of Place in Greek Anonymous Architecture". *Ekistics* 34, 334-340.

The First Men. 1973. The Emergence of Man. Time-Life Books. eds. London: Time-Life International (Nederland) B.V.

The Ibis. 1956. Volume 98, 340-530.

Thiessen, D. D. and Dawber, M. 1972. "Territorial Exclusion and Reproductive Isolation". *Psychonomic Science* 28, 159-160.

Thomlinson, R. 1969. *Urban Structure. The Social and Spatial Character of Cities.* New York: Random House.

Thompson, D. W. 1910. *Historia Animalium. The Works of Aristotle.* J. A. Smith and W. D. Ross, eds. Oxford: At the Clarendon Press.

Thompson, L. 1961. *Toward a Science of Mankind.* New York-Toronto-London: McGraw-Hill Book Company, Inc.

Thomson, G. 1946 (1941). *Aeschylus and Athens. A Study in the Social Origins of Drama.* London: Lawrence & Wishart.

Thorpe, W. H. 1961. "Introduction" to Part II and III. In: *Current Problems in Animal Behaviour.* W. H. Thorpe and O. L. Zangwill, eds. Cambridge: At the University Press. P. 87-101, 167-174.

Thorpe, W. H. 1956. *Learning and Instinct in Animals.* London: Methuen & Co. Ltd.

Thorpe, W. H. 1954. "Some Concepts of Ethology". *Nature* 174, 101-105.

Thorpe, W. H. 1944. "Some Problems of Animal Learning". *Proceedings of the Linnean Society of London* 156, 70-83.

Thrasher, F. M. 1968 (1927). *The Gang. A Study of 1,313 Gangs in Chicago.* Chicago-London: The University of Chicago Press.

Tiger, L. 1969. *Men in Groups.* London: Nelson.

Tiger, L. and Fox, R. 1971. *The Imperial Animal.* New York-Chicago-San Francisco: Holt, Rinehart & Winston.

Tiira, E. 1954. *Raft of Despair.* London: Hutchinson.

Timasheff, N. S. 1957 (1955). *Sociological Theory. Its Nature and Growth.* Revised Edition. New York: Random House.

Timms, D. 1971. *The Urban Mosaic. Towards a Theory of Residential Differentiation.* Cambridge: At the University Press.

Tinbergen, E. A. and Tinbergen, N. 1972. "Early Childhood Autism. An Ethological Approach". *Fortschritte der Verhaltensforschung. Beiheft zur Zeitschrift für Tierpsychologie* 10, 1-53.

Tinbergen, N. 1953. "Ein ethologischer Beitrag zur Tierpsychologie". *Archives Néerlandaises de Zoologie* 10: Supplément, 121-126.

Tinbergen, N. 1963. "On Aims and Methods of Ethology". *Zeitschrift für Tierpsychologie* 20, 410-433.

*Tinbergen, N. 1968. "On War and Peace in Animals and Man". *Science* 160, 1411-1418.

Tinbergen, N. 1955. "Psychology and Ethology as Supplementary Parts of a Science of Behavior". In: *Group Processes. Transactions of the First Conference, September 26, 27, 28, 29 and 30, 1954, Ithaca, New York.* B. Schaffner, ed. New York: Josiah Macy Jr. Foundation. P. 75-167.

Tinbergen, N. 1936. "The Function of Sexual Fighting in Birds; and the Problem of the Origin of 'Territory' " *Bird-Banding* 7, 1-8.

Tinbergen, N. 1957. "The Function of Territory". *Bird Study* 4, 14-27.

Tinbergen, N. 1958 (1951). *The Study of Instinct.* Oxford: At the Clarendon Press.

Tobias, P. V. 1964. "Bushman Hunter-Gatherers: A Study in Human Ecology". In: *Ecological Studies in Southern Africa.* D. H. S. Davis, ed. Monographiae Biologicae 14. The Hague: Dr. W. Junk. P. 67-86.

Tobias, P. V. 1965. "Early Man in East Africa". *Science* 149, 22-33.

Tolman, E. C. 1932. *Purposive Behavior in Animals and Men.* New York-London: The Century Co.

Townsend, P. 1962. *The Last Refuge. A Survey of Residential Institutions and Homes for the Aged in England and Wales.* London: Routledge & Kegan Paul.

Toynbee, A. 1967. "Town-Planning in the Ancient Greek World". *Ekistics* 145, 445-449.
Tregear, E. 1890. "The Maoris of New Zealand". *The Journal of the Anthropological Institute of Great Britain and Ireland* 19, 97-123.
Tremearne, A. J. N. 1912. "Notes on the Kagoro and other Nigerian Head-Hunters". *The Journal of the Royal Anthropological Institute of Great Britain and Ireland* 42, 136-199.
Trewartha, G. T. 1969. *A Geography of Population: World Patterns*. New York-London-Sydney-Toronto: John Wiley & Sons, Inc.
Trier, J. 1942. "Zaun und Mannring". *Beiträge zur Geschichte der Deutschen Sprache und Literatur* 66, 232-264.
Tuan, Y.-F. 1968. "A Preface to Chinese Cities". In: *Urbanization and its Problems. Essays in Honour of E. W. Gilbert*. R. P. Beckinsale and J. M. Houston, eds. Oxford: Basil Blackwell. P. 218-253.
Tuan, Y.-F. 1974. *Topohilia. A Study of Environmental Perception, Attitudes, and Values*. Englewood Cliffs, N.J.: Prentice-Hall, Inc.
Turnbull, C. B. 1965. *Wayward Servants. The Two Worlds of the African Pygmies*. Garden City, N.Y.: The Natural History Press.
Turner, J. C. 1971. "Barriers and Channels for Housing Development in Modernizing Countries". In: *The Growth of Cities*. Edited by D. Lewis. Architects' Year Book 13, 70-83.
Tyhurst, L. 1951. "Displacement and Migration. A Study in Social Psychiatry". *The American Journal of Psychiatry* 107, 561-568.

Uexküll, J. v. 1957 (1934). "A Stroll through the Worlds of Animals and Men. A Picture Book of Invisible Worlds". In: *Instinctive Behavior. The Development of a Modern Concept*. C. H. Schiller, ed. London: Methuen & Co. Ltd. P. 5-80.
Uexküll, J. v. 1909. *Umwelt und Innenwelt der Tiere*. Berlin: Julius Springer.
Unonius, G. 1950. *A Pioneer in Northwest America 1841-1858. The Memoirs of Gustaf Unonius. 1*. N. W. Olsson, ed. Minneapolis: The University of Minnesota Press.
Urban Core and Inner City. 1967. Proceedings of the International Study Week Amsterdam, 11-17 September 1966. Leiden: E. J. Brill.

Vallois, H. V. 1970 (1961). "The Social Life of Early Man: The Evidence of Skeletons". In: *Social Life of Early Man*. S. L. Washburn, ed. Chicago: Aldine Publishing Company. P. 214-235.
*Vieira, A. B. 1974. "De l'évolution de la schizophrénie considerée comme conflit territorial". *Acta Psychiatrica Belgica* 74, 57-79.
Viollet, P. 1872. "Caractère collectif des premières propriétés immobilières." *Bibliothèque de L'école des Chartes* 33, 455-504.
Vischer, A. L. 1918. *Die Stacheldraht-Krankheit. Beiträge zur Psychologie des Kriegsgefangenen*. Zürich: Rascher und Cie.
Vivrett, W. K. 1960. "Housing and Community Settings for Older People". In: *Handbook of Social Gerontology. Societal Aspects of Ageing*. C. Tibbits, ed. Chicago: The University of Chicago Press. P. 549-623.
Vogt, H.-H. 1964. *Wir Menschen sind ja gar nicht so! Vom Verhalten des Menschen und der Tiere*. Stuttgart: Frank'hsche Verlagshandlung.
Vold, G. B. 1958. *Theoretical Criminology*. New York: Oxford University Press.
Vowles, D. M. 1970. *The Psychobiology of Aggression*. A Lecture delivered at the University of Edinburgh on 15.4.1970. Edinburgh: At the University Press.

Waddington, C. H. 1972. "Density, Intensity and Stress". *Ekistics* 33, 266-267.
Wagley, C. and Harris, M. 1967 (1958). *Minorities in the New World. Six Case Studies*. New York-London: Columbia University Press.
Wagner, P. L. 1960. *The Human Use of the Earth*. Glencoe, Ill.: The Free Press of Glencoe.
Wallengren, H. 1927. "Om instinkten". In: *Festskrift tillägnad Hans Larsson*. Stockholm: Alb. Bonniers Boktryckeri. P. 251-273.

302   REFERENCES

Walther, F. 1967. "Huftierterritorien und ihre Markierung". In: *Die Strassen der Tiere*. H. Hediger, ed. Die Wissenschaft 125. Braunschweig: Friedr. Vieweg & Sohn. P. 26-45.

Walther-Büel, H. 1958. "Die soziale Problematik gestörten Seelenlebens". In: *Gestaltungen sozialen Lebens bei Tier und Mensch*. F. E. Lehmann, ed. Bern: Francke. P. 191-206.

Ward, B. 1964. "The Processes of World Urbanization". *Ekistics* 18, 274-280.

Warnock, G. J. 1960. "Philosophy". In: M. v. Senden. *Space and Sight*. London: Methuen & Co. Ltd. P. 319-325.

Washburn, S. L. and Avis, V. 1961. "Evolution of Human Behavior". In: *Behavior and Evolution*. A. Roe and G. G. Simpson, eds. New Haven: Yale University Press. P. 421-436.

Washburn, S. L. and DeVore, I. 1970 (1961). "Social Behavior of Baboons and Early Man". In: *Social Life of Early Man*. S. L. Washburn, ed. Chicago: Aldine. P. 91-105.

Washburn, S. L. and Harding, R. S. 1972. "Evolution of Primate Behavior". In: *Primate Patterns*. P. Dohlinow, ed. New York-Chicago-San Francisco-etc.: Holt, Rinehart & Winston. P. 338-351.

Washburn, S. L., Jay, P. C. and Lancaster, J. B. 1972. "Field Studies of Old World Monkeys and Apes". In: *Primate Patterns*. P. Dohlinow, ed. New York-Chicago-San Francisco-etc.: Holt, Rinehart & Winston. P. 246-260.

Watson, A. 1967. "Population Control by Territorial Behaviour in Red Grouse". *Nature* 215, 1274-1275.

Watson, A. and Jenkins, D. 1968. "Experiments on Population Control by Territorial Behaviour in Red Grouse". *The Journal of Animal Ecology* 37, 595-614.

Watson, A. and Miller, G. R. 1971. "Territory Size and Aggression in a Fluctuating Red Grouse Population". *The Journal of Animal Ecology* 40, 367-383.

*Watson, O. M. 1970. *Proxemic Behavior. A Cross-Cultural Study*. Approaches to Semiotics 8. T. A. Sebeok, ed. The Hague-Paris: Mouton.

*Watson, O. M. and Graves, T. D. 1966. "Quantitative Research in Proxemic Behavior". *American Anthropologist* 68, 971-985.

*Webber, M. M. 1964a. "Culture, Territoriality, and the Elastic Mile". *Papers and Proceedings of the Regional Science Association* 13, 59-69.

Webber, M. M. 1963. "Order in Diversity: Community without Propinquity." In: *Cities and Space. The Future Use of Urban Land. Essays from the Fourth RFF Forum*. L. Wingo Jr., ed. Baltimore: The John Hopkins Press. P. 23-54.

*Webber, M. M. 1964b. "The Urban Place and the Nonplace Urban Realm". In: *Explorations into Urban Structure* by M. M. Webber, J. W. Dyckman, D. L. Foley, A. Z. Guttenberg, W. L. C. Wheaton and C. B. Wurster. Philadelphia: University of Pennsylvania Press. P. 79-153.

Weeks, J. H. 1909. "Anthropological Notes on the Bangala of the Upper Congo River". *The Journal of the Royal Anthropological Institute of Great Britain and Ireland* 39, 97-136.

Wegrocki, H. J. 1964. "A Critique of Cultural and Statistical Concepts of Abnormality". In: *The Study of Abnormal Behavior. Selected Readings*. M. Zax and G. Stricker, eds. New York-London: Collier-MacMillan Ltd. P. 3-12.

Weinberg, S. K. 1967. "Urban Areas and Hospitalized Psychotics". In: *The Sociology of Mental Disorders*. S. K. Weinberg, ed. London: Staples Press. P. 22-26.

Wennberg, G. 1977. *Urbanisering, slum och kåkstäder*. Stockholm: Esselte Studium.

Werblowsky, R. J. Z. 1964. "Funerary Rites and Customs". In: *Encyclopaedia Britannica*, 9. Chicago-London-Toronto-etc.: Encyclopaedia Britannica. Inc. P. 1011-1017.

Werner, A. 1906. *The Natives of British Central Africa*. London: Archibald Constable and Company, Ltd.

Westin, A. F. 1968. *Privacy and Freedom*. New York: Atheneum.

Weybrew, B. B. 1963. "Psychological Problems of Prolonged Marine Submergence". In: *Unusual Environments and Human Behavior. Physiological and Psychological Problems of Man in Space*, N. M. Burns, R. M. Chambers and E. Hendler, eds. Glencoe, Ill.: The Free Press. P. 87-125.

Wheeler, G. C. 1910. *The Tribe, and Intertribal Relations, in Australia*. London: John Murray.

White, R. K. 1966. "Misperception and the Vietnam War". *The Journal of Social Issues* 22: 3, 1-167.

Whitman, C. O. 1898. "Animal Behavior". *Biological Lectures from the Marine Biological Station Woods Hole* 6, 285-338.

Whitrow, G. J. 1955-1956. "Why Physical Space has Three Dimensions". *The British Journal for the Philosophy of Science* 6, 13-31.

Whorf, B. L. 1956. *Language, Thought, and Reality. Selected Writings of Benjamin Lee Whorf.* Introduction by J. B. Carroll, ed. New York-London: John Wiley & Sons. Inc. and Chapman & Hall, Limited.

Whyte, W. F. 1964. "On Street Corner Society". In: *Contributions to Urban Sociology.* E. W. Burgess and D. J. Bogue, eds. Chicago-London: The University of Chicago Press. P. 256-268.

Wibberley, G. P. 1959. *Agriculture and Urban Growth. A Study of the Competition for Rural Land.* London: Michael Joseph.

*Willems, E. P. and Campbell, D. E. 1976. "One Path through the Cafeteria". *Environment and Behavior* 8, 125-140.

Williams G. C. 1966. *Adaptation and Natural Selection. A Critique of some Current Evolutionary Thought.* Princeton: Princeton University Press.

Wilner, D. M., Walkley, R. P., Pinkerton, T. C. and Tayback, M. 1962. *The Housing Environment and Family Life. A Longitudinal Study of the Effects of Housing on Morbidity and Mental Health.* Baltimore: The John Hopkins Press.

Wilson, A. 1959-1960. "Caravans as Homes". In: *Parliamentary Papers (House of Commons and Command).* 9. Session 20 October 1959-27 October 1960, 535-623.

Wilson, A. C. and Sarich, V. M. 1969. "A Molecular Time Scale for Human Evolution". *Proceedings of the National Academy of Sciences of the United States of America* 63, 1088-1093.

Wilson, E. O. 1971. "Competitive and Aggressive Behavior". In: *Man and Beast: Comparative Social Behavior.* J. F. Eisenberg and W. S. Dillon, eds. Smithsonian Annual III. City of Washington: Smithsonian Institution Press. P. 3-21.

Wingo, L. Jr. 1963. "Urban Space in a Policy Perspective: An Introduction". In: *Cities and Space. The Future Use of Urban Land. Essays from the Fourth RFF Forum.* L. Wingo Jr., ed. Baltimore: The John Hopkins Press. P. 3-21.

*Winick, C. and Holt, H. 1961. "Seating Position as Nonverbal Communication in Group Analysis". *Psychiatry* 24, 171-182.

Wirth, L. 1956. *Community Life and Social Policy. Selected Papers by L. Wirth.* E. W. Marvick and A. J. Reiss Jr., eds. Chicago: The University of Chicago Press.

Wirth, L. 1928. *The Ghetto.* Chicago: The University of Chicago Press.

Wohlwill, J. F. 1966. "The Physical Environment: A Problem for a Psychology of Stimulation". *The Journal of Social Issues* 22: 4, 29-38.

Wright, Q. 1942. *A Study of War 1-2.* Chicago. Ill.: The University of Chicago Press.

Wundt, W. 1892. *Vorlesungen ueber die Menschen- und Tierseele.* 2. revised edition. Hamburg-Berlin: Leopold Voss.

Wuttke, W. and Hoffmeister, F. 1967. "Differenzierungsmöglichkeiten tranquillisierender Wirkungen im Tierversuch". *Naunyn-Schmiedebergs Archiv für Pharmakologie und Experimentelle Pathologie* 257, 353-354.

Wynne-Edwards, V. C. 1962. *Animal Dispersion in Relation to Social Behavior.* Edinburgh-London: Oliver and Boyd.

Wynne-Edwards, V. C. 1972. "Ecology and the Evolution of Social Ethics". In: *Biology and the Human Sciences. The Herbert Spencer Lectures.* J. W. S. Pringle, ed. Oxford: Clarendon Press. P. 50-69.

Wynne-Edwards, V. C. 1969. "Self-Regulating Systems in Populations of Animals". In: *The Subversive Science. Essays toward an Ecology of Man.* P. Shepard and D. McKinley, eds. Boston: Houghton Mifflin Company. P. 99-111.

Wynne-Edwards, V. C. 1965. "Social Organization as a Population Regulator". *Symposium of the Zoological Society of London* 14, 173-178.

Yarrow, L. J. 1964. "Maternal Deprivation: Toward an Empirical and Conceptual Re- eva-luation". In: *The Study of Abnormal Behavior. Selected Readings*. M. Zax and G. Stricker, eds. New York-London: Collier-Macmillan Ltd. P. 320-350.

Yerkes, R. M. and Yerkes, A. W. 1935. "Social Behavior in Infrahuman Primates". In: *A Handbook of Social Psychology*. C. Murchinson, ed. Worcester, Mass.: Clark University Press. P. 973-1033.

Young, J. Z. 1971. *An Introduction to the Study of Man*. Oxford: At the Clarendon Press.

Zajonc, R. B. 1971. "Attraction, Affiliation and Attachment". In: *Man and Beast: Comparative Social Behavior*. J. F. Eisenberg and W. S. Dillon, eds. Smithsonian Annual III. Washington: Smithsonian Institution Press. P. 141-179.

Zeitschrift für Tierpsychologie 1973. Vol. 33, 429-430.

Ziegler, H. E. 1920 (1904). *Der Begriff des Instinktes einst und jetzt. Eine Studie über die Geschichte und die Grundlagen der Tierpsychologie*. 3. augmented edition. Jena: Gustav Fischer.

Zimbardo, P. G. 1969. "The Human Choice: Individuation, Reason, and Order versus Deindividuation, Impulses, and Chaos". *Nebraska Symposium on Motivation* 1969, 237-307.

Zimmerman, J. L. 1971. "The Territory and its Density Dependent Effect in Spiza americana". *The Auk* 88, 591-612.

Zisman, S. B. 1967. "Open Spaces in Urban Growth". In: *Taming Megalopolis 1. What is and what could be*. H. Wentworth Eldredge, ed. Garden City, N.Y.: Doubleday & Company, Inc. P. 286-296.

Zlutnick, S. and Altman, I. 1972. "Crowding and Human Behavior". In: *Environment and the Social Sciences: Perspectives and Applications*. J. F. Wohlwill and D. H. Carson, eds. Washington, D.C.: American Psychological Association. P. 44-58.

Zorbaugh, H. W. 1926. "The Natural Areas of the City". In: *The Urban Community*. E. W. Burgess, ed. Chicago: The University of Chicago Press. P. 219-229.

Zucker, P. 1959. *Town and Square. From the Agora to the Village Green*. New York: Columbia University Press.

Zuckerman, M. 1964. "Perceptual Isolation as a Stress Situation". *Archives of General Psychiatry* 11, 255-276.

Summary

1. Introduction
"Human territoriality" aims at a scientific survey of the present knowledge of physical behavioural territories in man together with a preliminary analysis and discussion of function and meaning.
2. Basic concepts

2.1. Space and its perception
Space is the four-dimensionality of the field, relative to a moving point of reference, e.g., the body of man. Environment is an open, dynamic, multidimensional system, to which living matter is sensitive and capable of reacting.

Space perception refers to the spatial attributes of objects. Vision is our most powerful organ for exploration, but locomotion in space seems to be crucial for conceptualization.

Physical space is not the same as life space, which is experienced in a specific way by every species and at least in man by every individual, the "Gestalt" and "cognitive map" conceptions being of great influence. Action space is built into the organism by behaviour.

2.2. Territory definitions
Behavioural territories are in principle subjective products, but their boundaries and markings often imply physical phenomena. Definitions involve personalization, ownership or defense of geographical areas with relation to different motives and needs.

The earlier quite dominating definition characteristic of defense has in recent times been questioned, exclusiveness of use now being stressed instead.

Territory definitions applicable only to man are still few but seem more and more to concentrate on territories as rooms for action, protection and identification.

Human behavioural territoriality is a phenomenon of ethological ecology with an instinctive nucleus, manifested as more or less exclusive spaces, to which individuals or groups of human beings are bound emotionally and which, for the possible avoidance of others, are distinguished by means of limits, marks or other kinds of structuring with adherent display, movements or aggressiveness.

In the past the term "home range" or "range", which refers to the total area occupied by an organism during a given period of time, has been used without distinction from that of "behavioural territory" which in French is called "*territoire*" and in German "*Revier*" or "*Heim*".

2.3. Sciences of territory
Behavioural territoriality is multidisciplinary, is often deemed peripheral and is thus not seldom neglected by the established sciences.

Anthropologists are among the pioneers in territory study, concentrating on cross-cultural observations. In geography territoriality particularly belongs to the political and behavioural subdepartments.

Earlier psychologists did not show much interest in behavioural territories, but the situation has now totally changed. Ethology as "the biological study of behaviour" is, of course, a basic science in the context.

Modern sociology has its roots in biological ecology and, functionally speaking, territory is an ecological phenomenon. Territorology might well deserve its name since it covers a distinct and important scientific area.

2.4. Instinct and aggression
Darwin was the first to imply, for the concept of instinct, some inherited modification of the brain, which functions within the fields of variation and natural selection and applies to both animals and men.

It is claimed, in the face of unending criticism, that in the machinery of behaviour there are quite considerable, self-contained units in which learning plays no role. This inflexible instinctive behaviour is so apparent that the reluctance to acknowledge it is incomprehensible.

Particularly for man the instinct controversy is heated, but it is concluded that major ends of human activity are rooted in instincts and that the description of man as lacking instincts is false.

Some scientists vindicate that aggression is wholly learned, but experiments with mammals showed that certain psychopharmacological agents can stop reactive fighting, however not spontaneous unprovoked aggression.

Ownership of territory is a frequent prerequisite for aggressive behaviour, but constraints on aggression are so great that it is brought into play only when it gives momentary advantage. Animal aggression is associated with competition according to the requirements of environment and can imply population regulation.

3. Animal territories

3.1. Characteristic features
Animal territories are dynamic, space-time systems with all gradations from exclusive, permanent to quite ephemeral units. They often function as series of significant, connected points and not always as bounded and marked two- or three-dimensional spaces.

More or less circular territories seem to predominate, if conditions permit. With increasing numbers most territories are compressed, but there are always minimum as well as maximum limits and, besides quantitative, also qualitative factors are in operation.

Animal territoriality is instinctive. It could have evolved if the pulsating halo of individual distance became attached to a particular place.

3.2. Territories in birds and mammals
From Aristotle onwards man has recognized avian territories. Birds are common and conspicuous, they proclaim their lands by singing and display and they not seldom chase each other and fight at the boundaries.

Among migrating passerine birds males usually establish territories in the breeding grounds before the arrival of the females. Territorial drives normally become less strong as reproduction proceeds but there are many species which also defend winter territories.

Mammals are macrosmatic and their scent marks places of special interest. The recognition of individuals by locality seems to be crucial, and neighbourliness is the keynote of organization, at least in territorially-established solitary species.

Opinions about primates still differ, but territoriality has now been demonstrated in at least twenty species. The two gibbons, closely connected with anthropoid apes, are strongly territorial.

Accounts indicate that apparent non-territoriality can be explained by factors such as small recent populations, well-acquainted groups and earlier settling of controversies. There is now also positive evidence for territoriality in all the three species of anthropoid apes.

How decisive numbers are in all these cases is shown by studies of hanuman langurs in districts of India with 20, 150 and 300 animals per square mile. In the first case there was no need for territoriality, in the second unchanging borders and defended territories and in the third poor territorial order because of disorganization.

3.3. Significance of animal territories

It seems to be unanimously agreed that territoriality as site attachment may assist in feeding, in escaping from predators and in augmenting fighting potentiality and that it can regulate density, at least in favoured habitats of birds and when situations are critical.

It is maintained that territories are important in determining the rate of spread of a species and that territoriality is in most cases equivalent to reproductive isolation. When population density increases, continued disruptions of homeostasis can transform a stable physiology into an unstable one. Territoriality leads to reduced rates of growth and suppressed final population.

Animal territoriality is employed to defend resources, depending on their cost in time and energy. The relation between dominance and spacing appears to be a general one. An individual territory has an owner dominant over all others entering but subordinate when he moves off this space. Such behaviour establishes the basic design of animal societies.

4. Territory in man

4.1. "Primitive" territories

Recent serological investigations suggest a separation between the lineages leading towards man and apes as late as four or five million years ago.

Man is outstanding in his capacity for conceptual thought. Further there is his great variability and non-speciality, his prolonging of foetal characters into postnatal development, his great tool-making skill as well as his self-domestication, exploratory behaviour and space perception.

Human beings are indubitably mammals, close relatives to other living primates and it is extremely improbable that whole groups of basic inborn behaviours, known from apes and other related animals, should be lacking in man and thus make comparisons impossible.

Homologies should always be possible as long as a common phylogenetic history for the compared organisms is admitted, whether structural correlates are present or not.

It is self-evident that there are differences between animal and human territories, e.g. more artificial structures in the latter, but the similarities seem to be still more obvious.

The child's awareness of proximity, enclosures and boundaries represent the beginning of an understanding of spatial relationships, developed by an active manipulation of nearby objects. At the age of 7 years full territoriality is evident, but observations of, e.g., personal space are made much earlier in life.

Imprinting is a form of learning centering on the broad characteristics of the species and confined to a brief period, possibly also to a particular environment, in the beginning of individual life. Parent-child relationship and territory are two important, closely interrelated themes of complementary interaction, probably strongly influenced by imprinting.

Refugee children placed in spacious community rooms displayed mental deficiency symptoms until the rooms were divided into separate compartments, or territories, where small groups of children could feel at home. Thus boundaries in the form of walls and corners were here necessary for territorial demarcation and territoriality was seen to be a necessity for psychic health.

Mental abnormality is defined as a tendency to choose a type of reaction which represents an escape from a conflict-producing situation. It is stressed that original instinctive behaviour is most often found in mental patients.

Lack of territory in children is followed by regression. Mentally deficient boys without exception took up territories in a playroom, independent of social reinforcement conditions. They had a tremendous need to gain control and territoriality offered a program which reduced complexity.

If any territorial behaviour, judged by its regularity, rigidity and affective performance, should have an innate background, it is that of the mentally abnormal, particularly the psychotic. Most psychiatric patients claim more personal space than healthy people, and they sometimes defend their territories fiercely.

About one million years ago *Homo habilis* placed a circle of stones in Olduvai Gorge, East Africa, the oldest still remaining area actively marked out by a man-like creature.

Some anthropologists claim that early man had an open, non-territorial society, others that territoriality already existed at the simplest levels of culture. The frequency of violent death among early men indicates an aggressively maintained territorial arrangement.

"Primitive" here only denotes peoples inhabiting a more natural environment and living more naturally than those of the great European and Asiatic cultures. Early anthropologists often denied territoriality for three reasons: colonial governments had provoked a lack of territorial feelings to justify driving "savages" away from valuable ground; theories of social history maintained that territorial phenomena had not occurred until the agricultural stage; differences of thinking and communication had biased or spoilt understanding.

Most authors report predominantly group territories from hunting and gathering societies. Tribes seem always to be territorial units, and territory-holding bands are probably older than the family. A claimed absence of territoriality can imply that boundaries are so well recognized by neighbours and populations so well adjusted to resources that there is no need of expansion or defense.

Even pastoralists hold territories, but mostly just when there is scarcity of resources and competition for ground. Agriculturalists are intimately bound to the soil and private ownership is here the most important form of land tenure. Property in land and behavioural territoriality are related but not identical concepts, the latter giving rights somewhere between individual ownership and communistic tenure.

The much debated pygmies of Africa were said to lack territorial rights or to defend just certain spots like water holes. Today it is confirmed that bushmen have strong areal territoriality, too, the differences seemingly dependent on varying history and resources.

For the nomadic peoples of northern and central Asia only critical winter-pastures are thought of as territorial possessions, marked off by features ranging from natural ridges to cattle dung. Notable are the hunting territories of the Veddahs in Ceylon, in principle forming a chess board but in practice being more like a net of hunting paths radiating from a centre.

Territoriality in Australian aborigines has been much discussed – tribe, band, family and individual units being known. Even desert nomads were so strongly attached to their territories socially, ritually and emotionally that after drought-caused absence they immediately returned with the rains.

Mostly hunting territories are reported from the Americas. The Maidu of California watched over their area using special armed guards, and it was never given up, even partly. The family hunting territories of the Algonkian bands in the northeastern U.S.A. were marked on maps of birch bark, and trespassing could be punished by death.

4.2. Rural territories

An ancient primate inheritance, ownership is today a universal trait of human culture. Land is the most important single object of property, which, however, meant originally merely having one's reserved location in a particular area.

It is stated that animals must meet any threat to their territory by exertion of physical force while humans are secured against this by their social order. However, behavioural territoriality serves to make acts of aggressiveness unnecessary in all kinds of vertebrates. The argument that only humans trade in land is not convincing, such trade is rather new in Western countries and practically unknown in "primitive" societies.

It seems that from the earliest times different land systems with both individual, family and tribe property have existed and that if any form has predominated, it is family possession. In fact, individual property in land is thought to have been as underestimated as the related concept of individual territoriality in "primitive" peoples.

Among territorial terms the Greek word for law, "*nomos*", also symbolizes the earliest division of land and the boundary space between households. That ownership alone cannot be equivalent to actual territoriality was demonstrated through a significant relation between territory defense and duration of residence, independent of ownership.

"Boundary" indicates the well-established limit of a given unit and holds together all that lies inside it. So this term is inner-oriented, centripetal, while "frontier" has an outer-oriented, centrifugal meaning.

In claiming virgin land the primary mark of territory is the human body. Felling of trees and cultivating of small patches are also common means of marking.

Without doubt fencing is an important way for man to stake out his share of land and increasing populations make people fence themselves in more carefully. As territorial marking we can also characterize the carving and painting of names or slogans on trees, caves, streets, houses, walls and desks.

Because excretion has a social function with all terrestrial mammals, at least traces of such behaviour should be found in man. Good examples are those cases in which boys and girls placed their excreta in the rooms or on the possessions of visiting strangers.

Of "*grumus merdae*", excrement left by burglars at the place of crime, the simplest explanation seems to be that it represents a marking of territory as an act of social release and personal integration. Profoundly retarded males, who exhibited chronic enuretic and encopretic behaviour and strong territoriality, improved after a decrease of crowding in their dormitory and when the floor space was divided by tape into equal areas around the beds.

Social vertebrates know each other personally and memories bound up with places are of great significance to them. The peasant proprietor was his own master: not even public officials had the right of intrusion.

Villages were regularly situated in relation to some natural or cultural advantage, often crossroad with an open place, surrounded by farms. The village could be fenced or provided with outer graves, and the small territory within had a large counterpart in the outer fields and pastures.

The German term "*Mark*" denoted originally a limiting mark, then the boundary itself and finally an enclosed area of land. Similarly the modern concept of the state was first a designation of a small territory, surveyable by the individual, developing by forming ever larger units, which engulf the older ones. It may be that the state is sound only if it represents a natural, behavioural group territory.

Sometimes real hierarchies of boundary walls are found, delimiting territorial units of increasing magnitude, as in ancient China. Probably the nation-state is the most territorial of political organizations.

We have no special war instinct but instead innate aggressive tendencies. This does not mean, however, that society must only be based on force, for there are adaptive features which can avert aggression. Thus territoriality is a mostly peaceful order of interaction.

The aggression instinct theory of war has some considerable degree of truth. Nations *can* fight because they are able to release the explosive stores of transformed aggression, but they *do* fight for any of a large number of particular reasons: acquisitiveness, frustration, displaced hatred or fear.

Nobody claims that territoriality is the only factor leading to war, but history is full of examples of human fighting over the same patch of land. In one actual war situation, American militants regarded South Vietnam as their own territory, invaded by North Vietnamese Communists.

The proverb "A man's home is his castle" strongly suggests that home is a defended territory, and an average Western person spends about three quarters of his lifetime at home. The home-binding forces are strong in both time and space and thus territoriality is normally dominant over the migratory urge, particularly in childhood.

Man has a greater or lesser power to take a movable territory with him or to build up new territories away from home, but the individual mental problems involved in migration are great, particularly in the case of refugees with no option of return.

The mental troubles connected with absence from the original, familiar territory are summarized as homesickness, which in children can sometimes lead to suicide, arson or murder. That it was called the "Swiss disease" may be explained by the strongly structured landscape in Switzerland, possibly imparting an unusually permanent territorial imprinting. Homesickness is endemic today, not only because of millions of migrants and refugees around us but also because many inhabitants of our towns and cities are displaced persons from the countryside.

4.3. Urban territories

Urban units are complex societies, the territorial element of which is meagre compared to that of its human content. Characterized by division of labour, social classes and service centres, they also have control over surrounding areas on which they depend for food and other supplies. Thus the city not only *is* a territory but *has* one, too.

The earliest meaning of "town" was an enclosed or fortified place, but material, technical, political and strictly human factors were behind the first urbanization. When the valleys of the Nile, the Tigris-Euphrates and the Indus had begun to yield a surplus supporting specialists, the growing villages of the region fought and combined until the result was a city-state.

The oldest town yet discovered is that fortified one next to modern Jericho, almost continously inhabited for about 10,000 years. A direct line leads from the Mesopotamian city-states to the Greek classical equivalent, called "*polis*", which was a walled enclosure on rising ground, dominated by a fortress or *acropolis*.

From the third century B.C. Rome took over as the centre of a strongly organized and urbanized empire, from which the city, the road and the law spread over Europe. The medieval period produced its own irregular city-states, political units with town-councils and guild-bodies, usually walled but not overcrowded. The city of the Renaissance with a core in the royal palace and wide, straight streets radiating therefrom was the "*città ideale*", influencing three centuries of urban planning up to modern times.

In the rural world nature dominates over artificial environment and agricultural over other occupations. Both the size of the community and the density of the population are comparatively less but the homogeneity of the human stock greater than in the urban world. Differentiation, stratification, mobility and contact interaction are less in the rural than in the urban habitat.

Urbanization is the process of city establishment and growth, which during the last century has reached proportions far greater than before all over the world. It is first and foremost characterized by the expansion of urban people and urban land.

Territorial problems are everywhere met with in the urbanization sector as demonstrated by the theories of central place and city region. The physical effects of contact between agricultural areas and towns can be bad or bearable depending on the type of farming and the type of settlement. Trespass problems can be settled and the movements of individuals regularised by careful marking of footpaths and good fencing.

The city is an open ecosystem which, like other multifactorial units of this kind, is poorly understood as a whole. Its two primary components are urban man and urban environment. It has always been obvious that cities consume space as they grow physically, but it has been less apparent until recently that living and working space for the individual inhabitant is also a significant need.

The city can be seen either as a point or as an area. The points are closely integrated into networks of cities on the local, regional, national and international level. In the areal conception, necessary if the urban region is conceived of as the node plus its hinterland, the most specialized cities serve the largest territories.

The Egyptian hieroglyph for town was a circle with a double-line cross inside, the first indicating a moat or wall and the second the convergence of roads. Circular towns dominated among the Hittites and were common in France during the Medieval Age. This form, the easiest to defend, has probably always been the primary one.

The differentiation and structure of the urban unit is of utmost importance. For the city should be imageable, so clearly organized that the resident can carry an accurate picture of its major spatial forms in his mind. The structured city is the consummate example of a territorial unit.

Cities involve a special kind of relation between population and area. The significance of this relationship does not, however, depend solely on the correlation of the sizes of population and urban space. Even though all cities had the same density, the spatial structure of large and small cities would undoubtedly differ.

A metropolitan area is most often defined as a concentration of more than 500,000 people living within an area in which the travelling time from the outskirts to the centre is no more than 40 minutes. In the past only a small fraction of mankind lived and worked at high densities, that is, above 1,000 persons per square mile, but today some Indian cities show densities ranging from 300,000 to over 450,000 persons per square mile.

Investigations show that big cities are rather unpopular. The first and most obvious reason is the burden of perceptual stress, the second a lack of visible identity, the third their illegibility, the fourth their rigidity, the fifth their lack of openness. The most immediate danger involved in megalopolis, the giant city, is that we might run short of territories, of enough space for living.

The spatial order of the city is founded on the desires and resources of its inhabitants as constrained and directed by society. A standard feature in the West is the concentration of administrative, financial, commercial, cultural and amusement facilities within a central city core, the qualities of which, however, have deteriorated i.a. with diminishing territorial value.

Suburbs are urbanized, residential communities outside the limits of a large central city but culturally and economically dependent upon it. Primarily suburbs are dormitory towns without own production, while satellites provide jobs for their own residents.

Suburbanites live where they do because of needs which are real and important, e.g., single family dwelling, home-ownership, private outdoor greens and open countryside. But suburbia is above all a residential nursery or reproduction territory, riding high on human multiplication and the protective instinct of parents.

Behind the modern garden city movement was not only the feudal park and farm garden models but still more a reaction against industrial society. A garden or other ground plot is a *sine qua non* for human habitation, as evidenced by the very strong drives for private space among congested city dwellers.

The garden colony movement started in Germany in 1822, a seemingly instinctive search for land and territory among industrialized citizens. The colony organization rented lots for cultivation during a certain time within special fenced areas at the outskirts of cities.

Double habitation is an old custom for wealthy people, but not until 1850 were villas for summer use built in the Swedish archipelago. It was probably not by chance that the garden colony movement started in Germany, and that Sweden has the world's highest percentage of summer villas. Not long ago both these countries had their dominant habitation in flats lacking territorial ground and garden.

The open space of the city has today become the object of new interest as a biological necessity and a social essential. Open space has three important functions: it is viewed, felt and used.

During the last decades the development of public parks has been unsatisfactory in many countries. Reasons for this are partly economic but particularly of a social nature: as the physical and human composition of the modern community has changed, enthusiasm for public parks has been superseded by other interests.

A Mexican gang intruding into a park in Chicago where Italian street-groups had their hangouts was harassed, ridiculed and insulted until they withdrew. Another park in Stockholm had two distinct territories at opposite ends, one dominated by immigrants, the other by students. Plans for a subway stop involved the cutting down of the elm trees of the park, but demonstrators occupied and defended their park territory until the plans were changed.

The square represents a psychological parking place within the urban landscape and consists often, as the Greek "*agora*", of a broadening of the main street. The Roman "*forum*" was a new creation of space, consciously rendered in three-dimensional design. Streets are the chief determining factors in the building of towns, but they have other functions than transportation. The open street space in the immediate vicinity of homes and workplaces is more frequented than all other urban areas. The street and its sidewalks have the character of a group territory, available for all but primarily for local inhabitants.

Comparisons of three streets in San Francisco with light, moderate and heavy traffic showed that residents on Moderate and Light Street considered part or all of the street as belonging to their territory. However, Heavy Street residents' sense of personal territory did not extend into the street.

Beggars, hawkers and pickpockets establish territories on sidewalks and occupy them to the exclusion of all others similarly employed. More or less criminal gangs in Chicago, stake out streets as home territories and defend them against invasion by rival groups. The strong territoriality must be viewed as a consequence of the lack of space of the dense neighbourhood population.

Local areas in cities have been demarcated since ancient times, not seldom circumvallated and sealed off, inhabited by particular ethnic or racial groups. The most significant city segment having territorial aspects is the neighbourhood, a small limited area of mostly personal, social relations and, not seldom, a historic growth.

The distinction between district and block is not always evident, even though the former is the larger area. Presupposed condition is in both cases propinquity, but still more decisive is familiarity with the area and its people. Strangers find only confused surroundings, while natives organize the environment and find similarities everywhere.

Minority enclaves may as a spatial phenomenon be best explained within the framework of social territory. Once a slice of physical space is identified as the territorial realm of a specific group, any attempt to alter this results in conflict. Segregation forced on one group by another has undesirable consequences, but is one form of accommodation between groups.

It is difficult to define the slum, but it always involves bad housing and aggregates those who are poor, unsuccessful and disreputable. Investigations showed that residents in spite of miserable conditions experienced profound satisfaction from living in their slum territories. In Chicago's "Gangland" feudal warfare is carried out continually on a territorial basis, each group being attached to one slum area through which it is dangerous for members of another gang to pass.

Millions of people live in squatter settlements – illegally occupied land at the outskirts of cities – which are crucial from a territoriality point of view. Lacking externally-imposed law or other regulative community actions, such squatters might be expected to treat all things in common, since all are in need. But rows of stones around houses, dividing lines between public and private, between the road and the squatter garden, belie this expectation.

The house is not only a structure but an institution with a complex set of purposes. Creating an environment best suited to the way of life of a people, it is thus a social unit of space. The demands of territoriality, basic to the house, most probably make life easier by making people feel more secure and better able to protect themselves.

Certainly the outer walls of the house are of special importance, detaching and almost sanctifying part of the outer space. Gates and doors mark the division between the sacred and the profane world outside. Particularly the passing over the threshold is in most countries accompanied by rituals of different kinds. Its sanctity is probably related to a constant need of maintaining territory.

The human settlement usually involves a piece of earth, even among squatters. Although here none of the property legally belongs to the residents, there is no doubt about the *de facto* ownership. Mostly there is neither post nor stones nor hedge since there is no need for them. A fence is used only to establish a boundary which might otherwise be in dispute, or as a security measure. Territoriality could not be more clearly manifested.

Few doubt that the best habitation for man is a free-standing one-family house with garden. Most people prefer such habitation, as private and isolated as possible. Even children who have always lived in flats draw homes this way.

Position, distance and symbolic decoration are the three basic spatial qualities which define the territorial value of rooms. That this value can be great is already evident from the fact that people spend so much time at home.

"The major space" of churches has long been subdivided according to religious, social and other parameters. Courtrooms and similar official localities have territorial divisions, and it is reported from dance-halls that when such separation is not automatically provided, musicians effectively segregate themselves behind instruments and the like.

Many office clerks use charts and equipment such as typewriters to define and protect their territories. In one case slightly increased regimentation and loss of primary status greatly decreased morale and nearly erased work efficiency. Alteration in shape, size, boundedness and differentiation of territorial cluster and unit thus caused marked alterations in the behaviour of its individual members.

Furniture not only demarcates but can function as territory itself, too. Specific chairs are regularly used by the same people in homes, clubs, seminars as well as on buses and trains. In an old people's home, despite rules to the contrary, chairs were stably occupied by specific individuals who defended "their" chairs in the face of intrusion.

When a library study area is opened, individual tables are each occupied by one person until no free tables are left. Studies at a seminar table showed that there were two territorially demarcated subgroups, one at each side of the table, that some members selected territories according to previously acquired hierarchical status while others gave priority just to staking out territory.

Human behaviour in confinement and isolation can be seen as an attempt to maintain some level of arousal since the nervous system requires constant, meaningful sensory input to function normally. As the length and severity of the confinement-isolation period increases the behaviour of the individual is quite likely to change towards the abnormal.

Navy recruits were run in dyads, living and working in a small room for 4-20 days with minimum outside contact. Half of them could not stand the longest isolation period. Aborters typically showed lower territorial interest early in isolation, compared with completers, and higher territorial behaviour later. If territoriality is important to integrity and identity then the manifestation of such behaviour early in a relationship can be taken as a sign that group members are behaving so as to create a viable relationship with one another.

Half of a group of schizophrenic males observed in a dayroom marked into square grids made use of all the available space and half occupied specific territories. The highest and lowest in rank did not show territorial behaviour, the highest because of total freedom to go unimpeded, the lowest because of total domination by others everywhere.

"Nestling" patients are persons who have recovered from a mental disease but have "taken root" in the hospital and want to remain there. It could be that these patients, who often lack their own homes, have acquired a new territory in the hospital during confinement. The ward setting has great influence in such cases, as also shown in comparisons of patient behaviour at home and in hospital.

In one prison each of twelve aggressive homosexuals lived in his territory with three or four other men known to engage in homosexual activity. Thus the penitentiary contained multiple territories where predators roamed unchallenged by other predators, surrounded by their prey. Measurements of the "body-buffer" zones of violent and non-violent prisoners showed that these zones were four times larger in the first than in the second group.

Most countries report growing criminality in parallel with increasing population density in small towns as well as big cities, and from the outskirts toward the urban core but there is hardly any consensus about the cause of this phenomenon.

General figures for magnitude of population, degree of urbanization and number of the mentally diseased in Belgium show that urbanization and psychiatric disorder are inseparable allies. The total insanity rate followed the ecological structure of the city, highest in the central areas of social disorder and steadily declining towards the periphery.

Two phenomena with territorial complications that could be involved in the pathology of the city are overcrowding and high density. The mostly psychological effects of crowding cannot, however, be evaluated solely in terms of population density but depend i.a. on structural and social organization and on the nature of relationships between individuals.

4.4. Special territories

Territories do not belong just to living humans but occur also among the dead in the form of tombs. The demand of open space for the dead now threatens to crowd the quarters of the living on a scale inconceivable in earlier cultures.

During the Stone Age tombs, sometimes marked by large stones, were often thought of as houses for the dead. In medieval Christian faith the tomb was considered an earthly symbol of a heavenly home, and Moslem countries still have cemeteries with Houses of the Dead visited by the owner families, who believe that the dead then come to their tomb territories.

It may be that the dead were the first to have permanent dwellings, to which wandering Paleolithic bands returned for sacrifice or communication with ancestral spirits. Thus the city of the dead antedates the city of the living. In any case it is remarkable how careful graves are marked out and protected, even the miniature ones from the world wars.

The nature and causal background of play is still not quite explained even though its similarity to usual instinctive behaviour is evident, e.g., as to exploration of the environment. Far from being a superfluous activity, it may be that play is necessary for the occurrence and success of all later social behaviour.

A common and striking form of play involves a child of four or five years who, by means of tables, chairs and clothing makes his own house, where he can retreat and feel private. Among other territorial play and games is "Territories": players take turns trying to stick a knife into each others delineated half-circle of ground in order to amass more territory.

Some of the oldest and most popular games are basically contests over ground, success marked by the scoring of goals. In football as in similar games it is the home team that most often wins the match. A strong instinctive territoriality is clearly awakened not only among players but among spectators too. Unable to be physically released by spectators pent up in the stands, the result of the territorial urge is not seldom overt aggression, vandalism and sometimes disaster during and after the match.

A double territorial fight is involved in chess. First, every square is the defended and often conquered territory of just one piece. Second and most important, the whole board is a contested territory, attacked from each side by the two players with sixteen pieces each.

Man not only has a portable "personal space" wherever he goes, but has also been able to construct vehicles which can function as mobile territories. Already the first and most simple boats suggested territoriality desires and larger ships have always been structured in such a way that they allow for territorial claims.

An elevator most often fills up in a particular way. First the four corners are taken up, then the rear wall and the centre, the maintaining of private space only later abandoned to indiscriminate packing. NASA recently decided that each crew member aboard Skylab should have a private sleeping compartment, satisfying individual needs for privacy and personal territory.

In the subway car spacing tendencies are most effectively satisfied by the occupation of areas which minimize boundary conflicts and the need to continually avoid contact with strangers, certain standing territories being preferred over available seats. The popularity of the automobile is remarkable, and the reasons are probably strongly instinctive. However, cars insulate man not only from the environment but from human contact as well, permitting only the most limited types of interaction, usually competitive, aggressive, and destructive.

The automobile not seldom functions as a dangerous weapon, probably as an extension of our personal space. Thus the car may be a movable and most effective territory, joining the otherwise irreconcilable centripetal and centrifugal tendencies, the drives towards staying at home or moving to foreign places.

A displaced group of people that fails to find a new territorial base will eventually lose its identity, usually by absorption into other cultures. Because of this it is often said that the Jewish people differ from all others in that their sense of unity is not based on territory but on faith and long and continuous tradition.

Probably the Babylonians as well as the Romans meant to destroy the Jews through their removal, knowing that no people can live without a land. But they failed, for it appears that the Jews were not without territory after all, but had taken it with them in the portable symbolic form of the Torah (handwritten parchment scrolls of the Law of Moses).

4.5. Fundamental facts of behavioural territoriality

Space and time are so closely related to each other that they can no longer be separated. In the case of the adult it is an individual history which is constantly confronted with a new situation composed of collective images, the product of a certain culture and therefore of a social history. But let us return to the world-before-knowledge, which is certainly that of the child and of the animal and seems also to be that in which the mentally sick and regressed individual lives. Then the situation is no longer the encounter between an individual history and a social history, but simply of a living organism and a world which derives its meaning from essentially spatial relationships rather than cultural layers.

If we suggest that this world-before-knowledge is also part of the basic mental constitution of normal man we are not far from the concept of instinct. In fact there is almost general agreement today that most human social behaviour is an interaction of cultural-environmental and biological influences. And, despite still vigorous criticism, it seems that association with and defense of territory resulted in a human behaviour pattern as thoroughly genetically determined as that in animals.

There is now clear evidence i.a. that males excel in spatial ability compared with females. Recent experiments show that spatial memory in mammals is located within the limbic system, where damage or disease was also demonstrated in connection with cases of extreme territorial aptitude. So it seems reasonable to assume that territoriality is innate and should be placed in the limbic system. These basal parts of the brain are old and unchanged enough to be responsible for a phenomenon common to all groups of vertebrates.

Territoriality probably reaches its highest development in the human species, and is found in a number of senses. Man has a personal space halo, notions of property in land, a willingness to defend areas of ground, and limits to the range of his activities. In one of the few systems of this fundamental human activity of controlling space there are presented four types of territory: public, home, interactional and body.

The area surrounding an individual, anywhere within which an intrusion is possible, causes him to feel encroached upon, to show displeasure and sometimes to withdraw. This is well known to us all, and it appears that implied physical threat and implicit threat in the form of status are among the most likely social releasers of territorial behaviour. All comprehensive social systems with recognizable political organization and some autonomous authority over an area have some form of territoriality in that there exist certain points, lines, or areas which elicit group identities and engender a sense of group exclusiveness against outsiders.

One of the many differences between cultures is that they extend different anatomical and behavioural features of the human organism. Indubitably what is fixed-feature space in one culture may be semi-fixed in another, and particularly proxemic patterns vary between different peoples. It may even be that man elaborates territoriality to such a degree that it hardly is recognizable as such.

One of its most characteristic features is the increasing spatial differentiation of the modern community e.g. the separation of house and work and thus the splitting of territorial areas. For the working class the street becomes an extension of the house, and in striking contrast to the middle-class, social organization territory is here equal to neighbourhood place. Conception of self and of place in society are thus subtly merged into conceptions of limited social interaction.

4.6. Effects and functions of behavioural territoriality

It seems possible to give plausible reasons for human behavioural territoriality, like other systems signified by order, constraint and communication. Man must be able to move freely within and between physical settings to satisfy not only his hunger, thirst, sex and other basic biological drives, but also his needs for affiliation, achievement, success, and other complex social desires.

Territory represents both information and action and is thus symbol as well as physical phenomenon. Biology, especially bio-cybernetics, ecology and ethology, offers an abundance of instances which illustrate how "goal-directed" behaviour is made possible by a complex organizational structure in which the vital environmental constraints are reflected. The point is that decoding and responding have been fixed once and for all, according to a preformed plan or program.

Most stressful encounters are avoided through spatial segregation. Avoidance is the first line of defense, physical barriers and social conventions offer other possibilities. In fact territories have been proposed as sources of appropriate sensory input to the nervous system, one primary object being to prevent understimulation as well as overstimulation of the limbic system, which is non-discriminatory as to external and internal stimuli and reacts in a diffuse and persistently lasting way.

A certain amount of ground or room is necessary for human living. Home and site attachment can be equated with the centripetal tendencies of nucleated territoriality, stressing the centre of the territory, while centrifugal forces are characteristic of exploratory behaviour in territorial areas far from the homebase. Thus an adequate territorial supply of some magnitude can in a way satisfy these two basic needs.

On the continuous spectrum from total anonymity to full identity, measurement of the precise degrees of acquaintance in cities and towns may help to explain the quality of life in each. Objects also express some aspects of the owner's identity so that the place in which objects are situated becomes associated with that person. A sense of spatial identity is fundamental for human functioning.

The need for privacy seems to grow with age and is most critical in the dwelling. A territory must be staked out that is peculiarly our own, the boundaries of which may be crossed by others only when we expressly invite them. Within the boundaries our own interests are sovereign, all initiative is ours, we are free to do our things, insulated against outside influence and observation. This is what we call privacy.

Psychiatrists nearly always find extensive insecurity in maladjusted and abnormal individuals and generally claim that feelings of security are necessary for mental health. Experiments with severely disturbed patients show a significant reduction of anxiety when the need for personal space diminishes. It is possible that frustration of the sense of territoriality may contribute far more importantly to the psychological problems of our age than we suspect.

There is now an exponential increase of the human world population. The first reaction to this is that we are in great risk of running short of space. Since world wide human population growth now shows a positive correlation with density, no density-dependent control seems to be in function.

Notable traits of humans in close association are an increase of emotionality and a decrease of responsibility. Extensive studies of children show that increased aggression and decreased interaction follow augmented density. It is further evident that overpopulation is highly relevant to questions of mental health because of increasing spatial constraints.

Normally animal populations are regulated by density-dependent factors. Exactly the same dynamic stability by means of homeostasis has always characterized the populations of "primitive" man. But the agricultural and still more the industrial revolution have strongly increased the material basis through overexploitation of our habitats. Because exploitable resources are limited and the proximate regulating factors cannot function in the long run without support of the ultimate factors, the recent rapid increase of human populations cannot go much farther without fatal consequences.

Two main reasons for the population height are: first, that resources of food and other needs have increased by means of more and more pronounced cultivation, exploitation and transport; second, that there is a great density-dependent adaptability of territoriality, demonstrated as the compartmentalization and structuring, above all, of settlements and habitations.

4.7. Behavioural territoriality in the past, the present and the future
Behavioural territoriality has an important place in the man-environment system of evolutionary adaptation. What evolved from environmental demands on our ancestors is now required by the individual from the milieu. Thus the only relevant criterion by which we can consider the natural adaptedness of any particular part of present-

day-man's behavioural equipment is the degree to which and the way in which it can contribute to population survival in his primeval environment.

Apparently the tendency to maintain territoriality is closely bound up with the differentiation of races, perhaps even of species, by selection and inbreeding. Certainly, human groups are rooted in the soil but have also a dynamic migratory urge which from time to time compels them to seek a new abode. For progressive evolutionary change both these moods are needed.

The age structure of the world's present population is highly favourable to growth and no one knows what total population we can expect before a net reproduction rate of one is achieved. Because crowding in animals leads to a decrease in reproduction, it could be that the lower rates of human population growth in urban as compared with rural areas is a reflection of the same tendency. In any case the situation is serious and a recent guide-line for social and political programs recommendable: Respect human territoriality and avoid overcrowding!

In a vertebrate community not governed by absolute hierarchy alone the individual acquires not only personality through his territory but also has some space where he is superior to all other members of the community. Thus, territoriality is not at all, as is sometimes claimed, a reactionary device, an antithesis to the open society. Instead, it offers perhaps the only natural and thus the only solid basis for the two cornerstones of a democracy: freedom and equality.

POSTSCRIPT

The manuscript of this book was finished in the first half of 1976. For various reasons the publication has been delayed, and it now seems appropriate to add a short postscript. This has been done in order to account for some pertinent, not earlier treated literature, as well as to provide some general reflections about the latest developments in territorology.

At the first international congress on human ecology held in Vienna in 1978, an effort was made to give a summary report on the modern study of human territoriality during the twenty-five years since the pioneer papers by Staehelin and Leyhausen in 1953-1954 (Malmberg, forthcoming). Most of the time, this particular form of investigation has uncovered well-known indications of a discipline still in the cradle: occasional, non-systematic work on very different matters without unitary theoretical foundation and nomenclature.

Doubtless, this situation was beginning to change already, when the first of about a dozen books now available on the subject appeared. But it does not seem adequate to talk about a new era of research before the 1976 introductory number of the journal *Environment and Behavior*, dedicated to the first, serious efforts made to give territoriality in man a theoretical platform.

As to the books mentioned above, it is unfortunate that three of them have fallen into my hands too late to be taken into full consideration in the text. Two are, however, mentioned before (p. 1), that by Bakker and Bakker-Rabdau, a valuable treatise on the psychological aspects of the matter, and that by Scheflen and Ashcraft, an interesting and well-illustrated description of proxemics. The third book, *Design for Diversity*, by B. B. Greenbie (1976), has some similarities with the present one, but the stress is there on architectural and other structural elements in territoriality.

Of particular importance is the recent breakthrough in the neurophysiological background of territorial behaviour, which augments and completes earlier given information (p. 220-222). P. D. MacLean made probable the idea that the human brain is a triune phenomenon, each part functioning as a biological computer, having, e.g., its own sense of time and space. The

three units are the reptilian brain (upper brain-stem, etc.), the paleomammalian brain (limbic system) and the neomammalian brain (neocortex).
It is thought that "the counterpart of the reptilian brain in mammals is
fundamental for such genetically constituted forms of behaviour as selecting
homesites, establishing territory .... The most explosive issue, of course,
is the problem of controlling man's reptilian intolerance and reptilian struggle for territory" (MacLean 1973: 8, 59).

We have repeatedly noted in the text how fundamental the emotional
load is in territorial contexts, and it could be that the paleomammalian
brain is so decisive that "it is questionable whether or not the human race
could survive without limbic emotions..." (op cit. p. 20). As further developed by Esser and Deutsch (1977) in a recent thought-provoking paper,
the neomammalian brain stands for conceptual and interaction territory.
As to general functions of the three brain parts, the authors summarize:
reptilian – biological; paleomammalian – emotional; neomammalian – intellectual.

It is stressed that the triune concept does not represent just a division but
also an integration, and this is true for the territorial behaviour as well.
Thus territoriality is not only a cross-disciplinary but also a cross-space
and cross-time topic, disclosing different natural and cultural as well as
phylogenetic levels. In this perspective, the relations between animal and
human ecology and territorology – treated in one of the few outstanding
European papers in the field from recent years (Paul 1976) – come into new
light. The differences and the unity are now better understood, the last-
named aspect, e.g., explained in the frame of information and communication (cf. Malmberg 1979).

However, for the moment there seem to be great risks that the integrative
study of territoriality splits up into separate sections. This would be tragic
because all the three units of brain and behaviour are necessary for a true
picture of the phenomenon. It looks as though the actual balance is already
strongly in favour of the investigation of features like that of personal
space related to social and other parameters. When looking for literature on basic seating preference in rooms (Malmberg and Malmberg
1979) – part of a plan to try to disclose the prerequisites of territoriality – we
realized that there were 1500-2000 papers in the category of "personal space"
and not more than three that could on the whole give some information
about the simple, fundamental preference named based on enough material.

In view of the great importance of human territoriality in all its phases
we stress the immediate need for international cooperation in this field.

It might initially be in the form of a congress, followed by some kind of organization, of a special journal and of bibliographies. The interest in these subjects seems to increase everywhere – if not hemmed in by more or less dogmatic misunderstanding. But the time for meaningful spatial research and its practical implementation is short in a still more crowded, shrinking and problem-filled world.

References

Esser, A. H. and Deutsch, R. D. 1977. "Private and Interaction Territories on Psychiatric Wards: Studies on Nonverbal Communication of Spatial Needs". In: *Ethological Psychiatry. Psychopathology in the Context of Evolutionary Biology.* M. T. Guire and L. A. Fairbanks, eds. New York: Grune and Stratton. P. 127-152.

Greenbie, B. B. 1976. *Design for Diversity. Planning for Natural Man in the Neotechnic Environment: An Ethological Approach.* Developments in Landscape Management and Urban Planning 2. Amsterdam-Oxford-New York: Elsevier Scientific Publishing Company.

MacLean, P. D. 1973. *A Triune Concept of the Brain and Behaviour.* The Clarence M. Hincks Memorial Lectures 1969. T. J. Boag and D. Campbell, eds. Toronto and Buffalo: University of Toronto Press.

Malmberg, O. and Malmberg, T. 1979. "Seating Preference in Male Adolescents: An Illustration of the Space-Behaviour Problem". *Man-Environment Systems* (in press).

Malmberg, T. 1979. "Territory as Information". In: *Perspectives on Adaptation, Environment and Population.* J. B. Calhoun, ed. New York: Praeger. P. 1271-1280.

Malmberg, T. (forthcoming). "The Study of Territoriality". In: *Proceedings of the First International Congress on Human Ecology. Vienna October 26-31, 1978.*

Paul, H. A. 1976. "Der Begriff der 'Territorialität' in der Allgemeinen Ökologie und in der Humanökologie". *Verhandlungen der Gesellschaft für Ökologie,* Göttingen 1976. P. 499-510.

Name Index

Subject Index

Due to lack of space, it was impossible to compile a complete subject index. Only general terms of special importance for human territoriality have been included. Please note that compound words are sometimes divided and that often several derived words in the text refer to one main entry in the index, usually a noun (e.g., adapt, adaptive, adaptively, adaptness, and adaptability are all listed under the heading Adaptation), and that synonyms should be sought for (e.g., automobile—car; boundary—limit). In some cases the second word in the entry occurs before and in some cases after the first one.